AMERICAN HOLOCAUST

AMERICAN HOLOCAUST

The Conquest of the New World

DAVID E. STANNARD

OXFORD UNIVERSITY PRESS
New York   *Oxford*

Oxford University Press

Oxford New York Toronto
Delhi Bombay Calcutta Madras Karachi
Kuala Lumpur Singapore Hong Kong Tokyo
Nairobi Dar es Salaam Cape Town
Melbourne Auckland Madrid

and associated companies in
Berlin Ibadan

First published in 1992 by Oxford University Press, Inc.,
198 Madison Avenue, New York, New York 10016-4314

First issued as an Oxford University Press paperback, 1993

Oxford is a registered trademark of Oxford University Press

Library of Congress Cataloging-in-Publication Data
Stannard, David E.
American holocaust : Columbus and the conquest of the
New World / David E. Stannard.
p. cm. Includes bibliographical references and index.
ISBN 0-19-507581-1
ISBN 0-19-508557-4 (PBK.)
1. Columbus, Christopher—Influence. 2. America—Discovery and
exploration—Spanish. 3. Indians, Treatment of. 4. Indians—First
contact with Europeans. I. Title.
E112.S82 1992
970.01'5—dc20 92-6922

4 6 8 10 9 7 5
Printed in the United States of America

For Florence Evelyn Harwood Stannard
—*the poet who gave me life and taught me that in kindness and charity there is strength*

and for Haunani-Kay Trask
—*the poet who sustains me and is unwavering in the struggle for justice*

CONTENTS

PROLOGUE

I N THE DARKNESS of an early July morning in 1945, on a desolate spot in the New Mexico desert named after a John Donne sonnet celebrating the Holy Trinity, the first atomic bomb was exploded. J. Robert Oppenheimer later remembered that the immense flash of light, followed by the thunderous roar, caused a few observers to laugh and others to cry. But most, he said, were silent. Oppenheimer himself recalled at that instant a line from the *Bhagavad-Gita:*

> I am become death,
> the shatterer of worlds.

There is no reason to think that anyone on board the *Niña*, the *Pinta*, or the *Santa María*, on an equally dark early morning four and a half centuries earlier, thought of those ominous lines from the ancient Sanskrit poem when the crews of the Spanish ships spied a flicker of light on the windward side of the island they would name after the Holy Saviour. But the intuition, had it occurred, would have been as appropriate then as it was when that first nuclear blast rocked the New Mexico desert sands.

In both instances—at the Trinity test site in 1945 and at San Salvador in 1492—those moments of achievement crowned years of intense personal struggle and adventure for their protagonists and were culminating points of ingenious technological achievement for their countries. But both instances also were prelude to orgies of human destructiveness that, each in its own way, attained a scale of devastation not previously witnessed in the entire history of the world.

Just twenty-one days after the first atomic test in the desert, the Japanese industrial city of Hiroshima was leveled by nuclear blast; never before had so many people—at least 130,000, probably many more—died from a single explosion.[1] Just twenty-one years after Columbus's first landing in the Caribbean, the vastly populous island that the explorer had re-named Hispaniola was effectively desolate; nearly 8,000,000 people—those Columbus chose to call Indians—had been killed by violence, disease, and despair.[2] It took a little longer, about the span of a single human generation, but what happened on Hispaniola was the equivalent of more than fifty Hiroshimas. And Hispaniola was only the beginning.

Within no more than a handful of generations following their first encounters with Europeans, the vast majority of the Western Hemisphere's native peoples had been exterminated. The pace and magnitude of their obliteration varied from place to place and from time to time, but for years now historical demographers have been uncovering, in region upon region, post-Columbian depopulation rates of between 90 and 98 percent with such regularity that an overall decline of 95 percent has become a working rule of thumb. What this means is that, on average, for every twenty natives alive at the moment of European contact—when the lands of the Americas teemed with numerous tens of millions of people—only one stood in their place when the bloodbath was over.

To put this in a contemporary context, the ratio of native survivorship in the Americas following European contact was less than half of what the human survivorship ratio would be in the United States today if every single white person and every single black person died. The destruction of the Indians of the Americas was, far and away, the most massive act of genocide in the history of the world. That is why, as one historian aptly has said, far from the heroic and romantic heraldry that customarily is used to symbolize the European settlement of the Americas, the emblem most congruent with reality would be a pyramid of skulls.[3]

Scholarly estimates of the size of the post-Columbian holocaust have climbed sharply in recent decades. Too often, however, academic discussions of this ghastly event have reduced the devastated indigenous peoples and their cultures to statistical calculations in recondite demographic analyses. It is easy for this to happen. From the very beginning, merely taking the account of so mammoth a cataclysm seemed an impossible task. Wrote one Spanish adventurer—who arrived in the New World only two decades after Columbus's first landing, and who himself openly reveled in the torrent of native blood—there was neither "paper nor time enough to tell all that the [conquistadors] did to ruin the Indians and rob them and destroy the land."[4] As a result, the very effort to describe the disaster's overwhelming magnitude has tended to obliterate both the writer's and the reader's sense of its truly horrific human element.

In an apparent effort to counteract this tendency, one writer, Tzvetan Todorov, begins his study of the events of 1492 and immediately thereafter with an epigraph from Diego de Landa's *Relación de las cosas de Yucatán:*

> The captain Alonso López de Avila, brother-in-law of the *adelantado* Montejo, captured, during the war in Bacalán, a young Indian woman of lovely and gracious appearance. She had promised her husband, fearful lest they should kill him in the war, not to have relations with any other man but him, and so no persuasion was sufficient to prevent her from taking her own life to avoid being defiled by another man; and because of this they had her thrown to the dogs.

Todorov then dedicates his book "to the memory of a Mayan woman devoured by dogs."[5]

It is important to try to hold in mind an image of that woman, and her brothers and sisters and the innumerable others who suffered similar fates, as one reads Todorov's book, or this one, or any other work on this subject—just as it is essential, as one reads about the Jewish Holocaust or the horrors of the African slave trade, to keep in mind the treasure of a single life in order to avoid becoming emotionally anesthetized by the sheer force of such overwhelming human evil and destruction. There is, for example, the case of a small Indian boy whose name no one knows today, and whose unmarked skeletal remains are hopelessly intermingled with those of hundreds of anonymous others in a mass grave on the American plains, but a boy who once played on the banks of a quiet creek in eastern Colorado—until the morning, in 1864, when the American soldiers came. Then, as one of the cavalrymen later told it, while his compatriots were slaughtering and mutilating the bodies of all the women and all the children they could catch, he spotted the boy trying to flee:

> There was one little child, probably three years old, just big enough to walk through the sand. The Indians had gone ahead, and this little child was behind following after them. The little fellow was perfectly naked, travelling on the sand. I saw one man get off his horse, at a distance of about seventy-five yards, and draw up his rifle and fire—he missed the child. Another man came up and said, "Let me try the son of a bitch; I can hit him." He got down off his horse, kneeled down and fired at the little child, but he missed him. A third man came up and made a similar remark, and fired, and the little fellow dropped.[6]

We must do what we can to recapture and to try to understand, in human terms, what it *was* that was crushed, what it *was* that was butchered. It is not enough merely to acknowledge that much was lost. So close to total was the human incineration and carnage in the post-Columbian Americas, however, that of the tens of millions who were killed, few individual lives left sufficient traces for subsequent biographical representation. The first two chapters to follow are thus necessarily limited in their concerns to the social and cultural worlds that existed in North and South America before Columbus's fateful voyage in 1492. We shall have to rely on our imaginations to fill in the faces and the lives.

The extraordinary outpouring of recent scholarship that has analyzed the deadly impact of the Old World on the New has employed a novel array of research techniques to identify introduced disease as the primary cause of the Indians' great population decline. As one of the pioneers in this research put it twenty years ago, the natives' "most hideous" enemies were not the European invaders themselves, "but the invisible killers which those men brought in their blood and breath."[7] It is true, in a plainly quantitative sense of body counting, that the barrage of disease unleashed by the Europeans among the so-called "virgin soil" populations of the Americas caused more deaths than any other single force of destruction. However, by focusing almost entirely on disease, by displacing responsibility for the mass killing onto an army of invading microbes, contemporary authors increasingly have created the impression that the eradication of those tens of millions of people was inadvertent—a sad, but both inevitable and "unintended consequence" of human migration and progress.[8] This is a modern version of what Alexander Saxton recently has described as the "soft-side of anti-Indian racism" that emerged in America in the nineteenth century and that incorporated "expressions of regret over the fate of Indians into narratives that traced the inevitability of their extinction. Ideologically," Saxton adds, "the effect was to exonerate individuals, parties, nations, of any moral blame for what history had decreed."[9] In fact, however, the near-total destruction of the Western Hemisphere's native people was neither inadvertent nor inevitable.

From almost the instant of first human contact between Europe and the Americas firestorms of microbial pestilence *and* purposeful genocide began laying waste the American natives. Although at times operating independently, for most of the long centuries of devastation that followed 1492, disease and genocide were interdependent forces acting dynamically—whipsawing their victims between plague and violence, each one feeding upon the other, and together driving countless numbers of entire ancient societies to the brink—and often over the brink—of total extermination. In the pages that lie ahead we will examine the causes and the consequences of both these grisly phenomena. But since the genocidal component has so often been neglected in recent scholarly analyses of the great American Indian holocaust, it is the central purpose of this book to survey some of the more virulent examples of this deliberate racist purge, from fifteenth-century Hispaniola to nineteenth-century California, and then to locate and examine the belief systems and the cultural attitudes that underlay such monstrous behavior.

. . .

History for its own sake is not an idle task, but studies of this sort are conducted not only for the maintenance of collective memory. In the Foreword to a book of oral history accounts depicting life in Germany during the Jewish Holocaust, Elie Wiesel says something that befits the present context as well: "The danger lies in forgetting. Forgetting, however, will not effect only the dead. Should it triumph, the ashes of yesterday will cover our hopes for tomorrow."[10]

To begin, then, we must try to remember. For at a time when quincentennial festivities are in full flower to honor the famed Admiral of the Ocean Sea—when hot disputes are raging, because of the quest for tourist dollars, over whether he first actually landed at Grand Turk Island, Samana Cay, or Watlings Island—the ashes of yesterday, and their implications for all the world's hopes for tomorrow, are too often ignored in the unseemly roar of self-congratulation.[11]

Moreover, the important question for the future in this case is not "can it happen again?" Rather, it is "can it be stopped?" For the genocide in the Americas, and in other places where the world's indigenous peoples survive, has never really ceased. As recently as 1986, the Commission on Human Rights of the Organization of American States observed that 40,000 people had simply "disappeared" in Guatemala during the preceding fifteen years. Another 100,000 had been openly murdered. That is the equivalent, in the United States, of more than 4,000,000 people slaughtered or removed under official government decree—a figure that is almost six times the number of American battle deaths in the Civil War, World War One, World War Two, the Korean War, and the Vietnam War combined.[12]

Almost all those dead and disappeared were Indians, direct descendants—as was that woman who was devoured by dogs—of the Mayas, creators of one of the most splendid civilizations that this earth has ever seen. Today, as five centuries ago, these people are being tortured and slaughtered, their homes and villages bombed and razed—while more than two-thirds of their rain forest homelands have now been intentionally burned and scraped into ruin.[13] The murder and destruction continue, with the aid and assistance of the United States, even as these words are being written and read. And many of the detailed accounts from contemporary observers read much like those recorded by the conquistadors' chroniclers nearly 500 years earlier.

"Children, two years, four years old, they just grabbed them and tore them in two," reports one witness to a military massacre of Indians in Guatemala in 1982. Recalls another victim of an even more recent assault on an Indian encampment:

> With tourniquets they killed the children, of two years, of nine months, of six months. They killed and burned them all. . . . What they did [to my

father] was put a machete in here (pointing to his chest) and they cut open his heart, and they left him all burned up. This is the pain we shall never forget. . . . Better to die here with a bullet and not die in that way, like my father did.[14]

Adds still another report, from a list of examples seemingly without end:

At about 1:00 p.m., the soldiers began to fire at the women inside the small church. The majority did not die there, but were separated from their children, taken to their homes in groups, and killed, the majority apparently with machetes. . . . Then they returned to kill the children, whom they had left crying and screaming by themselves, without their mothers. Our informants, who were locked up in the courthouse, could see this through a hole in the window and through the doors carelessly left open by a guard. The soldiers cut open the children's stomachs with knives or they grabbed the children's little legs and smashed their heads with heavy sticks. . . . Then they continued with the men. They took them out, tied their hands, threw them on the ground, and shot them. The authorities of the area were killed inside the courthouse. . . . It was then that the survivors were able to escape, protected by the smoke of the fire which had been set to the building. Seven men, three of whom survived, managed to escape. It was 5:30 p.m.[15]

In all, 352 Indians were killed in this massacre, at a time when 440 towns were being entirely destroyed by government troops, when almost 10,000 unarmed people were being killed or made to "disappear" annually, and when more than 1,000,000 of Guatemala's approximately 4,000,000 natives were being displaced by the deliberate burning and wasting of their ancestral lands. During such episodes of mass butchery, some children escape; only their parents and grandparents are killed. That is why it was reported in Guatemala in 1985 that "116,000 orphans had been tabulated by the judicial branch census throughout the country, the vast majority of them in the Indian townships of the western and central highlands."[16]

Reminders are all around us, if we care to look, that the fifteenth- and sixteenth-century extermination of the indigenous people of Hispaniola, brought on by European military assault and the importation of exotic diseases, was in part only an enormous prelude to human catastrophes that followed on other killing grounds, and continue to occur today—from the forests of Brazil and Paraguay and elsewhere in South and Central America, where direct government violence still slaughters thousands of Indian people year in and year out, to the reservations and urban slums of North America, where more sophisticated indirect government violence has precisely the same effect—all the while that Westerners engage in exultation over the 500th anniversary of the European discovery of America, the time and the place where all the killing began.

Other reminders surround us, as well, however, that there continues among indigenous peoples today the echo of their fifteenth- and sixteenth-century opposition to annihilation, when, despite the wanton killing by the European invaders and the carnage that followed the introduction of explosive disease epidemics, the natives resisted with an intensity the conquistadors found difficult to believe. "I do not know how to describe it," wrote Bernal Díaz del Castillo of the defiance the Spanish encountered in Mexico, despite the wasting of the native population by bloodbath and torture and disease, "for neither cannon nor muskets nor crossbows availed, nor hand-to-hand fighting, nor killing thirty or forty of them every time we charged, for they still fought on in as close ranks and with more energy than in the beginning."[17]

Five centuries later that resistance remains, in various forms, throughout North and South and Central America, as it does among indigenous peoples in other lands that have suffered from the Westerners' furious wrath. Compared with what they once were, the native peoples in most of these places are only remnants now. But also in each of those places, and in many more, the struggle for physical and cultural survival, and for recovery of a deserved pride and autonomy, continues unabated.

All the ongoing violence against the world's indigenous peoples, in whatever form—as well as the native peoples' various forms of resistance to that violence—will persist beyond our full understanding, however, and beyond our ability to engage and humanely come to grips with it, until we are able to comprehend the magnitude and the causes of the human destruction that virtually consumed the people of the Americas and other people in other subsequently colonized parts of the globe, beginning with Columbus's early morning sighting of landfall on October 12, 1492. That was the start of it all. This book is offered as one contribution to our necessary comprehension.

He'eia, O'ahu
January 1992

D.E.S.

The main islands were thickly populated with a peaceful folk when Christ-over found them. But the orgy of blood which followed, no man has written. We are the slaughterers. It is the tortured soul of our world.

—WILLIAM CARLOS WILLIAMS

I

BEFORE COLUMBUS

◀ **1** ▶

I T'S GONE NOW, drained and desiccated in the aftermath of the Spanish
conquest, but once there was an interconnected complex of lakes high
up in the Valley of Mexico that was as long and as wide as the city
of London is today. Surrounding these waters, known collectively as the
Lake of the Moon, were scores of towns and cities whose population,
combined with that of the outlying communities of central Mexico, totaled
about 25,000,000 men, women, and children. On any given day as many
as 200,000 small boats moved back and forth on the Lake of the Moon,
pursuing the interests of commerce, political intrigue, and simple pleasure.[1]

The southern part of the Lake of the Moon was filled with brilliantly
clear spring-fed water, but the northern part, in the rainy season, became
brackish and sometimes inundated the southern region with an invasion
of destructive salty currents. So the people of the area built a ten-mile long
stone and clay and masonry dike separating the lower third of the lake
from the upper two-thirds, blocking the salt water when it appeared, but—
through an ingenious use of sluice gates—allowing the heavy water traffic
on the lake to continue its rounds unobstructed by the massive levee wall.
This southern part of the great lake thus became, as well as a thorough-
fare, an immense fresh-water fish pond.

In the middle of this fresh-water part of the lake there were two reed-
covered mud banks that the residents of the area over time had built up
and developed into a single huge island as large as Manhattan, and upon
that island the people built a metropolis that became one of the largest
cities in the world. With a conventionally estimated population of about
350,000 residents by the end of the fifteenth century, this teeming Aztec

capital already had at least five times the population of either London or Seville and was vastly larger than any other European city.[2] Moreover, according to Hernando Cortés, one of the first Europeans to set eyes upon it, it was far and away the most beautiful city on earth.

The name of this magnificent metropolis was Tenochtitlán. It stood, majestic and radiant, in the crisp, clean air, 7200 feet above sea level, connected to the surrounding mainland by three wide causeways that had been built across miles of open water. To view Tenochtitlán from a distance, all who had the opportunity to do so agreed, was breathtaking. Before arriving at the great central city, travelers from afar had to pass through the densely populated, seemingly infinite, surrounding lands—and already, invariably, they were overwhelmed. Wrote Cortés's famous companion and chronicler Bernal Díaz del Castillo of their visit to one of the provincial cities at the confluence of Lake Chalco and Lake Xochimilco:

> When we entered the city of Iztapalapa, the appearance of the palaces in which they housed us! How spacious and well built they were, of beautiful stone work and cedar wood, and the wood of other sweet scented trees, with great rooms and courts, wonderful to behold, covered with awnings of cotton cloth. When we had looked well at all of this, we went to the orchard and garden, which was such a wonderful thing to see and walk in, that I was never tired of looking at the diversity of the trees, and noting the scent which each one had, and the paths full of roses and flowers, and the native fruit trees and native roses, and the pond of fresh water. There was another thing to observe, that great canoes were able to pass into the garden from the lake through an opening that had been made so that there was no need for their occupants to land. And all was cemented and very splendid with many kinds of stone [monuments] with pictures on them, which gave much to think about. Then the birds of many kinds and breeds which came into the pond. I say again that I stood looking at it and thought that never in the world would there be discovered lands such as these.[3]

Impressive as Iztapalapa was, the Spanish were seeking the heart of this great empire, so they pressed on. In addition to the cities that surrounded the Lake of the Moon, other towns were, like Tenochtitlán, built on smaller islands within it. As they neared the area that would take them to Tenochtitlán, Bernal Díaz wrote: "When we saw so many cities and villages built in the water and other great towns built on dry land and that straight and level causeway going towards [Tenochtitlán], we were amazed and said that it was like the enchantments they tell of in the legend of Amadis, on account of the great towers and [temples] and buildings rising from the water, and all built of masonry. And some of our soldiers even asked whether the things that we saw were not a dream."

Finally, they reached one of the causeways leading directly to Tenochtitlán. They pushed their way across it, although "it was so crowded with people that there was hardly room for them all, some of them going to and others returning from [Tenochtitlán]," said Bernal Díaz. Once in the city itself they were greeted by the Aztec ruler Montezuma and taken to the top of one of the temples, and from that vantage point they were afforded an almost aerial view of the surroundings through which they had just marched:

> [O]ne could see over everything very well [Bernal Díaz wrote], and we saw the three causeways which led into [Tenochtitlán], that is the causeway of Iztapalapa by which we had entered four days before, and that of Tacuba, and that of Tepeaquilla, and we saw the fresh water that comes from Chapultepec which supplies the city, and we saw the bridges on the three causeways which were built at certain distances apart through which the water of the lake flowed in and out from one side to the other, and we beheld on that great lake a great multitude of canoes, some coming with supplies of food and others returning with cargoes of merchandise; and we saw that from every house of that great city and of all the other cities that were built in the water it was impossible to pass from house to house, except by drawbridges which were made of wood or in canoes; and we saw in those cities [temples] and oratories like towers and fortresses and all gleaming white, and it was a wonderful thing to behold.

About 60,000 pale stucco houses filled the island metropolis, some of them single-story structures, some of them multi-storied, and "all these houses," wrote Cortés, "have very large and very good rooms and also very pleasant gardens of various sorts of flowers both on the upper and lower floors."[4] The many streets and boulevards of the city were so neat and well-swept, despite its multitude of inhabitants, that the first Europeans to visit never tired of remarking on the city's cleanliness and order: "There were even officials in charge of sweeping," recalled one awed observer. In fact, at least 1000 public workers were employed to maintain the city's streets and keep them clean and watered.[5]

Criss-crossed with a complex network of canals, Tenochtitlán in this respect reminded the Spanish of an enormous Venice; but it also had remarkable floating gardens that reminded them of nowhere else on earth.[6] And while European cities then, and for centuries thereafter, took their drinking water from the fetid and polluted rivers nearby, Tenochtitlán's drinking water came from springs deep within the mainland and was piped into the city by a huge aqueduct system that amazed Cortés and his men— just as they were astonished also by the personal cleanliness and hygiene of the colorfully dressed populace, and by their extravagant (to the Spanish) use of soaps, deodorants, and breath sweeteners.[7]

In the distance, across the expanse of shimmering blue water that extended out in every direction, and beyond the pastel-colored suburban towns and cities, both within the lake and encircling its periphery, the horizon was ringed with forest-covered hills, except to the southeast where there dramatically rose up the slopes of two enormous snow-peaked and smoldering volcanoes, the largest of them, Popocatepetl, reaching 16,000 feet into the sky. At the center of the city, facing the volcanoes, stood two huge and exquisitely ornate ceremonial pyramids, man-made mountains of uniquely Aztec construction and design. But what seems to have impressed the Spanish visitors most about the view of Tenochtitlán from within its precincts were not the temples or the other magnificent public buildings, but rather the marketplaces that dotted the residential neighborhoods and the enormous so-called Great Market that sprawled across the city's northern end. This area, "with arcades all around," according to Cortés, was the central gathering place where "more than sixty thousand people come each day to buy and sell, and where every kind of merchandise produced in these lands is found; provisions, as well as ornaments of gold and silver, lead, brass, copper, tin, stones, shells, bones, and feathers." Cortés also describes special merchant areas where timber and tiles and other building supplies were bought and sold, along with "much firewood and charcoal, earthenware braziers and mats of various kinds like mattresses for beds, and other, finer ones, for seats and for covering rooms and hallways."

"Each kind of merchandise is sold in its own street without any mixture whatever," Cortés wrote, "they are very particular in this." (Even entertainers had a residential district of their own, says Bernal Díaz, a place where there lived a great many "people who had no other occupation" than to be "dancers . . . and others who used stilts on their feet, and others who flew when they danced up in the air, and others like Merry-Andrews [clowns].") There were streets where herbalists plied their trade, areas for apothecary shops, and "shops like barbers' where they have their hair washed and shaved, and shops where they sell food and drink," wrote Cortés, as well as green grocer streets where one could buy "every sort of vegetable, especially onions, leeks, garlic, common cress and watercress, borage, sorrel, teasels and artichokes; and there are many sorts of fruit, among which are cherries and plums like those in Spain." There were stores in streets that specialized in "game and birds of every species found in this land: chickens, partridges and quails, wild ducks, fly-catchers, widgeons, turtledoves, pigeons, cane birds, parrots, eagles and eagle owls, falcons, sparrow hawks and kestrels [as well as] rabbits and hares, and stags and small gelded dogs which they breed for eating."

There was so much more in this mercantile center, overseen by officials who enforced laws of fairness regarding weights and measures and the quality of goods purveyed, that Bernal Díaz said "we were astounded at the number of people and the quantity of merchandise that it contained, and at the good order and control that it contained, for we had never seen such a thing before." There were honeys "and honey paste, and other dainties like nut paste," waxes, syrups, chocolate, sugar, wine. In addition, said Cortés:

There are many sorts of spun cotton, in hanks of every color, and it seems like the silk market at Granada, except here there is much greater quantity. They sell as many colors for painters as may be found in Spain and all of excellent hues. They sell deerskins, with and without the hair, and some are dyed white or in various colors. They sell much earthenware, which for the most part is very good; there are both large and small pitchers, jugs, pots, tiles and many other sorts of vessel, all of good clay and most of them glazed and painted. They sell maize both as grain and as bread and it is better both in appearance and in taste than any found in the islands or on the mainland. They sell chicken and fish pies, and much fresh and salted fish, as well as raw and cooked fish. They sell hen and goose eggs, and eggs of all the other birds I have mentioned, in great number, and they sell *tortillas* made from eggs.

At last Cortés surrendered the task of trying to describe it all: "Besides those things which I have already mentioned, they sell in the market everything else to be found in this land, but they are so many and so varied that because of their great number and because I cannot remember many of them nor do I know what they are called I shall not mention them." Added Bernal Díaz: "But why do I waste so many words in recounting what they sell in that great market? For I shall never finish if I tell it in detail. . . . Some of the soldiers among us who had been in many parts of the world, in Constantinople, and all over Italy, and in Rome, said that so large a marketplace and so full of people, and so well regulated and arranged, they had never beheld before."

And this was only the market. The rest of Tenochtitlán overflowed with gorgeous gardens, arboretums, and aviaries. Artwork was everywhere, artwork so dazzling in conception and execution that when the German master Albrecht Dürer saw some pieces that Cortés brought back to Europe he exclaimed that he had "never seen in all my days what so rejoiced my heart, as these things. For I saw among them amazing artistic objects, and I marveled over the subtle ingenuity of the men in these distant lands. Indeed, I cannot say enough about the things that were brought before me."[8]

If architectural splendor and floral redolence were among the sights and smells that most commonly greeted a stroller in the city, the most ever-present sounds (apart from "the murmur and hum of voices" from the mercantile district, which Bernal Díaz said "could be heard more than a league off") were the songs of the many multi-colored birds—parrots, hummingbirds, falcons, jays, herons, owls, condors, and dozens and dozens of other exotic species—who lived in public aviaries that the government maintained. As Cortés wrote to his king:

Most Powerful Lord, in order to give an account to Your Royal Excellency of the magnificence, the strange and marvelous things of this great city and of the dominion and wealth of this Mutezuma, its ruler, and of the rites and customs of the people, and of the order there is in the government of the capital as well as in the other cities of Mutezuma's dominions, I would need much time and many expert narrators. I cannot describe one hundredth part of all the things which could be mentioned, but, as best I can I will describe some of those I have seen which, although badly described, will I well know, be so remarkable as not to be believed, for we who saw them with our own eyes could not grasp them with our understanding.

In attempting to recount for his king the sights of the country surrounding Tenochtitlán, the "many provinces and lands containing very many and very great cities, towns and fortresses," including the vast agricultural lands that Cortés soon would raze and the incredibly rich gold mines that he soon would plunder, the conquistador again was rendered nearly speechless: "They are so many and so wonderful," he simply said, "that they seem almost unbelievable."

Prior to Cortés's entry into this part of the world no one who lived in Europe, Asia, Africa, or anywhere else beyond the Indies and the North and South American continents, had ever heard of this exotic place of such dazzling magnificence. Who were these people? Where had they come from? When had they come? How did they get where they were? Were there others like them elsewhere in this recently stumbled-upon New World?[9] These questions sprang to mind immediately, and many of the puzzlements of the conquistadors are with us still today, more than four and a half centuries later. But while scholarly debates on these questions continue, clear answers regarding some of them at last are finally coming into view. And these answers are essential to an understanding of the magnitude of the holocaust that was visited upon the Western Hemisphere—beginning at Hispaniola, spreading to Tenochtitlán, and then radiating out over millions of square miles in every direction—in the wake of 1492.

II

Where the first humans in the Americas came from and how they got to their new homes are now probably the least controversial of these age-old questions. Although at one time or another seemingly all the corners of Europe, Asia, the Middle East, and Africa fancifully have been suggested as the sources of early populations in the New World, no one any longer seriously doubts that the first human inhabitants of North and South America were the descendants of much earlier emigrants from ancestral homelands in northeastern Asia.

It conventionally is said that the migration (or migrations) to North America from Asia took place over the land bridge that once connected the two continents across what are now the Bering and Chukchi seas. "Land bridge" is a whopping misnomer, however, unless one imagines a bridge immensely wider than it was long, more than a thousand miles wide, in fact—about the distance between New York and Omaha—compared with a lengthwise span across the Bering Strait today of less than sixty miles.

During most, and perhaps all of the time from about 80,000 B.C. to about 10,000 B.C. (the geologic era known as the Wisconsin glaciation), at least part of the shallow floor of the Bering and Chukchi seas, like most of the world's continental shelves, was well above sea level due to the capture of so much of the earth's ocean water by the enormous continent-wide glaciers of this Ice Age epoch. The effect of this was, for all practical purposes, the complete fusion of Asia and North America into a single land mass whose place of connection was a huge chunk of earth—actually a subcontinent—hundreds of thousands of square miles in size, now called by geographers Berengia.[10] What we see today as a scattering of small islands in the ocean separating Alaska and northeast Asia as far south as the Kamchatka Peninsula are merely the tips of low mountains that, during the Wisconsin glaciation, rose from what at that time was an exposed floor of land.

The first humans in North America, then, appear to have been successor populations to groups of hunters from northern Asia who had moved, as part of the normal continuum of their boundary-less lives, into Berengia and then on to Alaska in pursuit of game and perhaps new vegetative sources of sustenance. During these many thousands of years much of Berengia, like most of Alaska at that time, was a grassland-like tundra, meandering through mountain valleys and across open plains that were filled with wooly mammoths, yaks, steppe antelopes, and many other animals and plants more than sufficient to sustain stable communities of late Paleolithic hunters and gatherers.

To say that the first people of the Americas "migrated" to North America from Asia is thus as much a misconception as is the image of the Berengian subcontinent as a "bridge." For although the origins of the earliest Americans can indeed ultimately be traced back to Asia (just as Asian and European origins ultimately can be traced back to Africa), the now-submerged land that we refer to as Berengia was the homeland of innumerable communities of these people for thousands upon thousands of years—for a span of time, for example, many times greater than that separating our world of today from the pre-Egyptian dawn of Near Eastern civilization more than fifty centuries ago. If anything, then, the direct precursors of American Indian civilizations were the Berengians, the ancient peoples of a once huge and bounteous land that now lies beneath the sea.

During most of the time that Berengia was above sea level, virtually the entire northernmost tier of North America was covered by an immensely thick mantle of glacial ice. As the earth's climate warmed, near the end of the geologic era known as the Pleistocene, the Wisconsin glaciation gradually began drawing to a close, a process that itself took thousands of years. It is estimated, for instance, that it took more than 4000 years for the dissolving ice barrier to creep north from what now is Hartford, Connecticut to St. Johnsbury, Vermont—a distance of less than 200 miles. With the partial melting of the great frozen glaciers, some of the water they had imprisoned was unlocked, trickling into the ocean basins and, over a great stretch of time, slowly lifting world-wide sea levels up hundreds of feet. As the water rose it began ebbing over and eventually inundating continental shelves once again, along with other relatively low-lying lands throughout the globe, including most of Berengia.

The natives of Berengia, who probably never noticed any of these gross geologic changes, so gradual were they on the scale of human time perception, naturally followed the climate-dictated changing shape of the land. Finally, at some point, Asia and North America became separate continents again, as they had been many tens of thousands of years earlier. Berengia was no more. And those of her inhabitants then living in the segregated Western Hemisphere became North America's indigenous peoples, isolated from the rest of the world by ocean waters on every side. Apart from the possible exception of a chance encounter with an Asian or Polynesian raft or canoe from time to time (possible in theory only, there is as yet no good evidence that such encounters ever actually occurred), the various native peoples of the Americas lived from those days forward, for thousands upon thousands of years, separate from the human life that was evolving and migrating about on the rest of the islands and continents of the earth.[11]

Much more controversial than the issue of where the first peoples of the Americas came from and how they got to the Western Hemisphere are the questions of when they originally moved from Berengia into North and South America—and how many people were resident in the New World when Columbus arrived in 1492. Both these subjects have been matters of intense scholarly scrutiny during the past several decades, and during that time both of them also have undergone revolutions in terms of scholarly knowledge. Until the 1940s, for example, it commonly was believed that the earliest human inhabitants of the Americas had migrated from the Alaskan portion of Berengia down into North and then South America no more than 6000 years ago. It is now recognized as beyond doubt, however, that numerous complex human communities existed in South America at least 13,000 years ago and in North America at least 6000 years before that. These are absolute minimums. Very recent and compelling archaeological evidence puts the date for earliest human habitation in Chile at 32,000 B.C. or earlier and North American habitation at around 40,000 B.C., while some highly respected scholars contend that the actual first date of human entry into the hemisphere may have been closer to 70,000 B.C.[12]

Similarly dramatic developments have characterized scholarly estimates of the size of the pre-Columbian population of the Americas. In the 1940s and 1950s conventional wisdom held that the population of the entire hemisphere in 1492 was little more than 8,000,000—with fewer than 1,000,000 people living in the region north of present-day Mexico. Today, few serious students of the subject would put the hemispheric figure at less than 75,000,000 to 100,000,000 (with approximately 8,000,000 to 12,000,000 north of Mexico), while one of the most well-regarded specialists in the field recently has suggested that a more accurate estimate would be around 145,000,000 for the hemisphere as a whole and about 18,000,000 for the area north of Mexico.[13]

III

In the most fundamental quantitative ways, then, recent scholarship has begun to redirect inquiry and expose falsehoods that have dominated characterizations of the Americas' native peoples for centuries—although very little of this research has yet found its way into textbooks or other nontechnical historical overviews. It now appears likely, for example, that the people of the so-called New World were already well-established residents of plains, mountains, forests, foothills, and coasts throughout the Western Hemisphere by the time the people of Europe were scratching their first carvings onto cave walls in the Dordogne region of France and northern Spain. It also is almost certain that the population of the Americas (and probably even Meso- and South America by themselves) exceeded the combined total of Europe and Russia at the time of Columbus's first voyage in 1492. And there is no doubt at all, according to modern linguistic analysis, that the cultural diversity of the Americas' pre-Columbian indigenous peoples was much greater than that of their Old World counterparts.[14] A bit of common sense might suggest that this should not be surprising. After all, North and South America are four times the size of Europe. But common sense rarely succeeds in combating cultural conceit. And cultural conceit has long been the driving force behind the tales most European and white American historians have told of the European invasion of the Americas.

The native peoples of the Americas are far from unique, of course, in traditionally having the basic elements of their historical existence willfully misperceived. In his sweeping and iconoclastic study of modern Africa, for instance, Ali A. Mazrui makes the cogent point that ethnocentrism has so shaped Western perceptions of geography that the very maps of the world found in our homes and offices and classrooms, based on the famous Mercator projection, dramatically misrepresent the true size of Africa by artificially deflating its land area (and that of all equatorial regions of the world) in comparison with the land areas of Europe and North America.[15] Because the Mercator map exaggerates the distance between the lines of latitude for those regions that lie closest to the poles, North America is made to appear one and a half times the size of Africa when in fact Africa contains in excess of 2,000,000 more square miles of land. A proportional cartographic distortion also affects the comparative depictions of Africa and Europe. Thus, the literal "picture" of Africa in relation to the rest of the world that schoolchildren have been taught for centuries is in fact an outright fraud.

A parallel ethnocentrism—this time historical, however, not geographic—traditionally has distorted conventional European and American views of the native American past. While texts on the subject routinely acknowledge the high civilizations of the Aztecs and the Incas (although the more sordid aspects of their religious rituals never fail to dominate discussion), the rest of North and South and Central America prior to the arrival of Europeans generally is seen as a barbaric wasteland.

Outside the perimeters of the Aztec and Inca empires, in that portion of the Americas lying south of the Rio Grande, most accounts tend to imply that there was nothing deserving of a modern reader's attention. One historian suggests that this myopia only indicates "that the geographical focus of modern scholarship parallels closely the political and economic realities of colonial times" in Meso- and South America, when the Europeans' hunger for gold caused them to focus their interests and concerns disproportionately on central Mexico and Peru.[16] As for the area north of the Rio Grande, the millions of Indians who lived for many centuries in permanently settled agricultural and sometimes urban communities on this vast continent are most often described as "handfuls of indigenous people" who were "scattered" across a "virgin land," "a vast emptiness," or even a "void," to cite the descriptions of some recently published, well-regarded, and symptomatic historical texts. The Indians themselves, according to these accounts, were simply "a part of the landscape" who lived, like other "lurking beasts," in a "trackless wilderness," where they had "no towns or villages" and either lived in "houses of a sort" or simply "roamed" across the land. The cultures of these "redskins" were, at best, "static and passive" (except when they were indulging in their "strange ceremonies" or taking advantage of their "compliant maidens"), though once encountered by Europeans, these living "environmental hazards" showed themselves to be "treacherous" and "belligerent," "savage foes" and "predators," for whom "massacre and torture were [the] rule," who introduced to Europeans the meaning of "total war," and whose threat of "nightly terror . . . haunted the fringes of settlement through the whole colonial era."[17]

This hostile attitude of stubbornly determined ignorance, it should be noted, is not confined to textbook writers. Recently, three highly praised books of scholarship on early American history by eminent Harvard historians Oscar Handlin and Bernard Bailyn have referred to thoroughly populated and agriculturally cultivated Indian territories as "empty space," "wilderness," "vast chaos," "unopened lands," and the ubiquitous "virgin land" that blissfully was awaiting European "exploitation." Bailyn, for his part, also refers to forced labor and slavery at the hands of the invading British as "population recruitment," while Handlin makes more references to the Indians' "quickly developed taste for firewater" than to any other single attribute.[18] And Handlin and Bailyn are typical, having been trained by the likes of the distinguished Samuel Eliot Morison who, a decade and a half earlier, had dismissed the indigenous peoples of the Americas as mere "pagans expecting short and brutish lives, void of hope for any future." (Earlier in his career Morison referred to Indians as "Stone Age savages," comparing their resistance to genocide with "the many instances today of backward peoples getting enlarged notions of nationalism and turning ferociously on Europeans who have attempted to civilize them.")[19]

It should come as no surprise to learn that professional eminence is no bar against articulated racist absurdities such as this, but if one example were chosen to stand for all the rest, perhaps the award would go to Hugh Trevor-Roper, the Regius Professor of Modern History at Oxford University, who wrote at the start of his book *The Rise of Christian Europe* of "the unrewarding gyrations of barbarous tribes in picturesque but irrelevant corners of the globe," who are nothing less than people without history. "Perhaps, in the future, there will be some African history to teach," he conceded, "but at present there is none, or very little: there is only the history of Europeans in Africa. The rest is largely darkness, like the history of pre-European, pre-Columbian America. And darkness is not a subject for history."[20]

The Eurocentric racial contempt for the indigenous peoples of North and South America, as well as Africa, that is reflected in scholarly writings of this sort is now so complete and second nature to most Americans that it has passed into popular lore and common knowledge of the "every schoolboy knows" variety. No intent to distort the truth is any longer necessary. All that is required, once the model is established, is the recitation of rote learning as it passes from one uncritical generation to the next.

As Mazrui points out with regard to the cartographic distortions that uniformly minimize Africa as a physical presence in the world, the historical distortions that systematically reduce in demographic and cultural and moral significance the native peoples of the Americas are part of a very old and enduring political design. They constitute what the historian of South Africa, Leonard Thompson, calls a "political mythology." In Thompson's words, a political myth is "a tale told about the past to legitimize or discredit a regime," whereas a political mythology is "a cluster of such myths that reinforce one another and jointly constitute the historical element in the ideology of the regime or its rival."[21] The occasion for these observations by Thompson was his book analyzing South Africa's system of *apartheid*. Two of the basic building blocks of this particular political mythology are the fabricated notions, embedded in Afrikaner imperialist history, that the blacks of South Africa—apart from being barbaric, so-called Hottentot brutes—were themselves fairly recent arrivals in the southern part of the continent, and that they were relatively few in number when the first European colonizers arrived.[22] Thus, in the Afrikaners' mythical version of the South African past, European settlers moved into a land that was largely empty, except for a small number of newly arrived savages who in time succumbed to progress and—thanks to the material comforts provided by the modern world, compared with the dark barbarism of their African ancestors—ultimately wound up benefiting from their own conquest.

One of the functions of this particular type of historical myth was described some years ago by the historian Francis Jennings. In addition to the fact that large and ancient populations commonly are associated with civilization and small populations with savagery, Jennings noted that, in cases where an invading population has done great damage to an existing native culture or cultures, small subsequent population estimates regarding the pre-conquest size of the indigenous population nicely serve "to smother retroactive moral scruples" that otherwise might surface.[23] Writing a few years after Jennings, Robert F. Berkhofer made much the same point regarding manufactured historical views of native barbarism: "the image of the savage," he stated flatly, serves "to rationalize European conquest."[24]

Jennings and Berkhofer could well have been writing about South Africa and its morally rationalizing post-conquest historians, but they were not; they were writing about America and *its* morally rationalizing post-conquest chroniclers. For the political mythology that long has served to justify the South African practice of *apartheid* finds a very close parallel in America's political mythology regarding the history of the Western Hemisphere's indigenous peoples. Indeed, this same form of official mendacity commonly underpins the falsified histories, written by the conquerors, of colonial and post-colonial societies throughout the world.

Employing what Edward W. Said has called "the moral epistemology of imperialism," the approved histories of such societies—the United States, Israel, South Africa, and Australia among them—commonly commence with what Said refers to as a "blotting out of knowledge" of the indigenous people. Adds another observer, native peoples in most general histories are treated in the same way that the fauna and flora of the region are: "consigned to the category of miscellaneous information. . . . they inhabit the realm of the 'etc.' "[25] Once the natives have thus been banished from collective memory, at least as people of numerical and cultural consequence, the settler group's moral and intellectual right to conquest is claimed to be established without question. As Frantz Fanon once put it: "The colonialist . . . reaches the point of no longer being able to imagine a time occurring without him. His irruption into the history of the colonized people is deified, transformed into absolute necessity."[26] Then, as Said has cogently observed, the *settler* group adorns itself with the mantle of the victim: the European homeland of the colonists—or the metropolitan European power that politically controls the settlement area—is portrayed as the oppressor, while the European settlers depict themselves as valiant seekers of justice and freedom, struggling to gain their deserved independence on the land that they "discovered" or that is theirs by holy right.

In such post-independence national celebrations of self, it is essential that the dispossessed native people not openly be acknowledged, lest they become embarrassingly unwelcome trespassers whose legacy of past and ongoing persecution by the celebrants might spoil the festivities' moral tone. This particular celebration, however, has gone on long enough. Before turning to an examination of the European invasion of the Americas, then, and the monumental Indian population collapse directly brought on by that genocidal siege, it is necessary that we survey, however briefly, some of the cultures of the Americas, and the people who created them, in the millennia that preceded the European conquest.

2

COMBINED, NORTH AMERICA and South America cover an area of 16,000,000 square miles, more than a quarter of the land surface of the globe. To its first human inhabitants, tens of thousands of years ago, this enormous domain they had discovered was literally a world unto itself: a world of miles-high mountains and vast fertile prairies, of desert shrublands and dense tropical rain forests, of frigid arctic tundra and hot murky swamps, of deep and fecund river valleys, of sparkling-water lakes, of canopied woodlands, of savannahs and steppes—and thousands upon thousands of miles of magnificent ocean coast. There were places where it almost never rained, and places where it virtually never stopped; there were places where the temperature reached 130 degrees Fahrenheit, and places where it dropped to 80 degrees below zero. But in all these places, under all these conditions, eventually some native people made their homes.

By the time ancient Greece was falling under the control of Rome, in North America the Adena Culture already had been flourishing for a thousand years. As many as 500 Adena living sites have been uncovered by modern archaeologists. Centered in present-day Ohio, they radiate out as far as Vermont, New York, New Jersey, Pennsylvania, Maryland, and West Virginia. We will never know how many hundreds more such sites are buried beneath the modern cities and suburbs of the northeastern United States, but we do know that these early sedentary peoples lived in towns with houses that were circular in design and that ranged from single-family dwellings as small as twenty feet in diameter to multi-family units up to eighty feet across. These residences commonly were built in close proximity to large public enclosures of 300 feet and more in diameter that modern archaeologists have come to refer to as "sacred circles" because of their presumed use for religious ceremonial purposes. The buildings they constructed for the living, however, were minuscule compared with the receptacles they built for their dead: massive tombs, such as that at Grave Creek in West Virginia, that spread out hundreds of feet across and reached seven stories in height—and that were commonplace structures throughout Adena territory as early as 500 B.C.[1]

In addition to the subsistence support of hunting and fishing, and gathering the natural fruit and vegetable bounty growing all around them, the ancient Adena people imported gourds and squash from Mexico and cultivated them along with early strains of maize, tubers, sunflowers, and other plant domesticates. Another import from the south—from South America—was tobacco, which they smoked through pipes in rituals of celebration and remembrance. From neighboring residents of the area that we now know as the Carolinas they imported sheets of mica, while from Lake Superior and beyond to the north they acquired copper, which they hammered and cut and worked into bracelets and rings and other bodily adornments.

Overlapping chronologically with the Adena was the Hopewell Culture that grew in time to cover an area stretching in one direction from the northern Great Lakes to the Gulf of Mexico, in the other direction from Kansas to New York. The Hopewell people, who as a group were physiologically as well culturally distinguishable from the Adena, lived in permanent communities based on intensive horticulture, communities marked by enormous earthen monuments, similar to those of the Adena, that the citizenry built as religious shrines and to house the remains of their dead.[2] Literally tens of thousands of these towering earthen mounds once covered the American landscape from the Great Plains to the eastern woodlands, many of them precise, geometrically shaped, massive structures of a thousand feet in diameter and several stories high; others—such as the famous quarter-mile long coiled snake at Serpent Mound, Ohio—were imaginatively designed symbolic temples.

No society that had not achieved a large population and an exceptionally high level of political and social refinement, as well as a sophisticated control of resources, could possibly have had the time or inclination or talent to design and construct such edifices. In addition, the Hopewell people had trade networks extending to Florida in one direction and Wyoming and North Dakota in the other, through which they acquired from different nations of indigenous peoples the copper, gold, silver, crystal, quartz, shell, bone, obsidian, pearl, and other raw materials that their artisans worked into elaborately embossed and decorative metal foil, carved jewelry, earrings, pendants, charms, breastplates, and other objets d'art, as well as axes, adzes, awls, and more. Indeed, so extensive were the Hopewell trading relationships with other societies throughout the continent that archaeologists have recovered from the centers of Hopewell culture in Ohio more materials originating from outside than from within the region.[3]

To the west of the Hopewell there emerged in time the innumerable villages of the seemingly endless plains—large, usually permanent communities of substantial, multi-family homes and common buildings, the villages themselves often fortified with stockades and dry, surrounding moats. These were the progenitors of the people—the Mandan, the Cree, the Blood, the Blackfoot, the Crow, the Piegan, the Hidatsa, the Arikara, the Cheyenne, the Omaha, the Pawnee, the Arapaho, the Kansa, the Iowa, the Osage, the Kiowa, the Wichita, the Commanche, the Plains Cree, various separate nations of Sioux, and others, including the Ute and Shoshoni to the west—who became the classic nomads on horseback that often serve as the popular American model for all Indian societies. But even they did not resort to that pattern of life until they were driven to it by invading armies of displaced Europeans.

Indeed, although the modern horse originated in the Americas, by 10,000 B.C. or so it had become extinct there as well. The only survivors from then until their reintroduction by the Spanish were the Old World breeds that long ago had moved across Berengia in the opposite direction from that of the human migrants, that is, from east to west and into Asia. Thus, there could not have been a nomadic life on horseback for the Indians of the plains prior to European contact, because there were no horses in North America to accommodate them. On the contrary, most of the people who lived in this region were successful hunters and farmers, well established in settled communities that were centered—as are most of today's midwestern towns—in conjunction with the rivers and adjoining fertile valleys of the Great Plains. Others did relocate their towns and villages on cyclical schedules dictated by the drastically changing seasons of this area, disassembling and reassembling their portable homes known as *tipis*. These dwellings were far different from the image most modern Americans have of them, however; when one of the earliest European explorers of the southwestern plains first came upon an Indian village containing scores of carefully arranged *tipis* "made of tanned hides, very bright red and white in color and bell-shaped . . . so large that in the most ordinary house, four different mattresses and beds are easily accommodated," he marveled at their comfort and extraordinary resistance to the elements, adding that "they are built as skillfully as any house in Italy."[4]

Since the land area supporting the people of the plains included about a million square miles of earth—that is, more than twice the area of formerly Soviet Central Asia—all generalizations about the societies and cultures that occupied the land are invariably rife with exceptions. Roughly speaking, however, the Indian peoples of the western plains thrived well into the post-Columbian era on the enormous herds of bison—along with elk, deer, bears, and other game—that these descendants of ancient wooly mammoth hunters had used as their primary means of sustenance for thousands of years. The same generally was true on the southern plains. But these varied peoples also were very active traders, principally with the other, more densely settled cultures of the plains to the north and to the east who raised advanced strains of maize and beans and other lesser-known plant crops, such as the unprepossessing but widely grown prairie turnip—which has three times the protein content of the potato and nearly the same level of vitamin C as most citrus fruits.[5]

Far to the north of the plains settlements, from Baffin and Ellesmere islands, off the coast of Greenland in the east, to the Yukon and beyond in the west, lay the enormous Arctic and Subarctic areas, inhabited by the Iglulik, the Nelsilik, and other Eskimo peoples, as well as the Aleut, the Koyukon, the Ingalik, the Tanana, the Kulchin, the Han, the Nabesna, the Tagish, the Hare, the Tahltan, the Kaska, the Tsetsaut, the Sekani, the Dogrib, the Salteaux, the Naskapi, the Beothuk, and others. If it were a country unto itself, this dominion today would be the seventh largest nation on earth in land area, just behind the entire continent of Australia, but larger than all of India including Kashmir.

The first people to migrate here had moved into what one archaeologist has called "the coldest, darkest, and most barren regions ever inhabited by man." But they were a hardy and tenacious lot whose varied and ingenious dwellings ranged from the well known *iglu* snow house (usually about 30 feet in diameter and often connected by domed passageways to clusters of other *iglus* as well as to large common rooms for feasting and dancing) to the huge semi-subterranean *barabara* structures of the Aleutian Islands, each of them up to 200 feet long and 50 feet wide, and housing more than 100 people. The residents of these northernmost regions survived the rigorous tests of the natural environment, and they flourished; as that same archaeologist who had described this area in terms of its cold, dark, and barren harshness later acknowledged, the early inhabitants of the Arctic and Subarctic possessed all the tools "that gave them an abundant and secure economy [and] they developed a way of life that was probably as rich as any other in the nonagricultural and nonindustrial world."[6] For subsistence, along with the fish that they caught, and the birds that sometimes flocked so thickly overhead that they threatened to cover the sky, the people of this land hunted polar bears, arctic fox, musk oxen, caribou, and narwhals, seals, and walruses.

Forbidding though this place may seem to residents of the rest of the world, to its native people there was nothing, apart from one another, that they treasured so much. Observes anthropologist Richard K. Nelson, writing of the Koyukon, a people still living there today:

> To most outsiders, the vast expanse of forest, tundra, and mountains in the Koyukon homeland constitute a wilderness in the absolute sense of the word.

. . . But in fact the Koyukon homeland is not a wilderness, nor has it been for millennia. This apparently untrodden forest and tundra country is thoroughly known by a people whose entire lives and cultural ancestry are inextricably associated with it. The lakes, hills, river bends, sloughs, and creeks are named and imbued with personal or cultural meanings. Indeed, to the Koyukon these lands are no more a wilderness than are farmlands to a farmer or streets to a city dweller.[7]

Nelson's point is affectingly well illustrated in a story told by environmental author Barry Lopez about "a native woman [of this region], alone and melancholy in a hospital room, [who] told another interviewer she would sometimes raise her hands before her eyes to stare at them: 'Right in my hand, I could see the shorelines, beaches, lakes, mountains, and hills I had been to. I could see the seals, birds, and game. . .' "[8]

From the panhandle of Alaska south through the upper northwest and on down to the California border lived so many different cultural communities, densely settled and thickly populated, that we have no hope of ever recovering anything close to a complete record of their vibrant pasts. The Makah, the Strait, the Quileute, the Nitinat, the Nooksack, the Chemakum, the Halkomelem, the Squamish, the Quinault, the Pentlatch, the Sechelt, the Twana, and the Luchootseet are a baker's dozen of linguistically and culturally separate peoples whose communities were confined to the relatively small area that today is bounded by Vancouver to the north and Seattle to the south, a distance of less than 150 miles. Overall, however, the native peoples of the northwest coast made their homes along more than 2000 miles of coastline. Compared with other regions, archaeological research has been minimal in the northwest. As a result, while traditional estimates of the population prior to European contact rarely exceed a third of a million people, many more than that probably lived along this strip of land that is more extensive than the coastline of Peru—an area that supported about 6,500,000 people in a much harsher environment during pre-Columbian times. Indeed, one recent study has put the population of British Columbia alone at over 1,000,000 prior to Western contact.[9] In addition to the coastal settlements, moreover, even as late as the nineteenth century, after many years of wholesale devastation, more than 100 tribes representing fifteen different language groups lived on in British Columbia, Washington, Oregon, and Idaho—including the Chelan, the Yakima, the Palouse, the Walla Walla, the Nez Perce, the Umatilla, the Cayuse, the Flathead, the Coeur D'Alene, the Kalispel, the Colville, the Kootenay, the Sanpoil, the Wenatchee, the Methow, the Okanagan, the Ntlakyapamuk, the Nicola, the Lillooct, the Shuswap, and more.

Similarly, from the northern California border down to today's Golden Gate Bridge in the west and Yosemite National Park in the east, an area barely 250 miles by 200 miles, there lived the Tolowa, the Yurok, the

Chilula, the Karok, the Shasta, the Wiyot, the Whilkut, the Hupa, the Mattole, the Chimariko, the Yana, the Nongatl, the Wintu, the Nomlaki, the Lassik, the Wailaki, the Sinkyone, the Yuki, the Cahto, the Modoc, the Achumawi, the Atsugewi, the Maidu, the Nisenan, the Washo, the Konkow, the Patwin, the Wappo, the Lake Miwok, the Coast Miwok, the Pomo, and a branch of the Northern Paiute—to name but some of the Indian nations of this region, again, all culturally and linguistically distinct peoples, a diversity in an area of that size that probably has never been equaled anywhere else in the world. And we have not even mentioned the scores of other independent native communities and cultures that once filled the land along the entire western seaboard of Oregon and central and southern California, thick populations of people living off a cornucopia of earth and marine resources.

As in so much of ancient America, the social and political systems of the west coast cultures varied dramatically from one locale to the next. Much of the northwest, for example, was inhabited by permanent settlements of fishing and intensive foraging peoples who lived in large wooden-planked houses that often were elaborately decorated with abstract designs and stylized animal faces; many of these houses and public buildings had an image of an animal's or bird's mouth framing their entryways, sometimes with huge molded wooden "beaks" attached that when open served as entrance and exit ramps. Northwest coast peoples are perhaps best known, however, for their rich and demonstrative ceremonial lives and their steeply hierarchical political systems. Thus, the most common symbolic associations we make with these cultures involve their intricately carved totem poles and ritual masks, as well as their great status-proclaiming feasts known as potlatches. Indeed, from the time of first European contact on down to contemporary ethnohistorical investigation, to outsiders the single most compelling aspect of these peoples' lives has always been their flamboyant display of wealth and their material extravagance. Given the natural riches of their surrounding environment—including lush and game-filled evergreen forests, salmon-thick rivers, and ocean waters warmed by the Japanese current—such festivals of conspicuous consumption are easily understood.

The peoples of resource rich California also were known for their complicated coastal-inland trade networks and for their large multi-cultural fiestas which apparently functioned in part to maintain and expand trade relationships.[10] But in addition—and in contrast to their neighbors to the north—the California peoples were noteworthy for their remarkably egalitarian and democratically ordered societies. As anthropologists long ago demonstrated, native California peoples such as the Wintu found it difficult even to express personal domination and coercion in their language, so foreign were those concepts to their ways of life.[11] And for most of California's Indian peoples those ways of life were directly tied to the great bounty nature had given them. Although many of them were, in a technical sense, hunter-gatherer societies, so rich in foodstuffs were the areas in which they settled that they had to move about very little in order to live well. Writing of the Ohlone peoples—a general name for forty or so independent tribes and many thousands of people who inhabited the coastal area between present-day San Francisco and Monterey—Malcolm Margolin has put it well:

> With such a wealth of resources, the Ohlones did not depend upon a single staple. If the salmon failed to run, the people moved into the marshes to hunt ducks and geese. If the waterfowl population was diminished by a drought, the people could head for the coast where a beached whale or a run of smelts might help them through their troubles. And if all else failed, there were always shellfish: mussels, clams, and oysters, high in nutrients and theirs for the collecting. . . . All around the Ohlones were virtually inexhaustible resources; and for century after century the people went about their daily life secure in the knowledge that they lived in a generous land, a land that would always support them.[12]

"In short," as Margolin writes, "the Ohlones did not practice agriculture or develop a rich material culture, not because they failed, but because they succeeded so well in the most ancient of all ways of life."[13]

Other California peoples did practice agriculture, however, and the very earliest European explorers found it and the numbers of people living in the region awe-inspiring. Describing his voyage along the southern California coast in 1542 and 1543, Juan Rodríguez Cabrillo repeatedly noted in his journal comments on the large houses he observed; the "very fine valleys [with] much maize and abundant food"; the "many savannahs and groves" and "magnificent valleys" that were "densely populated"—as was, he added, "the whole coastline." Again and again, wherever he went, he marveled at the "many pueblos," the "dense population," and the "thickly settled" coasts and plains. Even the small and subsequently uninhabited Santa Barbara islands, lying 25 to 70 miles off the coast—San Miguel, Santa Rosa, Santa Cruz, Santa Catalina, San Clemente, Santa Barbara, San Nicholas—were populated by "a great number of Indians" who greeted the Spanish ships in friendship and traded with them in ceremonies of peace. In all, from the islands to the coasts to the valleys and the plains that he observed, Cabrillo wrote, this "densely populated . . . country appears to be very fine."[14]

Just what the population of California was at this time is unknown. The most commonly cited estimate is something in excess of 300,000—while other calculations have put it at 700,000 and more.[15] Although the larger figure is regarded by many scholars as excessive, both it and the lower number represent estimates for California's Indian population only in 1769, the time of the founding of the Franciscan mission—that is, more than two centuries *after* initial Spanish incursions into the region. Even at the time of Cabrillo's voyage in 1542, however, the Indians reported to him the presence of other Spaniards in the area who, he wrote, "were killing many natives." And there is clear evidence that European diseases had a serious impact on California's native peoples throughout the sixteenth and seventeenth centuries.[16] Since, as we shall see in a later chapter, during those same two centuries the native population of Florida was reduced by more than 95 percent, primarily by Spanish-introduced diseases but also by Spanish violence, it is likely that the indigenous population of California also was vastly larger in the early sixteenth century than it was in 1769. A population of 300,000 for all of California, after all, works out to a population density somewhere between that of the Western Sahara and Mongolia today—hardly suggestive of Cabrillo's "thickly settled" and "densely populated" environs. Indeed, 700,000—rather than being excessive—will in time likely turn out to have been an excessively conservative estimate.

To the east of California lay the vast, dry spaces of the southwest, what is now southern Utah and Colorado, parts of northwestern Mexico, southern Nevada, west Texas, and all of Arizona and New Mexico. The Papago, the Pima, the Yuma, the Mojave, the Yavapai, the Havasupai, the Hualapai, the Paiute, the Zuni, the Tewa, the Navajo, the Hopi, the Towa, the Cocopa, the Tiwa, the Keres, the Piro, the Suma, the Coahuiltec, and various Apache peoples (the Aravaipa, the Coyotera, the Chiricahua, the Mimbreno, the Jicarella, the Mescalero, the Lipan) are just some of the major extant cultures of the southwest. And all these large cultural designations contain within them numerous smaller, but distinctive, indigenous communities. Thus, for example, the Coahuiltecs of the Texas-Mexico borderlands actually are more than 100 different independent peoples who are grouped together only because they speak the Coahuiltec language.[17]

The major ancient cultural traditions of this region were those of the Anasazi, the Hohokam, and the Mogollon. Together, these cultures influenced the lives of peoples living, from east to west, across the virtual entirety of modern-day Arizona and New Mexico, and from middle Utah and Colorado in the north to Mexico's Sonora and Chihuahua deserts in the south. This area has supported human populations for millennia, populations that were growing maize and squash more than 3000 years ago.[18] Indeed, agriculture in the pre-Columbian era attained a higher level of development among the people of the southwest than among any other group north of Mesoamerica. Beginning 1700 years ago, the Hohokam, for example, built a huge and elaborate network of canals to irrigate their crops; just one of these canals alone was 8 feet deep, 30 feet wide, 8 miles long, and was able to bring precious life to 8000 acres of arid desert land. Other canals carried water over distances of more than 20 miles.[19] The general lingering fame of these societies, however, rests predominantly on

their extraordinary artistry, craftsmanship, and architectural engineering—
from fine and delicate jewelry and pottery to massive housing complexes.

Among the numerous outstanding examples of southwest architectural
achievement are the Chacoan communities of the San Juan Basin in Colorado and New Mexico, within the Anasazi culture area. Chaco Canyon is
near the middle of the San Juan Basin, and here, more than a thousand
years ago, there existed the metropolitan hub of hundreds of villages and
at least nine large towns constructed around enormous multi-storied building complexes. Pueblo Bonito is an example of one of these: a single, four-
story building with large high-ceilinged rooms and balconies, it contained
800 rooms, including private residences for more than 1200 people and
dozens of circular common rooms up to 60 feet in diameter. No single
structure in what later became the United States housed this many people
until the largest apartment buildings of New York City were constructed
in the nineteenth century. But in its time Pueblo Bonito was far from unique.
Poseuinge, near present-day Ojo Caliente, is another example among many:
a complex of several adjoining three-story residential buildings, Poseuinge
(or Posi) contained more than 2000 rooms.[20]

In the dry surrounding countryside the people of this region—not only
the ancient Hohokam—constructed intricate canals and ditches, with
diversion dams, floodgates, and other runoff control systems, alongside
which they planted gardens.[21] So successful were these water management
systems that, as Peter Nabokov and Robert Easton have observed, "virtually all of the water that fell in the immediate vicinity was channeled
down spillways and troughs to feed their gardens and replenish their reservoirs."[22] And in recent decades aerial photography has revealed the
presence of great ancient roadways up to 30 feet wide that linked the
hundreds of Chaco Canyon communities with at least fifty so-called outlier
population centers up to 100 miles away, each of which contained its own
complex of large, masonry pueblos. In all, it appears that these roads connected together communities spread out over more than 26,000 square
miles of land, an area the size of Belgium and the Netherlands combined—
although recent studies have begun to suggest that the Chaco region was
even larger than the largest previous estimates have surmised. Indeed, as
an indication of how much remains to be learned about these ancient peoples and societies, in the Grand Canyon alone more than 2000 indigenous
habitation sites have thus far been identified, of which only three have
been excavated and studied intensively—while almost half of the canyon's
1,200,000 acres of land area has never even been seen at close range by
an archaeologist or a historian.[23]

Despite the enormous amount of organized labor that was necessary
to construct their carefully planned communities, the native people of the
southwest have always been known for their political egalitarianism and
their respect for personal autonomy. The earliest Spanish visitors to the

southwest—including Franciso Vásquez de Coronado in 1540 and Diego Pérez de Luxán in 1582—frequently commented on the widespread equality and codes of reciprocity they observed among such Pueblo peoples as the Hopi and the Zuni; the only significant class distinctions that could be discerned were those that granted power and prestige (but not excessive wealth) to the most elderly women and men.[24] Observing the descendants of these same peoples 400 years later, twentieth-century anthropologists continue to reach similar conclusions: it is "fundamentally indecent," anthropologist Clyde Kluckhohn once wrote of the Navajo, "for a single individual to make decisions for the group."[25] That was far from the case, however, for the Indians of the southeast who were encountered by Hernando de Soto in the early sixteenth century during his trek north through Florida in search of gold. Here, much more hierarchical political and personal arrangements prevailed.

At one location during his travels in the southeast de Soto was met by the female leader of the Cofitachequi nation who was carried in a sedan chair, was wrapped in long pearl necklaces, and rode in a cushion-filled and awning-covered boat. She commanded a large area of agriculturally productive land, once settled with dense clusters of towns and filled with impressively constructed ceremonial and burial sites. In plundering those sites de Soto's men found elegantly carved chests and art objects, pearl inlaid and copper-tipped weapons, and other valuables (including as many as 50,000 bows and quivers) that at least one of the conquistadors compared favorably with anything he had seen in fabulously prosperous Mexico or Peru. It was an apt comparison, not only because the jewelry and pottery from this area is distinctly similar in many respects to that of Mesoamerica and the Andes, but because large and dense city-like settlements, built in stockade fashion and surrounded by intensely cultivated agricultural plantations were common here, as were state and quasi-state organizations in the political realm. Major cultural centers here include those of the Caddo peoples, the Hasinai, the Bidai, the Atakapa, the Tunica, the Chickasaw, the Tuskegee, the Natchez, the Houma, the Chocktaw, the Creek, the Tohome, the Pensacola, the Apalachee, the Seminole, the Yamasee, the Cusabo, the Waccamaw, the Catawba, the Woccon—and again, as in other regions, many more. No other part of North America outside of Mesoamerica had such complex and differentiated societies, and no other area outside of the northwest coast and California was so linguistically diverse—much more diverse, in fact, than Western Europe is today.[26]

Pottery developed in this region at least 4000 years ago and true agriculture followed about 1000 years later. Although the people of the southeast did hunt and fish, they lived primarily in sedentary communities distinguished by clusters of towering temple mounds, large public buildings that each held scores and sometimes hundreds of assigned seats for political and religious gatherings, and assemblages of individual family houses that spread out over as many as fifteen to twenty miles. The people living in these state-like communities largely were nourished by enormous fields of corn, beans, and other produce that they harvested in two or even three crops each year and stored in corn cribs and granaries. They were superb basket-makers, carpenters, potters, weavers, tanners, and fishermen. Some, like the Calusa, fished from large canoes in the open ocean, while they and others also gathered clams and oysters from the coasts and used weirs and basket traps and spears and stupefying herbs to catch fish in rivers and in streams.[27]

The Calusa, in fact, are especially intriguing in that they defy conventional rules of political anthropology by having been a complex of hunting, fishing, and gathering societies that also were sedentary and highly stratified, with politically powerful and centralized governments. Paramount chiefs, who commanded standing armies of warriors who had no other work obligations, ruled directly over dozens of towns in their districts, while controlling dozens more through systems of tribute. Class rankings included nobles, commoners, and servants (who were military captives), while there were specialized roles for wood carvers, painters, engravers, navigators, healers, and the scores of dancers and singers who performed on ceremonial occasions. And such festivities were both frequent and major affairs: one European account from the sixteenth century describes a paramount chief's house as large enough to accommodate 2000 people "without being very crowded." Moreover, such buildings were not especially large by southeastern coast standards. As J. Leitch Wright, Jr., notes: "similar structures in Apalachee, Timucua, and Guale (coastal Georgia) held considerably more."[28]

Elaborate social and cultural characteristics of this nature are not supposed to exist among non-agricultural or non-industrial peoples, but like many of the hunting and gathering societies of the northwest, the Calusa lived in an environment so rich in easily accessible natural resources that agriculture was not needed to maintain large, stable, politically complex settlements. One measure of the great size of these communities can be seen in the middens—the refuse collections studied by archaeologists—that the Calusa left behind. Throughout the world, among the largest shellfish middens known to exist are those at Ertebølle in Denmark, where they range up to 30 acres in size and almost 10 feet in height. In comparison, shell middens from Calusa areas throughout southwest Florida have been found covering up to 80 acres of land and reaching to heights of 20 feet— that is, many times the cubic volume of the largest Ertebølle middens. And yet, enormous as these deposits are—testifying to extraordinary concentrations of population—ethnohistorical and archaeological evidence indicates that shellfish were not a major component of the Calusa diet.[29]

Far to the north of the Calusa and the hundreds of other cultural centers in what today are Florida, Georgia, Mississippi, Louisiana, Arkansas, Kentucky, South Carolina, North Carolina, Tennessee, and Virginia, resided the Tuscarora, the Pamlico, the Secotan, the Nottaway, the Weapemeoc, the Meherrin, the Powhatan, the Susquehannock, and the Delaware—to just begin a list that could be multiplied many times over. Beyond them, of course, were the great Northern Iroquoian nations—the Seneca, the Oneida, the Mohawk, the Onandaga, the Cayuga, the Wenro, the Erie, the Petun, the Neutral, the Huron, and the St. Lawrence Iroquois. And the New England Indian nations—the Pennacook, the Nipmuk, the Massachusett, the Wampanoag, the Niantic, the Nauset, the Pequot, the Mahican, the Narraganset, the Wappinger, the Mohegan, and more. Traditionally these native peoples were thought to have lived in very thinly populated settlements, but recent re-analyses of their population histories suggest that such separate nations as the Mohawk, the Munsee, the Massachusett, the Mohegan-Pequot, and others filled their territorial areas with as many or more residents per square mile as inhabit most western regions in the present-day United States. Overall, according to one estimate, the Atlantic coastal plain from Florida to Massachusetts supported more than 2,000,000 people before the arrival of the first Europeans.[30]

Probably the most common association that is made with the congregations of northeastern cultures concerns their sophisticated domestic political systems and their formal networks of international alliances, such as the Five Nation confederacy of the Iroquois League, founded in the middle of the fifteenth century and composed of the independent Mohawk, Oneida, Onondaga, Cayuga, and Seneca peoples. Many writers, both historians and anthropologists, have argued that the League was a model for the United States Constitution, although much controversy continues to surround that assertion. The debate focuses largely on the *extent* of Iroquois influence on Euro-American political thought, however, since no one denies there was some influence.[31] Indeed, as numerous historians have shown, overall American Indian political and social organization had a powerful impact on European social thought, particularly in seventeenth- and eighteenth-century France.[32] In any case, however the controversy over Iroquois influence on the U.S. Constitution eventually is decided, it will not minimize the Iroquois achievement, since—as one of the originators of the notion of a connection between the League and the Constitution, J.N.B. Hewitt of the Smithsonian Institution, admitted when he first propounded the hypothesis more than fifty years ago:

> Some of the ideas incorporated in the League of the Five Nations were far too radical even for the most advanced of the framers of the American Constitution. Nearly a century and a half was to elapse before the white men could reconcile themselves to woman suffrage, which was fundamental in the Indian government. They have not yet arrived at the point of abolishing capital punishment, which the Iroquois had accomplished by a very simple

legal device. And child welfare legislation, prominent in the Iroquois scheme of things, had to wait for a century or more before the white men were ready to adopt it.[33]

To limit a description of female power among the Iroquois to the achievement of "woman suffrage," however, is to not even begin to convey the reality of women's role in Iroquois society. As the Constitution of the Five Nations firmly declared: "The lineal descent of the people of the Five Nations shall run in the female line. Women shall be considered the progenitors of the Nation. They shall own the land and the soil. Men and women shall follow the status of the mother."[34] In her survey and analysis of the origins of sexual inequality among the major cultures of the world, this is how anthropologist Peggy Reeves Sanday describes the exception of the Iroquois:

> In the symbolic, economic, and familial spheres the Iroquois were matriarchal, that is, female dominated. Iroquoian women headed the family longhouse, and much of the economic and ceremonial life centered on the agricultural activities of women. Men were responsible for hunting, war, and intertribal affairs. Although women appointed men to League positions and could veto their decisions, men dominated League deliberations. This tension between male and female spheres, in which females dominated village life and left intertribal life to men, suggests that the sexes were separate but equal, at least during the confederacy. Before the confederacy, when the individual nations stood alone and consisted of a set of loosely organized villages subsisting on the horticultural produce of women, females may have overshadowed the importance of males.[35]

Perhaps this is why, as Sanday later remarks: "Archaeological excavations of pre-Iroquoian village sites show that they were unfortified, suggesting that if there was an emphasis on warfare, it lacked major economic motivation, and conquest was an unknown objective."[36] And perhaps this also helps account for the unusually strong egalitarianism even among later Iroquois people—as among other native peoples of the northeast—on which early European visitors invariably remarked. The Jesuit Pierre de Charlevoix, for instance, traveled throughout what today is New York, Michigan, and eastern Canada and marveled at the early age at which Indian children were encouraged, with success, in seemingly contradictory directions—toward both prideful independence and cooperative, communal socialization. Moreover, he noted, the parents accomplished this goal by using the gentlest and subtlest of techniques. While "fathers and mothers neglect nothing, in order to inspire their children with certain principles of honour which they preserve their whole lives," he wrote, "they take care always to communicate their instructions on this head, in an indirect manner." An emphasis on pride and honor—and thus on the avoidance of shame—was the primary means of adult guidance. For example, notes

Charlevoix: "A mother on seeing her daughter behave ill bursts into tears; and upon the other's asking her the cause of it, all the answer she makes is, Thou dishonourest me. It seldom happens that this sort of reproof fails of being efficacious." Some of the Indians, he adds, do "begin to chastise their children, but this happens only among those that are Christians, or such as are settled in the colony."[37] The most violent act of disapprobation that a parent might use on a misbehaving child, Charlevoix and other visitors observed, was the tossing of a little water in the child's face, a gesture obviously intended more to embarrass than to harm.

Children, not surprisingly, learned to turn the tables on their parents. Thus, Charlevoix found children threatening to do damage to themselves, or even kill themselves, for what he regarded as the slightest parental correction: "You shall not have a daughter long to use so," he cites as a typical tearful reaction from a chastised young girl. If this has a familiar ring to some late twentieth-century readers, so too might the Jesuit's concern about the Indians' permissive methods of child rearing: "It would seem," he says, "that a childhood so ill instructed should be followed by a very dissolute and turbulent state of youth." But that, in fact, is not what happened, he notes, because "on the one hand the Indians are naturally quiet and betimes masters of themselves, and are likewise more under the guidance of reason than other men; and on the other hand, their natural disposition, especially in the northern nations, does not incline them to debauchery."[38]

The Indians' fairness and dignity and self-control that are commented on by so many early European visitors manifested themselves in adult life in various ways, but none more visibly than in the natives' governing councils. This is evident, for example, in a report on the Huron's councils by Jean de Brebeuf during the summer of 1636. One of the most "remarkable things" about the Indian leaders' behavior at these meetings, he wrote, "is their great prudence and moderation of speech; I would not dare to say they always use this self-restraint, for I know that sometimes they sting each other,—but yet you always remark a singular gentleness and discretion. . . . [E]very time I have been invited [to their councils] I have come out from them astonished at this feature."[39] Added Charlevoix on this same matter:

It must be acknowledged, that proceedings are carried on in these assemblies with a wisdom and a coolness, and a knowledge of affairs, and I may add generally with a probity, which would have done honour to the areopagus of Athens, or to the Senate of Rome, in the most glorious days of those republics: the reason of this is, that nothing is resolved upon with precipitation; and that those violent passions, which have so much disgraced the politics even of Christians, have never prevailed amongst the Indians over the public good.[40]

Similar observations were made of other Indian societies up and down the eastern seaboard.[41] In addition, most natives of this region, stretching from the densely settled southern shores of the Great Lakes (with a pre-Columbian population that has been estimated at close to 4,000,000) across to northern Maine on down to the Tidewater area of Virginia and over to the Cumberland River in Tennessee, displayed to their neighbors, and to strangers as well, a remarkable ethic of generosity. As the Jesuit Joseph François Lafitau, who lived among the Indians for six years, observed: "If a cabin of hungry people meets another whose provisions are not entirely exhausted, the latter share with the newcomers the little which remains to them without waiting to be asked, although they expose themselves thereby to the same danger of perishing as those whom they help at their own expense so humanely and with such greatness of soul. In Europe we should find few [people] disposed, in like cases, to a liberality so noble and magnificent."[42]

As with our earlier enumerations and comments on native peoples across the length and breadth of the continent, these examples of eastern indigenous cultures are only superficial and suggestive—touching here on aspects of the political realm, there on intimate life, and elsewhere on material achievement, in an effort to point a few small spotlights into corners that conventionally are ignored by historians of America's past. Untold hundreds of other culturally and politically independent Indian nations and tribes that we have not even tried to survey filled the valleys and plains and woodlands and deserts and coastlines of what are now Canada and the United States. So many more, in fact, that to name the relative few that we have, this tiny percentage of the whole, risks minimizing rather than illustrating their numbers. Perhaps the best way to convey some sense of these multitudes and varieties of culture is simply to note that a recent listing of the extant Indian peoples of North America produced a compilation of nearly 800 separate nations—about half of which are formally recognized by the United States as semi-sovereign political entities—but then cautioned that the list "is not exhaustive with regard to their subdivisions or alternate names. There are thousands more of both."[43]

In the same way that in the villages and towns and nations of other continents—of Asia and Africa and Europe—the social structures and political networks and resource production systems of different communities varied greatly from place to place and from time to time, so too was there astounding diversity and multiformity among North America's aboriginal peoples. As on those other continents, both in the past and in the present, some communities were small, isolated, provincial, and poor, barely scraping subsistence from the soil. Others were huge urban and commercial centers where large numbers of people, entirely freed from the necessity of subsistence work, carried out other tasks of artistry, engineering, construction, religion, and trade. And, between these extremes, there was a rich variety of cultural organization, a great diversity of social design. But in all these communities, regardless of size or organizational complexity, human beings lived out the joys and sorrows, the mischief, the humor, the high seriousness and tragedy, the loves, fears, hatreds, jealousies, kindnesses, and possessed all the other passions and concerns, weaknesses and strengths, that human flesh throughout the world is heir to.

Over time (again as in the histories of the other continents), cultures and empires in North America rose and fell, only to be replaced by other peoples whose material and political successes also waxed and waned while the long centuries and millennia inexorably unfolded. Not all the cultures surveyed in the preceding pages were contemporaneous with one another; certain of them ascended or declined centuries apart. Some of the societies that we have mentioned here, and some that went unmentioned, have long since disappeared almost without a trace. Others continue on. Some have had their remains so badly plundered that virtually nothing of them any longer exists—such as the once-massive Spiro Mound, a monument of an eastern Oklahoma people, that was looted of its treasures in the 1930s by the farmer who owned the land on which it stood. Literally tons of shell, pearl, and other precious objects were hauled out in wheelbarrows and sold by the side of the road. And then, for good measure, once the mound was emptied, the farmer had it dynamited into rubble.[44]

In contrast, other large communities have left immense and permanent reminders of their past glories—such as the huge earthen mound at Cahokia, Illinois. At the center of a large community that sprawled down the banks of the Illinois River for a distance as great as that from one end of San Francisco to the other today, with houses spread out over more than 2000 acres of land, stood a gigantic man-made structure extending ten stories into the air and containing 22,000,000 cubic feet of earth. At its base this monument, which was larger than the Great Pyramid of Egypt, covered 16 acres of land. About 120 other temple and burial mounds rose up in and around Cahokia which acted as the urban core for more than fifty surrounding towns and villages in the Mississippi Valley, and which by itself probably had a population of well over 40,000 people. In size and social complexity Cahokia has been compared favorably with some of the more advanced Maya city-states of ancient Mesoamerica.[45] And it was fully flourishing almost 2000 years ago.

These, then, are just some examples of the great multitudes of permanently settled societies that constituted what commonly and incorrectly are thought of today as the small and wandering bands of nomads who inhabited North America's "virgin land" before it was discovered by Europeans. In fact, quite to the contrary of that popular image, as the eminent geographer Carl O. Sauer once pointed out:

> For the most part, the geographic limits of agriculture have not been greatly advanced by the coming of the white man. In many places we have not

passed the limits of Indian farming at all. . . . In general, it may be said that the plant domesticates of the New World far exceeded in range and efficiency the crops that were available to Europeans at the time of the discovery of the New World. . . . The ancient Indian plant breeders had done their work well. In the genial climates, there was an excellent, high yielding plant for every need of food, drink, seasoning, or fiber. On the climatic extremes of cold and drought, there still were a remarkable number of plant inventions that stretched the limits of agriculture about as far as plant growth permitted. One needs only to dip into the accounts of the early explorers and colonists, especially Spanish, to know the amazement with which the Europeans learned the quality and variety of crop plants of Indian husbandry.[46]

Still, wildly inaccurate though the popular historical perception of Indian America as an underpopulated virgin land clearly is, on one level—a comparative level—the myth does contain at least a shred of truth. For despite the large, prolific, sophisticated, permanently settled, and culturally varied populations of people who inhabited the Americas north of Mexico prior to the coming of Columbus, their numbers probably did not constitute more than 10 to 15 percent of the entire population of the Western Hemisphere at that time.

II

The number of people living north of Mexico in 1492 is now generally estimated to have been somewhere between what one scholar describes as "a conservative total" of more than 7,000,000 and another's calculation of about 18,000,000.[47] These figures are ten to twenty times higher than the estimates of scholars half a century ago, but even the largest of them is dwarfed by the population of central Mexico alone on the eve of European contact. As noted earlier, probably about 25,000,000 people, or about seven times the number living in all of England, were residing in and around the great Valley of Mexico at the time of Columbus's arrival in the New World.

But the Aztec empire, with its astonishing white city of Tenochtitlán, was at the end of the fifteenth century only the most recent in a long line of magnificent and highly complex cultures that had evolved in Mesoamerica—where more than 200 separate languages once were spoken—over the course of nearly three thousand years.

Some time around 2500 B.C. villages were being established in the Valley of Oaxaca, each of them containing probably no more than a dozen or so houses surrounding a plaza that served as the community's ceremonial center. After about 1000 years of increasing sophistication in the techniques of growing and storing foodstuffs, by 1500 B.C., around the time of Amenhotep I in Egypt and a thousand years before the birth of Pericles in Athens, these people had begun to merge into the Olmec Empire that was then forming in the lowlands off the southernmost point of the Gulf coast in Mexico. Very little detail is known about Olmec culture or social structure, nor about everyday life in the other complex societies that had begun to emerge in northwest Central America at an even earlier time. But there is no doubt that in both regions, between 1500 B.C. and 2000 B.C., there existed civilizations that provided rich cultural lives for their inhabitants and that produced exquisite works of art.[48]

The core of the Olmec population was situated in a river-laced crescent of land that stretched out across the Isthmus of Tehuantepec on Mexico's southern Gulf coast. At first glance this appears to be an inhospitable area for the founding of a major population center and civilization, but periodic flooding of the region's rivers created a marshy environment and the richest agricultural lands in Mexico—land that often has been compared to the Nile delta in Egypt. From about 1200 B.C. to 900 B.C. the center of Olmec culture was located in what is now known as San Lorenzo, after which it was moved to La Venta. Here, in the symbolic shadow of their Great Pyramid—about 3,500,000 cubic feet in volume, a construction project that is estimated to have taken the equivalent of more than 2000 worker-years to complete—the Olmecs farmed extensively, worshiped their gods, enjoyed athletic contests involving ball games and other sports, and produced art works ranging from tiny, meticulously carved, jade figurines to enormous basalt sculpted heads more than ten feet tall.

Neither the jade nor the basalt used for these carvings was indigenous to the areas immediately surrounding either of the Olmec capitals. The jade apparently was brought in, along with other items, through a complicated trade network that spread out across the region at least as far as Guatemala, Honduras, Nicaragua, and Costa Rica. The basalt, on the other hand, was available from quarries in the Tuxtla Mountains, a little more than fifty miles away. From here in the mountains, writes archaeologist Michael Coe, in all probability the stones designated to become the huge carvings "were dragged down to navigable streams and loaded on great balsa rafts, then floated first down to the coast of the Gulf of Mexico, then up the Coatzacoalcos River, from whence they would have to be dragged, probably with rollers, up the San Lorenzo plateau." Coe observes that "the amount of labor which must have been involved staggers the imagination," as indeed it does, considering that the finished sculptures formed from these enormous boulders themselves often weighed in excess of twenty tons.[49]

Before the dawn of the West's Christian era another great city was forming well north of the Olmec region and to the east of the Lake of the Moon—Teotihuacan. Built atop an enormous underground lava tube that the people of the area had expanded into a giant cave with stairways and large multi-chambered rooms of worship, this metropolis reached its pinnacle by the end of the second century A.D., about the time that, half a world away in each direction, the Roman Empire and the Han dynasty in China were teetering on the brink of ultimate collapse. Teotihuacan was divided into quarters, bisected from north to south and east to west by two wide, four-mile long boulevards. Constructed around a nine-square-mile urban core of almost wall-to-wall buildings made from white stucco that was brightly painted with religious and mythological motifs, the over-all alignment of the city—with everything consistently oriented to 15 degrees 25 minutes east of true north—evidently had religio-astronomical meaning that has yet to be deciphered.[50] At its peak, the city and its sur-roundings probably contained a population of about a quarter of a million people, making it at the time one of the largest cities in the world. The density of population in the city itself far exceeded that of all but the very largest American metropolises today.

Teotihuacan too had its great pyramids—the huge, twenty-story-high Pyramid of the Sun and slightly smaller Pyramid of the Moon. In addition, the city contained numerous magnificent palace compounds. Typical of these was the Palace of Xolalpan, with 45 large rooms and seven fore-courts arranged around a sunken central courtyard that was open to the sky. Smaller sunken courts existed in many of the surrounding rooms as well, with light and air admitted through openings in the high column-supported ceilings, a design reminiscent of Roman *atria*.[51] Those not for-tunate enough to live in one of Teotihuacan's palaces apparently lived in large apartment complexes, such as one that has been unearthed in the ruins on the eastern side of the city, containing at least 175 rooms, five courtyards, and more than twenty *atria*-like forecourts. So splendid and influential was the architecture and artwork of this immense urban center that a smaller, contemporary reproduction of it, a town that Michael Coe says is "in all respects a miniature copy of Teotihuacan," has been found in the highlands of Guatemala—650 miles away.[52]

Many other cultures were flourishing in Mesoamerica while Teotihu-acan was in its ascendancy, some in areas of lush farming potential, others in regions where complex irrigation techniques were devised to coax life from agriculturally marginal land. The Zapotec civilization in a previously almost uninhabited part of the Valley of Oaxaca is a prime example of this latter situation. And in the heart of Zapotec country another major city emerged—Monte Albán—an urban center that may have been unique in all the world as a politically neutral capital (a so-called disembedded capital) for a confederation of semi-independent and historically adversar-ial political states.[53] Politically neutral or not, however, Monte Albán clearly was an important ceremonial community, spread out over fifteen square miles of land, and containing public plazas, temple platforms, and public buildings, including the Palace of Los Danzantes, constructed around three towering central pyramids.

The city's many residents, for the most part, lived in homes built on more than 2000 terraces that they had carved into the hillsides from which Monte Albán later took its European name. Monte Albán's population usually is estimated to have been somewhat in excess of 30,000 (about what New York City's population was at the beginning of the nineteenth century), but a recent analysis of the agricultural potential of adjacent farmland has raised some questions about that number that have yet to be addressed: it shows the 30,000 figure to be less than 10 percent of the population that could have been supported by available foodstuffs.[54]

All of this, and much more, pre-dates by centuries the rise of classic Maya civilization during the time of what traditionally has been known in Europe as the Dark Ages. Indeed, with every passing year new discoveries are made suggesting that we have hardly even begun to recognize or understand the rich cultural intricacies of pre-Columbian Mesoamerican life. A recent example was the discovery in 1987 of a huge, four-ton basalt monument in a riverbed near the tiny Mexican village of La Mojarra. What made this find so confounding was that the monument is covered with a finely carved inscription of more than 500 hieroglyphic characters, surrounding an elaborate etching of a king—hieroglyphics of a type no modern scholar had ever seen, and dating back almost two centuries before the earliest previously known script in the Americas, that of the Maya. It has long been recognized that several less complex writing traditions existed in Mesoamerica as early as 700 B.C. (and simpler Olmec symbolic motifs date back to 1000 B.C. and earlier), but the monument found in La Mojarra is a complete writing system as sophisticated as that of the Maya, yet so different that epigraphers, who study and analyze hieroglyphics, don't know where to begin in trying to decipher it.

Whoever created the monument—and whatever other examples may exist of this unknown, but highly literate culture that otherwise has disappeared without a trace—was able to employ a complicated array of very stylized syllabic letters and other geometric symbols that acted as punctuation throughout the text. But as well as the task of attempting to decipher the writing, the concerns of archaeologists have quickly focused on the site itself. After all, La Mojarra today is but a small, remote village and has always been considered a fairly insignificant archaeological site. "Yet," says archaeologist Richard Diehl, "here we have this wonderful monument and incredible text. What happened at La Mojarra?" And how many other La Mojarras were there? For, as the initial published report on the La Mojarra discovery observes, at the very least "it has added another interesting piece to what has become a very complex mosaic. . . . [in that] scholars now suspect there must have been many sophisticated local writing traditions before the Maya."[55]

Until—if ever—questions like these are answered, however, popular interest in early Mesoamerican society will continue to focus on the Maya. And for good reason. The Maya, after all, created what has to be one of the most extraordinary civilizations the world has ever known, a civilization that governed fifty or more independent states and that lasted in excess of 1000 years.

The Maya empire stretched out over a vast land area of more than 100,000 square miles, beginning in the Yucatán region of southern Mexico, across and down through present-day Belize and Guatemala toward the borders of Honduras and El Salvador. No one knows how large the Maya population was at its zenith, but scholarly estimates have ranged as high as eight to ten to thirteen million for just the Yucatán portion of the empire, an area covering only one-third of Maya territory.[56] Scores of major cities, all of them filled with monumental works of art and architecture, blanketed the lands of the Maya. Cities such as Kaminaljuyú, the key center for the growth of early Maya culture; Yaxchilán, a vibrant arts community; Palenque, with its extraordinary palatial architecture; Copán, with its Acropolis and its elegant and serene statuary, totally absent of any martial imagery; Uxmal, with its majestic Quadrangle and mysterious Pyramid of the Magician; and the great Toltec-Maya cities like Tula and the grandly opulent Chichén Itzá—to name just some of the more magnificent of such urban complexes.

Maya cities were geographically larger and less densely populated than were other Mesoamerican urban centers, particularly those of central Mexico. Thus, for instance, the wondrous city of Tikal, in the middle of the luxuriant Peten rain forest, seems to have contained more than three times the land area of Teotihuacan (more than six times by one recent estimate), and also had a huge population, but a population less concentrated than Teotihuacan's because most of its buildings and residential compounds were separated by carefully laid out gardens and wooded groves. Current research also is demonstrating that Tikal's population—now estimated at between 90,000 and 100,000 people—was sustained by an elaborate system of immense catchment reservoirs that may have been constructed in other lowland urban areas as well. Combined with advanced agricultural techniques that allowed Tikal's farmers to coax enormous crop yields out of raised wetland gardens, the reservoir systems probably enabled population densities in rural Maya communities to exceed 500 people per square mile—that is, as high as the most intensively farmed parts of rural China (and the metropolitan areas of modern-day Albany, Atlanta, Dallas, and San Diego)—while urban core areas attained densities as high as 5000 persons per square mile, more than half the density of the high-rise city of Detroit today.[57]

It was with the support of this sort of extraordinary agricultural foundation that Maya populations fanned out well beyond the outer boundaries of their cities, filling thousands of square miles with non-urban peoples, in some cases virtually from the portals of one major city to the gates of the next. To use Tikal as an example once again, a detailed recent archaeological-demographic analysis has shown that at least 425,000 people—four to five times the population of the city itself, and a much higher number than ever before supposed—were under the city's direct control throughout the surrounding countryside.[58]

Many thick volumes have been written on the wonders of Maya culture and civilization—its economic organization and trade networks, its fabulous artworks, its religion and literature, its complex calendrical and astrological systems, and more. This is not the place to try to review any of this work, but it is important at least to point out how little we still know of these people. Their involved writing system, combining elements of both phonetic and ideographic script, for example, appears to have been fully expressive of the most intricate and abstract thinking and has been compared favorably to Japanese, Sumerian, and Egyptian—but it continues to defy complete translation.

Similarly, for many years the absence of a gridwork layout to streets, plazas, and buildings in Maya cities puzzled scholars. Right angles weren't where they logically should have been, buildings skewed off oddly and failed to line up in the expected cardinal directions; everything seemed to twist away from an otherwise generally northward presentation. Apparently, said some archaeologists, Maya builders were incompetent and couldn't construct simple right angles. Given the exquisite and precise alignments of every other aspect of Maya architecture, however, others thought this to be at best a hasty criticism. And now it is beginning to become evident that these seeming eccentricities of engineering had nothing to do with incompetence.

On the contrary, a complicated and original architectural pattern had always been present—the same pattern, some began to notice, in city after city after city—but its conceptual framework was so foreign to conventional Western perception and thought that it remained effectively invisible. Recently, the "code," as it were, of Maya engineering and construction has begun to be deciphered, and the story it reveals is mind-boggling. So precise were the Maya calendrical measurements and astronomical observations—and so central were these cosmic environmental calculations to their ritual and everyday lives—that the Maya constructed their cities in such a way that everything lined up exactly with specific celestial movements and patterns, particularly as they concerned the appearance and disappearance of the planet Venus in the evening sky.[59] We will never understand deeply the world of the ancient Maya. Too much has already been lost. But, in addition to what is known about their exceptional achievements in creating a vast and complex empire of trade, commerce, politics, urban planning, architecture, art, and literature, what anthropologist and astronomer Anthony Aveni has said about the life of the mind among the Maya surely is correct:

Their cosmology lacks the kind of fatalism present in our existential way of knowing the universe, one in which the purposeful role of human beings seems diminished. These people did not react to the flow of natural events by struggling to harness and control them. Nor did they conceive of themselves as totally passive observers in the essentially neutral world of nature. Instead, they believed they were active participants and intermediaries in a great cosmic drama. The people had a stake in all temporal enactments. By participating in the rituals, they helped the gods of nature to carry their burdens along their arduous course, for they believed firmly that the rituals served formally to close time's cycles. Without their life's work the universe could not function properly. Here was an enviable balance, a harmony in the partnership between humanity and nature, each with a purposeful role to play.[60]

If we were fully to follow the course of Mesoamerican culture and civilization after the Maya, we next would have to discuss the great Toltec state, and then the Mixtecs (some of whose history is recorded in those of their bark-paper and deerskin-covered books and codices that survived the fires of the Spanish conquest), and finally the Aztecs—builders of the great cities like Tenochtitlán, with which the previous chapter began. Of course, the empire of the Aztecs was much more extensive than that described earlier, centered on the Lake of the Moon. At its peak the empire reached well over 700 miles to the south of Tenochtitlán, across the Valley of Oaxaca, past the Isthmus of Tehuantepec, and into the piedmont and rich coastal plain of the province of Xoconocho on the border of modern-day Guatemala. Some provinces were completely subservient to the empire's might, while others, such as large and powerful Tlaxcallan to the east retained its nation-within-an-empire independence. Still others warded off Aztec control entirely, such as the immense Tarascan Kingdom to the north, about which little yet is known, but which once stretched out over 1000 miles across all of Mexico from the Gulf on one side to the Pacific Ocean on the other.

And then in Central America—beyond the reach of Maya or later Aztec influence—there were the culturally and linguistically independent Lenca peoples, the Jicaque, the Paya, the Sumu, and the Chorotega of present-day Honduras. In pre-Columbian times Honduras may easily have had a population in excess of 1,400,000 people—almost a third of what it contains even today.[61] Further to the south, Nicaragua's indigenous population probably reached at least 1,600,000 before the arrival of the Spanish—a little less than half of what the country's population is at present.[62] In all, current estimates of the size of pre-Columbian Central America's population (Guatemala, Honduras, Belize, El Salvador, Nicaragua, Costa Rica, and Panama) range from a low of about 5,650,000 to a high of more than 13,500,000.[63] The latter figure represents nearly half the 1990 population (around 29,000,000) of these turbulent and rapidly growing nations. And still we have not yet begun to discuss the entire continent of South America, by itself almost twice the size of China, larger than all of Europe and Australia combined.

A glance at the South American civilizations might begin with the cluster of independent chiefdoms that once dominated the northern Andes, where Ecuador and Colombia are today. These are commonly overlooked cultures in modern history texts, but they were not ignored by the first Europeans in the New World, who were drawn to them because of the fantastic wealth in gold and gems that they promised.

One story that the conquistadors had heard—and one that turned out to be true—concerned the Muisca people who lived in the vicinity of Lake Guatavita, a lake formed in the distant past by the impact of a falling meteor, high in the mountains of Colombia. Whenever a new leader of the Muisca acceded to power the coronation ritual involved his being anointed with a sticky gum or clay to which gold dust would adhere when sprayed on his body, apparently through tubes of cane stalk. Once thus transformed into a living statue of gold, the new leader stepped onto a raft that was laden down with gold and emerald jewelry. Specially garbed priests aboard the raft then directed it to the center of the lake. At the same time, the entire Muisca population surrounded the lake, playing musical instruments and holding many more gold and emerald implements in their hands. At an appointed moment, possibly as dawn broke and the lake's waters and the new leader's gilded body gleamed in the morning sun, he dove into the center of the lake, washing away the gold dust as his people threw their precious offerings into the sacred water-filled meteor crater.

A small fragment of the Muisca gold that survived the earliest Spanish depredations, along with some gold from other peoples of the region, is now housed in the Museo del Oro of the Banco de la República in Bogotá. It consists of about 10,000 golden artifacts, everything from small animal carvings and masks to spoons and nose rings. As one writer describes the experience of viewing this treasure house, unwittingly donated by a people about whom most of us have never heard:

> You walk down a corridor lined on both sides with display cases, each case packed with these opulent creations. You turn right, walk down another corridor past more of the same. Then more. And more. Finally, instead of going out, you are led into a dark room. After you have been there awhile the lights begin rising so gradually that you expect to hear violins, and you find yourself absolutely surrounded by gold. If all of Tut's gold were added to this accumulation, together with everything Schliemann plucked from Mycenae and Hissarlik, you could scarcely tell the difference.[64]

Turning from the northernmost parts of the Andes to the immediate south we encounter the region where, at the time of Columbus, the single most extensive empire on earth was located—the land of the Inca, stretching down the mountainous western spine of South America over a distance equivalent to that now separating New York and Los Angeles. This is a land with an ancient history. More than four thousand years before the flowering of the Incas, other cultures had existed in this region, some of which were built entirely on intricate systems of trade. The earliest of these seem to have been in the Andean highlands, communities—such as La Galgada, Huaricoto, Huacaloma, and others—characterized by large populations and extraordinary multi-storied works of monumental architecture. Many of these sites, just being uncovered and analyzed today, are causing excitement in archaeological circles because, as one scholar points out: "Mesoamerica, long thought to be the precocious child of the Americas, was still confined to the Mesoamerican village during the time we are talking about, and monumental architecture in Peru was a thousand years old when the Olmecs began their enterprise."[65] For the sake of world cultural context, this also means that Peruvian monumental architecture was in place by the time the Painted Pottery culture of neolithic northern China emerged, that it existed before England's Stonehenge was created, and that it was already about a thousand years old when Tutankhamen's body was being embalmed in Egypt.

These were societies, as noted, that developed in the Andean highlands. Others, also of ancient origin, emerged in coastal areas. One example, still being excavated by archaeologists today, is a complex of enormous stone structures known as El Paraíso that is located on the central Peruvian coast. Here, around 3800 years ago, there stood a large urban center that drew sustenance from fishing and the cultivation of some edible plants, such as beans and peppers, but whose dominant agricultural product was cotton. The inhabitants of El Paraíso used their cotton plantations to produce raw materials for the manufacture of fishing nets and clothing, which they traded with other coastal and highland communities to complement their limited variety of foodstuffs. Of especial interest to political historians is the fact that this large and complex society—whose residential and ceremonial buildings had required the quarrying of at least 100,000 tons of rock from the surrounding hillsides—apparently existed for centuries without a centralized political power structure; all the archaeological evidence uncovered thus far indicates that the people of El Paraíso built their huge stone structures and carried out their highly organized monocrop agriculture and trade while living under remarkably egalitarian political conditions.[66]

In contrast, during its relatively brief reign 3000 years later, the Inca empire was directed by a highly structured elite whose powers encompassed and governed, either directly or indirectly, nearly a hundred entirely different linguistic, ethnic, and political communities.[67] These included the people who built the splendid, cloud-enveloped, and almost otherworldly Andean city of Machu Picchu high in the remote forested mountains—so high and so remote that once Machu Picchu was deserted it was not found again (at least by non-Indians) until the twentieth century. And then there were and are the Nazca people, whose culture was flourishing 2000 years ago. These are the people who created on the barren desert floor south of present-day Lima enormous etchings of various living things—humming-birds, condors, dogs, plants, spiders, sharks, whales, and monkeys—as well as spiritual figures, domestic designs (such as a huge ball of yarn and a needle), and precisely aligned geometric patterns, including trapezoids, tri-angles, zigzags, and spirals. Because of their great size (a single line of a geometric figure may run straight as a ruler for more than half a mile) the full patterns of these perfectly drafted images can only be seen from the air or from very high ground. As a result, outlandish modern theories of origin have circulated widely, betraying once again our unthinking dispar-agement of the native peoples of this region who, it intuitively is thought, could not possibly have created anything so monumental and precise. In-terestingly (and conveniently overlooked by those who believe these great projects to be the work of outsiders), many of the same designs from the desert floor are found decorating ancient Nazca ceramics as well, and ad-ditional oversize animal representations and other designs, less famous and smaller in scale, have also been found in North American deserts, 3000 miles away.[68]

Compared with Mesoamerican cities, those of the Incas were almost austere. Even the fabulous city of Cuzco at first seemed most brilliant in its superb surface simplicity, its streets laid out on a cruciform plan, its houses mostly single-story affairs with steeply pitched roofs to fend off the heavy rains of the Andes. Apart from its gold, the first Europeans were most impressed with Cuzco's exceptional cleanliness, perhaps exemplified by the clear-water rivers and streams from the mountains that flowed through the center of the Inca capital. Before entering the city these waters' upstream pools and rivulets provided bathing and recreation for Cuzco's inhabitants; for years after the Spanish conquest, wrote one conquistador, it was common to find there "small gold ornaments or pins which [Inca women] forgot or dropped while bathing."[69] As the waters ran through Cuzco, however, they were captured and diverted into perfectly engineered stone gutters that followed the routes of the city's many streets, helping to wash away debris and keep the roadways clean.

At the center of Cuzco was an enormous plaza, large enough to accom-modate 100,000 people wrote the Spanish friar Martín de Murúa, and here any sense of the city's austerity ended. When the pleasure-loving peo-ple of this metropolis held their frequent dances and festivals in the square, it was roped off with a fine cable of gold, immensely long and fringed at both ends with bright red wool. Around the ceremonial square stood Cuz-co's palaces, each built by an Inca ruler during his reign. Here lay the dead leaders' mummified remains, along with all their furniture and treasures.

There were no locks or keys and nothing in the palaces was hidden: as John Hemming puts it,"the Incas were too confident of the security of their empire and the honesty of its citizens to hide their dead rulers' possessions."[70]

All the Inca palaces were different—made of various types of marble, rare woods, and precious metal—but each had at least one common characteristic: enormous halls and ballrooms capable of holding up to 4000 people for banquets and dances when the weather prevented such festivities from being held outdoors. One such hall, which "served on rainy days as a plaza for [Inca] festivals and dances . . . was so large," wrote Garcilaso de la Vega, "that sixty horsemen could very easily play *cañas* inside it." More exquisite even than the palaces, however, was the famed temple of the sun, Coricancha. A magnificent masonry structure with precisely curved and angled walls, Coricancha's majesty was crowned with an eight-inch-wide band of solid gold that encircled the entire building below the roof line. Along with all the other treasure that it held, at the temple's center was a ceremonial font and a massive altar of gold, surrounded by gold and silver images of the moon, of stars, of thunder—and the great Punchao, a massive golden sun, expertly crafted and encrusted with precious jewels. Of all this, though, it was the garden within its walls that most amazed the chroniclers who wrote about Coricancha: a simple garden of maize—but an artificial garden—with the stem and leaves of each perfect plant delicately fashioned in silver, while each crowning ear of corn was carved in gold.[71]

Cuzco's population in pre-Columbian times probably was somewhere between 150,000 and 200,000; beyond the city itself, many more people, living and working on vast maize plantations, filled the surrounding valleys. Although some Mesoamerican cities, such as Tenochtitlán, were larger, few cities in Europe at the time even approached the size of Cuzco. Nor would any of them have been able to compete with Cuzco in terms of the treasures it contained or the care with which it was laid out. For we now know that Cuzco was built following a detailed clay-model master plan, and that—as can be seen from the air—the outline of its perimeter was designed to form the shape of a puma with the famed temple-fortress of Sacsahuaman at its head.[72]

But if Cuzco was unique within Peru for the lavishness of its appointments, it was far from alone in the large number of its inhabitants. Other cities in other Andean locales were also huge; some are famous today, others are not. Among this latter group was the provincial city of Jauja. Here is a short description of it by Miguel de Estete, one of the earliest Spaniards to set eyes on it:

> The town of Jauja is very large and lies in a beautiful valley. A great river passes near it, and its climate is most temperate. The land is fertile. Jauja is

built in the Spanish manner with regular streets, and has several subject villages within sight of it. The population of the town and the surrounding countryside was so great that, by the Spaniards' reckoning, a hundred thousand people collected in the main square every day. The markets and streets were so full that every single person seemed to be there.[73]

A hundred thousand people gathered in the marketplace of a single provincial city each day? Many historians intuitively have supposed this to be an exaggeration, but after conducting the most detailed and exhaustive of Peru's population histories to date, Noble David Cook has concluded that the number "does not appear extravagant."[74]

To feed a population as enormous as this, and a population spread out over such a vast area, the Incas cut miles upon miles of intricate and precisely aligned canals and irrigated agricultural terraces from the steep Andean hillsides in their mountain home; and to move those foodstuffs and other supplies from one area to another they constructed more than 25,000 miles of wide highways and connecting roads. Both engineering feats astonished the Spaniards when they first beheld them. And for good reason: modern archaeologists and hydrologists are just as amazed, having discovered that most of these grand public works projects were planned, engineered, and constructed to within a degree or two of slope and angle that computer analyses of the terrain now regard as perfect. At the time of European contact, the thickly populated Andean valleys were criss-crossed with irrigation canals in such abundance, wrote one conquistador, that it was difficult, even upon seeing, to believe. They were found "both in upland and low-lying regions and on the sides of the hills and the foothills descending to the valleys, and these were connected to others, running in different directions. All this makes it a pleasure to cross these valleys," he added, "because it is as though one were walking amidst gardens and cool groves. . . . There is always verdure along these ditches, and grass grows beside many of them, where the horses graze, and among the trees and bushes there is a multitude of birds, doves, wild turkey, pheasants, partridge, and also deer. Vermin, snakes, reptiles, wolves—there are none."[75]

Describing the Incas' "grand and beautiful highway" that ran along the coast and across the plains was something in which all the early chroniclers delighted. From fifteen to twenty-four feet in width, and "bordered by a mighty wall more than a fathom high," this "carefully tended" roadway "ran beneath trees, and in many spots the fruit laden boughs hung over the road," recalled Pedro de Cieza de León, "and all the trees were alive with many kinds of birds and parrots and other winged creatures."[76] The great highway and other roads dipped through steep coastal valleys, hugged the edges of precipitous cliffs, tunneled through rock, and climbed in stepladder fashion up sheer stone walls.

Encountering rivers and lakes in the paths of their roadways, the people of the Andes built large ferries or had engineers design floating pontoon bridges: stretching thick, intertwined cables across the water over distances the length of a modern football field, secured on each side to underground foundations, workmen layered huge bundles of reeds with still more taut cables on top of the original bridge platforms, thus creating secure floating highways usually about fifteen feet in width and riding three feet or so above the water's surface. Even after the Spanish conquest these bridges remained in use, carrying men, horses, and supplies—as did the hundreds of suspension bridges that the Incas had strung across gorges and high mountain passes throughout the Andes. "Such magnificent roads could be seen nowhere in Christendom in country [as] rough as this," wrote Hernando Pizarro, a judgment echoed by modern scholars and engineers who have had an opportunity to study them.[77]

Inca roads and bridges were not built for horse traffic, however, but for men and women on foot, sometimes accompanied by trains of llamas. Thus, the ambivalent reactions of many conquistadors—ranging from admiration for Inca ingenuity to terror in the face of their environment—when they had to travel these roads in their quests for riches and power. After crossing a river, wrote one such Spaniard,

> we had to climb another stupendous mountainside. Looking up at it from below, it seemed impossible for birds to scale it by flying through the air, let alone men on horseback climbing by land. But the road was made less exhausting by climbing in zigzags rather than in a straight line. Most of it consisted of large stone steps that greatly wearied the horses and wore down and hurt their hooves, even though they were being led by their bridles.[78]

Under such exhausting conditions, the Spanish and other latter day intruders no doubt appreciated the more than one thousand large lodging houses and hostels and storehouses—some of them multi-storied, some built into hillside terraces—that had been provided for travelers along the Inca roadways. Like most Inca buildings, these generally were constructed by masons working with large, finely worked stones, carefully honed and finished to such a degree of smoothness that even when not secured by mortar the thinnest blade could not pass between them. "In all Spain I have seen nothing that can compare with these walls and the laying of their stone," wrote Cieza de León; they "were so extraordinary," added Bernabé Cobo, "that it would be difficult for anyone who has not actually seen them to appreciate their excellence."[79] So massive and stable were the Inca walls built in this way that many of them remain in place as the foundations for buildings throughout modern-day Peru. In Cuzco, after the conquest, the Spanish symbolically built their church of Santo Domingo atop the walls of the ruined Coricancha—and for centuries since, while earthquakes repeatedly have destroyed the church, the supporting walls of the great temple of the sun have never budged.

Although, as we shall see, the early Europeans appreciated the people of the Andes a good deal less than they did those people's engineering accomplishments, later visitors came to agree with the Spanish historian José de Acosta who, after spending many years in Peru, wrote in 1590: "Surely the Greeks and the Romans, if they had known the Republics of the Mexicans and the Incas, would have greatly esteemed their laws and governments." The more "profound and diligent" among the Europeans who have lived in this country, wrote Acosta, have now come to "marvel at the order and reason that existed among [the native peoples]."[80]

The life of the mind in the Inca-controlled Andes is beyond the scope or range of this brief survey, but like all the thousands of pre-Columbian cultures in the Americas it was deeply embedded both in the wonders and the cyclical rhythms of the surrounding natural world and in cultural affection for the unending string of genealogical forebears and descendants who had lived and who would live on indefinitely (or so it was thought) in these marvelous mountains and valleys and plains. As one recent analysis of Inca thought and philosophy puts it:

> The relationships Andeans perceived between life and death, and between humankind and the natural environment, were . . . profoundly different from Spanish and Christian equivalents. The land surrounding one told the story of one's first ancestors as much as it told one's own story and the story of those yet to come. It was right that the familiar dead were seen walking through the fields they had once cultivated, thus sharing them with both the living and with the original ancestors who had raised the first crops in the very same fields. Death was thus the great leveler not because, as in Christian thought, it reduced all human beings to equality in relation to each other and before God. Rather, death was a leveler because by means of it humans were reintegrated into a network of parents and offspring that embraced the entire natural order.[81]

To the east of the Inca homeland, down from the majestic peaks of the Andes, are the dense jungles of the Amazon, followed by the Brazilian highlands, and then the pampas of present-day Argentina—together, well over four million square miles of earth, an area larger than that of the United States today. Within this land the world's largest river rushes through the world's greatest forest—and within that forest lived peoples so numerous and so exotic to the first Western visitors that the Europeans seemed unable to decide whether they had stumbled onto the legendary Terrestrial Paradise or an evil confederacy of demons, or maybe both.

Disappointed that there were no great cities in this boundless part of their New World, the earliest travelers let their imaginations run riot. There was evidence, some of them claimed, that the Apostle Saint Thomas had visited Brazil and preached to the natives a millennium and a half ago; if you looked carefully enough, it was said, you still could see his footprints impressed into rock alongside various river banks. Apparently his preaching was successful, since the natives of this region were so generous and kind, the Jesuit missionary Father Manuel Nobrega reported, that "there are no people in all the world more disposed to receive the holy faith and the sweet yoke of the evangel than these," adding that "you can paint on the heart of this people at your pleasure as on a clean sheet of paper."[82]

Others thought they found evidence of somewhat stranger things. As one historian summarizes some of the first European reports:

> There were men with eight toes; the Mutayus whose feet pointed backwards so that pursuers tracked them in the wrong direction; men born with white hair that turned black in old age; others with dogs' heads, or one cyclopean eye, or heads between their shoulders, or one leg on which they ran very fast. . . . Then there was Upupiara, half man and half fish, the product of fish impregnated by the sperm of drowned men. . . . Brazil was also thought to contain giants and pygmies.[83]

And, of course, there were said to be Amazons, from which the great river derived its name. In fact, however, apart from the sheer mystery of this fabulous and seemingly primeval world, perhaps the thing that most amazed and unnerved the Europeans had nothing to do with fairy tales. It had to do with the fact that this land was covered with innumerable independent tribes and nations of people who seemed inordinately happy and content, and who lived lives of apparent total liberty: "They have neither kings nor princes," wrote the Calvinist missionary Jean de Léry in 1550, "and consequently each is more or less as much a great lord as the other."[84]

Many of the people of this vast region—including such linguistically distinct cultures as the Tupian, the Cariban, the Jívaroan, the Nambiquaran, the Arawakan, the Tucanoan, the Makuan, the Tupi-Guaraní, and others—lived in cedar planked houses, slept in hammocks or on large palm leaf mats, wore feather cloaks and painted cotton clothing, and played a variety of musical instruments. Very recent and continuing archaeological work in the Amazon lowlands indicates that the people living there have been making pottery for at least 7000 to 8000 years—that is, from about the same time that pottery also was first being made in ancient Iraq and Iran, and around 3000 years earlier than current evidence suggests it was being made in the Andes or in Mesoamerica. Some ancient Amazonian peoples hunted and fished and gathered, others farmed. But there is no doubt that organized communities lived in this locale at least 12,000 years ago, evolving into large agricultural chiefdoms and—more than 1000 years ago—into very populous and sophisticated proto-urban communities, such as Santarém, which, in the words of one recent study, "was a center for complex societies with large, nucleated settlements" in which "people made elaborate pottery vessels and statues, groundstone tools and ornaments of nephrite jade."[85]

Because the Amazon climate and land is not conducive to the preservation of the materials of village life, archaeological work is very difficult, and thus retrospective estimates of pre-Columbian population levels are quite controversial here. No one doubts, however, that the population was large—probably at least 5,000,000 to 7,000,000 people in just the Amazon basin within Brazil, which is only one part of tropical South America, although arguments have been made for individual tribes (such as Pierre Clastres's estimate of 1,500,000 for the Guaraní) that, if correct, would greatly enlarge that regional figure.[86]

One of the things that has most intrigued some modern anthropologists—Clastres in particular—about the people of the Amazon was their ability to sustain such large populations without resorting to steeply hierarchical political systems, something conventional political theory claims is impossible. In most respects, in fact, these people who appointed chiefs from among their ranks, but made sure that their leaders remained essentially powerless, were the classic exemplars of anthropologist Marshall Sahlins's "original affluent society," where people had relatively few material possessions, but also few material desires, and where there was no poverty, no hunger, no privation—where each person's fullest material wants were satisfied with the expenditure of about fifteen to twenty hours of work each week.[87]

Life was far more difficult for the natives of Tierra del Fuego, the cold and blustery islands off the southern tip of South America, between the Strait of Magellan and Cape Horn, and as close to the Antarctic Circle as Ketchikan, Alaska, is to the Arctic. Population densities had to be much thinner in this rugged environment, where the people lived largely off hunted marine mammals, fish, and shellfish that they pried loose from rocky headlands. Unlike the inhabitants of the Amazon, the residents of Tierra del Fuego—the Yahgan, the Alacaluf, the Ona, and the Haúsh—had to struggle constantly to sustain life. Indeed, so important were their sturdy, migratory canoes to them as they made their way through the icy waters, that they maintained permanent fires in beds of clay on board while they searched for the animal life on which they fed their families.

Harsh as life was for these peoples, the land and the water were their home. And, though we know little about them as they lived in pre-Columbian times, it is not difficult to imagine that they revered their homeland much as their relatives all over the hemisphere did, including those in the even more icy world of the far north. The people of Tierra del Fuego, after all, had lived in this region for at least 10,000 years before they were first visited by the wandering Europeans.[88]

Tierra del Fuego, along with Patagonia, its immediate mainland neighbor to the north, was the geographic end of the line for the great hemispheric migrations that had begun so many tens of thousands of years earlier. No one in human history has ever lived in permanent settlements further south on the planet than this. But those countless migrations did not invariably follow a north-to-south pathway. At various times (again, we must recall, over the course of tens of thousands of years) some groups decided to branch off and head east or west, or double back to the north. There is linguistic evidence, for example, seeming to suggest that during one historical epoch the Timucuan peoples of present-day Florida may gradually have migrated from the south (in Venezuela) across the island Caribbean to their new North American homeland. That also is what a people we have come to call the Arawak (they did not use the name themselves) decided to do a few thousand years ago, although, unlike the hypothesis regarding the Timucuans, they did not carry their travels as far as the northern mainland.[89]

Arawak is the general, post-Columbian name given to various peoples who made a long, slow series of migrations from the coast of Venezuela to Trinidad, then across open ocean perhaps first to Tobago, then Grenada, and on up the chain of islands that constitute the Antilles—St. Vincent, Barbados, St. Lucia, Martinique, Dominica, Guadeloupe, Montserrat, Antigua, Barbuda, St. Kitts, Anguilla, St. Croix, the Virgin Islands, Puerto Rico, Hispaniola, Jamaica, Cuba—then finally off to the Bahamas, leaving behind at each stop populations that grew and flourished and evolved culturally in their own distinctive ways. To use a comparison once made by Irving Rouse, the people of these islands who came to be known as Arawaks are analogous to those, in another part of the world, who came to be known as English: "The present inhabitants of southern Great Britain call themselves 'English,' and recognize that their ethnic group, the English people, is the product of a series of migrations from the continent of Europe into the British Isles, beginning with various prehistoric peoples and continuing with the Celts, Angles, Saxons, Vikings, and Normans of protohistoric time."[90]

Similarly, Arawak (sometimes "Taino," but that is a misnomer, as it properly applies only to a particular social and cultural group) is the name now given to the melange of peoples who, over the course of many centuries, carried out those migrations across the Caribbean, probably terminating with the Saladoid people sometime around two thousand years ago. By the time of their encounter with Columbus and his crews, the islands had come to be governed by chiefs or *caciques* (there were at least five paramount chiefdoms on Hispaniola alone, and others throughout the region) and the people lived in numerous densely populated villages both inland and along all the coasts. The houses in most of these villages were similar to those described by the Spanish priest Bartolomé de Las Casas:

> The inhabitants of this island . . . and elsewhere built their houses of wood and thatch in the form of a bell. These were very high and roomy so that in each there might be ten or more households. . . . On the inside designs and

symbols and patterns like paintings were fashioned by using wood and bark that had been dyed black along with other wood peeled so as to stay white, thus appearing as though made of some other attractive painted stuff. Others they adorned with very white stripped reeds that are a kind of thin and delicate cane. Of these they made graceful figures and designs that gave the interior of the houses the appearance of having been painted. On the outside the houses were covered with a fine and sweet-smelling grass.[91]

These large buildings conventionally were arranged to face the great house that was inhabited by the local *cacique,* and all of them in turn faced an open field or court where dances and ball games and other festivities and ceremonies were held. In larger communities, several such fields were placed at strategic locations among the residential compounds.

The people of these climate-blessed islands supported themselves with a highly developed level of agriculture—especially on Cuba and Hispaniola, which are among the largest islands on earth; Cuba, after all, is larger than South Korea (which today contains more than 42,000,000 people) and Hispaniola is nearly twice the size of Switzerland. In the infrequent areas where agricultural engineering was necessary, the people of the Indies created irrigation systems that were equal in sophistication to those existing in sixteenth-century Spain.[92] Their staple food was cassava bread, made from the manioc plant *yuca,* which they cultivated in great abundance. But also, through so many long generations in the same benign tropical environment, the Arawaks had devised an array of unique methods for more than satisfying their subsistence needs—such as the following technique which they used to catch green sea turtles weighing hundreds of pounds, large fish, and other marine life, including manatees:

> Noting that the remora or suckerfish, *Echeneis naucrates,* attached itself to the body of a shark or other larger fish by means of a suction disc in its head, the Arawaks caught, fed, and tamed the remora, training it to tolerate a light cord fastened to its tail and gill frame. When a turtle was sighted the remora was released. Immediately it swam to the turtle, attaching its suction disc to the under side of the carapace. The canoe followed the turtle, the Arawak angler holding a firm line on the remora which, in turn, held tightly to its quarry until the turtle could be gaffed or tied to the canoe.[93]

In addition to this technique, smaller fish were harvested by the use of plant derivatives that stupefied them, allowing the natives simply to scoop up large numbers as though gathering plants in a field. Water birds were taken by floating on the water's surface large calabashes which concealed swimmers who would seize individual birds, one at a time, without disturbing the larger flock. And large aquaculture ponds were created and walled in to maintain and actually cultivate enormous stocks of fish and turtles for human consumption. A single one of these numerous reed marine corrals held as many as 1000 large sea turtles. This yielded a quantity of meat equal to that of 100 head of cattle, and a supply that was rapidly replenished: a fertile female turtle would lay about 500 eggs each season. Still, the Arawaks were careful not to disturb the natural balance of these and other creatures; the evidence for this is that for millennia they sustained in perpetuity their long-term supply of such natural foodstuffs. It was only after the coming of the Spanish—and, in particular, their release of dogs and pigs that turned feral and ran wild—that the wildlife ecology of the islands found itself in serious trouble.[94]

In sum, as Caribbean expert Carl Sauer once put it, "the tropical idyll of the accounts of Columbus and Peter Martyr was largely true" regarding the Arawak. "The people suffered no want. They took care of their plantings, were dextrous at fishing and were bold canoeists and swimmers. They designed attractive houses and kept them clean. They found aesthetic expression in woodworking. They had leisure to enjoy diversion in ball games, dances, and music. They lived in peace and amity."[95]

III

Much the same thing that Sauer says about the Arawak can be said for many of the other peoples we have surveyed here, and for countless others we had neither the time nor the space to mention. Certainly not all of them, however. And again, this is what would be expected on any large body of land containing such remarkable geographic and cultural diversity. Some of the native peoples of the Americas did indeed suffer from want, at least from time to time, and some lived hard and difficult lives. Some had little time or talent for great art or architecture, or for elaborate games or music or dance. Others lived in societies that, far from being characterized by peace and amity, frequently were at odds with their neighbors.

There is no benefit to be gained from efforts to counter the anti-Indian propaganda that dominates our textbooks with pro-Indian propaganda of equally dubious veracity. For the very plain fact is that the many tens of millions of people who lived in the Americas prior to 1492 were human— neither subhuman, nor superhuman—just human. Some of the social practices of selected groups of them we would find abhorrent to our cultural tastes and attitudes at present, in the same way that we would find loathsome certain social practices of earlier European and Asian cultures. Thus, for example, few of us today would countenance the practice of human sacrifice as a way of propitiating an angry god, as was done by a few of the highest urban cultures in Mesoamerica during the fifteenth- and early sixteenth-century. However, neither would many of us support the grisly torture and killing of thousands of heretics or the burning of tens of thousands of men and women as witches, in a similar effort to mollify a jealous deity, as was being done in Europe, with theocratic approval, at precisely the same time that the Aztecs were sacrificing enemy warriors.

Conversely, other social practices of certain native Americans in the pre-Columbian era—from methods of child rearing and codes of friendship and loyalty, to worshiping and caring for the natural environment—appear far more enlightened than do many of the dominant ideas that we ourselves live with today. (Even in the sixteenth century the conquering Spanish wrote "with undisguised admiration" of Aztec childrearing customs, notes historian J.H. Elliott. "Nothing has impressed me more," commented the Jesuit José de Acosta, "or seemed to me more worthy of praise and remembrance, than the care and order shown by the Mexicans in the upbringing of their children.")[96] If these attitudes and behaviors varied in emphasis from one native group to another, one characteristic of America's indigenous peoples that does seem almost universal, transcending the great diversity of other cultural traits, was an extraordinary capacity for hospitality. We have noted this in our discussion of the Iroquois and the Indians of California, but in fact, the native peoples' affectionate and fearless cordiality in greeting strangers was mentioned by almost all the earliest European explorers, from Vespucci in South America in 1502, where the Indians "swam out to receive us . . . with as much confidence as if we had been friends for years," to Cartier in Canada in 1535, where the Indians "as freely and familiarly came to our boats without any fear, as if we had ever been brought up together."[97]

And these were more than ceremonial, more than passing generosities. Indeed, without the assistance of the Indians in everything from donated food supplies to instruction in the ways of hunting and fishing and farming, the earliest European settlements, particularly in North America, could not have taken root. As Edmund S. Morgan has shown, with regard to Roanoke in the 1580s:

> Wingina [the local chief] welcomed the visitors, and the Indians gave freely of their supplies to the English, who had lost most of their own when the *Tyger* [their ship] grounded. By the time the colonists were settled, it was too late to plant corn, and they seem to have been helpless when it came to living off the land. They did not know the herbs and roots and berries of the country. They could not or would not catch fish in any quantity, because they did not know how to make weirs. And when the Indians showed them, they were slow learners: they were unable even to repair those that the Indians made for them. Nor did they show any disposition for agriculture. Hariot admired the yields that the Indians got in growing maize; but the English, for lack of seed, lack of skill, or lack of will, grew nothing for themselves, even when the new planting season came round again. Superior English technology appeared, for the moment at least, to be no technology at all, as far as food production was concerned.[98]

Indeed, Morgan later notes, "the Indians . . . could have done the English in simply by deserting them."[99] They did not desert them, however, and in that act they sealed their fate. The same was true throughout the Americas: the cultural traits and the material achievements of the native people were turned against them once the European invasion began. Indian openness and generosity were met with European stealth and greed. Ritualized Indian warfare, in which few people died in battle, was met with the European belief in devastating holy war. Vast stores of grain and other food supplies that Indian peoples had lain aside became the fuel that drove the Europeans forward. And in that drive they traveled quickly, as they could not otherwise have done, on native trails and roadways from the northeast and northwest coasts to the dizzying heights of the Andes in Peru.

Some who have written on these matters—such as one historian who recently has shown how the Spanish conquest of Mexico was literally fed by the agricultural abundance that the Aztecs had created—have commented on the irony of native achievement being turned against itself.[100] Perhaps the greatest and most tragic irony of all, however, was that the extraordinary good health of the native people throughout the Americas prior to the coming of the Europeans would become a key ingredient in their disastrous undoing. For in their tens of thousands of years of isolation from the rest of the earth's human populations, the indigenous peoples of the Americas were spared from contact with the cataclysms of disease that had wreaked such havoc on the Old World, from China to the Middle East, from the provinces of ancient Rome to the alleyways of medieval Paris.

This is not to say that there were no diseases in the pre-Columbian Americas. There were, and people died from them. But the great plagues that arose in the Old World and that brought entire Asian, African, and European societies to their knees—smallpox, measles, bubonic plague, diphtheria, influenza, malaria, yellow fever, typhoid, and more—never emerged on their own among the Western Hemisphere's native peoples and did not spread to them across the oceans' barriers until 1492. Thus, when smallpox was introduced among Cree Indians in Canada as late as the eighteenth century, one native witnessing the horrifying epidemic that was destroying his people exclaimed that "we had no belief that one man could give it to another, any more than a wounded man could give his wound to another."[101] Such devastating contagion was simply unknown in the histories of the Cree or other indigenous peoples of the Americas.

Debate continues as to the existence or extent of tuberculosis and syphilis among native peoples in the pre-Columbian era, with most recent research suggesting that at least some sort of "tuberculosis-like pathology" was present in some parts of the New World prior to 1492, though of a type not associated with pulmonary disease, as well as a relatively benign nonvenereal (that is, not sexually transmitted) treponemal infection that was related to syphilis.[102] However, there is no evidence that either disease (whatever it may have been) was at all widespread in either North or South America. And the most detailed recent studies of large-scale sedentary societies in the Americas—where such diseases would have taken hold if they were to do so anywhere—have found no evidence of either tuberculosis or syphilis (or anything like them) as causing significant damage prior to European contact.[103] Similarly, ancient small-scale migratory societies, even in such harsh environments as those of the frigid northwestern plains, produced people who, in the words of the most recent and extensive study of the subject, "appear to have lived very long lives without significant infectious conditions, or even much serious injury."[104] Moreover, the limited range of potentially serious diseases that did exist among the Americas' indigenous peoples (primarily gastrointestinal disease and various minor infections) had long since been mitigated by millennia of exposure to them, as well as by generally beneficent living environments and more than adequate nutrition.[105]

All that was to change, however, with shocking and deadly suddenness, once those first three Spanish ships bobbed into view on the rim of the Caribbean horizon. For it was then only a matter of months before there would begin the worst series of human disease disasters, combined with the most extensive and most violent programs of human eradication, that this world has ever seen.

NATIVE PEOPLES

For 40,000 years, hundreds of millions of the Americas' native peoples have built their homes and their societies on a land mass equal to one-fourth of the earth's ground surface. Consistent with the great diversity of their natural environments, some of these original inhabitants of the Western Hemisphere lived in relatively small communities that touched only lightly on the land, while others resided in cities that were among the largest and most sophisticated to be found anywhere in the world. So numerous, varied, ancient, and far-flung were these peoples that at one time they spoke as many as two thousand distinct and mutually unintelligible languages.

Only a few of the societies that once existed in the New World are illustrated on the following pages. Thousands of others filled North and South and Central America's 16,000,000 square miles of land, most of them as distinctive and different from one another as were the peoples represented here. By the end of the nineteenth century, photographers had become interested in preserving images of what they erroneously thought were the soon-to-be-extinct native peoples of North America. The photographs reproduced at the end of this section are from that era.

The drawings of Maya cities were done by Tatiana Proskouriakoff in collaboration with archaeologists who excavated the sites. They are reprinted here with the permission of the Peabody Museum of Archaeology and Ethnology at Harvard University. Theodor de Bry's engravings of Florida's and Virginia's native peoples, based on first-hand paintings by Jacques Le Moyne and John White, appeared in de Bry's multi-volume *Great and Small Voyages* (1590–1634), from which the illustrations and quoted portions of captions printed here are taken. The photographs following the de Bry illustrations are all from the Smithsonian Institution, with the exception of the last one, which is from the Library of Congress.

The Acropolis at Copán, Honduras. Constructed at a bend of the Copán River, the city's enormous rectangular plazas were surrounded by pyramids with steps on which the populace sat in review of ceremonies and to witness athletic events. Although the countryside outside Copán was thick with other towns and villages, the city contained no military fortifications and its elaborate art and architecture carried no hint of martial imagery.

Chichén Itzá, Yucatán: View from the North. A paved boulevard led from the sacred well of the city in the north (lower left of the drawing) to the four-sided, eight-story-high Temple of Kukulcan in the center. To the east, the Group of the Thousand Columns, made up of plazas and temples and colonnades, once was a busy marketplace. To the west lay a huge ballcourt and athletic compound.

Temple Group at Uaxactún, Guatemala. The temple clusters of this city were
built on eight hilltops, which were leveled in some places and fortified in others
to support large monuments and plazas. Paved roadways, raised to the heights of
the hilltops, connected the temple groups, while residential areas and minor
courts and plazas were placed on adjacent hillsides and low ground.

The Patio of the Mercado, Chichén Itzá. The Mercado was the marketplace of the city, and this small patio, surrounding a recessed interior court, was at the rear of one of the Mercado's main buildings. Masonry walls and plaster-covered columns, set into a plaster-and-flagstone floor, supported wooden rafters and a steeply pitched roof, designed to resist the high winds and heavy rains of the region.

The Gallery of the Mercado, Chichén Itzá. This building directly faced the large quadrangle that held the numerous kiosks and stalls of Chichén Itzá's busy marketplace. The building itself apparently served as something of a courthouse where commercial disputes were settled by presiding judges. The façade of the gallery was a colonnade of alternating round columns and rectangular piers, each painted with bands of brightly contrasting colors. Interior walls and doorways were decorated with elaborate carvings, paintings, and sculpture.

"When the king is ready to take a wife," says the sixteenth-century caption for this illustration from Florida, "he gives orders that from among the daughters of his principal men the tallest and most beautiful shall be chosen. The newly selected queen is brought to him on a litter covered with the skin of some rare animal and fitted with a canopy of boughs to shade her head." Some early European explorers in this region favorably compared the precious jewelry and artwork of these peoples to those of the fabulously wealthy societies of Mexico and Peru.

"While hunting with some of my comrades in the forest, I once saw Chief Saturiba and his queen taking an evening walk. He was clad in a deerskin so exquisitely prepared and painted with so many colors that I have never seen anything more lovely. Two young men walked by his side carrying fans, while a third one, with little gold and silver balls hanging at his belt, followed close behind him holding up his train. The queen and her maidens were adorned with belts worn either at the shoulder or at the waist, made of a kind of moss that grows on the trees. This moss is woven into slender threads of a bluish-green color and is so delicate in texture as to be mistaken for filaments of silk."

"Many of the islands produce an abundance of fruits. These are gathered twice a
year, carried home in canoes, and stored in low and roomy granaries, built of
stone and earth and thickly roofed with palm branches and a kind of soft earth.
. . . There the Indians store everything they wish to preserve, and there they go
for supplies whenever they need anything—no one fears being cheated. Indeed, it
would be good if among Christians there were as little greed to torment men's
minds and hearts."

The town of Secotan in Virginia, where "the people live happily together without envy or greed." De Bry's engraving, following John White's painting, artificially reduces the number and size of buildings and compresses the many activities and features of village life here—from fields of corn and squash and pumpkins, to patches of tobacco and sunflowers; from a firelit nighttime dance ceremony near the bottom of the illustration, to hunting in the cleared and canopied forest at the upper left. The accompanying text describes such villages as usually containing from ten to thirty houses, ranging in size from about forty feet long and twenty feet wide to roughly seventy-five feet long and thirty-five feet wide.

Unlike Secotan, the Virginia town of Pomeioc was enclosed and guarded, made up of about two dozen longhouses. This stylized engraving, entitled "An Old Man in His Winter Clothes," shows Pomeioc in the background surrounded by carefully tended cornfields and groves of fruit trees. The accompanying caption says: "The country round Pomeiock is far more fruitful than England."

A young Seri Indian woman of southwest Texas or nothern Mexico.

A young Navajo man of Arizona or New Mexico.

A family from an unknown (possibly Bannock) southeastern Idaho people.

A girl of the Kiowa nation who lived in the Colorado, Texas, and Oklahoma Great Plains.

A Nez Perce boy from the Columbia Plateau region of Washington and Idaho.

A man of the Kansa people who lived in the Oklahoma, Nebraska, and Kansas Great Plains.

A Sioux camp in South Dakota within days of the massacre at Wounded Knee.

II

PESTILENCE AND GENOCIDE

◀3▶

THE SPAIN THAT Christopher Columbus and his crews left behind just before dawn on August 3, 1492, as they sailed forth from Palos and out into the Atlantic, was for most of its people a land of violence, squalor, treachery, and intolerance. In this respect Spain was no different from the rest of Europe.

Epidemic outbreaks of plague and smallpox, along with routine attacks of measles, influenza, diphtheria, typhus, typhoid fever, and more, frequently swept European cities and towns clean of 10 to 20 percent of their populations at a single stroke. As late as the mid-seventeenth century more than 80,000 Londoners—one out of every six residents in the city—died from plague in a matter of months. And again and again, as with its companion diseases, the pestilence they called the Black Death returned. Like most of the other urban centers in Europe, says one historian who has specialized in the subject, "every twenty-five or thirty years—sometimes more frequently—the city was convulsed by a great epidemic."[1] Indeed, for centuries an individual's life chances in Europe's pesthouse cities were so poor that the natural populations of the towns were in perpetual decline that was offset only by in-migration from the countryside—in-migration, says one historian, that was "vital if [the cities] were to be preserved from extinction."[2]

Famine, too, was common. What J. H. Elliott has said of sixteenth-century Spain had held true throughout the Continent for generations beyond memory: "The rich ate, and ate to excess, watched by a thousand hungry eyes as they consumed their gargantuan meals. The rest of the population starved."[3] This was in normal times. The slightest fluctuation in food prices could cause the sudden deaths of additional tens of thousands who lived on the margins of perpetual hunger. So precarious was the existence of these multitudes in France that as late as the seventeenth century each "average" increase in the price of wheat or millet directly killed a proportion of the French population equal to nearly twice the percentage of Americans who died in the Civil War.[4]

That was the seventeenth century, when times were getting better. In the fifteenth and sixteenth centuries prices fluctuated constantly, leading people to complain as a Spanish agriculturalist did in 1513 that "today a pound of mutton costs as much as a whole sheep used to, a loaf as much as a *fanega* [a bushel and a half] of wheat, a pound of wax or oil as much as an *arroba* [25 Spanish pounds]."[5] The result of this, as one French historian has observed, was that "the epidemic that raged in Paris in 1482 fits the classic pattern: famine in the countryside, flight of the poor to the city in search of help, then outbreak of disease in the city following upon the malnutrition."[6] And in Spain the threat of famine in the countryside was especially omnipresent. Areas such as Castile and Andalusia were wracked with harvest failures that brought on mass death repeatedly during the fifteenth century.[7] But since both causes of death, disease and famine, were so common throughout Europe, many surviving records did not bother (or were unable) to make distinctions between them. Consequently, even today historians find it difficult or impossible to distinguish between those of the citizenry who died of disease and those who merely starved to death.[8]

Roadside ditches, filled with stagnant water, served as public latrines in the cities of the fifteenth century, and they would continue to do so for centuries to follow. So too would other noxious habits and public health hazards of the time persist on into the future—from the practice of leaving the decomposing offal of butchered animals to fester in the streets, to London's "special problem," as historian Lawrence Stone puts it, of "poor's holes." These were "large, deep, open pits in which were laid the bodies of the poor, side by side, row upon row. Only when the pit was filled with bodies was it finally covered over with earth." As one contemporary, quoted by Stone, delicately observed: "How noisome the stench is that arises from these holes so stowed with dead bodies, especially in sultry seasons and after rain."[9]

Along with the stench and repulsive appearance of the openly displayed dead, human and animal alike, a modern visitor to a European city in this era would be repelled by the appearance and the vile aromas given off by the living as well. Most people never bathed, not once in an entire lifetime. Almost everyone had his or her brush with smallpox and other deforming diseases that left survivors partially blinded, pock-marked, or crippled, while it was the norm for men and women to have "bad breath from the rotting teeth and constant stomach disorders which can be documented from many sources, while suppurating ulcers, eczema, scabs, running sores and other nauseating skin diseases were extremely common, and often lasted for years."[10]

Street crime in most cities lurked around every corner. One especially popular technique for robbing someone was to drop a heavy rock or chunk of masonry on his head from an upper-story window and then to rifle the body for jewelry and money. This was a time, observes Norbert Elias, when "it was one of the festive pleasures of Midsummer Day to burn alive one or two dozen cats," and when, as Johan Huizinga once put it, "the continuous disruption of town and country by every kind of dangerous rabble [and] the permanent threat of harsh and unreliable law enforcement . . . nourished a feeling of universal uncertainty."[11] With neither culturally developed systems of social obligation and restraint in place, nor effective police forces in their stead, the cities of Europe during the fifteenth and sixteenth centuries were little more than chaotic population agglomerates with entire sections serving as the residential turf of thieves and brigands, and where the wealthy were forced to hire torch-bearing bodyguards to accompany them out at night. In times of famine, cities and towns became the setting for food riots. And the largest riot of all, of course—though the word hardly does it justice—was the Peasants' War, which broke out in 1524 following a series of local revolts that had been occurring repeatedly since the previous century. The Peasants' War killed over 100,000 people.

As for rural life in calmer moments, Jean de La Bruyère's seventeenth-century description of human existence in the French countryside gives an apt summary of what historians for the past several decades have been uncovering in their research on rustic communities in Europe at large during the entire late medieval to early modern epoch: "sullen animals, male and female [are] scattered over the country, dark, livid, scorched by the sun, attached to the earth they dig up and turn over with invincible persistence; they have a kind of articulate speech, and when they rise to their feet, they show a human face, and, indeed, they are men. At night they retire to dens where they live on black bread, water, and roots."[12]

To be sure, La Bruyère was a satirist and although, in the manner of all caricaturists, his portrait contains key elements of truth, it also is cruel in what it omits. And what it omits is the fact that these wretchedly poor country folk, for all their life-threatening deprivations, were not "sullen animals." They were, in fact, people quite capable of experiencing the same feelings of tenderness and love and fear and sadness, however constricted by the limitations of their existence, as did, and do, all human beings in every corner of the globe.

But what Lawrence Stone has said about the typical English village also was likely true throughout Europe at this time—that is, that because of the dismal social conditions and prevailing social values, it "was a place filled with malice and hatred, its only unifying bond being the occasional episode of mass hysteria, which temporarily bound together the majority in order to harry and persecute the local witch." Indeed, as in England, there were towns on the Continent where as many as a third of the population were accused of witchcraft and where ten out of every hundred people were executed for it in a single year. In one small, remote locale within reputedly peaceful Switzerland, more than 3300 people were killed in the late sixteenth- and seventeenth-century for allegedly Satanic activities. The tiny village of Wiesensteig saw sixty-three women burned to death in one year alone, while in Obermarchtal fifty-four people—out of a total population of barely 700—died at the stake during a three-year period. Thus, while it is true that the Europeans of those days possessed the same range of emotions that we do, as Stone puts it, "it is noticeable that hate seems to have been more prominent an emotion than love."[13]

At the time La Bruyère was writing (which was a good bit later than the time of Columbus, during which time conditions had improved), the French "knew every nuance of poverty," says one modern historian, and they had a battery of formal terms to describe precise levels of indigence: *pauvre, le vrai pauvre, le mauvais pauvre, pauvre valide ou invalide, pauvre honteux, indigent, misérable, nécessiteux, mendiant de profession, mendiant de bonne foi, mendiant volontaire, mendiant sédentaire,* and more. At the top were those who "at best lived at subsistence level, at worst fell far below," while at the bottom were those described as *dans un état d'indigence absolue,* meaning that "one had no food or adequate clothing or proper shelter, that one had parted with the few battered cooking-pots and blankets which often constituted the main assets of a working-class family."[14] Across the whole of France, between a third and half the population fell under one of these categories of destitution, and in regions such as Brittany, western Normandy, Poitou, and the Massif the proportion ascended upwards of two-thirds. In rural areas in general, between half and 90 percent of the population did not have land sufficient for their support, forcing them to migrate out, fall into permanent debt, or die.[15]

And France was hardly unique. In Genoa, writes historian Fernand Braudel, "the homeless poor sold themselves as galley slaves every winter." They were fortunate to have that option. In more northern climes, during winter months, the indigent simply froze to death. The summer, on the other hand, was when the plague made its cyclical visitations. That is why, in summer months, the wealthy left the cities to the poor: as Braudel points out elsewhere, Rome along with other towns "was a graveyard of fever" during times of warmer weather.[16]

Throughout Europe, about half the children born during this time died before reaching the age of ten. Among the poorer classes—and in Spain particularly, which had an infant mortality rate almost 40 percent higher even than England's—things were much worse.[17] In addition to exposure, disease, and malnutrition, one of the causes for such a high infant mortality rate (close to three out of ten babies in Spain did not live to see their first birthdays) was abandonment. Thousands upon thousands of children who could not be cared for were simply left to die on dungheaps or in roadside ditches.[18] Others were sold into slavery.

East European children, particularly Romanians, seem to have been favorites of the fourteenth- and fifteenth-century slave trade, although many thousands of adults were enslaved as well. Child slaves, however, were as expensive as adults, for reasons best left to the imagination, as is indicated by a fourteenth-century letter from a man involved in the business: "We are informed about the little slave girl you say you personally need," he wrote to his prospective client, "and about her features and age, and for what you want her. . . . Whenever ships come from Romania, they should carry some [slave girls]; but keep in mind that little slave girls are as expensive as the grown ones, and there will be none that does not cost 50 to 60 florins if we want one of any value."[19] Those purchasing female slaves of child-bearing age sometimes were particularly lucky and received a free bonus of a baby on the way. As historian John Boswell has reported: "Ten to twenty percent of the female slaves sold in Seville in the fifteenth century were pregnant or breast-feeding, and their infants were usually included with them at no extra cost."[20]

The wealthy had their problems too. They hungered after gold and silver. The Crusades, begun four centuries earlier, had increased the appetites of affluent Europeans for exotic foreign luxuries—for silks and spices, fine cotton, drugs, perfumes, and jewelry—material pleasures that required pay in bullion. Thus, gold had become for Europeans, in the words of one Venetian commentator of the time, "the sinews of all government . . . its mind, soul . . . its essence and its very life." The supply of the precious metal, by way of the Middle East and Africa, had always been uncertain. Now, however, the wars in eastern Europe had nearly emptied the Continent's coffers. A new supply, a more regular supply—and preferably a cheaper supply—was needed.[21]

Violence, of course, was everywhere, as alluded to above; but occasionally it took on an especially perverse character. In addition to the hunting down and burning of witches, which was an everyday affair in most locales, in Milan in 1476 a man was torn to pieces by an enraged mob and his dismembered limbs were then eaten by his tormenters. In Paris and Lyon, Huguenots were killed and butchered, and their various body parts were sold openly in the streets. Other eruptions of bizarre torture, murder, and ritual cannibalism were not uncommon.[22]

Such behavior, nonetheless, was not officially condoned, at least not usually. Indeed, wild and untrue accusations of such activities formed the basis for many of the witch hunts and religious persecutions—particularly of Jews—during this time.[23] In precisely those years when Columbus was trekking around Europe in search of support for his maritime adventures, the Inquisition was raging in Spain. Here, and elsewhere in Europe, those out of favor with the powerful—particularly those who were believed to be un-Christian—were tortured and killed in the most ingenious of fashions: on the gallows, at the stake, on the rack—while others were crushed, beheaded, flayed alive, or drawn and quartered.

On the very day that Columbus finally set forth on his journey that would shake the world, the port of the city he sailed from was filled with ships that were deporting Jews from Spain. By the time the expulsion was complete between 120,000 and 150,000 Jews had been driven from their homes (their valuables, often meager, having first been confiscated) and then they were cast out to sea. As one contemporary described the scene:

> It was pitiful to see their sufferings. Many were consumed by hunger, especially nursing mothers and their babies. Half-dead mothers held dying children in their arms. . . . I can hardly say how cruelly and greedily they were treated by those who transported them. Many were drowned by the avarice of the sailors, and those who were unable to pay their passage sold their children.[24]

This was the world an ex-trader of African slaves named Christopher Columbus and his shipmates left behind as they sailed from the city of Palos in August of 1492. It was a world wracked by disease—disease that killed in massive numbers, but, importantly, that also tended to immunize survivors. A world in which all but the wealthy often could not feed themselves, and in which the wealthy themselves hungered after gold.[25] It was a world, as well, of cruel violence and certainty of holy truth. Little wonder, then, that the first report back from that Atlantic voyage, purportedly to the Orient, caused such sensations across the length and breadth of Europe.

In a letter composed aboard the *Niña,* as the returning ships passed through the Azores, Columbus described his discovery, during the previous fall and winter, of what he thought was the Indian Sea and its "many islands filled with people without number." One of the first major islands, which he called Juana, known to us today as Cuba, "was so long that I thought it must be the mainland, the province of [Cathay]." Another large island—the one we now know as Hispaniola, containing the nations of Haiti and the Dominican Republic—he called La Spañola. Columbus had reason to be impressed with the size of these two islands, since together they were two-thirds as large as his home country of Italy.

The Admiral continued his description of the wonders he had seen, in a passage that must be quoted at length if we are to achieve even a small understanding of the impact his voyage almost immediately had on the people of Europe, living under the wretched conditions of their time and just coming out of another cold and miserable winter:

As Juana, so all the other [islands] are very fertile to an excessive degree, and this one especially. In it there are many harbors on the sea coast, beyond comparison with others which I know in Christendom, and numerous rivers, good and large, which is marvelous. Its lands are lofty and in it there are many sierras and very high mountains, to which the island Tenerife is not comparable. All are most beautiful, of a thousand shapes, and all accessible, and filled with trees of a thousand kinds and tall, and they seem to touch the sky; and I am told that they never lose their foliage, which I can believe, for I saw them as green and beautiful as they are in Spain in May, and some of them were flowering, some with fruit . . . . And there were singing the nightingale and other little birds of a thousand kinds in the month of November, there where I went. There are palm trees of six or eight kinds, which are a wonder to behold because of their beautiful variety, and so are the other trees and fruits and plants; therein are marvelous pine groves, and extensive meadow country; and there is honey, and there are many kinds of birds and a great variety of fruits. Upcountry there are many mines of metals, and the population is innumerable. *La Spañola* is marvelous, the sierras and the mountains and the plains and the meadows and the lands are so beautiful and rich for planting and sowing, and for livestock of every sort, and for building towns and villages. The harbors of the sea here are such as you could not believe it without seeing them; and so the rivers, many and great, and good streams, the most of which bear gold.[26]

If it sounded like Paradise, that was no accident. Paradise filled with gold. And when he came to describe the people he had met, Columbus's Edenic imagery never faltered:

The people of this island and of all the other islands which I have found and seen, or have not seen, all go naked, men and women, as their mothers bore them, except that some women cover one place only with the leaf of a plant or with a net of cotton which they make for that purpose. They have no iron or steel or weapons, nor are they capable of using them, although they are well-built people of handsome stature, because they are wondrous timid. . . . [T]hey are so artless and free with all they possess, that no one would believe it without having seen it. Of anything they have, if you ask them for it, they never say no; rather they invite the person to share it, and show as much love as if they were giving their hearts; and whether the thing be of value or of small price, at once they are content with whatever little thing of whatever kind may be given to them.[27]

For years to come Columbus repeatedly would insist that his expeditions and adventures in the New World had nothing to do with "mere reason, mathematics, and maps," as two scholars of the subject put it, but rather that "his 'execution of the affair of the Indies' was a fulfillment of prophecies in Isaiah."[28] In addition to helping explain, if taken seriously, why Columbus in many respects was a less successful navigator and helmsman than is commonly supposed (once into the Caribbean he rarely seemed to know where he was and routinely lost ships that were under his command), this rhetorical claim of biblical guidance is a clue to understanding the European reaction to his reported find.[29]

Columbus finished his letter, describing what he had seen on his voyage, on March 4th of 1493. A printed version of it was published in Barcelona and was widely circulated less than a month later. A month after that a translated edition was circulating in Rome. A month after that a version that set the letter to verse appeared. Others followed in Antwerp, Basel, Paris, Florence, Strassburg, Valladolid, and elsewhere, most of them going back for second and third and fourth printings. At least seventeen different translated editions appeared throughout Europe within five years following Columbus's return from that first voyage.

If not the biblical Eden, or the fabled Fortunate Isles of classical myth, Columbus, it seemed, at least had found some sort of paradise on earth. Such places had long filled the legends and dreams of all the peoples of Europe, as they would on into the future: it is no coincidence that during the next two centuries the invented utopias of Bacon and More and Harrington and others invariably would be located in distant oceanic lands to the west.

But myths of paradise and utopia were complex—and often confused—affairs. On the one hand, in some versions, they represented a rediscovered time of innocent perfection dating from *before* the biblical Fall from Grace; on the other hand, some dreams of such perfection envisioned and were built upon the expectation of a *future* time of anticipated peace and harmony. And bound up with every myth, past, present, or future, was still another and contradictory vision of the primordial world, a Satanic vision of savagery and wildness and the dark.

Before long, reports were circulating that Satan himself resided on one of those islands in the Caribbean Sea. Perhaps it was only natural then, as Lewis Hanke has said, that "the popular image, in the first feverish months, of a terrestrial paradise was soon succeeded by that of a hostile continent peopled with armed warriors rushing out of the tropical forests or strange cities to resist the advance of the Spanish soldiers and the missionary efforts of their companion friars."[30]

It was only a matter of time before that stereotype of barbarically hostile natives had metamorphosed once again. As best described by its most famous proponent, the eminent Spanish scholar Juan Ginés de Sepúlveda, the next representation of the New World's Indians was as creatures of a subhuman, Caliban-like nature who were intended by God "to be placed under the authority of civilized and virtuous princes or nations, so that they may learn, from the might, wisdom, and law of their conquerors, to practice better morals, worthier customs and a more civilized way of life."[31] That the visions of the ferocious Indian assailant or the inferior natural slave were fictions, as much as the image of a prelapsarian American Eden had been, mattered not one bit to anyone. The myths were simply formed and re-formed, shaped and re-shaped, and made to do whatever work their propagators at any given moment wanted done.

Numerous modern scholars have dissected and analyzed the effects of both biblical and classical myth on the minds of Europeans during this so-called Age of Discovery. But at least as strong as all the mixed-up imaginings of terrestrial heavens and Elysian fields, of lusty maidens and cannibalistic human beasts, was a fervent, and in many cases a truly maniacal, European craving for raw power and the wealth of gold and silver. Among the clergy, meanwhile, there was the promise of God's favor should they successfully introduce the New World's "pagan innocents" to the glory of his grace. It is not surprising, then, that in the very first sentence of his celebrated letter to the Spanish Crown Columbus says of the lands that he has found, "and of them all have I taken possession for Their Highnesses, by proclamation and with the royal standard displayed, and nobody objected." Consider the picture: standing alone with a few of his fellow officers in the white coral sand of a tiny island whose identification remains disputed to this day, an island "discovered" by Columbus despite the fact that it was well populated and had in fact been discovered by others thousands of years earlier, the admiral "took possession" of it—and of all the people it contained. And "nobody objected." Clearly, God was on the Spaniards' side.

So it went, from island to island, small and large, throughout the Caribbean. Wherever he went Columbus planted a cross, "making," as he said, "the declarations that are required," and claiming ownership of the land for his royal patrons back in Spain. Despite the fact that Columbus noted in his own journal of the voyage that "the people of these lands do not understand me nor I them," it seems to have been of particular satisfaction to him that never once did any of the onlooking Arawak-speaking islanders object to his repeated proclamations in Spanish that he was taking control of their lands away from them.[32] Ludicrous though this scene may appear to us in retrospect, at the time it was a deadly serious ritual, similar in ways equally ludicrous and deadly to the other famous ritual the Spanish bestowed upon the non-Spanish-speaking people of the Americas, the *requerimiento*.

Following Columbus, each time the Spanish encountered a native individual or group in the course of their travels they were ordered to read to the Indians a statement informing them of the truth of Christianity and the necessity to swear immediate allegiance to the Pope and to the Spanish crown. After this, if the Indians refused or even delayed in their acceptance (or, more likely, their understanding) of the *requerimiento*, the statement continued:

I certify to you that, with the help of God, we shall powerfully enter into your country and shall make war against you in all ways and manners that we can, and shall subject you to the yoke and obedience of the Church and of Their Highnesses. We shall take you and your wives and your children, and shall make slaves of them, and as such shall sell and dispose of them as Their Highnesses may command. And we shall take your goods, and shall do you all the mischief and damage that we can, as to vassals who do not obey and refuse to receive their lord and resist and contradict him.[33]

In practice, the Spanish usually did not wait for the Indians to reply to their demands. *First* the Indians were manacled; then, as it were, they were read their rights. As one Spanish conquistador and historian described the routine: "After they had been put in chains, someone read the *Requerimiento* without knowing their language and without any interpreters, and without either the reader or the Indians understanding the language they had no opportunity to reply, being immediately carried away prisoners, the Spanish not failing to use the stick on those who did not go fast enough."[34]

In this perverse way, the invasion and destruction of what many, including Columbus, had thought was a heaven on earth began. Not that a reading of the *requerimiento* was necessary to the inhuman violence the Spanish were to perpetrate against the native peoples they confronted. Rather, the proclamation was merely a legalistic rationale for a fanatically religious and fanatically juridical and fanatically brutal people to justify a holocaust. After all, Columbus had seized and kidnapped Indian men, women, and children throughout his first voyage, long before the *requerimiento* was in use, five at one stop, six at another, more at others, filling his ships with varied samples of Indians to display like exotic beasts in Seville and Barcelona upon his return.

On at least one occasion Columbus sent a raiding party ashore to capture some women with their children to keep his growing excess of captured native males company, "because," he wrote in his journal, his past experience in abducting African slaves had taught him that "the [Indian] men would behave better in Spain with women of their country than without them." On this date he also records the vignette of "the husband of one of these women and father of three children, a boy and two girls," who followed his captured family onto Columbus's ship and said that if they had to go "he wished to come with them, and begged me hard, and they all now remain consoled with him."[35]

But not for long. As a harbinger of things to come, only a half-dozen or so of those many captured native slaves survived the journey to Spain, and of them only two were alive six months later. On his second voyage Columbus tried an even more ambitious kidnapping and enslavement scheme. It is described by an Italian nobleman, Michele de Cuneo, who accompanied Columbus on this voyage:

When our caravels in which I wished to go home had to leave for Spain, we gathered together in our settlement 1600 people male and female of those Indians, of whom, among the best males and females, we embarked on our caravels on 17 February 1495, 550 souls. Of the rest who were left the announcement went around that whoever wanted them could take as many as he pleased; and this was done. And when everybody had been supplied there were some 400 of them left to whom permission was granted to go wherever they wanted. Among them were many women who had infants at the breast. They, in order the better to escape us, since they were afraid we would turn to catch them again, left their infants anywhere on the ground and started to flee like desperate people.[36]

No one knows what happened to those six hundred or so left-over natives who were enslaved, on the Admiral's orders, by "whoever wanted them," or the four hundred or so who fled in terror, or their abandoned infants—but by the time Columbus's ships entered the waters outside Spain, of the 550 captured Indians he took with him two hundred had died. Says Cuneo: "We cast them into the sea." When they reached Cadiz, half of the remaining 350 slaves were sick and dying. Only a relative few survived much longer, because, Cuneo surmised, "they are not working people and they very much fear cold, nor have they long life."[37]

This final point—"nor have they long life"—would not have been true a few years earlier: the health and life expectancy of the natives had been far superior to that of the Europeans prior to the Columbian invasion. But by the time Cuneo was writing he was certainly correct. Once the first Spanish settlements had taken root, the hold on life that any Indian had, at any given moment, was tenuous at best. Spanish diseases had begun their own invasion of the Americas almost from the moment Columbus and his crews first breathed upon their New World hosts. But the systematic, genocidal destruction of the Indians did not begin until Columbus's return.

II

Columbus's second voyage was the true beginning of the invasion of the Americas. The royal instructions authorizing the expedition had directed that the finest ships in Andalusia be outfitted for the trip and that they be commanded by the most expert pilots and navigators in the realm. Seventeen ships made the voyage and aboard those ships were more than 1200 soldiers, sailors, and colonists—including a cavalry troop of lancers and half a dozen priests. Along the way, at the Canary Islands, some other passengers were boarded: goats and sheep and cattle, and eight pigs, were placed on deck and in the holds below.

In early January of 1494 the fleet arrived at the place on the northern coast of Hispaniola that Columbus had chosen to build his New World capital, his town of Isabela. No sooner were the ships unloaded, however, than sickness broke out among the crews. It quickly spread among the natives, who had come to greet the ships with gifts of fish and fruits, "as if we had been their brothers," recalled one of the men on board.[38] Within a few days, the Admiral's surgeon reported, a third of the Spaniards had fallen ill, while natives everywhere were dead. Columbus directed groups of the healthy among his crews to explore the island's inland regions and find the fabulous gold mines they all were sure existed. But many of those men returned to the ships, having come down with the mysterious illness along the way.

For years historians have speculated as to what the epidemic was that laid low so many Spaniards and killed so many native people. Carl Sauer thought it might have been some sort of intestinal infection, while Samuel Eliot Morison diagnosed it as either malaria or something caused by "drinking well water and eating strange fish." Most recently, Kirkpatrick Sale has opted for bacillic dysentery—although he too lists malaria or even syphilis as among the likely culprits.[39] Others have thought it everything from smallpox to yellow fever. While it is possible (even probable) that more than one disease was causing the afflictions, the reported symptoms had nothing of the signs of syphilis, and malaria was not then present in the Indies or the Americas, nor would it be for many years to come.[40] For the same reasons, it could not have been yellow fever or smallpox that was wreaking all this havoc, and it certainly did not derive from something the Spanish ate or drank, because it spread like wildfire not only among the Spanish, but with particular virulence among the Indian people all across the island.[41] No, the most recent and original medically informed hypothesis—and the one that goes the furthest in explaining reported symptoms, including high mortality, and the extraordinary contagiousness—identifies influenza as the cause, influenza carried by those Canary Islands pigs.[42]

If, as the Spanish physician and medical historian Francisco Guerra now contends, the epidemic that ravaged Hispaniola in 1494 was swine influenza, it would have been a pestilence of devastating proportions. For it now appears that it was swine flu that swept the world in 1918, killing off at least 20,000,000 people before it finally dissipated. Like other people in the Americas, and unlike the Spanish, the natives of Hispaniola had no previous exposure to the virus—nor to the numerous other diseases that historically, in other parts of the world, had spread from domesticated animal hosts. Other than small dogs in some locations and llamas in the Andes, few animals were domesticated anywhere in the hemisphere. And of the many plagues that in time would overwhelm the Americas' native peoples, influenza—of various types, from both humans and non-human vectors—was second only to smallpox and maybe measles as the most rapid epidemic killer of them all.[43]

Whatever it was, in any case, the imported pathogen moved among the native people with a relentlessness that nothing ever had in all their history. "So many Indians died that they could not be counted," wrote Gonzalo Fernández de Oviedo, adding that "all through the land the Indians lay dead everywhere. The stench was very great and pestiferous."[44] And in the wake of the plague they had introduced, the Spanish soldiers followed, seeking gold from the natives, or information as to where to find it. They were troubled by the illness, and numbers of them died from it. But unlike the island natives the European invaders and their forebears had lived with epidemic pestilence for ages. Their lungs were damaged from it, their faces scarred with pocks, but accumulations of disease exposure allowed them now to weather much. So they carried infections with them everywhere they went—burdensome, but rarely fatal, except to the natives that they met.

Following the Admiral's orders, reconnaissance parties were sent out across the island and off to Cuba, Jamaica, and to other nearby lands. The Spanish plagues raced on ahead. Still, the natives, as Columbus had observed during his first voyage, continued to be kind and generous to their guests, and so innocent in the use of dangerous weapons that when Columbus "showed them swords," he said, "they grasped them by the blade and cut themselves through ignorance."[45]

Wherever the marauding, diseased, and heavily armed Spanish forces went out on patrol, accompanied by ferocious armored dogs that had been trained to kill and disembowel, they preyed on the local communities—already plague-enfeebled—forcing them to supply food and women and slaves, and whatever else the soldiers might desire. At virtually every previous landing on this trip Columbus's troops had gone ashore and killed indiscriminately, as though for sport, whatever animals and birds and natives they encountered, "looting and destroying all they found," as the Admiral's son Fernando blithely put it.[46] Once on Hispaniola, however, Columbus fell ill—whether from the flu or, more likely, from some other malady—and what little restraint he had maintained over his men disappeared as he went through a lengthy period of recuperation. The troops went wild, stealing, killing, raping, and torturing natives, trying to force them to divulge the whereabouts of the imagined treasure-houses of gold.

The Indians tried to retaliate by launching ineffective ambushes of stray Spaniards. But the combined killing force of Spanish diseases and Spanish military might was far greater than anything the natives could ever have imagined. Finally, they decided the best response was flight. Crops were left to rot in the fields as the Indians attempted to escape the frenzy of the conquistadors' attacks. Starvation then added its contribution, along with pestilence and mass murder, to the native peoples' woes.

Some desperate Hispaniola natives fled to other islands. One of these, a *cacique* named Hatuey, brought with him to Cuba as many of his surviving people as he could—and what little gold that they possessed. Once there, in a place called Punta Maisi, he assembled his followers together and displayed for them the treasures that they had, explaining that this was what the Spanish troops were after, that these apparently were objects of worship to the murderous invaders. Whereupon, to protect his people from the greed and savagery of these vile strangers, he threw the gold to the bottom of a nearby river.

It didn't work. The Spanish found Hatuey and his people, killed most of them, enslaved the others, and condemned their leader to be burned alive. Reportedly, as they were tying him to the stake, a Franciscan friar urged him to take Jesus to his heart so that his soul might go to heaven, rather than descend into hell. Hatuey replied that if heaven was where the Christians went, he would rather go to hell.[47]

The massacres continued. Columbus remained ill for months while his soldiers wandered freely. More than 50,000 natives were reported dead from these encounters by the time the Admiral had recovered from his sickness.[48] And when at last his health and strength had been restored, Columbus's response to his men's unorganized depredations was to organize them. In March of 1495 he massed together several hundred armored troops, cavalry, and a score or more of trained attack dogs. They set forth across the countryside, tearing into assembled masses of sick and unarmed native people, slaughtering them by the thousands. The pattern set by these raids would be the model the Spanish would follow for the next decade and beyond. As Bartolomé de Las Casas, the most famous of the accompanying Spanish missionaries from that trip recalled:

> Once the Indians were in the woods, the next step was to form squadrons and pursue them, and whenever the Spaniards found them, they pitilessly slaughtered everyone like sheep in a corral. It was a general rule among Spaniards to be cruel; not just cruel, but extraordinarily cruel so that harsh and bitter treatment would prevent Indians from daring to think of themselves as human beings or having a minute to think at all. So they would cut an Indian's hands and leave them dangling by a shred of skin and they would send him on saying "Go now, spread the news to your chiefs." They would test their swords and their manly strength on captured Indians and place bets on the slicing off of heads or the cutting of bodies in half with one blow. They burned or hanged captured chiefs.[49]

At least one chief, the man considered by Columbus to be Hispaniola's ranking native leader, was not burned or hanged, however. He was captured, put in chains, and sent off by ship for public display and imprisonment in Spain. Like most of the Indians who had been forced to make that voyage, though, he never made it to Seville: he died en route.

With the same determination Columbus had shown in organizing his troops' previously disorganized and indiscriminate killings, the Admiral then set about the task of systematizing their haphazard enslavement of the natives. Gold was all that they were seeking, so every Indian on the island who was not a child was ordered to deliver to the Spanish a certain amount of the precious ore every three months. When the gold was delivered the individual was presented with a token to wear around his or her neck as proof that the tribute had been paid. Anyone found without the appropriate number of tokens had his hands cut off.

Since Hispaniola's gold supply was far less than what the Spaniards' fantasies suggested, Indians who wished to survive were driven to seek out their quotas of the ore at the expense of other endeavors, including food production. The famines that had begun earlier, when the Indians attempted to hide from the Spanish murderers, now grew much worse, while new diseases that the Spanish carried with them preyed ever more intensely on the malnourished and weakened bodies of the natives. And the soldiers never ceased to take delight in killing just for fun.

Spanish reports of their own murderous sadism during this time are legion. For a lark they "tore babes from their mother's breast by their feet, and dashed their heads against the rocks." The bodies of other infants "they spitted . . . together with their mothers and all who were before them, on their swords." On one famous occasion in Cuba a troop of a hundred or more Spaniards stopped by the banks of a dry river and sharpened their swords on the whetstones in its bed. Eager to compare the sharpness of their blades, reported an eyewitness to the events, they drew their weapons and

> began to rip open the bellies, to cut and kill those lambs—men, women, children, and old folk, all of whom were seated, off guard and frightened, watching the mares and the Spaniards. And within two credos, not a man of all of them there remains alive. The Spaniards enter the large house nearby, for this was happening at its door, and in the same way, with cuts and stabs, begin to kill as many as they found there, so that a stream of blood was running, as if a great number of cows had perished. . . . To see the wounds which covered the bodies of the dead and dying was a spectacle of horror and dread.[50]

This particular slaughter began at the village of Zucayo, where the townsfolk earlier had provided for the conquistadors a feast of cassava, fruit, and fish. From there it spread. No one knows just how many Indians the Spanish killed in this sadistic spree, but Las Casas put the number at well over 20,000 before the soldiers' thirst for horror had been slaked.

Another report, this one by a group of concerned Dominican friars, concentrated on the way the Spanish soldiers treated native infants:

> Some Christians encounter an Indian woman, who was carrying in her arms a child at suck; and since the dog they had with them was hungry, they tore the child from the mother's arms and flung it still living to the dog, who

proceeded to devour it before the mother's eyes. . . . When there were among
the prisoners some women who had recently given birth, if the new-born
babes happened to cry, they seized them by the legs and hurled them against
the rocks, or flung them into the jungle so that they would be certain to die
there.[51]

Or, Las Casas again, in another incident he witnessed:

The Spaniards found pleasure in inventing all kinds of odd cruelties, the
more cruel the better, with which to spill human blood. They built a long
gibbet, low enough for the toes to touch the ground and prevent strangling,
and hanged thirteen [natives] at a time in honor of Christ Our Saviour and
the twelve Apostles. When the Indians were thus still alive and hanging, the
Spaniards tested their strength and their blades against them, ripping chests
open with one blow and exposing entrails, and there were those who did
worse. Then, straw was wrapped around their torn bodies and they were
burned alive. One man caught two children about two years old, pierced
their throats with a dagger, then hurled them down a precipice.[52]

If some of this has a sickeningly familiar ring to readers who recall the
massacres at My Lai and Song My and other Vietnamese villages in the
not too distant past, the familiarity is reinforced by the term the Spanish
used to describe their campaign of terror: "pacification."[53] But as horrific
as those bloodbaths were in Vietnam, in sheer magnitude they were as
nothing compared with what happened on the single island of Hispaniola
five hundred years ago: the island's population of about eight million people at the time of Columbus's arrival in 1492 already had declined by a
third to a half before the year 1496 was out. And after 1496 the death
rate, if anything, accelerated.

In plotting on a graph the decline of Hispaniola's native population
there appears a curious bulge, around the year 1510, when the diminishing
numbers seemed to stabilize and even grow a bit. Then the inexorable
downward spiral toward extinction continues. What that little blip on the
demographic record indicates is not, however, a moment of respite for the
island's people, nor a contradiction to the overall pattern of Hispaniola's
population free-fall following Columbus's arrival. Rather, it is a shadowy
and passing footnote to the holocaust the Spanish at the same time were
bringing to the *rest* of the Caribbean, for that fleeting instant of population
stabilization was caused by the importation of tens of thousands of slaves
from surrounding islands in a fruitless attempt by the Spanish to replace
the dying natives of Hispaniola.[54]

But death seized these imported slaves as quickly as it had Hispaniola's
natives. And thus, the islands of the Bahamas were rapidly stripped of
perhaps half a million people, in large part for use as short-lived replace-
ments by the Spanish for Hispaniola's nearly eradicated indigenous inhabitants. Then Cuba, with its enormous population, suffered the same fate.

With the Caribbean's millions of native people thereby effectively liqui-dated in barely a quarter of a century, forced through the murderous vor-tex of Spanish savagery and greed, the slavers turned next to the smaller islands off the mainland coast. The first raid took place in 1515 when natives from Guanaja in the Bay Islands off Honduras were captured and taken to forced labor camps in depopulated Cuba. Other slave expeditions followed, and by 1525, when Cortés arrived in the region, all the Bay Islands themselves had been entirely shorn of their inhabitants.[55]

In order to exploit most fully the land and its populace, and to satisfy the increasingly dangerous and rebellion-organizing ambitions of his well-armed Spanish troops, Columbus instituted a program called the *repartim-iento* or "Indian grants"—later referred to, in a revised version, as the system of *encomiendas*. This was a dividing-up, not of the land, but of entire peoples and communities, and the bestowal of them upon a would-be Spanish master. The master was free to do what he wished with "his people"—have them plant, have them work in the mines, have them do anything, as Carl Sauer puts it, "without limit or benefit of tenure."[56]

The result was an even greater increase in cruelty and a magnification of the firestorm of human devastation. Caring only for short-term material wealth that could be wrenched up from the earth, the Spanish overlords on Hispaniola removed their slaves to unfamiliar locales—"the roads to the mines were like anthills," Las Casas recalled—deprived them of food, and forced them to work until they dropped. At the mines and fields in which they labored, the Indians were herded together under the supervi-sion of Spanish overseers, known as *mineros* in the mines and *estancieros* on the plantations, who "treated the Indians with such rigor and inhuman-ity that they seemed the very ministers of Hell, driving them day and night with beatings, kicks, lashes and blows and calling them no sweeter names than dogs." Needless to say, some Indians attempted to escape from this. They were hunted down with mastiffs. When found, if not torn apart on the spot, they were returned and a show-trial was held for them, and for the edification of other Indians who were made to stand and watch. The escapees were

> brought before the *visitador* [Spanish inspector-magistrate] and the accuser, that is, the supposedly pious master, who accused them of being rebellious dogs and good-for-nothings and demanded stiff punishment. The *visitador* then had them tied to a post and he himself, with his own hands, as the most honorable man in town, took a sailor's tarred whip as tough as iron, the kind they use in galleys, and flogged them until blood ran from their naked bodies, mere skin and bones from starvation. Then, leaving them for dead, he stopped and threatened the same punishment if they tried it again.[57]

Occasionally, when slaves were so broken by illness, malnutrition, or exhaustion unto death that they became incapable of further labor output, they were dismissed from the mines or the fields where they worked. Las Casas estimated that perhaps 10 percent of the Indian conscripts survived long enough for this to happen. However, he continued:

> When they were allowed to go home, they often found it deserted and had no other recourse than to go out into the woods to find food and to die. When they fell ill, which was very frequently because they are a delicate people unaccustomed to such work, the Spaniards did not believe them and pitilessly called them lazy dogs, and kicked and beat them; and when illness was apparent they sent them home as useless, giving them some cassava for the twenty- to eighty-league journey. They would go then, falling into the first stream and dying there in desperation; others would hold on longer, but very few ever made it home. I sometimes came upon dead bodies on my way, and upon others who were gasping and moaning in their death agony, repeating "Hungry, hungry."[58]

In the face of utter hopelessness, the Indians began simply surrendering their lives. Some committed suicide. Many refused to have children, recognizing that their offspring, even if they successfully endured the Spanish cruelties, would only become slaves themselves. And others, wrote Las Casas,

> saw that without any offence on their part they were despoiled of their kingdoms, their lands and liberties and of their lives, their wives, and homes. As they saw themselves each day perishing by the cruel and inhuman treatment of the Spaniards, crushed to the earth by the horses, cut in pieces by swords, eaten and torn by dogs, many buried alive and suffering all kinds of exquisite tortures . . . [they] decided to abandon themselves to their unhappy fate with no further struggles, placing themselves in the hands of their enemies that they might do with them as they liked.[59]

Other natives, in time, did find ways to become reunited with whatever remained of their families. But when most wives and husbands were brought back together,

> they were so exhausted and depressed on both sides that they had no mind for marital communication and in this way they ceased to procreate. As for the newly born, they died early because their mothers, overworked and famished, had no milk to nurse them, and for this reason, while I was in Cuba, 7,000 babies died in three months. Some mothers even drowned their babies from sheer desperation, while others caused themselves to abort with certain herbs that produced stillborn children. In this way husbands died in the mines, wives died at work, and children died from lack of milk, while others had not time or energy for procreation, and in a short time this land which was so great, so powerful and fertile, though so unfortunate, was depopulated.[60]

By 1496, we already have noted, the population of Hispaniola had fallen from eight million to between four and five million. By 1508 it was down to less than a hundred thousand. By 1518 it numbered less than twenty thousand. And by 1535, say the leading scholars on this grim topic, "for all practical purposes, the native population was extinct."[61]

In less than the normal lifetime of a single human being, an entire culture of millions of people, thousands of years resident in their homeland, had been exterminated. The same fate befell the native peoples of the surrounding islands in the Caribbean as well. Of all the horrific genocides that have occurred in the twentieth century against Armenians, Jews, Gypsies, Ibos, Bengalis, Timorese, Kampucheans, Ugandans, and more, none has come close to destroying this many—or this great a proportion—of wholly innocent people.[62]

And then the Spanish turned their attention to the mainland of Mexico and Central America. The slaughter had barely begun. The exquisite city of Tenochtitlán was next.

III

Unlike most of the Caribbean peoples the Spanish encountered, the inhabitants of Mexico had a good deal of experience with warfare. To be sure, Aztec warriors were trained in highly individualistic fighting techniques, since the aim of battle was not to kill masses of the enemy, but rather to capture and bring back a single worthy opponent to be sacrificed at the following year's ceremonies of fertility.[63] Still, those fighting skills were formidable. And when combined with the Aztecs' enormous numerical advantage, they were more than a match for any invading army out of Europe. As the European interlopers' own accounts make clear, individual Indian warriors repeatedly showed themselves the equal, and more, of any among the Spanish militia. The story of one Aztec soldier who, in hand-to-hand combat, fought off a handful of Spanish horsemen—"when they could not bring him down, one of the Spaniards threw his lance at the Indian, who caught it and fought for another hour before being shot by two archers and then stabbed"—was but one among innumerable such reports from the conquistadors themselves.[64]

The Indians' battlefield experience, however, was the result of complex political rivalries that had existed in the region for centuries, rivalries the Spanish under Hernando Cortés were able to turn to their advantage. As one scholar of Aztec military strategy recently has emphasized, "while the Spanish conquest is now seen as a major watershed in the history of the New World," to the various competing Indian polities at the time "the Spanish were simply another group, albeit an alien one, seeking to gain political dominance in central Mexico." As such, although the first people the Spanish confronted, the Tlaxcaltecs, could easily have defeated the conquistadors, they saw in them instead potential confederates against their traditional adversaries.[65] It was thus with a formidable army of Indian allies—at one point Cortés refers to 150,000 warriors who accompanied his band of less than a thousand Spanish soldiers—that the conquistadors marched on Tenochtitlán.[66]

Rather than meeting resistance when he approached the great city, Cortés was greeted in friendship and was welcomed by Montezuma. In retrospect this behavior of the Aztec leader has usually seemed foolish or cowardly or naïve to Western historians. But Mesoamerican political traditions had always dictated that war was to be announced before it was launched, and the reasons for war were always made clear well beforehand. War was a sacred endeavor, and it was sacrilegious to engage in it with treachery or fraud. In fact, as Inga Clendinnen recently has noted: "So important was this notion of fair testing that food and weapons were sent to the selected target city as part of the challenge, there being no virtue in defeating a weakened enemy."[67] In this case, therefore, not only was there no reason for Montezuma to suppose Cortés intended to launch an invasion (the Tlaxcaltec troops who accompanied him could have been part of an effort to seek political alliance), but Cortés had plainly announced in advance that his purposes were not warlike, that he came as an ambassador of peace.

Once the Spanish were inside the city's gates, however, it soon became apparent that this was a far from conciliatory mission. In the midst of a great public celebration of the feast of the god Huitzilopochtli, the Spanish, led by Cortés's ruthless lieutenant Pedro de Alvarado, entered and surrounded the ceremonial arena. It was filled, recalled the sixteenth-century Spanish historian Bernardino de Sahagún, with "nobles, priests, and soldiers, and throngs of other people." Still unaware of the conquistadors' intentions, says Sahagún, "the Indians thought that [the Spanish] were just admiring the style of their dancing and playing and singing, and so continued with their celebration and songs." Then the assault began:

> The first Spaniards to start fighting suddenly attacked those who were playing the music for the singers and dancers. They chopped off their hands and their heads so that they fell down dead. Then all the other Spaniards began to cut off heads, arms, and legs and to disembowel the Indians. Some had their heads cut off, others were cut in half, and others had their bellies slit open, immediately to fall dead. Others dragged their entrails along until they collapsed. Those who reached the exits were slain by the Spaniards guarding them; and others jumped over the walls of the courtyard; while yet others climbed up the temple; and still others, seeing no escape, threw themselves down among the slaughtered and escaped by feigning death. So great was the bloodshed that rivulets [of blood] ran through the courtyard like water in a heavy rain. So great was the slime of blood and entrails in the courtyard and so great was the stench that it was both terrifying and heartrending. Now that nearly all were fallen and dead, the Spaniards went searching for

those who had climbed up the temple and those who had hidden among the dead, killing all those they found alive.[68]

As word spread of what was happening, Aztec soldiers appeared and drove the Spanish into the royal quarters where they held Montezuma prisoner. Before this event had occurred, the ruling nobles and priests had expressed unhappiness with Montezuma's apparent weakness when confronted with these heavily armed strangers. Now, when Montezuma appeared on the palace rooftop, in chains and accompanied by Spanish soldiers, and appealed through a spokesman for peace, the populace revolted. According to Sahagún: "One of them spoke out, 'What is he saying, this whore of the Spaniards?' " And a siege of the palace began. Montezuma was killed in the ensuing battle. Two weeks or so of intermittent struggle later, says Sahagún, Cortés demonstrated the "courage and skill" that all "brave captains [do] in the time of greatest need." He ordered a retreat from the city under cover of night.[69]

In retreat, however, Cortés left behind an invisible killer that would prevent the Aztecs from following and destroying his broken army, and that would begin the process of wreaking his revenge: the microscopic smallpox bacillus. Smallpox was a fearsome killer wherever it existed, but among a people with no previous exposure to the disease it was catastrophic. It first had appeared in the New World in 1518 on the huge and dying island of Hispaniola, a sort of dreadful *coup de grâce* to that once enchanting place's dwindling few survivors.[70] After being released among the Aztecs, wrote Cortés's secretary Francisco Lopez de Gomara, "it spread from one Indian to another, and they, being so numerous and eating and sleeping together, quickly infected the whole country. In most houses all the occupants died, for, since it was their custom to bathe as a cure for all diseases, they bathed for the smallpox and were struck down." Gomara continues:

> Those who did survive, having scratched themselves, were left in such a condition that they frightened the others with the many deep pits on their faces, hands and bodies. And then came famine, not because of a want of bread, but of meal, for the women do nothing but grind maize between two stones and bake it. The women, then, fell sick of the smallpox, bread failed, and many died of hunger. The corpses stank so horribly that no one would bury them; the streets were filled with them; and it is even said that the officials, in order to remedy this situation, pulled the houses down to cover the corpses.[71]

The epidemic seems to have lasted for about two months, during which time, and for months after, Cortés was reorganizing his defeated forces and marching on and burning smaller towns in the region.[72] Once the disease dissipated—having devastated the city's residents and killed off most of the Aztec leaders—Cortés prepared to attack again. First, he had ships constructed that were used to intercept and cut off food supplies to the island capital. Then he destroyed the great aqueduct that brought fresh water to the city. Finally, the Spanish and their Indian allies laid siege to the once brilliant white metropolis and its dwindling population of diseased and starving people.

"Siege," as Inga Clendinnen has observed, was for the Aztecs "the antithesis of war." Viewing it as cowardly and dishonorable, "the deliberate and systematic weakening of opposition before engagement, and the deliberate implication of noncombatants in the contest, had no part in their experience."[73] But it had been the European mode of battle for many centuries, deriving its inspiration from the Greek invention of ferocious and massively destructive infantry warfare.[74] To the Spanish, as to all Europeans when committed to battle, victory—by whatever means—was all that mattered. On the other side, for reasons equally steeped in ancient tradition, the people of Tenochtitlán had no other option than to resist dishonor and defeat until the very end.

The ensuing battle was furious and horrifying, and continued on for months. Tenochtitlán's warriors, though immensely weakened by the deadly bacteria that had been loosed in their midst, and at least initially hobbled by what Clendinnen calls their "inhibition against battleground killing," were still too formidable an army for direct military confrontation. So Cortés extended his martial strategy by destroying not only the Aztecs' food and water supplies, but their very city itself. His soldiers burned magnificent public buildings and marketplaces, and the aviaries with their thousands of wondrous birds; they gutted and laid waste parks and gardens and handsome boulevards. The metropolis that the Spanish had just months earlier described as the most beautiful city on earth, so dazzling and beguiling in its exotic and brilliant variety, became a monotonous pile of rubble, a place of dust and flame and death.

Because of the way the city was built on canals, however, burning was not always the most efficient means of despoliation. Often "we levelled the houses to the ground," recalled Bernal Díaz, "for if we set fire to them they took too long to burn, and one house would not catch fire from another, for each house stood in the water, and one could not pass from one to the other without crossing bridges or going in canoes."[75] Every day the Spanish crushed houses and other buildings in the city, and piled the debris into the canals; and each night the Aztecs dredged the canals in a desperate effort to keep the waters running free. Some captured Indians finally told the Spanish just how bad things were for the city's residents. Recalled Cortés:

> We now learnt from two wretched creatures who had escaped from the city and come to our camp by night that they were dying of hunger and used to

come out at night to fish in the canals between the houses, and wandered through the places we had won in search of firewood, and herbs and roots to eat. . . . I resolved to enter the next morning shortly before dawn and do all the harm we could. . . . and we fell upon a huge number of people. As these were some of the most wretched people and had come in search of food, they were nearly all unarmed, and women and children in the main. We did them so much harm through all the streets in the city that we could reach, that the dead and the prisoners numbered more than eight hundred.[76]

With the advantage finally theirs—even if it was against "wretched . . . unarmed . . . women and children in the main"—Cortés and the Spanish pressed on. "That day," wrote Cortés, "we did nothing save burn and raze to the ground the houses on either side of that main street, which indeed was a sad sight; but we were obliged to do it, there being no other way of accomplishing our aims." They moved their forces to another section of the city where they slaughtered and captured more than twelve thousand people. Within a day or two they had another multitude of helpless citizens penned in: "They no longer had nor could find any arrows, javelins or stones with which to attack us." More than forty thousand were killed in that single day, and "so loud was the wailing of the women and children that there was not one man amongst us whose heart did not bleed at the sound." Indeed, because "we could no longer endure the stench of the dead bodies that had lain in those streets for many days, which was the most loathsome thing in all the world," recalled Cortés, "we returned to our camps."[77]

But not for long. The next morning the Spanish were in the streets again, mopping up the starving, dehydrated, and disease-wracked Indians who remained. "I intended to attack and slay them all," said Cortés, as he observed that:

> The people of the city had to walk upon their dead while others swam or drowned in the waters of that wide lake where they had their canoes; indeed, so great was their suffering that it was beyond our understanding how they could endure it. Countless numbers of men, women and children came out toward us, and in their eagerness to escape many were pushed into the water where they drowned amid that multitude of corpses; and it seemed that more than fifty thousand had perished from the salt water they had drunk, their hunger and the vile stench. . . . And so in those streets where they were we came across such piles of the dead that we were forced to walk upon them.[78]

In all their writings on the Aztecs, the Inquisition-loving Spanish—like most Western writers who have followed them—expressed indignant horror at their enemies' religious rituals involving human sacrifice. And indeed, the Aztec toll in that regard was great. Perhaps as many as 20,000 enemy warriors, captured in battle, were sacrificed each year during the peak of the Aztecs' brief reign as the lords of central Mexico—although what one conquistador said of the reports of Inca human sacrifice may hold true here as well: "These and other things are the testimony we Spaniards raise against these Indians," wrote Pedro de Cieza de León in 1553, "endeavoring by these things we tell of them to hide our own shortcomings and justify the ill treatment they have suffered at our hands. . . . I am not saying that they did not make sacrifices . . . but it was not as it was told."[79] Las Casas claimed the same was true of the reports from Mexico—"the estimate of brigands," he claimed, "who wish to find an apology for their own atrocities,"—and modern scholars have begun to support the view that the magnitude of sacrifice was indeed greatly exaggerated by the New World's conquerors, just as it was, for the same reasons, by Western conquerors in other lands.[80] Even if the annual figure of 20,000 were correct, however, in the siege of Tenochtitlán the invading Spaniards killed twice that many people in a single day—including (unlike Aztec sacrifice) enormous numbers of innocent women, children, and the aged. And they did it day after day after day, capping off the enterprise, once Tenochtitlán had been razed, by strip-searching their victims for any treasure they may have concealed before killing them. As an Aztec chronicler recalled: "The Christians searched all the refugees. They even opened the women's skirts and blouses and felt everywhere: their ears, their breasts, their hair."[81] Lastly, they burned the precious books salvaged by surviving Aztec priests, and then fed the priests to Spanish dogs of war.

This initial phase of the Spanish bloodbath in the region finally over, Cortés now returned to camp where he spent three or four days "attending to many items of business . . . . concerning myself with the good order, government and pacification of these parts." What this meant, first of all, as he says in his very next sentence, was the collecting and dividing up of the gold ("and other things, such as slaves") that were the spoils of the carnage. Although much had been destroyed or lost in the fury of the battle, these valuables included "many gold bucklers," which he promptly melted down, "plumes, feather headdresses and things so remarkable that they cannot be described in writing nor would they be understood unless they were seen."[82]

Through prior arrangement with his king, Cortés's share of the loot was one-fifth. In gold and jewelry and artwork, that was a fortune, probably more than $10,000,000 in 1990 American currency. In terms of slaves, it meant at least 3000 human beings for his personal and private use, not counting about 23,000 Indian "vassals," even after the Crown reduced his holdings in 1529. Immediately setting his slaves to labor in the placer mines, he drove them until they dropped. Before long, almost all of them had died from neglect and overwork. No matter how quickly he moved to replenish his human capital (an individual slave cost only six or seven pesos because they were so plentiful), Cortés killed faster than he could purchase or commandeer. By the time of his own death in 1547 his personal holdings in Indian slaves, despite constant infusions of new bodies was barely one-tenth of what he started with.[83]

Meanwhile, Tenochtitlán effectively was no more. About a third of a million people dead, in a single city in a single lake in the center of Mexico. And still this was just the beginning.

Smallpox and other new diseases—new, at least to the Indians—were now rippling out in currents of destruction across the Mexican and Central American landscape. The microbes moved even faster than the ambitious conquistadors on their horses, but the conquistadors moved as quickly as they could. And few if any were as ambitious as Pedro de Alvarado, who had led the temple massacre during the feast day ceremonies for the god Huitzilopochtli. Alvarado and his compatriots headed south, seeking gold for their coffers and flesh for their mines. Others headed north. Like parasites feeding on the remains of whatever was left alive once the winds of epidemic fever had passed over the native populations they encountered, the Spanish adventurers invaded, conquered, and enslaved the peoples living in the rest of Mexico and in what today is Guatemala, Belize, Honduras, El Salvador, Nicaragua, Costa Rica, and Panama.

No one knows how many they killed, or how many died of disease before the conquistadors got there, but Las Casas wrote that Alvarado and his troops by themselves "advanced killing, ravaging, burning, robbing and destroying all the country wherever he came." In all, he said:

> By other massacres and murders besides the above, they have destroyed and devastated a kingdom more than a hundred leagues square, one of the happiest in the way of fertility and population in the world. This same tyrant wrote that it was more populous than the kingdom of Mexico; and he told the truth. He and his brothers, together with the others, have killed more than four or five million people in fifteen or sixteen years, from the year 1525 until 1540, and they continue to kill and destroy those who are still left; and so they will kill the remainder."[84]

Alvarado, of course, was but one among many engaged in this genocidal enterprise. Nuño Beltrán de Guzmán was one of those who led armies to the north, torturing and burning at the stake native leaders, such as the Tarascan king, while seizing or destroying enormous native stores of food. Guzmán later was followed by Alvar Nuñez Cabeza de Vaca, by Francisco Vásquez de Coronado, by Francisco de Ibarra, and countless other conquerors and marauders. As elsewhere, disease, depredation, enslavement, and outright massacres combined to extinguish entire Indian cultures in Mexico's northwest. Among the region's Serrano culture groups, in barely more than a century the Tepehuán people were reduced in number by 90 percent; the Irritilla people by 93 percent; the Acaxee people by

95 percent. It took a little longer for the various Yaqui peoples to reach this level of devastation, but they too saw nearly 90 percent of their numbers perish, while for the varied Mayo peoples the collapse was 94 percent. Scores of other examples from this enormous area followed the same deadly pattern.[85]

To the south the story was the same—and worse. By 1542 Nicaragua alone had seen the export of as many as half a million of its people for slave labor (in effect, a death sentence) in distant areas whose populations had been destroyed. In Honduras about 150,000 were enslaved. In Panama, it was said, between the years of 1514 and 1530 up to 2,000,000 Indians were killed. But again, since numbers such as these are so overwhelming, sometimes it is the smaller incident that best tells what it was like—such as the expedition to Nicaragua in 1527 of Lopez de Salcedo, the colonial governor of Honduras. At the start of his trip Salcedo took with him more than 300 Indian slaves to carry his personal effects. Along the way he killed two-thirds of them, but he also captured 2000 more from villages that were in his path. By the time he reached his destination in León only 100 of the more than 2300 Indian slaves he had begun with or acquired during his journey were still alive.[86] All this was necessary to "pacify" the natives.

As Bishop Diego de Landa (who was a brutal overlord himself) described the process in his region of the Yucatán: "the Spaniards pacified [the Indians of Cochua and Chetumal] in such a way, that these provinces which were formerly the thickest settled and most populous, remained the most desolate of all the country." In these besieged provinces, added Fray Lorenzo de Bienvenida, "the Indians fled from all this and did not sow their crops, and all died of hunger. I say all, because there were pueblos of five hundred and one thousand houses, and now one which has one hundred is large."[87] The Spanish had a saying, recalled Alonso de Zorita, that it was easy to find one's way from province to province, because the paths were marked with the bones of the dead. There are "certain birds," he added, "that, when an Indian falls, pick out his eyes and kill and eat him; it is well known that these birds appear whenever the Spaniards make an incursion or discover a mine."[88] Indeed, to this day there exist in Yucatán towns and villages Spanish buildings and monuments that celebrate the sixteenth-century slaughter. One example is Montejo house in Mérida—on the coast, near the sites of the ancient Maya cities of Uxmal and Chichén Itzá—whose façade is decorated with two proud and preening conquistadors, each of whom has his feet planted atop the severed heads of Indians.[89]

The gratuitous killing and outright sadism that the Spanish soldiers had carried out on Hispaniola and in central Mexico was repeated in the long march to the south. Numerous reports, from numerous reporters, tell of Indians being led to the mines in columns, chained together at the neck, and decapitated if they faltered. Of children trapped and burned alive in their houses, or stabbed to death because they walked too slowly. Of the routine cutting off of women's breasts, and the tying of heavy gourds to their feet before tossing them to drown in lakes and lagoons. Of babies taken from their mothers' breasts, killed, and left as roadside markers. Of "stray" Indians dismembered and sent back to their villages with their chopped-off hands and noses strung around their necks. Of "pregnant and confined women, children, old men, as many as they could capture," thrown into pits in which stakes had been imbedded and "left stuck on the stakes, until the pits were filled."[90] And much, much more.

One favorite sport of the conquistadors was "dogging." Traveling as they did with packs of armored wolfhounds and mastiffs that were raised on a diet of human flesh and were trained to disembowel Indians, the Spanish used the dogs to terrorize slaves and to entertain the troops. An entire book, Dogs of the Conquest, has been published recently, detailing the exploits of these animals as they accompanied their masters throughout the course of the Spanish depredations. "A properly fleshed dog," these authors say, "could pursue a 'savage' as zealously and effectively as a deer or a boar. . . . To many of the conquerors, the Indian was merely another savage animal, and the dogs were trained to pursue and rip apart their human quarry with the same zest as they felt when hunting wild beasts."[91]

Vasco Núñez de Balboa was famous for such exploits and, like others, he had his own favorite dog—Leoncico, or "little lion," a reddish-colored cross between a greyhound and a mastiff—that was rewarded at the end of a campaign for the amount of killing it had done. On one much celebrated occasion, Leoncico tore the head off an Indian leader in Panama while Balboa, his men, and other dogs completed the slaughter of everyone in a village that had the ill fortune to lie in their journey's path. Heads of human adults do not come off easily, so the authors of Dogs of the Conquest seem correct in calling this a "remarkable feat," although Balboa's men usually were able to do quite well by themselves.[92] As one contemporary description of this same massacre notes:

> The Spaniards cut off the arm of one, the leg or hip of another, and from some their heads at one stroke, like butchers cutting up beef and mutton for market. Six hundred, including the cacique, were thus slain like brute beasts. . . . Vasco ordered forty of them to be torn to pieces by dogs.[93]

Just as the Spanish soldiers seem to have particularly enjoyed testing the sharpness of their yard-long rapier blades on the bodies of Indian children, so their dogs seemed to find the soft bodies of infants especially tasty, and thus the accounts of the invading conquistadors and the padres who traveled with them are filled with detailed descriptions of young Indian children routinely taken from their parents and fed to the hungry animals. Men who could take pleasure in this sort of thing had little trouble with less sensitive matters, such as the sacking and burning of entire cities and towns, and the destruction of books and tablets containing millennia of accumulated knowledge, wisdom, and religious belief.

Even when supposedly undoing the more extreme acts of violence perpetrated by their compatriots, the conquistadors seemed unable to restrain themselves from one last act of savagery. For a number of years Indians who were enslaved had their chattel status burned into their faces with branding irons that stamped them with the initials of their owners. When sold from one Spaniard to another, a replacement brand was made. Consequently, some slaves' faces were scarred with two or three or four branding mutilations identifying them as transferable pieces of property. Once, however, writes William Sherman, "when a ship put in at a Nicaraguan port loaded with illegally enslaved encomienda Indians, the governor freed them and sent them home. But first the natives, some of whom were women and suckling children, had their face brands canceled. Fresh letters spelling 'libre' were burned into their scarred faces." [94]

The treatment of Indian females is particularly revealing, in light of the Catholic *machismo* ideology of the Spanish that celebrated the purity of their own women. The tone for such treatment was set at the start, with the first description that exists of a sexual encounter between a European and an Indian woman. It occurred during Columbus's second voyage and was described by the protagonist himself, not a Spaniard in this case, but the Italian nobleman Michele de Cuneo:

> While I was in the boat I captured a very beautiful Carib woman, whom the said Lord Admiral gave to me, and with whom, having taken her into my cabin, she being naked according to their custom, I conceived desire to take pleasure. I wanted to put my desire into execution but she did not want it and treated me with her finger nails in such a manner that I wished I had never begun. But seeing that, (to tell you the end of it all), I took a rope and thrashed her well, for which she raised such unheard of screams that you would not have believed your ears. Finally we came to an agreement in such manner that I can tell you she seemed to have been brought up in a school of harlots. [95]

Cuneo here expresses an attitude toward raped women that soon would become a staple of violent pornography and male sadistic fantasy: she enjoyed it. While still in the Caribbean, a report to the king's minister by a group of Dominicans provides a different, but equally vivid, example of the other classic function and fantasy of rape—the demonstration of power and the degradation of both the victim and her loved ones. Typically, when an enslaved workman returned from the mines at the end of a day, the friars reported, "not only was he beaten or whipped because he had not brought up enough gold, but further, most often, he was bound hand and foot and flung under the bed like a dog, before the [Spanish] foreman lay down, directly over him, with his wife."[96]

These were just precursors to the open trade in enslaved women that the Spanish delighted in as the decades wore on. Native women—or *indias*—were gambled away in card games and traded for other objects of small value, while stables of them were rented out to sailors who desired sexual accompaniment during their travels up and down the coast. If an *india* attempted to resist, she was whipped or tortured or burned alive. Even when laws were passed to curb the more extreme of such atrocities, the penalties were a joke. When, for example, an uncooperative Nicaraguan Indian woman was burned to death in her hut by a Spaniard who tried to rape her, he was prosecuted by the governor—and fined five pesos.[97]

Those women who were not valued as enslaved concubines were forced to do back-breaking work. Writes one modern historian:

> Some of the *indias* even as late as the 1580s were being broken physically, their insides literally bursting in some instances from the heavy loads they had to carry. Unable to endure more, some of them committed suicide by hanging, starving themselves, or by eating poisonous herbs. Encomenderos forced them to work in open fields where they tried to care for their children. They slept outside and there gave birth to and reared their babies, who were often bitten by poisonous insects. Mothers occasionally killed their offspring at birth to spare them future agonies. . . . [Other] working mothers present a poignant image when we hear of them returning home after weeks or months of separation from their children, only to find that they had died or had been taken away.[98]

Concludes this writer: "All of those factors help explain the fact that on tribute rolls married couples were frequently entered as having no children at all or only one, and seldom more than two."[99] In even the most healthful of environments birth rates of this level will mean zero population growth at first, and then increasingly precipitous decline. In an environment of such enormous mortality from genocide and firestorms of disease, as was the rule in the Americas during the Spanish conquest, birth rates this low were a blueprint for extinction.

And that is precisely what happened in community after community. Almost everyone was killed. There were, of course, exceptions. But overall in central Mexico the population fell by almost 95 percent within seventy-five years following the Europeans' first appearance—from more than 25,000,000 people in 1519 to barely 1,300,000 in 1595. And central Mexico was typical. Even using moderate estimates of the pre-1492 population, in southeastern Mexico the number of inhabitants dropped from 1,700,000 to less than 240,000 in a century and a half. In northern Mexico, over a somewhat longer period, the native population fell from more than 2,500,000 to less than 320,000. Wherever the invaders went, the pattern was the same. On the island of Cozumel, off the eastern coast of Mexico, more than 96 percent of the population had been destroyed less than 70 years after the Spaniards' first arrival. In the Cuchumatan Highlands of Guatemala the population fell by 82 percent within the first half-century following European contact, and by 94 percent—from 260,000 to 16,000—in less than a century and a half. In western Nicaragua 99 percent of the people were dead (falling in number from more than 1,000,000 to less than 10,000) before sixty years had passed from the time of the Spaniards' initial appearance. In western and central Honduras 95 percent of the people were exterminated in half a century. In Córdoba, near the Gulf of Mexico, 97 percent of the population was extinguished in little more than a century, while simultaneously, in neighboring Jalapa, the same lethal pattern held: 97 percent of the Jalapa population was destroyed— falling from 180,000 people in 1520 to 5000 in 1626. With dreary regularity, in countless other locales across the length and breadth of Mexico and down into Central America, the European intrusion meant the sudden and near total disappearance of populations that had lived and flourished there for thousands upon thousands of years.[100]

Those natives who survived remembered, however, and in poetry they passed on to posterity the dreadful tale of what had happened. Recalled an Aztec poet:

> Broken spears lie in the roads;
> we have torn our hair in grief.
> The houses are roofless now, and their walls
> are red with blood.
>
> Worms are swarming in the streets and plazas,
> and the walls are splattered with gore.
> The water has turned red, as if it were dyed,
> and when we drink it,
> it has the taste of brine.
>
> We have pounded our hands in despair
> against the adobe walls,
> for our inheritance, our city, is lost and dead.[101]

The Maya book of *Chilam Balam* adds "what the white lords did when they came to our land":

> They taught fear and they withered the flowers. So that their flower should live, they maimed and destroyed the flower of others. . . . Marauders by day, offenders by night, murderers of the world.[102]

Then the Spanish, joined now by other European adventurers and their military escorts, pushed on into South America.

IV

Peru and Chile, home of the Incas and one of the wealthiest and largest empires anywhere, covering virtually the entire western coast of the South American continent, had contained at least 9,000,000 people only a few years before the Europeans arrived, possibly as many as 14,000,000 or more. As elsewhere, the conquistadors' diseases preceded them—smallpox, and probably other epidemics swept down through Mexico and across the Andes in the early 1520s, even before Pizarro's first foray into the region— but also as elsewhere the soldiers and settlers who followed wreaked terrible havoc and destruction themselves. Long before the close of the century, barely 1,000,000 Peruvians remained alive. A few years more and that fragment was halved again. At least 94 percent of the population was gone—somewhere between 8,500,000 and 13,500,000 people had been destroyed.[103]

Here, as in the Caribbean and Mexico and Central America, one could fill volumes with reports of murderous European cruelties, reports derived from the Europeans' own writings. As in those other locales, Indians were flogged, hanged, drowned, dismembered, and set upon by dogs of war as the Spanish and others demanded more gold and silver than the natives were able to supply. One ingenious European technique for getting what they wanted involved burying Indian leaders in earth up to their waists after they had given the Spanish all the goods that they possessed. In that helpless position they then were beaten with whips and ordered to reveal the whereabouts of the rest of their treasure. When they could not comply, because they had no more valuable possessions, more earth was piled about them and the whippings were continued. Then more earth. And more beating. At last, says the Spanish informant on this particular matter, "they covered them to the shoulders and finally to the mouths." He then adds as an afterthought: "I even believe that a great number of natives were burned to death."[104]

Pedro de Cieza de León, in what is justly regarded as the best first-hand account of the conquest of the Incas, describes in page after page the beautiful valleys and fields of this part of the world, the marvelous cities, the kind and generous native people—and the wholesale slaughter of them by the Spanish "as though a fire had gone, destroying everything in its path."[105] Cieza de León was himself a conquistador, a man who believed in the right of the Spaniards to seize Indians and set them to forced labor, but only, he wrote, "when it is done in moderation." He explains:

I would not condemn the employment of Indian carriers . . . but if a man had need of one pig, he killed twenty; if four Indians were wanted, he took a dozen . . . and there were many Spaniards who made the poor Indians carry their whores in hammocks borne on their shoulders. Were one ordered to enumerate the great evils, injuries, robberies, oppression, and ill treatment inflicted on the natives during these operations . . . there would be no end of it . . . for they thought no more of killing Indians than if they were useless beasts.[106]

But, like many others, Cieza de León's point is better made in incidentals of detail than with grand pronouncements—as in the offhand reference, in his immediately succeeding sentence, to "a Portuguese named Roque Martin, who had the quarters of Indians hanging on a porch to feed his dogs with, as if they were wild beasts."

Despite all the savage face-to-face cruelties, however, it was enslavement on the Spaniards' plantations and in their silver mines, in addition to the introduced diseases and starvation, that killed the most Indians directly. Immediately upon entering this region, the conquistadors laid waste the Incas' roads and bridges, agricultural terraces, and canals. They looted heavily stocked storehouses and granaries, and gratuitously slaughtered llamas by the thousands. "It is said," wrote one later Spanish official, "that [the soldiers] killed great numbers of llamas simply to eat the marrow-fat, and the rest [of the meat] was wasted." Others described the Spaniards' almost unbelievable destruction of agriculture and animal life, and "in this way," wrote one, "all the food, the vegetables, llamas and alpacas that were in that valley and district were totally consumed." Added Pascual de Andagoya as early as 1539: "The Indians are being totally destroyed and lost. . . . They [beg] with a cross to be given food for the love of God. . . . [The soldiers are] killing all the llamas they want for no greater need than to make tallow candles. . . . The Indians are left with nothing to plant, and since they have no cattle and can never obtain any, they cannot fail to die of hunger."[107]

Believing that El Dorados existed in the Amazon, the conquistadors drove thousands of natives before them in their desperate searches for gold mines in the jungles. "Some two or three hundred Spaniards go on these expeditions," wrote Domingo de Santo Tomas, but "they take two or three thousand Indians to serve them and carry their food and fodder. . . . Few or no Indians survive, because of lack of food, the immense hardships of the long journeys through wastelands, and from the loads themselves." Added Diego de Almagro—in an account that was typical of countless others—Hernando Pizarro would "take Indians in chains to carry what [the conquistadors] had pillaged. . . . When the Indians grew exhausted, they cut off their heads without untying them from the chains, leaving the roads full of dead bodies, with the utmost cruelty." Entire towns and provinces were wiped out by these and similar practices.[108]

Those who did survive the Spanish gifts of plague and famine and massacre, and who were not force-marched into jungles as the conquistadors' enslaved beasts of burden, were subject to being herded together and driven from their highland residences in the Andes to coca plantations on the sweltering peripheries of low-lying tropical rain forests. There, their lungs—long adapted to the cool, thin air of mountain altitudes—were assaulted by a barrage of still more strange, debilitating, and murderous diseases, including uta or *mal de los Andes,* which ate away at noses, mouths, and throats before bringing on terrifyingly painful death. So many were succumbing at such a rapid rate, in fact, that even the Spanish Crown began worrying about the long-term success of their enterprise should too many Indians be destroyed. Because "an infinite number of Indians perish," observed King Philip himself in a belated imperial decree, "and others emerge so sick and weak that they never recuperate," the coca trade, he urged, must be moderated or discouraged. The Spanish on the scene, trying for more precision than their king regarding the matter of Indian mortality, estimated that "between a third and half of the annual quota of coca workers died as a result of their five month service" in the fields. And those who did survive, and the fewer still who lived out the remainder of the year, had only the next round of lethal work to face in the coming season ahead. Still, despite the urgings of the Crown, the trade in coca grew—because, as Hernando de Santillan put it, "down there [in the coca plantations] there is one disease worse than all the rest: the unrestrained greed of the Spaniards."[109]

Work in the silver mines, if anything, was worse. Dropped down a shaft bored as far as 750 feet into the earth, taking with them only "some bags of roasted maize for their sustenance," observed Rodrigo de Loaisa, the miners remained below ground for a week at a time. There, in addition to the dangers of falling rocks, poor ventilation, and the violence of brutal overseers, as the Indian laborers chipped away at the rock faces of the mines they released and inhaled the poisonous vapors of cinnabar, arsenic, arsenic anhydride, and mercury. "If twenty healthy Indians enter [a mine] on Monday," wrote Loaisa, "half may emerge crippled on Saturday." Crippled, if they were lucky. To enter a mine, wrote Santo Tomás, was to enter "a mouth of hell."[110]

For as long as there appeared to be an unending supply of brute labor it was cheaper to work an Indian to death, and then replace him or her with another native, than it was to feed and care for either of them properly. It is probable, in fact, that the life expectancy of an Indian engaged in forced labor in a mine or on a plantation during these early years of Spanish terror in Peru was not much more than three or four months—about the same as that of someone working at slave labor in the synthetic rubber manufacturing plant at Auschwitz in the 1940s.[111]

So immense was the indigenous population of the Andes that the Spanish seemed to think at first that the supply of labor was infinite and inexhaustible. Whole valleys, once filled with thriving villages and hundreds of thousands of native people, were picked clean of human life. But at last the friars and some settlers began writing to their king in Spain, asking him to use his influence to moderate the holocaust, lest the absence of any Indians—a prospect that was beginning to seem imminent—serve to shut their enterprises down.[112]

The Crown consented. On Christmas Day in 1551, the king decreed that henceforth all Indian labor in the mines must be voluntary. The mine owners countered by using forced Indian laborers to carry supplies to the remote and isolated mining regions (that form of involuntary servitude was unaffected by the king's decree) and then trying to coax those laborers into working "voluntarily" in the mines. Others "rented out" Indian workers from Spanish labor overlords. But still the supply of workers, along with all the native people, continued to disappear.

Finally, in the 1560s, the Spanish viceroy on the scene countermanded the royal decree and declared that "for the good of the realm" one-seventh of the native tributary population living within approximately 150 miles of a mine would be drafted to labor in the mine pits. After four months that group would be replaced by another collection of conscripts from the same area. Although such draftees were treated better than the earlier slaves, and were allowed to spend each night above ground rather than in the mines—they were, after all, now a much scarcer and thus more valuable commodity—conditions during the day below ground were as bad as they had always been. Indeed, even the trek up the mountains to reach the mines remained a murderous journey. One Spaniard described a march he witnessed of "more than seven thousand souls" from the province of Chuquito to the "silver mountain" of Potosí. It covered a "distance of about one hundred leagues [and] takes two months" he wrote, because the cattle which were driven up the mountain alongside the people "cannot travel quicker, nor [can] their children of five and six years whom they take with them." He continues:

> Of all this mankind and common wealth which they take away from Chuquito, no more than two thousand souls ever return, and the remainder, about five thousand, in part, they die, and in part they remain in Potosí. . . . And for this, and the work, so excessive that, of six months, four in the mines, working twelve hours a day, going down four hundred and twenty and at times seven hundred feet, down to where night is perpetual, for it is always necessary to work by candlelight, the air thick and ill-smelling being enclosed in the entrails of the earth, the going up and down most dangerous, for they come up loaded with their small sack of metal tied up to their backs, taking quite four to five hours, step by step, and if they make the slightest false step they may fall seven hundred feet; and when they arrive at the top out of breath, find as shelter a mineowner who scolds them because they did

not come quickly enough or because they did not bring enough load, and for the slightest reason makes them go down again.[113]

These were the "improved" conditions in the Spaniards' Andean silver mines, where still two-thirds of those who ascended the mountains soon died or withered away. Even the initial survivors' lives were brief, however, since most of them soon developed *mal de la mina,* or mine sickness, which—before it killed—began with ulcers on the gums and soon progressed to rotting and destruction of the mouth and jaw, while its victims coughed up sputum mixed with mercury and blood. Understandably, before too long, likely draftees started moving out of the conscription zones around the mining regions, which only heightened the Spaniards' need for more recruits—recruits whose terms of labor then also necessarily grew longer, which in turn drove still more of them to migrate from the area. As Felipe Guaman Poma de Ayala explained:

Some absent themselves from their communities to avoid going to the mines where they would suffer agony and martyrdom, and in order to avoid experiencing such hell, hardship and torment of the devils, others flee the mines, and still others take to the roads to avoid the mines and would rather chance dying suddenly than to suffer a slow death. They say that they reach such a state because contracting mercury sickness one dries up as a stick and has asthma, and cannot live day or night. It goes on in this manner a year or two and they die.[114]

But by moving away from the reach of the Spanish mine recruiters, Indians had to break up their families and communities and move down to the lowlands where the Europeans' epidemic diseases—such as measles, mumps, typhus, influenza, diphtheria, scarlet fever, and hemorrhagic smallpox, to mention only those diseases that are known to have broken out here during these years—spread more easily in the warm and muggy air. The would-be conscripts, therefore, were trapped: they could either be drafted and destroyed in the torture of the mines, or they could move down to a hot and humid seething pesthouse—where, recent research has shown, the population was disintegrating at about twice the speed that it was even in the mining regions.[115]

Whether or not to migrate from the highland regions, then, was an agonizing individual and family decision. For Andean society as a whole, however, no alternatives were afforded. Within a century following their first encounter with the Spanish, 94 to 96 percent of their once-enormous population had been exterminated; along their 2000 miles of coastline, where once 6,500,000 people had lived, everyone was dead.

And then there was Brazil. Here, the Englishman Anthony Knivet once had said, you could travel from the Atlantic coast across the continent to Potosí in the Andes "and all the way as you go, you shall have great townes of Indians. . . . You shall have five hundred of these Indians by the way as you travell readie with Nets [hammocks] to carry you." So thick with a vast variety of cultures and peoples were Brazil's coastal and riverine areas that the first Portuguese governor of the region, Tomé de Sousa, declared that it was impossible for there ever to be a lack of natives, "even if we were to cut them up in slaughterhouses."[116] It was one of those rare statements that was both prescient and wrong: the effect of European conquest in Brazil was indeed as damaging as if the people had been cut up in slaughterhouses; but the number of natives was not inexhaustible.

The Portuguese governorship of Brazil was established with Sousa's arrival in the Bay of Bahia in March of 1549. Within just twenty years— when, in 1570, King Sebastião emptily declared that natives should not be enslaved unless they were captured in "just wars"—the native peoples of Brazil already were well along the road to extinction. From the first days of the colony, in 1549 and on into the 1550s, as Pero de Magalhães Gandavo wrote at the time, "the governors and captains of the land destroyed [the natives] little by little and killed many, and others fled into the interior." In 1552, and again in 1554, and again in 1556, and again in 1559 through 1561, epidemic diseases brought by the Europeans swept the coasts and countryside, preying heavily on the weakened bodies of enslaved Indians whose ancestors had never encountered such pestilences. In 1552, wrote Francisco Pires, of those natives who came down with the fever "almost none of these has survived." In 1554 an epidemic of "bloody fluxes," reported Simão de Vasconcellos, "struck with such violence that as soon as it appeared it laid them low, unconscious, and within three or four days it carried them to the grave." In 1556 another epidemic destroyed "an infinite number of savages," recalled André Thevet. And for two years, from 1559 to 1561, horrifying hemorrhagic fevers, dysentery, and influenza or whooping cough, raked the populace that remained. The natives everywhere "were terrified and almost stunned by what was happening to them," wrote António Blásques: "They no longer performed their songs and dances. Everything was grief. . . . there was nothing to be heard but weeping and groaning by the dying."[117]

In the midst of all this the enslavement and forced labor continued. King João III had earlier divided the 2500 miles of the Indians' Brazilian coastline into fourteen so-called "captaincies," or private grants of land, each one extending inland from a coastal strip that might be anywhere from 100 to 400 miles long.[118] In the captaincy with the best existing records, the Bahia captaincy, at least 40,000 Indians toiled in forced plantation labor as the decade of the 1560s began. Other captaincies had similar numbers of Indian slaves.

Meanwhile, in Europe, bubonic plague and smallpox both were raging once again. With case mortality rates as high as 60 percent and more for either of the scourges by itself—and with most deaths occurring within a week of first infection, even among people with centuries of exposure and thus a measure of resistance—the Continent was reeling.[119] About 40,000 people died in Lisbon alone from this single epidemic. People with no history of the maladies, of course, would succumb at an even greater rate. The 100,000 natives who had died in the Rio de la Plata two years earlier were mute testament to that. And so, in January of 1563, the plague and smallpox left a ship that was anchored off the coast and accompanied their human hosts onto the mainland of Brazil.

The resulting carnage beggared all description. The plague was first. It seemed as though everyone was infected. At least everyone who was a native. As is common when a contagion invades a people with no previous exposure to it, the first generation of symptoms are like nothing anyone, even anyone with long experience with the infection, has ever seen: "The disease began with serious pains inside the intestines," wrote Simão de Vasconcellos, "which made the liver and the lungs rot. It then turned into pox that were so rotten and poisonous that the flesh fell off them in pieces full of evil-smelling beasties." Thousands died in a matter of days, at least 30,000 within three months. Then, among the plague's survivors, the smallpox was discovered. Wrote Leonardo do Vale:

> When this tribulation was past and they wanted to raise their heads a little, another illness engulfed them, far worse than the other. This was a form of smallpox or pox so loathsome and evil-smelling that none could stand the great stench that emerged from them. For this reason many died untended, consumed by the worms that grew in the wounds of the pox and were engendered in their bodies in such abundance and of such great size that they caused horror and shock to any who saw them.[120]

As had been the case in the Caribbean and Mexico and Central America and Peru before, the secondary consequences of the epidemic were as bad or worse than the monstrous diseases themselves. With no one healthy enough to prepare food or to draw water or even to comfort the others, multitudes starved to death, died of dehydration, or of outright despair, even before the infection could run its deadly course. Children were the worst afflicted. "In the end," recalled Vale, "the thing grew so bad that there was no one to make graves and some were buried in dunghills and around the huts, but so badly that the pigs routed them up."[121]

If enslavement had weakened the Indians, increasing their susceptibility to the fatal microbes, the destruction of their ways of life by armadas of disease in turn made them more susceptible to enslavement. For many, whose crops now were gone, because there was no one strong enough to tend them while the epidemic raged, giving themselves over to servitude became the only way they could even hope to eat. They approached plantation masters and begged to be taken in. "There are some who were not even wanted as slaves," wrote Vale, so they "had themselves shackled so that they would be taken: it seemed less likely that they would be rejected if already in irons." Added Vasconcellos: "One man surrendered his liberty for only one gourd of flour to save his life. Others hired themselves out to work all or part of their lives, others sold their own children." Within three decades at least 90 percent of the region's native people had been destroyed.[122]

This was, of course, far from the last of it. An unending rhythm of attack from slaving parties, punctuated by furious epidemic disease episodes brought by those same slavers, as well as by missionaries, and then military assault again, became the norm of Brazilian Indian life for most of the next two centuries. Even when nominally free, the natives were being systematically destroyed. Thus, for example, by the 1630s those Indians still living in the municipal council of Salvador who were able to work for wages earned on average between one-eighth and one-sixteenth of what black slaves were paid—and often such "wages" were doled out in flour, cloth, and alcohol, if they were paid at all. Frequently they were not. Even if paid, however, and paid in hard currency, such earnings were far from sufficient for survival.[123] If there is anything that now seems surprising in light of all this, it is the extraordinary level of resistance the natives continued to mount even as they watched their own populations falling rapidly toward non-existence. The story of Ajuricaba, heroic eighteenth-century chief of the powerful Manau tribe, who fought ferociously to preserve his people from abduction and enslavement—and who leapt to his own death rather than be captured—is still remembered today among Brazilians who care about such things. But, in fact, Ajuricaba was only one of many.

From the very beginning—from at least that day in 1493 when a "very beautiful Carib woman" fought off the violent advances of Michele de Cuneo, before being thrashed with a rope and then raped by him—the people of the Americas resisted. None did so more successfully than the Maya, who combined retreats into the deep jungle cover of the Yucatán lowlands—where, as one historian puts it, the pursuing conquistadors "soon found themselves adrift in a green expanse of forest without food to eat, souls to convert, or labor to exploit"—with relentless military counterattacks that finally led to temporary expulsion of the Spanish in 1638.[124] And neither did any people resist with more symbolism than the Maya, who made a practice of destroying not only Spanish soldiers but whatever foreign things the Spanish had brought with them—horses, cattle, cats, dogs, trees, and plants.[125] In the end, however, the Maya too lost 95 of every 100 of their people—a price for their resistance that most outsiders, if they know of it, can hardly hope to comprehend.[126]

By the time the sixteenth century had ended perhaps 200,000 Spaniards had moved their lives to the Indies, to Mexico, to Central America, and points further to the south. In contrast, by that time, somewhere between 60,000,000 and 80,000,000 natives from those lands were dead. Even then, the carnage was not over.[127]

4

I N THE AREA around the town of Barquicimeto, in the lowlands near the northern coast of Venezuela, a mysterious fire like a will o' the wisp sometimes seems to be burning in the marshes. It is, tradition has it, the "soul of the traitor Lope de Aguirre [who] wanders in the savannahs, like a flame that flies the approach of men."[1]

Aguirre's 1561 expedition from Peru, across the Andes and down to the Venezuelan seacoast, has become "a byword for sensational horror," writes one historian, adding that "no pirates who infested the Caribbean before or since proved more rapacious and merciless," and no military campaign was more "notorious for its atrocities" than the one driven by "Aguirre's mad rage."[2] In fact, Aguirre's rampage through South America was a good deal less destructive than those of any number of long-forgotten conquistadors. What has made it so memorable, so worthy of evocation in books and poems and films, was Aguirre's propensity for killing Spaniards as well as Indians. This is what made him "the traitor Aguirre"—a traitor to nothing less than his race.

For this reason there never has been any doubt that Aguirre was an evil man. For this reason also, when he was captured, Aguirre's fellow Spaniards cut off his head and placed it on display in an iron cage. Beyond Aguirre, however, debate has gone on almost non-stop for four centuries about the behavior of other conquistadors—about what in some quarters has come to be called the "Black Legend." Proponents of this idea hold that the Spanish have been unduly and unfairly criticized for their behavior in the New World. They base this contention on two general principles: first, that the stories of Spanish cruelties toward the Indians, almost entirely traceable, it is said, to the writings of Bartolomé de Las Casas, are untrue, or at least are exaggerations; and, second, that the cruelties of other European nations against the native peoples of the Americas were just as condemnable.[3]

The first of these charges has now largely fallen into disuse as historian after historian has shown not only that Las Casas's reports were remarkably accurate (and often, in quantitative terms, even underestimates) but that they were supported by a host of other independent observers who, like Las Casas, spent a good deal of time in the Caribbean, Mexico, and Central and South America during the sixteenth century.[4] It is the second of the complaints by Black Legend advocates that remains worthy of consideration—that is, as one supporter of this view puts it, that "the Spaniards were no more and no less human, and no more and no less humane" than were other Europeans at that time.[5] Of particular concern to those who hold this position is the behavior of the British and, later, the Americans. To be sure, on occasion this line of Spanish defense has been stretched to the point of absurdity. One historian, for example, has suggested quite seriously that—apart from their murderous treatment of the Indians—the Spaniards' public torture and burning of Jews and other alleged heretics and heathens was simply "pageantry," comparable, albeit on a different level, to American Fourth of July celebrations.[6] But the larger argument that the Spanish were not unique in their murderous depredations—that others of European ancestry were of equally genocidal temperament—is, we shall see, both responsible and correct.

II

During the latter half of the sixteenth century, while the Spanish and Portuguese were busy "pacifying" the indigenous peoples in Mexico and on to the south (with additional forays up into Florida and Virginia), the English were preoccupied with their own pacification of the Irish. From the vantage point of the present it may seem absurd that the English of this time were accusing anyone of savagery or barbarism. After all, this was a society in which a third of the people lived at the bare margin of subsistence, a society in which conditions of health and sanitation were so appalling that it was rare for an individual to survive into his or her mid-thirties.[7] As for the superior qualities of the English cast of mind, in the closing years of the sixteenth century (the era that British historians of philosophy call the dawn of the Age of Reason) the courts of Essex County alone brought in about 650 indictments for more than 1500 witchcraft-related crimes. And this, says the historian who has studied the subject most closely, "was only the projecting surface of far more widespread suspicions."[8]

Still, Britain's people considered themselves the most civilized on earth, and before long they would nod approvingly as Oliver Cromwell declared

God to be an Englishman. It is not surprising, then, that English tracts and official minutes during this time described the "wild Irish" as "naked rogues in woods and bogs [whose] ordinary food is a kind of grass." Less ordinary food for the Irish, some reported, was the flesh of other people, sometimes their own mothers—which, perhaps, was only fair, since still other tall tales had it that Irish mothers ate their children. The Irish were, in sum, "unreasonable beasts," said William Thomas, beasts who "lived without any knowledge of God or good manners, in common of their goods, cattle, women, children and every other thing."[9]

Such brutishness was beyond the English capacity for tolerance. Especially when the vulgarians in question occupied such lovely lands. So, as they had for centuries, the English waged wars to pacify and civilize the Irish. One of the more successful English soldiers in the Irish wars was the Oxford-educated half-brother of Sir Walter Raleigh, one Humphrey Gilbert—himself later knighted for his service to the Crown. Gilbert devised a particularly imaginative way of bringing the Irish to heel. He ordered that

> the heddes of all those (of what sort soever thei were) which were killed in the daie, should be cutte off from their bodies and brought to the place where he incamped at night, and should there bee laied on the ground by eche side of the waie ledyng into his owne tente so that none could come into his tente for any cause but commonly he muste passe through a lane of heddes which he used *ad terrorem*.[10]

Needless to say, this "lane of heddes" leading to Gilbert's tent did indeed cause "greate terrour to the people when thei sawe the heddes of their dedde fathers, brothers, children, kinsfolke, and freinds" laid out "on the grounde before their faces."[11] Lest anyone think to quibble over such extreme methods of persuasion, however, the British frequently justified their treatment of the Irish by referring to the Spanish precedent for dealing with unruly natives.[12]

In the meantime, a few English expeditions had gone forth to explore the lands of the New World, but they concentrated on areas far to the north of where the Spanish were engaged in their exploits. The first serious attempt by the English to set up a colony in America was on Baffin Island, where they thought they had discovered gold. As it turned out, the mineral they discovered was fool's gold and the colony was abandoned, but not before the leader of the expedition, Martin Frobisher, had captured and kidnapped a handful of the "sundry tokens of people" he found there.

On his first trip to the area Frobisher seized a native man who approached his ship in a kayak and returned with him and his kayak to England. The man soon died, however, so on his next voyage Frobisher took on board an old woman and a young woman with her child—this, after he and his men had "disposed ourselves, contrary to our inclination, something to be cruel," and destroyed an entire native village. After stripping the old woman naked "to see if she were cloven footed," they sent her on her way, but kept the young woman and child, along with a man they also had captured in a separate raid.[13] They then brought the man and woman together, with the crew assembled "to beholde the manner of their meeting and entertainment," as though they were two animals. The crew was disappointed, however, for instead of behaving in bestial fashion, the captive Indians showed themselves to be more restrained and dignified and sensitive than their captors.

> At theyr first encountering, they behelde eache the other very wistly a good space, withoute speeche or worde uttered, with greate change of coloure and countenance, as though it seemed the greefe and disdeyne of their captivitie had taken away the use of their tongues and utterance: the woman of the first verie suddaynely, as though she disdeyned or regarded not the man, turned away and beganne to sing, as though she minded another matter: but being agayne broughte togyther, the man brake up the silence first, and with sterne and stayed countenance beganne to tell a long solemne tale to the woman, whereunto she gave good hearing, and interrupted him nothing till he had finished, and, afterwards being growen into more familiar acquaintance by speech, were turned togither, so that (I think) the one would hardly have lived without the comfort of the other.[14]

Much to the surprise of the inquiring English, however, the captive Indians maintained their sexual distance. Although they frequently comforted one another, reported a member of the crew, "only I thinke it worth the noting the continencie of them both; for the man would never shifte himselfe, except he had first caused the woman to depart out of his cabin, and they both were most shamefast least anye of their privie parts should be discovered, eyther of themselves or any other body."[15]

Upon their arrival in England the kidnapped man unsurprisingly displayed "an Anglophobia," reported one observer who disapproved. And when it was discovered that he was seriously ill from broken ribs that had punctured a lung, the presiding physician recommended blood-letting, but "the foolish, and only too uncivilised, timidity of this uncivilised man forbade it." He died soon thereafter, as had the man they captured on their previous expedition. This was very upsetting to all concerned. As the physician in charge recalled: "I was bitterly grieved and saddened, not so much by the death of the man himself as because the great hope of seeing him which our most gracious Queen had entertained had now slipped through her fingers, as it were, for a second time."[16] His body was dissected and buried, by which time the native woman had also fallen ill. Before long, she was dead as well, and her child followed soon thereafter.

If the fate of Indians captured by the English for display and viewing in London was routinely the same as that suffered by natives in Spanish captivity, there also was a similarity in the fate of those Indians, north and south, who remained at home. By the time the English announced the settlement of Jamestown in Virginia (marking their dominion, as did the Spanish, with a cross), the lands the Spanish and Portuguese had conquered already were an immense and bone-strewn graveyard. Indians in the many tens of millions had died horribly from the blades and germs of their Iberian invaders. As far north as Florida and southern Georgia, for every ten Timucuan Indians who were alive in 1515 only one was alive in 1607. And by 1617, a short decade later, that number was halved again. According to the most detailed population analysis of this region that ever has been done, in 1520 the number of Timucuan people in the area totaled over 720,000; following a century of European contact they numbered barely 36,000. Two-thirds of a million native people—95 percent of the enormous and ancient Timucuan society—had been obliterated by the violence of sword and plague.[17]

But the Spanish didn't stop at Florida and Georgia. As early as the summer of 1521, while Cortés and his army were still completing the destruction of Tenochtitlán, Spanish ships under the command of Pedro de Quejo and Francisco Gordillo landed on the coast of what is now South Carolina, near Winyah Bay, north of Charleston. Each man independently claimed possession of the land for his particular employer—and each one also denounced the other for doing so. But on one thing, at least, they agreed. Their mission was to find and capture as many Indians as possible and to bring them back to labor in the Bahamas, whose millions of native people by then—less than 30 years after Columbus's first voyage—had largely been exterminated. They did their job well. After two weeks of friendly contact with the Indians living around Winyah Bay, Quejo and Gordillo invited them to visit their ships. Once the natives were on board, however, the two captains raised anchor and set sail for Santo Domingo.

There is some dispute as to how many Indians were captured that day by the Spanish—somewhere between 60 and 130—but there is no disagreement about what happened next. Upon their arrival in Santo Domingo the natives were enslaved and put to work on plantations, though for food they had to fend for themselves. They were reduced to scavenging through decaying garbage and eating dead and decomposing dogs and donkeys. By 1526, four years after their capture, only one of them was still alive.[18]

It was a fitting start for all that was to follow. For the next half-century and beyond, the Spanish and French and English plied the waters off the coast of Florida, Georgia, the Carolinas, and Virginia—with raiding parties marching inland to capture slaves and spread disease and depredation. Before the last of the slaves from the Quejo-Gordillo expedition had been killed, Giovanni de Verrazzano was leading a fleet of French ships into the area, followed by Jacques Cartier in 1534, and numerous others after him. Their impact on the lives of the native peoples they encountered varied, as did their specific intentions. But for most, their intentions were clear in what they brought with them. Thus, in 1539, Hernando de Soto landed with a force of 600 armed men, more than 200 horses, hundreds of wolfhounds, mastiffs, and greyhounds, a huge supply of neck chains for the slaves they planned to capture, and a portable forge in case that supply proved inadequate.[19]

By the 1560s and 1570s European militiamen were traveling throughout the southeast, spreading disease and bloody massacre everywhere they went. Still, in the early 1570s—even after a series of devastating European diseases had attacked the Virginia Indians for more than half a decade—the Jesuit Juan Rogel, generally regarded as the most reliable of all the early Spanish commentators on this region, wrote of coastal Virginia: "There are more people here than in any of the other lands I have seen so far along the coast explored. It seemed to me that the natives are more settled than in other regions I have been."[20] And Father Rogel previously had lived in densely populated Florida. Twenty-five years later, when the British colonizing troops arrived at Jamestown, they found "a lande," wrote one of them, "that promises more than the Lande of promisse: In steed of mylke we fynde pearl. / & golde Inn steede of honye." But by now the people they found were greatly reduced in number from what they had been before the coming of the earlier Europeans. The signs of the previous invaders' calling cards could not be missed, "for the great diseaze reignes in the [native] men generally," noted an anonymous correspondent, "full fraught with noodes botches and pulpable appearances in their forheades."[21]

A decade earlier, in 1596, an epidemic of measles—or possibly bubonic plague—had swept through Florida, killing many native people. It may have made its way to Virginia as well, since on previous occasions the two locales had been nearly simultaneous recipients of European pestilence: in 1586, for instance, Thomas Hariot's English troops left disease and death throughout Virginia at the same time that Francis Drake had loosed some "very foul and frightful diseases" (at least one of which appears to have been typhus) among the Indians at St. Augustine; and in 1564, a six-year siege of disease and starvation began that reduced Virginia's population drastically, at the same time that a devastating plague of some sort was killing large numbers of Florida's Timucuan people.[22]

Invariably, in the New World as in the Old, massive epidemics brought starvation in their wake, because the reduced and debilitated populations were unable to tend their crops. As one Jesuit wrote of Virginia in the fall of 1570:

> We find the land of Don Luis [the Spanish name given an Indian aboard ship who had been taken from Virginia to Spain some years earlier] in quite an-

other condition than expected, not because he was at fault in his description of it, but because Our Lord has chastised it with six years of famine and death, which has brought it about that there is much less population than usual. Since many have died and many also have moved to other regions to ease their hunger [and unwittingly spread disease inland] there remain but few of the tribe, whose leaders say that they wish to die where their fathers have died. . . . They seemed to think that Don Luis had risen from the dead and come down from heaven, and since all who remained are his relatives, they are greatly consoled in him. . . . Thus we have felt the good will which this tribe is showing. On the other hand, as I have said, they are so famished that all believe they will perish of hunger and cold this winter.[23]

It was not likely an exaggeration, then, when the British settlers in Jamestown were told in 1608, by the elderly leader of the Indians whose land they were there to take, that he had witnessed "the death of all my people thrice, and not one living of those 3 generations, but my selfe."[24] England's formal contribution to this holocaust was next.

Despite the horrors they had endured in recent decades, the Indians' continuing abilities to produce enormous amounts of food impressed and even awed many of the earliest British explorers. Beans, pumpkins, and many other vegetables, especially corn, which was greatly superior in its yield (about double that of wheat) and in its variety of uses to anything Europeans had ever seen, were grown in fields tended with such care that they looked more like huge gardens, it was said, than farmlands. So too did at least some British, despite their general disdain for the Indians, initially praise their technological ingenuity, marveling as well at their smooth-functioning but complex machineries of government—government that was commonly under the control of democratic councils, but that also produced individual leaders of dignity and civility. As one historian has noted, the contrast in regal manner between the Indian and British leaders was especially extreme at the time of the British settlement of Virginia, because England was then ruled by King James I who was notorious for his personal filthiness, his excessive and slobbering ways of eating and drinking, and his vulgar and boorish style of speech and overall behavior.[25]

Admiration of Indian ways of living—particularly their peacefulness, generosity, trustworthiness, and egalitarianism, all of which were conspicuously absent from English social relations of the time—led to some eloquent early praise of Virginia's native people, albeit from a distinct minority of British observers. But if those who spoke with their pens are sometimes regarded skeptically, those who voted with their feet cannot be. And it is especially telling that throughout the seventeenth and on into the eighteenth and nineteenth centuries, while almost no Indians voluntarily lived among the colonists, the number of whites who ran off to live with the Indians was a problem often remarked upon. After a century and a half of permanent British settlement in North America, Benjamin Franklin joined numerous earlier commentators in lamenting that

When an Indian child has been brought up among us, taught our language and habituated to our Customs, yet if he goes to see his relations and make one Indian Ramble with them, there is no perswading him ever to return. [But] when white persons of either sex have been taken prisoners young by the Indians, and lived a while among them, tho' ransomed by their Friends, and treated with all imaginable tenderness to prevail with them to stay among the English, yet in a Short time they become disgusted with our manner of life, and the care and pains that are necessary to support it, and take the first good Opportunity of escaping again into the Woods, from whence there is no reclaiming them.[26]

Children brought up among the Indians were not the only problem. Adult men and women also turned their backs on Western culture, leading J. Hector St. John de Crèvecoeur to exclaim: "Thousands of Europeans are Indians, and we have no examples of even one of these Aborigines having from choice become Europeans!"[27] After surveying and analyzing this literature and the narratives of those Europeans who wrote about their experiences with the Indians, James Axtell has concluded that the whites who chose to remain among the natives

stayed because they found Indian life to possess a strong sense of community, abundant love, and uncommon integrity—values that the European colonists also honored, if less successfully. But Indian life was attractive for other values—for social equality, mobility, adventure, and, as two adult converts acknowledged, "the most perfect freedom, the ease of living, [and] the absence of those cares and corroding solicitudes which so often prevail with us."[28]

The first colonial leaders, however, would have none of this. Most of them were military men, trained in the Irish wars. Whatever they thought of the Indian way of life, they never failed to regard the Indians themselves as peoples fated for conquest. As a counterweight to that relative handful of writers who were praising the native peoples and their governments, these British equivalents of the conquistadors viewed the Indians as, in John Smith's words, "craftie, timerous, quicke of apprehension, and very ingenuous. Some," he added, "are of disposition fearefull, some bold, most cautelous [deceitful], all Savage. . . . Their chiefe God they worship is the Divell"[29] For men like Smith, having learned how to deal with what they regarded as the savage people of Ireland was a lesson of importance when they turned their attention to the Indians; as Howard Mumford Jones once put it, the "English experience with one wild race conditioned their expectation of experience with another."[30]

And so, based on that experience, founding colonial leaders like Smith and Ralph Lane routinely carried out a policy of intimidation as the best means of garnering their hosts' cooperation. Observing the closeness of Indian parents and children, for example, and the extraordinary grief suffered by Indian mothers and fathers when separated from their offspring, Smith and Lane made it a practice to kidnap and hold hostage Indian children whenever they approached a native town.[31] As for those Englishmen among them who might be tempted to run off and live with the Indians, the colonial governors made it clear that such behavior would not be tolerated. For example, when in the spring of 1612, some young English settlers in Jamestown "being idell . . . did runne away unto the Indyans," Governor Thomas Dale had them hunted down and executed: "Some he apointed to be hanged Some burned Some to be broken upon wheles, others to be staked and some to be shott to deathe."[32]

This was the treatment for those who wished to act like Indians. For those who had no choice in the matter, because they were the native people of Virginia, the tone had been set decades earlier in the "lost colony" of Roanoke. There, when an Indian was accused by an Englishman of stealing a cup and failing to return it, the English response was to attack the natives in force, burning the entire community and the fields of corn surrounding it.[33]

Such disproportionate responses to supposed affronts was to mark English dealings with the Indians throughout the seventeenth century. Thus, in Jamestown in the summer of 1610, Governor Thomas West De la Warr requested of the Indian chief Powhatan (Wahunsonacock) that he return some runaway Englishmen—presumably to be hanged, burned, "broken upon wheles," staked, and shot to death—whom De la Warr thought Powhatan was harboring. Powhatan responded in a way that De la Warr considered unsatisfactory, giving "noe other than prowde and disdaynefull Answers." So De la Warr launched a military campaign against Powhatan headed by George Percy, the brother of the Earl of Northumberland and De la Warr's second in command. Here is Percy's own description of what he did:

> Draweinge my sowldiers into Battalio placeinge a Capteyne or Leftenante att every fyle we marched towards the [Indians'] Towne. . . . And then we fell in upon them putt some fiftene or sixtene to the Sworde and Almost all the reste to flyghte. . . . My Lieftenantt bringeinge with him the Quene and her Children and one Indyann prisoners for the Which I taxed him becawse he had Spared them his Answer was thatt haveinge them now in my Custodie I might doe with them whatt I pleased. Upon the same I cawsed the Indians head to be cutt of. And then dispersed my fyles Apointeinge my Sowldiers to burne their howses and to cutt downe their Corne groweinge aboutt the Towne.[34]

With the Indians thus dead or dispersed, their village destroyed, and their food supplies laid waste, Percy sent out another raiding party to do the same to another Indian town and then marched back to his boats with the Indian "queen" and her children in tow. There, however, his soldiers "did begin to murmur becawse the quene and her Children weare spared." This seemed a reasonable complaint to Percy, so he called a council together and "it was Agreed upon to putt the Children to deathe the which was effected by Throweinge them overboard shoteinge owtt their Braynes in the water." Upon his return to Jamestown, however, Percy was informed that Governor De la Warr was unhappy with him because he had not yet killed the queen. Advised by his chief lieutenant that it would be best to burn her alive, Percy decided instead to end his day of "so mutche Blood-shedd" with a final act of mercy: instead of burning her, he had the queen quickly killed by stabbing her to death.[35]

From this point on there would be no peace in Virginia. Indians who came to the English settlements with food for the British (who seemed never able to feed themselves) were captured, accused of being spies, and executed. On other occasions Indians were enticed into visiting the settlements on the pretence of peace and the sharing of entertainment, whereupon they were attacked by the English and killed. Peace treaties were signed with every intention to violate them: when the Indians "grow secure uppon the treatie," advised the Council of State in Virginia, "we shall have the better Advantage both to surprise them, & cutt downe theire Corne." And when at last the Indians retaliated strongly, killing more than three hundred settlers, the attack, writes Edmund S. Morgan, "released all restraints that the company had hitherto imposed on those who thirsted for the destruction or enslavement of the Indians."[36] Not that the restraints had ever been particularly confining, but from now on the only controversy was over whether it was preferable to kill all the native peoples or to enslave them. Either way, the point was to seize upon the "right of Warre [and] invade the Country and destroy them who sought to destroy us," wrote a rejoicing Edward Waterhouse at the time, "whereby wee shall enjoy their cultivated places . . . [and] their cleared grounds in all their villages (which are situate in the fruitfullest places of the land) shall be inhabited by us."[37]

Hundreds of Indians were killed in skirmish after skirmish. Other hundreds were killed in successful plots of mass poisoning. They were hunted down by dogs, "blood-Hounds to draw after them, and Mastives to seaze them." Their canoes and fishing weirs were smashed, their villages and agricultural fields burned to the ground. Indian peace offers were accepted by the English only until their prisoners were returned; then, having lulled the natives into false security, the colonists returned to the attack. It was the colonists' expressed desire that the Indians be exterminated, rooted "out from being longer a people uppon the face of the earth." In a single raid the settlers destroyed corn sufficient to feed four thousand people for a year. Starvation and the massacre of non-combatants was becoming the preferred British approach to dealing with the natives. By the end of the winter of 1623 the Indians acknowledged that in the past year alone as many of their number had been killed as had died since the first arrival of the British a decade and a half earlier.[38]

The slaughter continued. In 1624—in a single battle—sixty heavily armed Englishmen cut down 800 defenseless Indian men, women, and children in their own village. And, of course, as elsewhere, British diseases were helping to thin out whatever resistance the Indians could hope to muster. Long before the middle of the century was reached the region's largest and most powerful Indian confederation, known to historians retrospectively as Powhatan's Empire, was "so rowted, slayne and dispersed," wrote one British colonist, "that they are no longer a nation." At the end, Powhatan's successor chief, Opechancanough, was captured. An old man now, "grown so decrepit that he was not able to walk alone . . . his Flesh all macerated, his Sinews slacken'd, and his Eye-lids become so heavy that he could not see," Opechancanough was thrown into a cell in Jamestown and displayed like the captive beast that the colonists thought he was. But not for long. Within two weeks a British soldier shot him in the back and killed him.[39]

When the first 104 English settlers arrived at Jamestown in April of 1607, the number of Indians under Powhatan's control was probably upwards of 14,000—a fraction of what it had been just a few decades earlier, because of English, French, and Spanish depredations and disease. (Estimates of the region's native population prior to European contact extend upwards of 100,000.) By the time the seventeenth century had passed, those 104 settlers had grown to more than 60,000 English men and women who were living in and harvesting Virginia's bounty, while Powhatan's people had been reduced to about 600, maybe less.[40] More than 95 percent of Powhatan's people had been exterminated—beginning from a population base in 1607 that already had been drastically reduced, perhaps by 75 percent or more, as a result of prior European incursions in the region.

Powhatan's Empire was not the only Indian nation in Virginia, of course, but his people's fate was representative of that of the area's other indigenous societies. In 1697 Virginia's Lieutenant Governor Andros put the number of Indian warriors in the entire colony at just over 360, which suggests a total Indian population of less than 1500, while John Lawson, in his *New Voyage to Carolina,* claimed that more than 80 percent of the colony's native people had been killed off during the previous fifty years alone. In time, a combination plan of genocide and enslavement, as initially proposed by the colony's Governor William Berkeley, appeared to quiet what had become a lingering controversy over whether it was best to kill all the Indians or to capture them and put them to forced labor: Berkeley's plan was to slaughter all the adult Indian males in a particular locale, "but to spare the women and children and sell them," says Edmund

Morgan. This way the war of extermination "would pay for itself," since it was likely that a sufficient number of female and child slaves would be captured "to defray the whole cost."[41]

By the time this clever enterprise was under way in Virginia, the British had opened colonies in New England as well. As usual, earlier visits by Europeans already had spread among the Indians a host of deadly plagues. The Patuxet peoples, for example, were effectively exterminated by some of these diseases, while other tribes disappeared before they were even seen by any white men. Others were more fortunate, suffering death rates of 50 and 60 percent—a good deal greater than the proportion of Europeans killed by the Black Death pandemic of the fourteenth century, but still far short of total liquidation. These were rates, however, for any given *single* epidemic, and in New England's sixteenth and seventeenth centuries few epidemics traveled by themselves.[42] The extant descriptions of what life and death were like at times like these are rare, but the accounts we do have of the viral and bacteriological assaults are sobering indeed, reminiscent of the earlier Spanish and Portuguese accounts from Mesoamerica and Brazil. Wrote Plymouth Colony's Governor William Bradford, for instance, of a smallpox epidemic from which huge numbers of Indians "died most miserably":

> For want of bedding and linen and other helps they fall into a lamentable condition as they lie on their hard mats, the pox breaking and mattering and running one into another, their skin cleaving by reason thereof to the mats they lie on. When they turn them, a whole side will flay off at once as it were, and they will be all of a gore blood, most fearful to behold. And then being very sore, what with cold and other distempers, they die like rotten sheep. The condition of this people was so lamentable and they fell down so generally of this disease as they were in the end not able to help one another, no not to make a fire nor to fetch a little water to drink, nor any to bury the dead. But would strive as long as they could, and when they could procure no other means to make fire, they would burn the wooden trays and dishes they ate their meat in, and their very bows and arrows. And some would crawl out on all fours to get a little water, and sometimes die by the way and not be able to get in again.[43]

While "very few" of the Indians escaped this scourge, including "the chief sachem . . . and almost all his friends and kindred," Bradford reported, "by the marvelous goodness and providence of God, not one of the English was so much as sick or in the least measure tainted with this disease." Time and again Old World epidemics such as this coursed through the veins of the native peoples of the North Atlantic coast, even before the arrival of the first great waves of British settlers, leaving in their wake so many dead that they could not be buried, so many piles of skeletal remains that one early colonist referred to the land as "a new found Golgotha."[44] But it was a Golgotha the Puritans delighted in discovering, not only because the diseases they brought with them from England left the Puritans themselves virtually unaffected, but because the destruction of the Indians by these plagues was considered an unambiguous sign of divine approval for the colonial endeavor. As the first governor of the Massachusetts Bay Colony wrote in 1634, the Puritan settlers, numbering at the time "in all about four thousand souls and upward," were in remarkably good health: "through the Lord's special providence . . . there hath not died above two or three grown persons and about so many children all the last year, it being very rare to hear of any sick of agues or other diseases." But, he noted in passing, as "for the natives, they are near all dead of the small-pox, so as the Lord hath cleared our title to what we possess."[45]

God, however, was not enough. At some point the settlers would have to take things into their own hands. For, terribly destructive though the Old World diseases were, some Indians remained alive. The danger posed by these straggling few natives was greatly exaggerated by the English (as it remains exaggerated in most history textbooks today), not only because their numbers had been so drastically reduced, but because their attitudes toward the colonists and their very means of warfare were so comparatively benign.

We have seen in an earlier chapter that the native peoples of this region (as elsewhere) combined in their everyday lives a sense of individual autonomy and communal generosity that the earliest Europeans commented on continuously. This was a great cultural strength, so long as the people they were dealing with shared those values and accepted the array of culturally correct reciprocal responses to them. However, just as their isolation from Old World diseases made the Indians an exceptionally healthy people as long as they were not contacted by disease-bearing outsiders, once Europeans invaded their lands with nothing but disdain for the native regime of mutual respect and reciprocity, the end result was doomed to spell disaster.

This probably is seen most dramatically in the comparative Indian and European attitudes toward warfare. We already have observed one consequence of the differing rituals that were conventional to Europe and the Americas in Montezuma's welcoming Cortés into Tenochtitlán in part because Cortés claimed he was on a mission of peace; and one inviolable code of Mesoamerican warfare was that it was announced, with its causes enumerated, in advance. Cortés's declared intentions of peace, therefore, were supposed by Montezuma to be his true intentions. A similar attitude held among Indians in much of what is now the United States. Thus, as a seventeenth-century Lenape Indian explained in a discussion with a British colonist:

We are minded to live at Peace: If we intend at any time to make War upon you, we will let you know of it, and the Reasons why we make War with you; and if you make us satisfaction for the Injury done us, for which the War is intended, then we will not make War on you. And if you intend at any time to make War on us, we would have you let us know of it, and the Reasons for which you make War on us, and then if we do not make satisfaction for the Injury done unto you, then you may make War on us, otherwise you ought not to do it.[46]

The simplicity of this seems naïve and even quaint to modern observers, as it did to seventeenth-century Britishers, but it made perfect sense to native peoples who simply did not wage war for the same reasons that Europeans did. "Given ample land and a system of values by and large indifferent to material accumulation," writes a scholar of military law, "the New England tribes rarely harbored the economic and political ambitions that fueled European warfare." Instead, an Indian war usually was a response to personal insults or to individual acts of inter-tribal violence. As such, it could be avoided by "making satisfaction for the injury done" (as noted in the quotation above), but even when carried out "native hostilities generally aimed at symbolic ascendancy, a status conveyed by small payments of tribute to the victors, rather than the dominion normally associated with European-style conquest." Moreover, given the relative lack of power that Indian leaders had over their highly autonomous followers, Indian warriors might choose not to join in battle for this or that cause, and it was even common for an Indian war party on the march to "melt away as individual warriors had second thoughts and returned home."[47]

Prior to the European assaults on their lands, Indians throughout the continent held similar attitudes toward the proper conduct of war. The idea of large-scale battle, wrote Ruth Benedict more than half a century ago, was "alien" to all these peoples. Of the California Indians, even long after they had almost been exterminated by white malevolence, Benedict wrote: "Their misunderstanding of warfare was abysmal. They did not have the basis in their own culture upon which the idea could exist."[48] As for the Indians of the Plains, who have been turned into the very portrait of aggression and ferocity by purveyors of American popular culture (and by far too many serious historians as well), wrote George Bird Grinnell:

Among the plains tribes with which I am well acquainted—and the same is true of all the others of which I know anything at all—coming in actual personal contact with the enemy by touching him with something held in the hand or with a part of the person was the bravest act that could be performed . . . [This was known as] to count coup on—to touch or strike—a living unhurt man and to leave him alive, and this was frequently done. . . . It was regarded as an evidence of bravery for a man to go into battle carrying no weapon that would do any harm at a distance. It was more creditable to carry a lance than a bow and arrows; more creditable to carry a hatchet or war club than a lance; and the bravest thing of all was to go into a fight with nothing more than a whip, or a long twig—sometimes called a coup stick. I have never heard a stone-headed war club called coup stick.[49]

Commenting on this passage, and on the generality of its application to indigenous warfare, anthropologist Stanley Diamond has noted that to people such as the American Indians "taking a life was an *occasion*," whereas warfare of the type described "is a kind of play. No matter what the occasion for hostility, it is particularized, personalized, ritualized." In contrast, by the time of the invasion of the Americas, European warfare had long since been made over into what Diamond describes as "an abstract, ideological compulsion" resulting in "indiscriminate, casual, unceremonious killing."[50]

Not surprisingly, then, the highly disciplined and ideologically motivated British expressed contempt for what Captain John Mason called the Indians' "feeble manner . . . [that] did hardly deserve the name of fighting." Warfare among the native peoples had no "dissipline" about it, complained Captain Henry Spelman, so that when Indians fought there was no great "slawter of nether side"; instead, once "having shott away most of their arrows," both sides commonly "weare glad to retier." Indeed, so comparatively harmless was inter-tribal fighting, noted John Underhill, that "they might fight seven yeares and not kill seven men."[51] Added Roger Williams: "Their Warres are farre lesse bloudy, and devouring than the cruell Warres of Europe; and seldome twenty slain in a pitcht field. . . . When they fight in a plaine, they fight with leaping and dancing, that seldome an Arrow hits, and when a man is wounded, unlesse he that shot followes upon the wounded, they soone retire and save the wounded." In addition, the Indians' code of honor "ordinarily spared the women and children of their adversaries."[52]

In contrast, needless to say, the British did very little in the way of "leaping and dancing" on the field of battle, and more often than not Indian women and children were consumed along with everyone and everything else in the conflagrations that routinely accompanied the colonists' assaults. Their purpose, after all, was rarely to avenge an insult to honor—although that might be the stipulated rationale for a battle—but rather, when the war was over, to be able to say what John Mason declared at the conclusion of one especially bloody combat: that "the Lord was pleased to smite our Enemies in the hinder Parts, and *to give us their Land for an Inheritance*."[53] Because of his readers' assumed knowledge of the Old Testament, it was unnecessary for Mason to remind them that this last phrase is derived from Deuteronomy, nor did he need to quote the words that immediately follow in that biblical passage: "Thou shalt save alive nothing that breatheth. . . . But thou shalt utterly destroy them."

The brutish and genocidal encounter to which Mason was referring was the Pequot War. Its first rumblings began to be heard in July of 1636— two years after a smallpox epidemic had devastated the New England natives "as far as any Indian plantation was known to the west," said John Winthrop—when the body of a man named John Oldham was found, apparently killed by Narragansett Indians on Block Island, off the Rhode Island coast.[54] Although he held positions of some importance, Oldham was not held in high regard by many of the English settlers—he had been banished from Plymouth Colony and described by its Governor Bradford as "more like a furious beast than a man"—and those whites who found his body had proceeded to murder more than a dozen Indians who were found at the scene of the crime, whether or not they were individually responsible.[55] Even in light of the colonists' grossly disproportionate sense of retribution when one of their own had been killed by Indians, this should have been sufficient revenge, but it was not. The colonists simply wanted to kill Indians. Despite the pledge of the Narragansetts' chief to mete out punishment to Oldham's murderers—a pledge he began to fulfill by sending 200 warriors to Block Island in search of the culprits—New England's Puritan leaders wanted more.

Led by Captain John Endicott, a heavily armed and armored party of about a hundred Massachusetts militiamen soon attacked the Block Island Indians. Their plan was to kill the island's adult males and make off with the women and children; as with Governor Berkeley's later scheme in Virginia, the venture would pay for itself since, as Francis Jennings puts it, "the captured women and children of Block Island would fetch a tidy sum in the West Indies slave markets."[56] The Indians scattered, however, realizing they had no hope against the colonists' weapons and armor, so the frustrated soldiers, able to kill only an odd few Narragansetts here and there, had to content themselves with the destruction of deserted villages. "We burnt and spoiled both houses and corn in great abundance," recalled one participant.[57]

From Block Island the troops headed back to the mainland where, following the directions of their colony's governor, they sought out a confrontation with some Pequot Indians. The Pequots, of course, had nothing to do with Oldham's death (the excuse for going after them was the allegation that, two years earlier, some among them may have killed two quarrelsome Englishmen, one of whom had himself tried to murder the Governor of Plymouth Colony), so when the soldiers first appeared along the Pequots' coastline the Indians ran out to greet them. As Underhill recalled: "The Indians spying of us came running in multitudes along the water side, crying, what cheere, Englishmen, what cheere, what doe you come for: They not thinking we intended warre, went on cheerefully untill they come to Pequeat river."[58] It soon became evident to the Pequots what the soldiers had come for, even if the cause of their coming remained a mystery, so after some protracted efforts at negotiation, the Pequots melted back into the forest to avoid a battle. As they had on Block Island, the troops then went on a destructive rampage, looting and burning the Indians' villages and fields of corn.

Once the Massachusetts troops left the field and returned to Boston, the Pequots came out of the woods, made a few retaliatory raids in the countryside, and then attacked nearby Fort Saybrook. Casualties were minimal in all of this, as was normal in Indian warfare, and at one point— presumably feeling that their honor had been restored—the Pequots fell back and asked the fort's commander if he felt he had "fought enough." The commander, Lieutenant Lion Gardiner, made an evasive reply, but its meaning was clear: from that day forward there would be no peace. Next, the Pequots asked if the English planned to kill Indian women and children. Gardiner's reply was that "they should see that hereafter."[59]

For a time small troubles continued in the field, while in Hartford the Connecticut General Court met and declared war against the Pequots. John Mason was appointed commander of the Connecticut troops. Rather than attack frontally, as the Massachusetts militia had, Mason led his forces and some accompanying Narragansetts (who long had been at odds with the Pequots) in a clandestine assault on the main Pequot village just before dawn. Upon realizing that Mason was planning nothing less than a wholesale massacre, the Narragansetts dissented and withdrew to the rear. Mason regarded them with contempt, saying that they could "stand at what distance they pleased, and see whether *English Men* would now fight or not." Dividing his forces in half, Mason at the head of one party, Underhill leading the other, under cover of darkness they attacked the unsuspecting Indians from two directions at once. The Pequots, Mason said, were taken entirely by surprise, their "being in a dead indeed their last Sleep."[60]

The British swarmed into the Indian encampment, slashing and shooting at anything that moved. Caught off guard, and with apparently few warriors in the village at the time, some of the Pequots fled, "others crept under their Beds," while still others fought back "most courageously," but this only drove Mason and his men to greater heights of fury. "*We must burn them*," Mason later recalled himself shouting, whereupon he "brought out a Fire Brand, and putting it into the Matts with which they were covered, set the Wigwams on Fire."[61] At this, Mason says, "the Indians ran as Men most dreadfully Amazed":

And indeed such a dreadful Terror did the Almighty let fall upon their Spirits, that they would fly from us and run into the very Flames, where many of them perished. . . . [And] God was above them, who laughed his Enemies and the Enemies of his People to Scorn, making them as a fiery Oven: Thus were the Stout Hearted spoiled, having slept their last Sleep, and none of their Men could find their Hands: Thus did the Lord judge among the Heathen, filling the Place with dead Bodies![62]

It was a ghastly sight—especially since we now know, as Francis Jennings reminds us, that most of those who were dying in the fires, and who were "crawling under beds and fleeing from Mason's dripping sword were women, children, and feeble old men."[63] Underhill, who had set fire to the other side of the village "with a traine of Powder" intended to meet Mason's blaze in the center, recalled how "great and doleful was the bloudy sight to the view of young soldiers that never had been in war, to see so many souls lie gasping on the ground, so thick, in some places, that you could hardly pass along." Yet, distressing though it may have been for the youthful murderers to carry out their task, Underhill reassured his readers that "sometimes the Scripture declareth women and children must perish with their parents."[64] Just because they were weak and helpless and unarmed, in short, did not make their deaths any less a delight to the Puritan's God. For as William Bradford described the British reaction to the scene:

> It was a fearful sight to see them thus frying in the fire and the streams of blood quenching the same, and horrible was the stink and scent thereof; but the victory seemed a sweet sacrifice, and they gave the praise thereof to God, who had wrought so wonderfully for them, thus to enclose their enemies in their hands and give them so speedy a victory over so proud and insulting an enemy.[65]

Added the Puritan divine Cotton Mather, as he celebrated the event many years later in his *Magnalia Christi Americana*: "In a little more than one hour, five or six hundred of these barbarians were dismissed from a world that was burdened with them." Mason himself counted the Pequot dead at six or seven hundred, with only seven taken captive and seven escaped. It was, he said joyfully, "the just Judgment of God."[66]

The Narragansetts who had accompanied the Puritans on their march did not share the Englishmen's joy. This indiscriminate carnage was not the way warfare was to be carried out. "Mach it, mach it," Underhill reports their shouting; "that is," he translates, "It is naught, it is naught, because it is too furious, and slays too many men."[67] Too many Indians, that was. Only two of the English died in the slaughter.

From then on the surviving Pequots were hunted into near-extermination. Other villages were found and burned. Small groups of warriors were intercepted and killed. Pockets of starving women and children were located, captured, and sold into slavery. If they were fortunate. Others were bound hand and foot and thrown into the ocean just beyond the harbor. And still more were buried where they were found, such as one group of three hundred or so who tried to escape through a swampland, but could make "little haste, by reason of their Children, and want of Provision," said Mason. When caught, as Richard Drinnon puts it, they "were literally run to ground," murdered, and then "tramped into the mud or buried in swamp mire."[68]

The comparative handful of Pequots who were left, once this series of massacres finally ended, were parceled out to live in servitude. John Endicott and his pastor, for example, wrote to the governor asking for "a share" of the captives, specifically "a yong woman or girle and a boy if you thinke good."[69] The last of them, fifteen boys and two women, were shipped to the West Indies for sale as slaves, the ship captain who carried them there returning the next year with what he had received in exchange: some cotton, some salt, some tobacco, "and Negroes, etc." The word "Pequot" was then removed from New England's maps: the river of that name was changed to the Thames and the town of that name became New London.[70] Having virtually eradicated an entire people, it now was necessary to expunge from historical memory any recollection of their past existence.[71]

Some, however, remembered all too well. John Mason rode the honor of his butchery to the position of Major General of Connecticut's armed forces. And Underhill, as Drinnon notes, "put his experience to good use" in selling his military prowess to the Dutch. On one subsequent occasion "with his company of Dutch troops Underhill surrounded an Indian village outside Stamford, set fire to the wigwams, drove back in with saber thrusts and shots those who sought to escape, and in all burned and shot five hundred with relative ease, allowing only about eight to escape—statistics comparable to those from the Pequot fort."[72]

Meanwhile, the Narragansetts, who had been the Pequots' rivals, but who were horrified at this inhuman carnage, quietly acknowledged the English domination of the Pequots' lands—their "widowed lands," to borrow a phrase from Jennings. That would not, however, prove sufficient. The English towns continued to multiply, the colonists continued to press out into the surrounding fields and valleys. The Narragansetts' land, and that of other tribes, was next.

To recount in detail the story of the destruction of the Narragansetts and such others as the Wampanoags, in what has come to be known as King Philip's War of 1675 and 1676, is unnecessary here. Thousands of native people were killed, their villages and crops burned to the ground. In a single early massacre 600 Indians were destroyed. It was, says the recent account of two historians, "a seventeenth-century My Lai" in which the English soldiers "ran amok, killing the wounded men, women, and children indiscriminately, firing the camp, burning the Indians alive or dead in their huts." A delighted Cotton Mather, revered pastor of the Second Church in Boston, later referred to the slaughter as a "barbeque."[73] More butchery was to follow. Of these, one bloodbath alongside the Connecticut River was typical. It is described by an eyewitness:

Our souldiers got thither after an hard March just about break of day, took most of the Indians fast asleep, and put their guns even into their Wigwams, and poured in their shot among them, whereupon the Indians that durst and were able did get out of their Wigwams and did fight a little (in which fight one Englishman only was slain) others of the Indians did enter the River to swim over from the English, but many of them were shot dead in the waters, others wounded were therein drowned, many got into Canoes to paddle away, but the paddlers being shot, the Canoes over-set with all therein, and the stream of the River being very violent and swift in the place near the great Falls, most that fell over board were born by the strong current of that River, and carryed upon the Falls of Water from those exceeding high and steep Rocks, and from thence tumbling down were broken in pieces; the English did afterwards find of their bodies, some in the River and some cast a-shore, above two hundred.[74]

The pattern was familiar, the only exception being that by the latter seventeenth century the Indians had learned that self-defense required an understanding of some English ideas about war, namely, in Francis Jennings's words: "that the Englishmen's most solemn pledge would be broken whenever obligation conflicted with advantage; that the English way of war had no limit of scruple or mercy; and that weapons of Indian making were almost useless against weapons of European manufacture. These lessons the Indians took to heart," so for once the casualties were high on both sides.[75] There was no doubt who would win, however, and when raging epidemics swept the countryside during the peak months of confrontation it only hastened the end.

Once the leader of the Indian forces, "a doleful, great, naked, dirty beast," the English called him, was captured—and cut in pieces—the rest was just a mop-up operation. As one modern celebrant of the English puts it: "Hunting redskins became for the time being a popular sport in New England, especially since prisoners were worth good money, and the personal danger to the hunters was now very slight."[76] Report after report came in of the killing of hundreds of Indians, "with the losse only of one man of ours," to quote a common refrain. Equally common were accounts such as that of the capture of "about 26 Indians, most Women and Children brought in by our Scouts, as they were ranging the Woods about Dedham, almost starved." All this, of course, was "God's Will," says the British reporter of these events, "which will at last give us cause to say, How Great is his Goodness! and how great is his Beauty!"[77] As another writer of the time expressed the shared refrain, "thus doth the Lord Jesus make them to bow before him, and to lick the Dust."[78]

Typical of those being made to bow and lick the dust by this time was "a very decrepit and harmless Indian," too old and too weak to walk, who was captured by the Puritan troops. For a time, says the eyewitness account of John Easton, the soldiers contented themselves with merely "tormenting" the old man. Finally, however, they decided to kill him: "some would have had him devoured by dogs," wrote Easton, "but the tenderness of some of them prevailed to cut off his head."[79]

The only major question remaining as King Philip's war drew to its inevitable close was how to deal with the few natives who still were alive. So many Indians had been "consumed . . . by the Sword & by Famine and by Sickness," wrote Cotton Mather's father Increase, "it being no unusual thing for those that traverse the woods to find dead Indians up and down . . . there hath been none to bury them," that there now were "not above an hundred men left of them who last year were the greatest body of Indians in New England."[80] As to what to do with that handful of survivors, only two choices—as always—enjoyed any support among the English colonists: annihilation or enslavement. Both approaches were tried. Allegedly dangerous Indians (that is, adult males) were systematically executed, while women and children were either shipped off to the slave markets of Spain or the West Indies, or were kept as servants of the colonists themselves. The terms of captured child slaves within Connecticut were to end once they reached the age of twenty-six. But few saw their day of liberation. Either they died before reaching their twenty-sixth birthday, or they escaped. And those who escaped and were caught usually then were sold into foreign slavery, with the blessing of the Connecticut General Court that had passed specific postwar legislation with this end in mind.

One final bit of business that required clearing up concerned the fates of those scattered Indians who had been able to hide out on islands in Narragansett Bay that were under the colonial jurisdiction of Rhode Island. Rhode Island had remained neutral during the war, and both the Indians and the leaders of the other colonies knew there was less likelihood of homicidal or other barbarous treatment for native refugees found in Rhode Island's domain. This infuriated the colonists in Connecticut, Massachusetts, and Plymouth, not only because of their continuing blood lust, but because the Rhode Islanders were themselves reducing escaped Indians to servitude, even if they were not methodically executing them. The other colonies, "mindful of the cash value of prisoners," writes Douglas Edward Leach, felt that the Rhode Islanders were thus unfairly "now reaping the benefits which others had sowed in blood and treasure." Rhode Island's response was that the number of Indians within their territory was greatly exaggerated. And it appears that they were right, so successful had been the extermination campaign against the native people.[81]

By the beginning of the eighteenth century the indigenous inhabitants of New England, and of most other northeastern Indian lands, had been reduced to a small fraction of their former number and were living in isolated, squalid enclaves. Cotton Mather called these defeated and scattered people "tawny pagans" whose "inaccessible" homes were now nothing more than "kennels."[82] And Mather's views, on this at least, were widely shared among the colonists. The once-proud native peoples, who had shown the English how to plant and live in the difficult environs of New England, were now regarded as animals, or at most, to quote one Englishwoman who traveled from Boston to New York in 1704, as "the most salvage of all the salvages of that kind that I have ever Seen."[83]

It had started with the English plagues and ended with the sword and musket. The culmination, throughout the larger region, has been called the Great Dispersal. Before the arrival of the English—to choose an example further north from the area we have been discussing—the population of the western Abenaki people in New Hampshire and Vermont had stood at about 12,000. Less than half a century later approximately 250 of these people remained alive, a destruction rate of 98 percent. Other examples from this area tell the same dreary tale: by the middle of the seventeenth century, the Mahican people—92 percent destroyed; the Mohawk people—75 percent destroyed; the eastern Abenaki people—78 percent destroyed; the Maliseet-Passamaquoddy people—67 percent destroyed. And on, and on. Prior to European contact the Pocumtuck people had numbered more than 18,000; fifty years later they were down to 920—95 percent destroyed. The Quiripi-Unquachog people had numbered about 30,000; fifty years later they were down to 1500—95 percent destroyed. The Massachusett people had numbered at least 44,000; fifty years later they were down to barely 6000—81 percent destroyed.[84]

This was by mid-century. King Philip's War had not yet begun. Neither had the smallpox epidemics of 1677 and 1678 occurred yet. The devastation had only started. Other wars and other scourges followed. By 1690, according to one count, the population of Norridgewock men was down to about 100; by 1726 it was down to 25. The same count showed the number of Androscoggin men in 1690 reduced to 160; by 1726 they were down to 10. And finally, the Pigwacket people: by 1690 only 100 men were left; by 1726 there were 7. These were the last ones, those who had fled to Canada to escape the English terrors. Once hostilities died down they were allowed to return to the fragments of their homelands that they still could say were theirs. But they hesitated "and expressed concern," reports a recent history of the region, "lest the English fall upon them while they were hunting near the Connecticut and Kennebec Rivers."[85] The English—who earlier had decorated the seal of the Massachusetts Bay Colony with an image of a naked Indian plaintively urging the colonists to "Come over and help us"—had taught the natives well.

III

The European habit of indiscriminately killing women and children when engaged in hostilities with the natives of the Americas was more than an atrocity. It was flatly and intentionally genocidal. For no population can survive if its women and children are destroyed.

Consider the impact of some of the worst instances of modern warfare. In July of 1916, at the start of the First World War, General Douglas Haig sent his British troops into combat with the Germans at the Battle of the Somme. He lost about 60,000 men the very first day—21,000 in just the first hour—including half his officers. By the time that battle finally ended, Haig had lost 420,000 men.[86] And the war continued for two more years. This truly was, far and away, the worst war in Britain's history. To make matters worse, since the start of the decade England had been experiencing significant out-migration, and at the end of the decade it was assaulted by a deadly influenza pandemic. Yet, between 1911 and 1921, Britain's population *increased* by about two million people.[87]

Or take Japan. Between 1940 and 1950, despite the frenzy of war in the Pacific, capped by the nuclear destruction of Hiroshima and Nagasaki, the population of Japan *increased* by almost 14 percent. Or take Southeast Asia. Between 1960 and 1970, while B-52s were raining destruction from the sky and a horrific ground war was spilling across every national boundary in the region, Southeast Asia's population *increased* at an average rate of almost 2.5 percent each year.[88]

The reason these populations were able to increase, despite massive military damage, was that a greatly disproportionate ratio of men to women and children was being killed. This, however, is not what happened to the indigenous people in the Caribbean, in Mesoamerica, in South America, or in what are now the United States and Canada during the European assault against them. Neither was this slaughter of innocents anything but intentional in design, nor did it end with the close of the colonial era.

As Richard Drinnon has shown, in his book *Facing West: The Metaphysics of Indian-Hating and Empire-Building,* America's revered founding fathers were themselves activists in the anti-Indian genocide. George Washington, in 1779, instructed Major General John Sullivan to attack the Iroquois and "lay waste all the settlements around . . . that the country may not be merely overrun but destroyed," urging the general not to "listen to any overture of peace before the total ruin of their settlements is effected." Sullivan did as instructed, he reported back, "destroy[ing] everything that contributes to their support" and turning "the whole of that beautiful region," wrote one early account, "from the character of a garden to a scene of drear and sickening desolation." The Indians, this writer said, "were hunted like wild beasts" in a "war of extermination," something Washington approved of since, as he was to say in 1783, the Indians, after all, were little different from wolves, "both being beasts of prey, tho' they differ in shape."[89]

And since the Indians were mere beasts, it followed that there was no cause for moral outrage when it was learned that, among other atrocities, the victorious troops had amused themselves by skinning the bodies of some Indians "from the hips downward, to make boot tops or leggings." For their part, the surviving Indians later referred to Washington by the nickname "Town Destroyer," for it was under his direct orders that at least 28 out of 30 Seneca towns from Lake Erie to the Mohawk River had been totally obliterated in a period of less than five years, as had *all* the towns and villages of the Mohawk, the Onondaga, and the Cayuga. As one of the Iroquois told Washington to his face in 1792: "to this day, when that name is heard, our women look behind them and turn pale, and our children cling close to the necks of their mothers."[90]

They might well have clung close to the necks of their mothers when other names were mentioned as well—such as Adams or Monroe or Jackson. Or Jefferson, for example, who in 1807 instructed his Secretary of War that any Indians who resisted American expansion into their lands must be met with "the hatchet." "And . . . if ever we are constrained to lift the hatchet against any tribe," he wrote, "we will never lay it down till that tribe is exterminated, or is driven beyond the Mississippi," continuing: "in war, they will kill some of us; we shall destroy all of them." These were not offhand remarks, for five years later, in 1812, Jefferson again concluded that white Americans were "obliged" to drive the "backward" Indians "with the beasts of the forests into the Stony Mountains"; and one year later still, he added that the American government had no other choice before it than "to pursue [the Indians] to extermination, or drive them to new seats beyond our reach." Indeed, Jefferson's writings on Indians are filled with the straightforward assertion that the natives are to be given a simple choice—to be "extirpate[d] from the earth" or to remove themselves out of the Americans' way.[91] Had these same words been enunciated by a German leader in 1939, and directed at European Jews, they would be engraved in modern memory. Since they were uttered by one of America's founding fathers, however, the most widely admired of the South's slaveholding philosophers of freedom, they conveniently have become lost to most historians in their insistent celebration of Jefferson's wisdom and humanity.

In fact, however, to the majority of white Americans by this time the choice *was* one of expulsion or extermination, although these were by no means mutually exclusive options. Between the time of initial contact with the European invaders and the close of the seventeenth century, most eastern Indian peoples had suffered near-annihilation levels of destruction; typically, as in Virginia and New England, 95 percent or more of their populations had been eradicated. But even then the carnage did not stop. One recent study of population trends in the southeast, for instance, shows that east of the Appalachians in Virginia the native population declined by 93 percent between 1685 and 1790—that is, *after* it already had declined by about 95 percent during the *preceding* century, which itself had followed upon the *previous* century's whirlwind of massive destruction. In eastern North and South Carolina the decline between 1685 and 1790 was 97 percent—again, following upon two earlier centuries of genocidal devastation. In Louisiana the 1685–1790 figure for population collapse was 91 percent, and in Florida 88 percent. As a result, when the eighteenth century was drawing to its close, less than 5000 native people remained alive in all of eastern Virginia, North Carolina, South Carolina, and Louisiana combined, while in Florida—which alone contained more than 700,000 Indians in 1520—only 2000 survivors could be found.[92]

Overwhelmingly, these disasters were the result of massively destructive epidemics and genocidal warfare, while a small portion of the loss in numbers derived from forced expulsion from the Indians' traditional homelands. How these deadly phenomena interacted can be seen clearly by examining the case of the Cherokee. After suffering a calamitous measure of ruination during the time of their earliest encounters with Europeans, the Cherokee population continued to decline steadily and precipitously as the years unfolded. During the late seventeenth and major part of the eighteenth century alone, for example, the already devastated Cherokee nation endured the loss of another three-fourths of its population.[93] Then, just as the colonies were going to war in their quest for liberation from the British, they turned their murderous attention one more time to the quest for Indian liquidation; the result for the Cherokee was that "their towns is all burned," wrote one contemporary, "their Corn cut down and Themselves drove into the Woods to perish and a great many of them killed."[94] Before long, observed James Mooney, the Cherokee were on "the verge of extinction. Over and over again their towns had been laid in ashes and their fields wasted. Their best warriors had been killed and their women and children had sickened and starved in the mountains."[95] Thus, the attempt at straightforward extermination. Next came expulsion.

From the precipice of non-existence, the Cherokee slowly struggled back. But as they did, more and more white settlers were moving into and onto their lands. Then, in 1828 Andrew Jackson was elected President. The same Andrew Jackson who once had written that "the whole Cherokee Nation ought to be scurged." The same Andrew Jackson who had led troops against peaceful Indian encampments, calling the Indians "savage dogs," and boasting that "I have on all occasions preserved the scalps of my killed." The same Andrew Jackson who had supervised the mutilation of 800 or so Creek Indian corpses—the bodies of men, women, and children that he and his men had massacred—cutting off their noses to count and preserve a record of the dead, slicing long strips of flesh from their bodies to tan and turn into bridle reins. The same Andrew Jackson who— after his Presidency was over—still was recommending that American troops specifically seek out and systematically kill Indian women and children who were in hiding, in order to complete their extermination: to do otherwise, he wrote, was equivalent to pursuing "a wolf in the hamocks without knowing first where her den and whelps were."[96]

Almost immediately upon Jackson's ascension to the Presidency, the state of Georgia claimed for itself enormous chunks of Cherokee property, employing a fraudulent legal technique that Jackson himself had once used to justify dispossession. The Cherokee and other Indian nations in the region—principally the Chickasaw, the Choctaw, and the Creek—stood fast, even taking their case to the United States Supreme Court. But all the while that they were trying to hold their ground, a flood tide of white immigrants (probably about 40,000 in Cherokee country alone) swarmed over the hills and meadows and woods, their numbers continuing to swell as gold was discovered in one section of the territory.[97]

The white settlers, in fact, were part of the government's plan to drive the Indians off their land. As Michael Paul Rogin has demonstrated, the "intruders entered Indian country only with government encouragement, after the extension of state law." And once on the Indians' land, they overran it. Confiscating the farms of wealthy and poor Indians alike, says Rogin, "they took possession of Indian land, stock, and improvements, forced the Indians to sign leases, drove them into the woods, and acquired a bonanza in cleared land." They then destroyed the game, which had supplemented the Indians' agricultural production, with the result, as intended, that the Indians faced mass starvation.[98]

Still, the Cherokee resisted. And by peaceful means. They won their case before the U.S. Supreme Court, with a ruling written by Justice John Marshall, a ruling that led to Jackson's famous remark: "John Marshall has made his decision, now let him enforce it." The Court, of course, had no direct means of enforcement, so the drive against the Cherokee and the other Indians of the region continued unabated.

Finally, a treaty was drawn up, ceding the Cherokee lands to the American government in exchange for money and some land in what had been designated Indian Territory far to the west. Knowing that neither the Cherokee elders, nor the majority of the Cherokee people, would approve the treaty, the U.S. government held the most influential Cherokee leader in jail and shut down the tribal printing press while negotiations took place between American officials and a handful of "cooperative" Indians. Even the American military official who was on hand to register the tribe's members for removal protested to the Secretary of War that "that paper . . . called a treaty, is no treaty at all, because not sanctioned by the great body of the Cherokee and made without their participation or assent. I solemnly declare to you that upon its reference to the Cherokee people it would be instantly rejected by nine-tenths of them, and I believe by nineteen-twentieths of them."[99]

But the President had what he wanted—someone's signature on a piece of paper. This was what the great French observer of American life, Alexis de Tocqueville, was speaking of when he remarked sarcastically that, in contrast with the sixteenth-century Spanish, in the nineteenth century—and, we might add here, the twentieth—"the conduct of the United States Americans toward the natives was inspired by the most chaste affection for legal formalities. . . . It is impossible to destroy men with more respect to the laws of humanity."[100]

Soon the forced relocation, what was to become known as the Trail of Tears, began under the direction of General Winfield Scott. In fact, the "relocation" was nothing less than a death march—a Presidentially ordered death march that, in terms of the mortality rate directly attributable to it, was almost as destructive as the Bataan Death March of 1942, the most notorious Japanese atrocity in all of the Second World War.[101] About 22,000 Cherokee then remained in existence, 4000 of whom had already broken under the pressures of white oppression and left for Indian Territory. Another thousand or so escaped and hid out in the Carolina hills. The remaining 17,000 were rounded up by the American military and herded into detention camps—holding pens, really—where they waited under wretched and ignominious conditions for months as preparations for their forced exile were completed. James Mooney, who interviewed people who had participated in the operation, described the scene:

> Under Scott's orders the troops were disposed at various points throughout the Cherokee country, where stockade forts were erected for gathering in and holding the Indians preparatory to removal. From these, squads of troops were sent to search out with rifle and bayonet every small cabin hidden away in the coves or by the sides of mountain streams, to seize and bring in as prisoners all the occupants, however or wherever they might be found. Families at dinner were startled by the sudden gleam of bayonets in the doorway and rose up to be driven with blows and oaths along the weary miles of trail that led to the stockade. Men were seized in their fields or going along the road, women were taken from their wheels and children from their play. In many cases, on turning for one last look as they crossed the ridge, they saw their homes in flames, fired by the lawless rabble that followed on the heels of the soldiers to loot and pillage. So keen were these outlaws on the scent that in some instances they were driving off the cattle and other stock of the Indians almost before the soldiers had fairly started their owners in the other direction. Systematic hunts were made by the same men for Indian graves, to rob them of the silver pendants and other valuables deposited with the dead. A Georgia volunteer, afterward a colonel in the Confederate service, said: "I fought through the civil war and have seen men shot to pieces and slaughtered by thousands, but the Cherokee removal was the cruelest work I ever knew."[102]

An initial plan to carry the Cherokee off by steamboat, in the hottest part of the summer, was called off when so many of them died from disease and the oppressive conditions. After waiting for the fall season to begin, they were then driven overland, in groups upwards of about a thousand, across Tennessee, Kentucky, Illinois, and Missouri. One white traveler from Maine happened upon several detachments from the death march, all of them "suffering extremely from the fatigue of the journey, and the ill health consequent upon it":

> The last detachment which we passed on the 7th embraced rising two thousand Indians. . . . [W]e found the road literally filled with the procession for about three miles in length. The sick and feeble were carried in waggons—about as comfortable for traveling as a New England ox cart with a covering over it—a great many ride on horseback and multitudes go on foot—even aged females, apparently nearly ready to drop into the grave, were traveling with heavy burdens attached to the back—on the sometimes frozen ground, and sometimes muddy streets, with no covering for the feet except what nature had given them. . . . We learned from the inhabitants on the road where the Indians passed, that they buried fourteen or fifteen at every stopping place, and they make a journey of ten miles per day only on an average.[103]

Like other government-sponsored Indian death marches, this one intentionally took native men, women, and children through areas where it was known that cholera and other epidemic diseases were raging; the government sponsors of this march, again as with the others, fed the Indians spoiled flour and rancid meat, and they drove the native people on through freezing rain and cold. Not a day passed without numerous deaths from the unbearable conditions under which they were forced to travel. And when they arrived in Indian Territory many more succumbed to fatal illness and starvation.

All told, by the time it was over, more than 8000 Cherokee men, women, and children died as a result of their expulsion from their homeland. That is, about half of what then remained of the Cherokee nation was liquidated under Presidential directive, a death rate similar to that of other southeastern peoples who had undergone the same process—the Creeks and the Seminoles in particular. Some others who also had been expelled from the lands of their ancestors, such as the Chickasaw and the Choctaw, fared better, losing only about 15 percent of their populations during their own forced death marches.[104] For comparative purposes, however, that "only" 15 percent is the approximate equivalent of the death rate for German combat troops in the closing year of World War Two, when Germany's entire southern front was collapsing and its forces in the field everywhere were being overwhelmed and more than decimated. The higher death rate of the Creeks, Seminoles, and Cherokee was equal to that of Jews in Germany, Hungary, and Rumania between 1939 and 1945.[105] And all these massacres of Indians took place, of course, only *after* many years of preliminary slaughter, from disease and military assault, that already had reduced these peoples' populations down to a fragment of what they had been prior to the coming of the Europeans.

The story of the southeastern Indians, like that of the northeastern tribes, was repeated across the entire expanse of the North American continent, as far south as Mexico, as far north as Canada and the Arctic, as far west as the coasts of Washington, Oregon, and California. Just as we have had to overlook many native peoples in Maryland, Pennsylvania, New Jersey, and elsewhere, who regularly suffered depopulation rates of 90 to 95 percent and more—as well as numerous New England and southern tribes who passed into total extinction with less drama than did those we have surveyed here—our references to the holocaust that swept the rest of the continent can be little more than suggestive of the devastation that occurred.

We can speak of small but illustrative incidents. For example, the total destruction in 1792 of a far northwest coast Nootka Indian village called Opitsatah, half a mile in diameter and containing more than 200 elaborately carved homes (and many times that number of people) under the command of a man who later said he "was in no ways tenacious of" carrying out such mass murder, and that he "was grieved to think" that his commander "should let his passions go so far." But he did it anyway, because he was ordered to. Every door the American killers entered, he said, "was in resemblance to a human and beasts head, the passage being through the mouth, besides which there was much more rude carved work about the dwellings, some of which by no means inelegant. This fine village, the work of ages, was in a short time totally destroyed." [106] Or there is the case of the Moravian Delaware Indians who had converted to Christianity, as demanded by their white conquerors, in order to save their lives. It didn't matter. After destroying their corn and reducing them to starving scavengers, American troops under Colonel David Williamson rounded up those tribal members who were still clinging to life and, as reported after the events,

> assured them of sympathy in their great hunger and their intention to escort them to food and safety. Without suspicion . . . the Christians agreed to go with them and after consultations, hastened to the Salem fields to bring in their friends. The militia relieved the Indians of their guns and knives, promising to restore them later. The Christians felt safe with these friendly men whose interest in their welfare seemed genuine. Too late they discovered the Americans' treachery. Once defenseless, they were bound and charged with being warriors, murderers, enemies and thieves . . . . After a short night of prayer and hymns . . . twenty-nine men, twenty-seven women, and thirty-four children were ruthlessly murdered. Pleas, in excellent English, from some of the kneeling Christians, failed to stop the massacre. Only two escaped by feigning death before the butchers had completed their work of scalping. [107]

Massacres of this sort were so numerous and routine that recounting them eventually becomes numbing—and, of course, far more carnage of this sort occurred than ever was recorded. So no matter how numbed—or even, shamefully, bored—we might become at hearing story after story after story of the mass murder, pillage, rape, and torture of America's native peoples, we can be assured that, however much we hear, we have heard only a small fragment of what there was to tell.

The tale of the slaughter at Wounded Knee in South Dakota is another example too well known to require detailed repeating here, but what is less well known about that massacre is that, a week and a half before it happened, the editor of South Dakota's *Aberdeen Saturday Pioneer*—a gentle soul named L. Frank Baum, who later became famous as the author of *The Wizard of Oz*—urged the wholesale extermination of *all* America's native peoples:

> The nobility of the Redskin is extinguished, and what few are left are a pack of whining curs who lick the hand that smites them. The Whites, by law of conquest, by justice of civilization, are masters of the American continent, and the best safety of the frontier settlements will be secured by the total annihilation of the few remaining Indians. Why not annihilation? Their glory has fled, their spirit broken, their manhood effaced; better that they should die than live the miserable wretches that they are.[108]

Baum reflected well the attitudes of his time and place, for ten days later, after hundreds of Lakota men, women, and children at Wounded Knee had been killed by the powerful Hotchkiss guns (breech-loading cannons that fired an explosive shell) of the Seventh Cavalry, the survivors were tracked down for miles around and summarily executed—because, and only because, the blood running in their veins was Indian. "Fully three miles from the scene of the massacre we found the body of a woman completely covered with a blanket of snow," wrote one eyewitness to the butchery, "and from this point on we found them scattered along as they had been relentlessly hunted down and slaughtered while fleeing for their lives. . . . When we reached the spot where the Indian camp had stood, among the fragments of burned tents and other belongings we saw the frozen bodies lying close together or piled one upon another."[109] Other women were found alive, but left for dead in the snow. They died after being brought under cover, as did babies who "were found alive under the snow, wrapped in shawls and lying beside their dead mothers."[110] Women and children accounted for more than two-thirds of the Indian dead. As one of the Indian witnesses—a man named American Horse, who had been friendly to the American troops for years—recalled:

> They turned their guns, Hotchkiss guns, etc., upon the women who were in the lodges standing there under a flag of truce, and of course as soon as they

were fired upon they fled. . . . There was a woman with an infant in her arms who was killed as she almost touched the flag of truce, and the women and children of course were strewn all along the circular village until they were dispatched. Right near the flag of truce a mother was shot down with her infant; the child not knowing that its mother was dead was still nursing, and that especially was a very sad sight. The women as they were fleeing with their babes were killed together, shot right through, and the women who were very heavy with child were also killed. . . . After most all of them had been killed a cry was made that all those who were not killed or wounded should come forth and they would be safe. Little boys who were not wounded came out of their places of refuge, and as soon as they came in sight a number of soldiers surrounded them and butchered them there. . . . Of course it would have been all right if only the men were killed; we would feel almost grateful for it. But the fact of the killing of the women, and more especially the killing of the young boys and girls who are to go to make up the future strength of the Indian people, is the saddest part of the whole affair and we feel it very sorely.[111]

Four days after this piece of work the *Aberdeen Saturday Pioneer*'s editor Baum sounded his approval, asserting that "we had better, in order to protect our civilization, follow it up . . . . and wipe these untamed and untamable creatures from the face of the earth."[112]

Some native people did survive at Wounded Knee, however, including "a baby of about a year old warmly wrapped and entirely unhurt," recalled an Indian witness to the carnage. "I brought her in, and she was afterward adopted and educated by an army officer."[113] This was the child named Zintka Lanuni—or Lost Bird—who in fact was taken by General William Colby against the other survivors' objections, not to educate her but to display her thereafter for profit as a genuine Indian "war curio." When Colby first showed off "his newly acquired possession," reported his home town newspaper, "not less than 500 persons called at his house to see it." Finally put on display in Buffalo Bill's Wild West Show, Lost Bird died at age twenty-nine in Los Angeles. In July 1991, the Lakota had her remains moved from Los Angeles back to Wounded Knee, where she was interred, a hundred years after the massacre, next to the mass grave that still marks the killing field where the rest of her family lies buried.[114]

Sometimes it was raw slaughter, sometimes it was the raging fire of exotic introduced disease. But, year in and year out, in countless places across the length and breadth of the continent, the "scene of desolation" described by one observer of events in western Canada was repeated over and over again:

In whatever direction you turn, nothing but sad wrecks of mortality meet the eye; lodges standing on every hill, but not a streak of smoke rising from them. Not a sound can be heard to break the awful stillness, save the ominous croak of ravens, and the mournful howl of wolves fattening on the human carcasses that lie strewed around. It seems as if the very genius of desolation had stalked through the prairies, and wreaked his vengeance on everything bearing the shape of humanity.[115]

Or we can speak of statistics. They are, on the surface, less emotional evidence, and are simple to enumerate. Take Illinois, for example. Between the late seventeenth and late eighteenth century the number of Illinois Indians fell by about 96 percent; that is, for every one hundred Illinois Indians alive in 1680, only four were alive a century later. That massive destruction was the result of war, disease, and despair—despair in the face of apparently imminent extinction from a siege the likes of which cannot be imagined by those who have not endured it. A fragmentary selection of examples from every corner of the continent—in addition to the instances already discussed—tells the same depressing tale over and over again. The Kansa people of northeast Kansas suffered about the same level of devastation as the Illinois, though stretched over a somewhat longer period of time: it took a bit more than a century and a half—from the early eighteenth century to the late nineteenth century for the Kansa population to fall to 4 percent of its former size. A higher rate of collapse has been calculated for the ten tribes of Kalapuya Indians of Oregon's Willamette Valley: for every hundred Kalapuya alive prior to Western contact, about 25 or 30 remained alive in the late eighteenth century; only five were left by the late 1830s; and only one was left at the close of the nineteenth century. In Baja, California up to 60,000 Indians were alive at the end of the seventeenth century; by the middle of the nineteenth century there were none. Further north in California, the Tolowa peoples' population had collapsed by 92 percent after fifty years of Western contact. In less than half a century, between 1591 and 1638, two out of three people in northwestern Mexico died. In western Arizona and eastern New Mexico, within fifty years following European contact at least half of the Zuni, two-thirds of the Acoma, and 80 percent of the Hopi people had been liquidated. In Delaware, half the Munsee tribe was wiped out in the thirty-five years between 1680 and 1715. Two-thirds of New York's Huron nation were killed in a single decade. In Oklahoma, 50 percent of the Kiowa people died in a period of just two years. Ninety percent of the Upper Missouri River Mandan died in less than a year. From a population of up to 20,000 in 1682, the Quapaw people of the lower Mississippi and Arkansas River valleys were reduced in number to 265 by 1865—a 99 percent destruction rate. In Alaska, in part because of its vastness and the relative remoteness of its population centers, statistics are less clear. However, as a detailed recent study shows, from the earliest days of Western contact Aleut and other native peoples were "systematically exterminated"—first by Russians, later by Americans—when they weren't being destroyed by introduced epidemics of smallpox, typhoid, measles, or influenza (which carried away as much as a third of the region's population in individual assaults), and by the lethal gifts of syphilis and tuberculosis, which rotted away more slowly from within.[116]

Controlled studies of tribal populations across the Lower Mississippi Valley, Central New York, and the Middle Missouri region replicate these patterns: drastic and often catastrophic population crashes, occasionally plunging to extinction levels, occurred repeatedly.[117] In all these cases— and in literally hundreds more of equal magnitude—the observed population collapses occurred *after* previous population declines that are known to have happened, but whose numbers went unrecorded. Thus, even figures of 95 and 98 and 99 percent destruction may time and again be too low. For this same reason, many entire tribes will never even be mentioned in lists of Indian population decline because they disappeared before any whites were around to record their existence for posterity. In 1828, for example, the French biologist Jean Louis Berlandier traveled through Texas and noted that of fifty-two Indian nations recorded by members of the La Salle expedition a century and a half earlier only three or four nations remained. But we will never know how many of Texas's native peoples or tribes were wiped out by the swarms of violence and deadly infectious disease that arrived from Europe, by way of Spanish troops, before *La Salle's* expedition appeared upon the scene. For when he was in Louisiana in 1682, LaSalle repeatedly questioned whether the maps and chronicles he had inherited from the earlier De Soto expedition were accurate, since they referred to the presence of large numbers of Indian peoples and populations that LaSalle could not find, because they already had long since been destroyed.[118]

Among all these instances of horror visited upon America's native peoples, however, one episode perhaps stands out. It occurred in eastern Colorado in November of 1864, at a small and unarmed Cheyenne and Arapaho village known as Sand Creek. It is not that so many Indians died there. Rather, it is how they died—and the political and cultural atmosphere in which they died—that is so historically revealing. It is, moreover, representative in its savagery of innumerable other events that differ from it only because they left behind less visible traces.

Colorado at this time was the quintessence of the frontier west. Various incidents had earlier raised tensions between the Indians there and the seemingly endless flow of white settlers who came as squatters on Cheyenne and Arapaho lands. As tempers flared, so did the settlers' rhetoric, which became inflamed with genocidal threats and promises. During the year preceding the incident that has come to be known as the Sand Creek Massacre, a local newspaper, the *Rocky Mountain News,* launched an incendiary campaign that urged the Indians' extermination. "They are a dissolute, vagabondish, brutal, and ungrateful race, and ought to be wiped from the face of the earth," wrote the *News's* editor in March of 1863. In that year, of twenty-seven stories having anything at all to do with Indians, ten went out of their way to urge extermination.[119]

The following year was election time in Colorado. In addition to political offices that were up for grabs, a constitution was on the ballot that would have opened the door for statehood—something that was not especially popular with most settlers. The faction allied with the *Rocky Mountain News* (which included the incumbent governor) supported statehood and apparently perceived political gain to be had in whipping up hatred for the Indians. As a rival newspaper put it, the pro-statehood forces believed that if they "cooked up" enough settler fear of the Indians they would be able to "prove [to the voters] that only as a state could Colorado get sufficient troops to control her Indians." While the election year wore on, stories in the *News* continued to stir those fears: wild rumors of Indian conspiracies were heralded as fact; any violence at all between whites and Indians was reported as an Indian "massacre."[120]

The public and the military began taking up the chant. After a skirmish between Indians and soldiers in which two soldiers died, the military replied by killing twenty-five Indians. "Though I think we have punished them pretty severely in this affair," stated the troops' commander, "yet I believe now is but the commencement of war with this tribe, which must result in exterminating them." More skirmishes followed. Groups of Indians, including women and children, were killed here and there by soldiers and bands of vigilantes. To many whites it had become abundantly clear, as the *News* proclaimed in August of 1864, that the time was at hand when the settlers and troops must "go for them, their lodges, squaws and all."[121]

Then, at last, the excuse was at hand. A family of settlers was killed by a group of Indians—which Indians, no one knew, nor did anyone care. The governor issued an emergency proclamation: regiments of citizen soldiers were authorized to form and to kill any and all hostile Indians they could find. Their compensation would be "whatever horses and other property they may capture, and, in addition, [the Governor] promises to use his influence to procure their payment by the general government." In effect, this was an official government license to kill any and all Indians on sight, to seize their horses and other property, and then—after the fact—to claim they had been "hostiles." In the event that this point might be missed by some, the governor's journalistic ally, the *News,* urged all out "extermination against the red devils," making no distinction between those Indians who were friendly and those who were not. With identical intent the governor issued another proclamation—a clarification: the evidence was now "conclusive," he declared, that "most" of the Indians on the Plains were indeed "hostile"; it was, therefore, the citizens' and the military's right and obligation—for which they would be duly paid—to "pursue, kill, and destroy" them all.[122]

This, then, was the mood and the officially sanctioned setting when about 700 heavily armed soldiers, under the command of a former Methodist missionary (and still an elder in the church), Colonel John Chivington, rode into Sand Creek village. Several months earlier Chivington, who that year was also a candidate for Congress, had announced in a speech that his policy was to "kill and scalp all, little and big." "Nits make lice," he was fond of saying—indeed, the phrase became a rallying cry of his troops; since Indians were lice, their children were nits—and the only way to get rid of lice was to kill the nits as well. Clearly, Colonel Chivington was a man ahead of his time. It would be more than half a century, after all, before Heinrich Himmler would think to describe the extermination of another people as "the same thing as delousing." [123]

The air was cold and crisp, the early morning darkness just beginning to lift, when they entered the snowy village on November 29. The creek was almost dry, the little water in it crusted over with ice, untouched yet by the dawn's first rays of sun. The cavalrymen paused and counted well over a hundred lodges in the encampment. Within them, the native people were just stirring; as had been the case with the Pequots in Connecticut, more than 200 years earlier—and with countless other native peoples across the continent since then—the village was filled almost entirely with women and children who had no inkling of what was about to happen. Most of the men were away on a buffalo hunt. One of the colonel's guides, Robert Bent, later reported that there were about 600 Indians in camp that morning, including no more than "thirty-five braves and some old men, about sixty in all." The rest were women and children. [124]

A few days before riding into the Indian camp Colonel Chivington had been informed that the village at Sand Creek could be taken with a small fraction of the troops at his command, not only because most of the Cheyenne men were away on the hunt, but because the people had voluntarily disarmed themselves to demonstrate that they were not hostile. They had turned in all but their essential hunting weapons to the commander at nearby Fort Lyon. Technically, the colonel was informed, the government considered the Indians at Sand Creek to be harmless and disarmed prisoners of war. Witnesses later reported that Chivington—who just then had been going on at length about his desire for taking Indian scalps—dismissed this news, drew himself up in his chair, and replied: "Well, I long to be wading in gore." [125]

His wish was soon fulfilled. As Chivington and his five battalions moved into the village that morning, two whites who were visiting the camp tied a tanned buffalo hide to a pole and waved it to signal the troops that this was a friendly town. They were met with a fusillade of gunfire. Then old chief Black Kettle, the principal leader of the Cheyenne, tied a white flag to a lodge pole, and above that he tied an American flag that had been given him by the Commissioner of Indian Affairs. He gathered his family around him and he held the pole high—again, in an effort to show the American soldiers that his was not a hostile camp. He "kept calling out" to his people "not to be frightened," Robert Bent's brother George recalled, "that the camp was under protection and there was no danger. Then suddenly the troops opened fire on this mass of men, women, and children, and all began to scatter and run."[126]

The massacre was on. Chivington ordered that cannons be fired into the panicked groups of Indians first; then the troops charged on horseback and on foot. There was nowhere for the native people to hide. The few Cheyenne and Arapaho men in camp tried to fight back, and Robert Bent says they "all fought well," but by his own count they were outnumbered twenty to one and had virtually no weapons at their disposal. Some women ran to the riverbank and clawed at the dirt and sand, frantically and hopelessly digging holes in which to conceal themselves or their children.

From this point on it is best simply to let the soldiers and other witnesses tell what they did and what they saw, beginning with the testimony of Robert Bent:[127]

> After the firing the warriors put the squaws and children together, and surrounded them to protect them. I saw five squaws under a bank for shelter. When the troops came up to them they ran out and showed their persons, to let the soldiers know they were squaws and begged for mercy, but the soldiers shot them all. . . . There were some thirty or forty squaws collected in a hole for protection; they sent out a little girl about six years old with a white flag on a stick; she had not proceeded but a few steps when she was shot and killed. All the squaws in that hole were afterwards killed, and four or five bucks outside. The squaws offered no resistance. Every one I saw dead was scalped. I saw one squaw cut open with an unborn child, as I thought, lying by her side. Captain Soule afterwards told me that such was the fact. . . . I saw quite a number of infants in arms killed with their mothers.

> I went over the ground soon after the battle [reported Asbury Bird, a soldier with Company D of the First Colorado Cavalry]. I should judge there were between 400 and 500 Indians killed. . . . Nearly all, men, women, and children were scalped. I saw one woman whose privates had been mutilated.

> The bodies were horribly cut up [testified Lucien Palmer, a Sergeant with the First Cavalry's Company C] skulls broken in a good many; I judge they were broken in after they were killed, as they were shot besides. I do not think I saw any but what was scalped; saw fingers cut off [to get the rings off them], saw several bodies with privates cut off, women as well as men.

> Next morning after the battle [said Corporal Amos C. Miksch, also of Company C], I saw a little boy covered up among the Indians in a trench, still alive. I saw a major in the 3rd regiment take out his pistol and blow off the top of his head. I saw some men unjointing fingers to get rings off, and cutting off ears to get silver ornaments. I saw a party with the same major

take up bodies that had been buried in the night to scalp them and take off ornaments. I saw a squaw with her head smashed in before she was killed. Next morning, after they were dead and stiff, these men pulled out the bodies of the squaws and pulled them open in an indecent manner. I heard men say they had cut out the privates, but did not see it myself.

I saw some Indians that had been scalped, and the ears were cut off of the body of White Antelope [said Captain L. Wilson of the First Colorado Cavalry]. One Indian who had been scalped had also his skull all smashed in, and I heard that the privates of White Antelope had been cut off to make a tobacco bag out of. I heard some of the men say that the privates of one of the squaws had been cut out and put on a stick.

The dead bodies of women and children were afterwards mutilated in the most horrible manner [testified David Louderback, a First Cavalry Private]. I saw only eight. I could not stand it; they were cut up too much . . . they were scalped and cut up in an awful manner. . . . White Antelope's nose, ears, and privates were cut off.

All manner of depredations were inflicted on their persons [said John S. Smith, an interpreter], they were scalped, their brains knocked out; the men used their knives, ripped open women, clubbed little children, knocked them in the head with their guns, beat their brains out, mutilated their bodies in every sense of the word . . . worse mutilated than any I ever saw before, the women all cut to pieces. . . . [C]hildren two or three months old; all ages lying there, from sucking infants up to warriors.

In going over the battle-ground the next day I did not see a body of man, woman, or child but was scalped, and in many instances their bodies were mutilated in the most horrible manner—men, women, and children's privates cut out, &c. [reported First Lieutenant James D. Cannon of the New Mexico Volunteers]. I heard one man say that he had cut out a woman's private parts and had them for exhibition on a stick; I heard another man say that he had cut the fingers off an Indian to get the rings on the hand. . . . I also heard of numerous instances in which men had cut out the private parts of females and stretched them over the saddle-bows, and wore them over their hats while riding in the ranks. . . . I heard one man say that he had cut a squaw's heart out, and he had it stuck up on a stick.

Once the carnage was over, and the silence of death had descended on the killing-field, Colonel Chivington sent messages to the press that he and his men had just successfully concluded "one of the most bloody Indian battles ever fought" in which "one of the most powerful villages in the Cheyenne nation" was destroyed. There was exultation in the land. "Cheyenne scalps are getting as thick here now as toads in Egypt," joked the *Rocky Mountain News.* "Everybody has got one and is anxious to get another to send east." [128]

Outside of Colorado, however, not everyone was pleased. Congressional investigations were ordered, and some among the investigators were shocked at what they found. One of them, a senator who visited the site of the massacre and "picked up skulls of infants whose milk-teeth had not yet been shed," later reported that the concerned men of Congress had decided to confront Colorado's governor and Colonel Chivington openly on the matter, and so assembled their committee and the invited general public in the Denver Opera House. During the course of discussion and debate, someone raised a question: Would it be best, henceforward, to try to "civilize" the Indians or simply to exterminate them? Whereupon, the senator wrote in a letter to a friend, "there suddenly arose such a shout as is never heard unless upon some battlefield—a shout almost loud enough to raise the roof of the opera house—'EXTERMINATE THEM! EXTERMINATE THEM!' "[129]

The committee, apparently, was impressed. Nothing ever was done to Chivington, who took his fame and exploits on the road as an after-dinner speaker. After all, as President Theodore Roosevelt said later, the Sand Creek Massacre was "as righteous and beneficial a deed as ever took place on the frontier."[130]

IV

Meanwhile, there was California to the west, the last stop before the holocaust that had begun on Hispaniola in 1492 would move out across the Pacific, in the wake of eighteenth-century voyages to Australia, Polynesia, and beyond by Captains Cook, Wallis, Bougainville, and others. Spanish troops had entered California overland early in the sixteenth century, while Cortés and Pizarro were still alive and basking in the glory of their conquests of the Aztecs and the Incas. Indeed, Juan Rodríguez Cabrillo, who heard stories of Spanish troops and violence in California while he was sailing off the coast in 1542, probably had been with Cortés at the fall of Tenochtitlán and with the infamous Alvarado further south.[131] In any case, wherever there was Spanish violence there was bound to be disease. In raping native women and merely breathing on native men, the marching Spanish soldiers spread syphilis and gonorrhea, smallpox and influenza, everywhere they went. And Cabrillo was not likely innocent himself: his crews were mostly conscripts, the dregs of the Spanish settlements in Mexico; there can be little doubt that diseases festered in those men that became explosive epidemics when spread among the natives.

It once was thought that syphilis did not arrive in California until Don Juan Bautista de Anza's introduction of the "putrid and contagious" plague in 1777, but there is no longer any doubt that the disease was present throughout the region well before de Anza's visit.[132] As for smallpox, influenza, and other lethal infections, they spread early and they spread far. Martin de Aguilar explored the northern California and Oregon coasts for Spain in 1603, following by twenty-four years Sir Francis Drake who had sailed up the Pacific coast and landed with his crews on the Oregon shore in 1579. And Drake may not have been the first European to venture that far north. But whoever was the first among the sixteenth-century adventurers, eighteenth-century explorers found old smallpox scars on the bodies of the native people there.[133]

In 1602 and 1603 Sebastián Vizcaino led an expedition of three ships up and down the California coast, with frequent stops on shore where his men spent time with various Indian peoples. There was sickness on Vizcaino's ships from the moment they set sail, and before the voyage was complete it combined with scurvy to literally shut the voyage down. Scores of men were incapacitated. At one point Vizcaino wrote: "All the men had fallen sick, so that there were only two sailors who could climb to the maintopsail." The ship that he was on, Vizcaino later added, "seemed more like a hospital than a ship of an armada." Fray Antonio de la Ascensión, one of three clergymen who made the voyage with Vizcaino, feared the whole crew was close to death. But fortunately for the Spanish—and unfortunately for the natives—the Indians helped the crippled sailors, offering them "fish, game, hazel nuts, chestnuts, acorns, and other things. . . . for though but six of our men remained in the said frigate, the rest having died of cold and sickness, the Indians were so friendly and so desirous of our friendship . . . that they not only did them no harm, but showed them all the kindness possible."[134] There can be no doubt that for their kindness the Indians were repaid by plagues the likes of which nothing in their history had prepared them.

The earliest European mariners and explorers in California, as noted in a previous chapter's discussion of Cabrillo, repeatedly referred to the great numbers of Indians living there. In places where Vizcaino's ships could approach the coast or his men could go ashore, the Captain recorded, again and again, that the land was thickly filled with people. And where he couldn't approach or go ashore "because the coast was wild," the Indians signaled greetings by building fires—fires that "made so many columns of smoke on the mainland that at night it looked like a procession and in the daytime the sky was overcast." In sum, as Father Ascensión put it, "this realm of California is very large and embraces much territory, nearly all inhabited by numberless people."[135]

But not for very long. Throughout the late sixteenth and the seventeenth and eighteenth centuries, Spanish disease and Spanish cruelty took a large but mostly uncalculated toll. Few detailed records of what happened during that time exist, but a wealth of research in other locales has shown the early decades following Western contact to be almost invariably the worst for native people, because that is when the fires of epidemic disease burn most freely. Whatever the population of California was before the Spanish came, however, and whatever happened during the first few centuries following Spanish entry into the region, by 1845 the Indian population of California had been slashed to 150,000 (down from many times that number prior to European contact) by swarming epidemics of influenza, diphtheria, measles, pneumonia, whooping cough, smallpox, malaria, typhoid, cholera, tuberculosis, dysentery, syphilis, and gonorrhea—along with everyday settler and explorer violence.[136] As late as 1833 a malaria epidemic brought in by some Hudson's Bay Company trappers killed 20,000 Indians by itself, wiping out entire parts of the great central valleys. "A decade later," writes one historian, "there still remained macabre reminders of the malaria epidemic: collapsed houses filled with skulls and bones, the ground littered with skeletal remains."[137]

Terrible as such deaths must have been, if the lives that preceded them were lived outside the Spanish missions that were founded in the eighteenth century, the victims might have counted themselves lucky. Two centuries earlier the Puritan minister John Robinson had complained to Plymouth's William Bradford that although a group of massacred Indians no doubt "deserved" to be killed, "Oh, how happy a thing had it been, if you had converted some before you had killed any!"[138] That was probably the only thing the New England Puritans and California's Spanish Catholics would have agreed upon. So, using armed Spanish troops to capture Indians and herd them into the mission stockades, the Spanish padres did their best to convert the natives before they killed them.

And kill they did. First there were the Jesuit missions, founded early in the eighteenth century, and from which few vital statistics are available. Then the Franciscans took the Jesuits' place. At the mission of Nuestra Señora de Loreto, reported the Franciscan chronicler Father Francisco Palóu, during the first three years of Franciscan rule 76 children and adults were baptized, while 131 were buried. At the mission of San José Cumundú during the same time period 94 were baptized, while 241 died. At the mission of Purisima de Cadegomó, meanwhile, 39 were baptized—120 died. At the mission of Nuestra Señora de Guadalupe the figures were similar: 53 baptisms, 130 deaths. The same held true at others, from the mission of Santa Rosaliá de Mulegé, with 48 baptisms and 113 deaths, to the mission of San Ignacio, with 115 baptisms and 293 deaths—all within the same initial three-year period.[139]

For some missions, such as those of San José del Cabo and Santiago de las Coras, no baptism or death statistics were reported, because there were so few survivors ("nearly all are ill with syphilis," Father Palóu wrote) that there was no reason to do any counting. Overall, however, during those three years alone, between a quarter and a third of the California Indians died who were under Franciscan control. We will never know how many died during the earlier decades when the Jesuits were in charge. However, "if it goes on at this rate," lamented Father Palóu, "in a short time Old California will come to an end."[140]

Old California, perhaps, but not the missions. Not if anything within the padres' power could be done. And what was done was that they simply brought more natives in, under military force of arms. Although the number of Indians within the Franciscan missions increased steadily from the close of those first three disastrous years until the opening decade or so of the nineteenth century, this increase was entirely attributable to the masses of native people who were being captured and force-marched into the mission compounds. Once thus confined, the Indians' annual death rate regularly exceeded the birth rate by more than two to one. This is an overall death-to-birth ratio that, in less than half a century, would completely exterminate a population of any size that was not being replenished by new conscripts. The death rate for children in the missions was even worse. Commonly, the child death rate in these institutions of mandatory conversion ranged from 140 to 170 per thousand—that is, three to four times the birth rate—and in some years it climbed to 220 and 265 and even 335 per thousand. Year in and year out, then, from one of every six to one of every three Indian children who were locked up in the missions perished.[141]

In fact, it may have been even worse than that. The figures above were generated from available resources in the late 1930s. Recently, an analysis has been conducted on data from more than 11,000 Chumash Indians who passed through the missions of Santa Bárbara, La Purísima, and Santa Inés in the late eighteenth and early nineteenth century. Perhaps the most complete data set and detailed study ever done on a single mission Indian group's vital statistics, this analysis shows that 36 percent of those Chumash children who were not yet two years old when they entered the mission died in less than twelve months. Two-thirds died before reaching the age of five. Three of four died before attaining puberty. At the same time, adolescent and young adult female deaths exceeded those of males by almost two to one, while female fertility rates steadily spiraled downward. Similar patterns—slightly better in some categories, slightly worse in others—have been uncovered in another study of 14,000 mission Indians in eight different Franciscan missions.[142]

In short, the missions were furnaces of death that sustained their Indian population levels for as long as they did only by driving more and more natives into their confines to compensate for the huge numbers who were being killed once they got there. This was a pattern that held throughout California and on out across the southwest. Thus, for example, one survey of life and death in an early Arizona mission has turned up statistics showing that at one time an astonishing 93 percent of the children born within its walls died before reaching the age of ten—and yet the mission's total population did not drastically decline.[143]

There were various ways in which the mission Indians died. The most common causes were the European-introduced diseases—which spread like wildfire in such cramped quarters—and malnutrition. The personal living space for Indians in the missions averaged about seven feet by two feet per person for unmarried captives, who were locked at night into sex-segregated common rooms that contained a single open pit for a toilet. It was perhaps a bit more space than was allotted a captive African in the hold of a slave ship sailing the Middle Passage. Married Indians and their children, on the other hand, were permitted to sleep together—in what Russian visitor V.M. Golovnin described in 1818 as "specially constructed 'cattle-pens.' " He explained:

> I cannot think of a better term for these dwellings that consist of a long row of structures not more than one *sagene* [seven feet] high and 1½—2 *sagenes* wide, without floor or ceiling, each divided into sections by partitions, also not longer than two *sagenes,* with a correspondingly small door and a tiny window in each—can one possibly call it anything but a barnyard for domestic cattle and fowl? Each of these small sections is occupied by an entire family; cleanliness and tidiness are out of the question: a thrifty peasant usually has a better-kept cattle-pen.[144]

Under such conditions Spanish-introduced diseases ran wild: measles, smallpox, typhoid, and influenza epidemics occurred and re-occurred, while syphilis and tuberculosis became, as Sherburne F. Cook once said, "totalitarian" diseases: virtually all the Indians were afflicted by them.[145]

As for malnutrition, despite agricultural crop yields on the Indian-tended mission plantations that Golovnin termed "extraordinary" and "unheard of in Europe," along with large herds of cattle and the easily accessible bounty of sea food, the food given the Indians, according to him, was "a kind of gruel made from barley meal, boiled in water with maize, beans, and peas; occasionally they are given some beef, while some of the more diligent [Indians] catch fish for themselves."[146] On average, according to Cook's analyses of the data, the caloric intake of a field-laboring mission Indian was about 1400 calories per day, falling as low as 715 or 865 calories per day in such missions as San Antonio and San Miguel. To put this in context, the best estimate of the caloric intake of nineteenth-century African American slaves is in excess of 4000 calories per day, and almost 5400 calories per day for adult male field hands. This seems high by modern Western standards, but is not excessive in terms of the caloric expenditure required of agricultural laborers. As the author of the estimate puts it: "a diet with 4206 calories per slave per day, while an upper limit [is] neither excessive nor generous, but merely adequate to provide sufficient energy to enable one to work like a slave." Of course, the mission Indians also worked like slaves in the padres' agricultural fields, but they did so with far less than half the caloric intake, on average, commonly provided a black slave in Mississippi, Alabama, or Georgia.[147]

Even the military commanders at the missions acknowledged that the food provided the Indians was grossly insufficient, especially, said one, given "the arduous strain of the labors in which they are employed"; labors, said another, which last "from morning to night"; and labors, noted a third, which are added to the other "hardships to which they are subjected." [148] Caloric intake, of course, is but one part of the requirement for a sufficient diet. The other part is nutritional value. And the most thorough study of the composition of the mission Indians' diets reveals them to have been seriously deficient in high-quality protein, and in Vitamins A and C, and riboflavin. [149] The resulting severe malnutrition, of course, made the natives all the more susceptible to the bacterial and viral infections that festered in the filthy and cramped living conditions they were forced to endure—just as it made them more likely to behave lethargically, something that would bring more corporal punishment down upon them. Not surprisingly, osteological analyses of California mission Indian skeletal remains, compared with those of Indians who lived in the same regions prior to European contact, show the long bones of the mission Indians to be "significantly smaller than those of their prehistoric and protohistoric predecessors," leading to the conclusion that such differences "reflect retarded growth, possibly attributable to the nutritional deficiency of the mission diet or the combined effects of poor nutrition and infectious disease." [150]

When not working directly under the mission fathers' charge, the captive natives were subject to forced labor through hiring-out arrangements the missions had with Spanish military encampments. The only compensation the natives received for this, as for all their heavy daily labors, was the usual inadequate allotment of food. As one French visitor commented in the early nineteenth century, after inspecting life in the missions, the relationship between the priest and his flock "would . . . be different only in name if a slaveholder kept them for labor and rented them out at will; he too would feed them." But, we now know, he would have fed them better. [151]

In short, the Franciscans simultaneously starved and worked their would-be converts to death, while the diseases they and others had imported killed off thousands more. The similarity of this outcome to what had obtained in the slave labor camps of Central and South America should not be surprising, since California's Spanish missions, established by Father Junípero Serra (aptly dubbed "the last conquistador" by one admiring biographer and currently a candidate for Catholic sainthood), were directly modeled on the genocidal encomienda system that had driven many millions of native peoples in Central and South America to early and agonizing deaths. [152]

Others died even more quickly, not only from disease, but from grotesque forms of punishment. To be certain that the Indians were spiritually prepared to die when their appointed and rapidly approaching time came, they were required to attend mass in chapels where, according to one mission visitor, they were guarded by men "with whips and goads to enforce order and silence" and were surrounded by "soldiers with fixed bayonets" who were on hand in case any unruliness broke out. These were the same soldiers, complained the officially celibate priests, who routinely raped young Indian women. If any neophytes (as the Spanish called Indians who had been baptized) were late for mass, they would have "a large leathern thong, at the end of a heavy whip-staff, applied to their naked backs."[153] More serious infractions brought more serious torture.

And if ever some natives dared attempt an escape from the padres' efforts to lead them to salvation—as, according to the Franciscans' own accounts, the Indians constantly did—there would be little mercy shown. From the time of the missions' founding days, Junípero Serra traveled from pulpit to pulpit preaching fire and brimstone, scourging himself before his incarcerated flock, pounding his chest with heavy rocks until it was feared he would fall down dead, burning his breast with candles and live coals in imitation of San Juan Capistrano.[154] After this sort of self-flagellating exertion, Father Serra had no patience for Indians who still preferred not to accept his holy demands of them. Thus, on at least one occasion when some of his Indian captives not only escaped, but stole some mission supplies to support them on their journey home, "his Lordship was so angered," recalled Father Palóu, "that it was necessary for the fathers who were there to restrain him in order to prevent him from hanging some of them. . . . He shouted that such a race of people deserved to be put to the knife."[155]

It was not necessary for starving and desperate Indians to steal food or supplies, however, to suffer the perverse punishments of the mission fathers. The padres also were concerned about the continuing catastrophic decline in the number of babies born to their neophyte charges. At some missions the priests decided the Indians intentionally were refraining from sex, as the natives of the Caribbean supposedly had done, in an effort to spare their would-be offspring the tortures of life as a slave. Some of the Indians may indeed have been purposely avoiding sex, although by themselves the starvation-level diets, along with the disease and enormous stress of the Indians' mission existence, were more than sufficient to cause a collapse in the birth rate.[156] In either case, here is a first-hand account of what happened at mission Santa Cruz when a holy and ascetic padre named Ramon Olbés came to the conclusion that one particular married couple was behaving with excessive sexual inhibition, thereby depriving him of another child to enslave and another soul to offer up to Christ:

> He [Father Olbés] sent for the husband and he asked him why his wife hadn't borne children. The Indian pointed to the sky (he didn't know how to speak Spanish) to signify that only God knew the cause. They brought an interpreter. This [one] repeated the question of the father to the Indian, who

answered that he should ask God. The Fr. asked through the interpreter if he slept with his wife, to which the Indian said yes. Then the father had them placed in a room together so that they would perform coitus in his presence. The Indian refused, but they forced him to show them his penis in order to affirm that he had it in good order. The father next brought the wife and placed her in the room. The husband he sent to the guardhouse with a pair of shackles. . . . Fr. Olbés asked her if her husband slept with her, and she answered that, yes. The Fr. repeated his question "why don't you bear children?" "Who knows!" answered the Indian woman. He had her enter another room in order to examine her reproductive parts.

At this point the woman resisted the padre's attempted forced inspection; for that impertinence she received fifty lashes, was "shackled, and locked in the nunnery." He then gave her a wooden doll and ordered her to carry it with her, "like a recently born child," wherever she went. Meanwhile, her husband remained in jail, only leaving once each day to attend mass—and during all the time he was outside the guardhouse he was required to undergo the public humiliation of wearing on his head "cattle horns affixed with leather."[157]

From time to time some missions permitted certain of their captives to return home for brief visits, under armed guard. "This short time is the happiest period of their existence," wrote one foreign observer, "and I myself have seen them going home in crowds, with loud rejoicings." He continues:

> The sick, who can not undertake the journey, at least accompany their happy countrymen to the shore where they embark and sit there for days together mournfully gazing on the distant summits of the mountains which surround their homes; they often sit in this situation for several days, without taking any food, so much does the sight of their lost home affect these new Christians. Every time some of those who have the permission run away, and they would probably all do it, were they not deterred by their fears of the soldiers.[158]

There was, of course, good reason for the Indians to fear the consequences of running away and being caught. Since even the most minor offenses in the missions carried a punishment of fifteen lashes, while middling infractions, including fighting, "brought one hundred lashes and a set of shackles at the guard house," those who were captured while trying to break free of mission captivity might count themselves lucky to be whipped 100 times and clapped in irons affixed to a heavy log. For as one traveler described the condition of some attempted escapees he had seen: "They were all bound with rawhide ropes and some were bleeding from wounds and some children were tied to their mothers." He went on:

Some of the run-away men were tied on sticks and beaten with straps. One chief was taken out to the open field and a young calf which had just died was skinned and the chief was sewed into the skin while it was yet warm. He was kept tied to a stake all day, but he died soon and they kept his corpse tied up.[159]

If this was early California's version of what Spanish defenders later would disingenuously dismiss as merely another Black Legend, it did not last as long as did its counterpart on the continent to the south. In 1846 the United States militarily occupied California, and two years later, at Guadalupe Hidalgo, Mexico ceded the land over to American control. In addition to the two centuries of previous evidence adducing the genocidal practices of Britain and the United States toward America's native peoples across the length and breadth of the continent, we therefore have in California a unique opportunity to test informally one part of the Spaniards' Black Legend defense, the part alleging that other whites treated Indians just as badly as did the Spanish. And what we find is that, on this point at least—difficult though it may be to believe—the Spanish are correct.

By 1845 the Indian population of California was down to no more than a quarter of what it had been when the Franciscan missions were established in 1769. That is, it had declined by at least 75 percent during seventy-five years of Spanish rule. In the course of just the next twenty-five years, under American rule, it would fall by another 80 percent. The gold rush brought to California a flood of American miners and ranchers who seemed to delight in killing Indians, miners and ranchers who rose to political power and prominence—and from those platforms not only legalized the enslavement of California Indians, but, as in Colorado and elsewhere, launched public campaigns of genocide with the explicitly stated goal of all-out Indian extermination.

Governmentally unsanctioned enslavement of the Indians began as soon as California became an American possession and continued for many years. It seemed an excellent idea in a land where free labor was in short supply and white wages were high. Moreover, as whites who had lived in the southern United States repeatedly asserted, California's Indians—who already had suffered a savage population loss at the hands of the Spanish— "make as obedient and humble slaves as the negroes in the south," wrote one former New Orleans cotton broker. In fact, they were even better than blacks, claimed a ranch owner in 1846, because they accepted "flagellation with more humility than negroes."[160]

Indian docility was believed to be particularly assured "when caught young." So a thriving business in hunting and capturing Indian children developed. Newspapers frequently reported sightings of men driving Indian children before them on back-country roads to the slave markets in Sacramento and San Francisco. As with black slaves in the South, prices varied "according to quality," said the *Ukiah Herald,* but they sometimes climbed as high as two-hundred dollars each. Bargains could be had in some areas, however, as "in Colusa County in 1861 [where] Indian boys and girls aged three and four years were sold at fifty dollars apiece." Especially "good little" Indians—or, as the *Sacramento Daily Union* described them, "bright little specimens"—might even fetch a straight trade for a horse. Given the shortage of women in California during these early years of white settlement, "a likely young girl" might cost almost double that of a boy, because, as the *Marysville Appeal* phrased it, girls served the double duty "of labor and of lust."[161]

Not surprisingly, the parents of these valuable children could be a problem. The prospect of losing their beloved offspring to slave traders, said the *Humboldt Times,* "has the effect of making Indians very shy of coming into the Reservations, as they think it is a trick to deprive them of their children."[162] And, indeed, it often was. Thus inconvenienced, the slave traders had to pursue their prey into the hills. There, when they cornered the objects of their desire, reported the California Superintendent of Indian Affairs in 1854, they frequently murdered the troublesome parents as they were gathering up the children, a tactic that allowed the slavers to sell their little charges as "orphans" without possibility of contradiction.[163]

Should Indian adults attempt to use the California courts to bring such killers to justice, they invariably were frustrated because the law of the land prohibited Indians from testifying against whites. Even some otherwise unsympathetic settler newspapers observed and protested this situation (to no avail), since in consequence it encouraged and legalized the open-season hunting of Indians. As one San Francisco newspaper put it in 1858, following the unprovoked public murder of an Indian, and the release of the known killer because the only eyewitnesses to the event were native people: the Indians "are left entirely at the mercy of every ruffian in the country, and if something is not done for their protection, the race will shortly become extinct."[164]

Nothing was done, however, and so enslavement and murder, carried out by entrepreneurial and genocide-minded whites, continued on for many years. One of the more well-known incidents, described in Theodora Kroeber's popular *Ishi in Two Worlds,* occurred in 1868. Part of a series of massacres of Yahi Indians, in which ultimately all but one member of this tiny fragment of a tribe were scalped and murdered, this particular assault is distinguished by the perverse concern shown by one of the attackers for the bodies of his victims: "as he explained afterwards, [he] changed guns during the slaughter, exchanging his .56–caliber Spencer rifle for a .38–caliber Smith and Wesson revolver, because the rifle 'tore them up so bad,' particularly the babies."[165]

It would be a mistake, however, to think of the destruction of California's Indians—or most of the Indians of the Americas—as the work of renegades. As early as 1850 the first session of the California legislature passed a law entitled "Act for the Government and Protection of Indians" that in fact did little more than give the imprimatur of legality to the kidnapping and enslavement of native people. Among other provisions, the law provided for the forced indenture of any Indian child to any white person who could convince a justice of the peace that the child in his possession had not been obtained by force. Justices of the peace were easily convinced, especially if the abducted child's parents had been murdered or terrorized into silence and were therefore not on hand to provide contradictory testimony. In 1860 the legislature expanded the law, extending the duration of terms of forced service and permitting the law's use to cover adult Indians as well as children.

The problem the whites were facing by this time, and that the new legislation was intended to address, was a shortage of Indian labor. About ten thousand of the rapidly dwindling numbers of Indians had been put to forced labor legally, under the provisions of the 1850 and 1860 laws (many more, of course, were enslaved without going through the niceties of a justice of the peace's approval), but this was nothing compared with the thousands who had been killed.[166] The shortage of menial workers, despite large numbers of Mexican, Hawaiian, and Asian contract laborers in California, led the *Humboldt Times* to champion the 1860 enslavement law while exclaiming in an editorial: "What a pity the provisions of the law are not extended to greasers, Kanakas, and Asiatics. It would be so convenient to carry on a farm or mine, when all the hard and dirty work is performed by apprentices!"[167]

Considering the California legislature's concern for cheap—indeed, slave—labor in the 1850s, it would in retrospect seem mindless for the lawmakers simultaneously to encourage the destruction of that same Indian labor force. But that is precisely what happened. Because some Indians, who in the late 1840s had been driven into the mountains by marauding slave catchers, were thereby forced to poach on white-owned livestock for their existence, the governor of California in his 1851 message to the legislature announced the necessity for a total eradication of the natives: "the white man, to whom time is money, and who labors hard all day to create the comforts of life, cannot sit up all night to watch his property," Governor Peter Burnett said; "after being robbed a few times he becomes desperate, and resolves upon a war of extermination." Such a war to annihilate the Indians had already begun by then, Burnett recognized, but, he added, it must "continue to be waged between the races until the Indian becomes extinct." A year later the governor's successor to that office, John McDougal, renewed the charge: if the Indians did not submit to white demands to relinquish their land, he said, the state would "make war upon the [Indians] which must of necessity be one of extermination to many of the tribes." [168]

This straightforward advocacy of genocide by the highest American officials in the land emerged in a cultural milieu that habitually described the California Indians as ugly, filthy, and inhuman "beasts," "swine," "dogs," "wolves," "snakes," "pigs," "baboons," "gorillas," and "orangutans," to cite only a few of the press's more commonly published characterizations. Some whites gave the Indians the benefit of the doubt and declared them to be not quite animals, but merely "the nearest link, of the sort, to the quadrupeds" in North America, while others not inclined to such lofty speculations said that simply touching an Indian created "a feeling of repulsion just as if I had put my hand on a toad, tortoise, or huge lizard." [169] The eradication of such abominable creatures could cause little trouble to most consciences.

Between 1852 and 1860, under American supervision, the indigenous population of California plunged from 85,000 to 35,000, a collapse of about 60 percent within eight years of the first gubernatorial demands for the Indians' destruction. By 1890 that number was halved again: now 80 percent of the natives who had been alive when California became a state had been wiped out by an official policy of genocide. Fewer than 18,000 California Indians were still living, and the number was continuing to drop. In the late 1840s and 1850s one observer of the California scene had watched his fellow American whites begin their furious assault "upon [the Indians], shooting them down like wolves, men, women, and children, wherever they could find them," and had warned that this "war of extermination against the aborigines, commenced in effect at the landing of Columbus, and continued to this day, [is] gradually and surely tending to the final and utter extinction of the race." While to most white Californians such a conclusion was hardly lamentable, to this commentator it was a major concern—but only because the extermination "policy [has] proved so injurious to the interests of the whites." That was because the Indians' "labor, once very useful, and, in fact, indispensable in a country where no other species of laborers were to be obtained at any price, and which might now be rendered of immense value by pursuing a judicious policy, has been utterly sacrificed by this extensive system of indiscriminate revenge." [170]

Three hundred years earlier, writing from Peru, the Dominican priest Santo Tomás had expressed exactly the same concern. The ongoing slaughter of the Incas and other Andean peoples was so intense, he warned his sovereign, that unless orders were given to reduce the genocide "the natives will come to an end; and once they are finished, your Majesty's rule over [this land] will cease." Explained Diego de Robles Cornejo, from the same region a few years later: "If the natives cease, the land is finished. I mean its wealth: for all the gold and silver that comes to Spain is extracted by means of these Indians." [171]

Like the sixteenth-century Spanish in Peru, then, to some critics the genocidal Californians were simply bad businessmen, liquidating their own best draft animals in an unceasing pique of racist passion. In time, however, these critics turned out to be wrong. Other labor was found. And by the end of the nineteenth century California's population was surging past one and a half million persons, of whom only 15,000—or one percent— were Indians, most of them stored safely away on remote and impoverished reservations, suffering from disease, malnutrition, and despair.

As had happened in Virginia two hundred years earlier—and as happened across the entire continent during the intervening years—between 95 and 98 percent of California's Indians had been exterminated in little more than a century. And even this ghastly numerical calculation is inadequate, not only because it reveals nothing of the hideous suffering endured by those hundreds of thousands of California native peoples, but because it is based on decline only from the estimated population for the year 1769—a population that already had been reduced savagely by earlier invasions of European plague and violence. Nationwide by this time only about one-third of one percent of America's population—250,000 out of 76,000,000 people—were natives. The worst human holocaust the world had ever witnessed, roaring across two continents non-stop for four centuries and consuming the lives of countless tens of millions of people, finally had leveled off. There was, at last, almost no one left to kill.

GENOCIDE

During the course of four centuries—from the 1490s to the 1890s—Europeans and white Americans engaged in an unbroken string of genocide campaigns against the native peoples of the Americas. Pictured on the following pages are the results of the first of these slaughters—the Spanish depredations in the West Indies and Mesoamerica under the initial command of Christopher Columbus—and what conventionally, though incorrectly, is regarded as the last of them—the United States Army's massacre of Sioux Indians near a creek called Wounded Knee in South Dakota. These scenes are representative of thousands of other such incidents that occurred (and in some places continue to occur) in the Indies and in South, Central, and North America, most of them bloodbaths that have gone unnamed and are long forgotten.

The illustrations of the Spanish cruelties are by Jean Theodore and Jean Israel de Bry, from a 1598 edition of Bartolomé de Las Casas's *Brief Account of the Destruction of the Indies*. The accompanying captions are drawn from Las Casas's descriptions of the events he witnessed. With two exceptions, the photographs from the Wounded Knee massacre are printed here with the permission of the Nebraska State Historical Society. The exceptions are the photograph of Big Foot, from the National Anthropological Archives of the Smithsonian Institution, and the photograph of General Colby and Zintka Lanuni, which is printed by courtesy of the Denver Public Library's Western History Collection. Quotations in the captions for the Wounded Knee photographs are from Richard E. Jensen, R. Eli Paul, and John E. Carter, *Eyewitness at Wounded Knee* (Lincoln: University of Nebraska Press, 1991).

"[The Spaniards] took babies from their mothers' breasts, grabbing them by the feet and smashing their heads against rocks. . . . They built a long gibbet, low enough for the toes to touch the ground and prevent strangling, and hanged thirteen [natives] at a time in honor of Christ Our Saviour and the twelve Apostles. . . . Then, straw was wrapped around their torn bodies and they were burned alive."

"As the Spaniards went with their war dogs hunting down Indian men and women, it happened that a sick Indian woman who could not escape from the dogs, sought to avoid being torn apart by them, in this fashion: she took a cord and tied her year-old child to her leg, and then she hanged herself from a beam. But the dogs came and tore the child apart; before the creature expired, however, a friar baptized it."

"They would cut an Indian's hands and leave them dangling by a shred of skin . . . [and] they would test their swords and their manly strength on captured Indians and place bets on the slicing off of heads or the cutting of bodies in half with one blow. . . . [One] cruel captain traveled over many leagues, capturing all the Indians he could find. Since the Indians would not tell him who their new lord was, he cut off the hands of some and threw others to the dogs, and thus they were torn to pieces."

"The Spanish treated the Indians with such rigor and inhumanity that they
seemed the very ministers of Hell, driving them day and night with beatings,
kicks, lashes and blows, and calling them no sweeter names than dogs. . . .
Women who had just given birth were forced to carry burdens for the Christians
and thus could not carry their infants because of the hard work and weakness of
hunger. Infinite numbers of these were cast aside on the road and thus perished."

"They threw into those holes all the Indians they could capture of every age and kind. . . . Pregnant and confined women, children, old men [were] left stuck on the stakes, until the pits were filled. . . . The rest they killed with lances and daggers and threw them to their war dogs who tore them up and devoured them."

"Because he did not give the great quantity of gold asked for, they burned him and a number of other nobles and caciques . . . with the intention of leaving no prince or chieftain alive in the entire country."

"When the Spaniards had collected a great deal of gold from the Indians, they shut them up in three big houses, crowding in as many as they could, then set fire to the houses, burning alive all that were in them, yet those Indians had given no cause nor made any resistance."

"With my own eyes I saw Spaniards cut off the nose, hands and ears of Indians, male and female, without provocation, merely because it pleased them to do it. . . . Likewise, I saw how they summoned the caciques and the chief rulers to come, assuring them safety, and when they peacefully came, they were taken captive and burned."

"Big Foot lay in a sort of solitary dignity," wrote Carl Smith, a reporter for the *Chicago Inter-Ocean*. "He was shot through and through. A wandering photographer propped the old man up, and as he lay there defenseless his portrait was taken."

"In one square of less than half an acre there were forty-eight bodies stiffened by the frost," observed reporter Carl Smith. "One had a face which was hideous to view. . . . He had originally fallen on his face, and he must have lain in that position for some time, as it was flattened on one side. His hands were clenched, his teeth were clenched. . . . One hand was raised in the air . . . frozen in that position." A rifle was placed as a prop at the dead medicine man's side, to suggest that a battle, rather than a massacre, had occurred. The photograph later was retouched to conceal the dead man's genitals, exposed when his trousers were shot away.

"I was badly wounded and pretty weak too," recalled Dewey Beard, a Miniconjou Indian. "While I was lying on my back, I looked down the ravine and saw a lot of women coming up and crying. When I saw these women, girls and little girls and boys coming up, I saw soldiers on both sides of the ravine shoot at them until they had killed every one of them." The photograph shows a burial party collecting corpses from that ravine.

Mass burials followed the carnage. One hundred forty-six bodies were thrown into this pit, dug on the same hillside from which the Army's Hotchkiss guns, with their exploding shells, had been fired.

Survivors were placed in a makeshift hospital, "a pitiful array of young girls and women and babes in arms, little children, and a few men, all pierced with bullets," recalled Elaine Goodale Eastman in her *Memoirs*. Observed the wife of a correspondent who was on the scene: "There was a little boy with his throat apparently shot to pieces . . . and when they feed him now the food and water come out the side of his neck." Still, wrote Dr. Charles Eastman, "they objected very strenuously to being treated by army surgeons . . . and [said] they never wanted to see a uniform again."

In the wake of the carnage, whites descended on Wounded Knee in search of souvenirs. In this photograph, the seated man in the middle is wearing what appears to be a sacred Ghost Dance shirt, while the standing man is modeling a woman's beaded dress. It is not known whether the seated man on the left kept the trophy he is holding in his lap.

General Leonard W. Colby showing off his Lakota Sioux war curio, Zintka Lanuni or Lost Bird. After privately putting her on display for personal profit, Colby
eventually released her to Buffalo Bill's Wild West Show. She died in Los Angeles
at age 29. In 1991 the Lakota people had Zintka Lanuni's remains moved back
to Wounded Knee for interment with the rest of her family.

◄ III ►

SEX, RACE, AND HOLY WAR

◄5►

THERE IS A MOMENT in Toni Morrison's moving novel, *Beloved,* when Stamp Paid, a black man in the mid-nineteenth-century American South, notices something red stuck to the bottom of his flatbed boat as he is tying it up alongside a river bank. It was a particularly bad time for black people in a century of particularly bad times for them. "White-folks were still on the loose," writes Morrison: "Whole towns wiped clean of Negroes; eighty-seven lynchings in one year alone in Kentucky; four colored schools burned to the ground; grown men whipped like children; children whipped like adults; black women raped by the crew; property taken, necks broken." And the smell of "skin, skin and hot blood . . . cooked in a lynch fire" was everywhere.

At first when he saw the red thing stuck to his boat Stamp Paid thought it was a feather. Reaching down to retrieve it,

> he tugged and what came loose in his hand was a red ribbon knotted around a curl of wet woolly hair, clinging still to its bit of scalp. He untied the ribbon and put it in his pocket, dropped the curl in the weeds. On the way home, he stopped, short of breath and dizzy. He waited until the spell passed before continuing on his way. A moment later, his breath left him again. This time he sat down by a fence. Rested, he got to his feet, but before he took a step he turned to look back down the road he was traveling and said, to its frozen mud and the river beyond, "What *are* these people? You tell me, Jesus. What *are* they?" [1]

It is a question many have asked, many times, during the course of the past millennium. What *were* those people whose minds and souls so avidly fueled genocides against Muslims, Africans, Indians, Jews, Gypsies, and other religious, racial, and ethnic groups? What *are* they who continue such wholesale slaughter still today?

It is tempting, when discussing the actions described in the two preceding chapters, as well as genocides from other times and places, to describe the behavior of the crimes' perpetrators as insane. But as Terrence Des Pres once pointed out with regard to the Nazis' attempted mass extermination of Europe's Jews, "demonic" seems a better word than "insane" to characterize genocidal behavior. Des Pres's semantic preference here, he said, was based upon his sense that "insanity is without firm structure, not predictable, something you cannot depend upon." And while "what went on in the [Nazi] killing centers was highly organized and very dependable indeed," thereby not qualifying as insanity, at least according to Des Pres's informal definition, "the dedication of life's energies to the production of death is a demonic principle of the first degree."[2]

Des Pres continued on in this essay to distinguish between the Nazi effort to extinguish from the earth Europe's Jewish population and other examples of genocide "from the thick history of mankind's inhumanity," including "the slaughter of the American Indians." The difference he found was that "the destruction of the European Jews had no rational motive whatsoever, neither politics nor plunder, neither military strategy nor the moment's blind expediency. . . . This was genocide for the sake of genocide."[3] Had Des Pres pursued these distinctions further, however—that is, had he been as concerned with the mass destruction of native peoples as he was with Europeans—he may well have realized that his posited contrasts were more apparent than they were real. On the one hand, much (though not all) of the European and American slaughter of American Indians—from fifteenth-century Hispaniola to sixteenth-century Peru to seventeenth-century New England to eighteenth-century Georgia to nineteenth-century California—was not driven by reasons of politics or plunder, nor by military strategy or blind expediency, but by nothing more than, to use Des Pres's phraseology, genocide for the sake of genocide. On the other hand, much (though not all) of the Nazi slaughter of Europe's Jews *was* driven by what the perpetrators of that holocaust regarded as rational motives—however perverse or bizarre or sick or hateful those motives appear to others.[4]

To say this is not to say that the Jewish Holocaust—the inhuman destruction of 6,000,000 people—was not an abominably unique event. It was. So, too, for reasons of its own, was the mass murder of about 1,000,000 Armenians in Turkey a few decades prior to the Holocaust.[5] So, too, was the deliberately caused "terror-famine" in Stalin's Soviet Union in the 1930s, which killed more than 14,000,000 people.[6] So, too, have been each of the genocidal slaughters of many millions more, decades after the Holocaust, in Burundi, Bangladesh, Kampuchea, East Timor, the Brazilian Amazon, and elsewhere.[7] Additionally, within the framework of the Holocaust itself, there were aspects that were unique in the campaign of genocide conducted by the Nazis against Europe's Romani (Gypsy) people, which resulted in the mass murder of perhaps 1,500,000 men, women, and children.[8] Of course, there also were the unique horrors of the African slave trade, during the course of which at least 30,000,000—and possibly as many as 40,000,000 to 60,000,000—Africans were killed, most of them in the prime of their lives, before they even had a chance to begin working as human chattel on plantations in the Indies and the Americas.[9] And finally, there is the unique subject of this book, the total extermination of many American Indian peoples and the near-extermination of others, in numbers that eventually totaled close to 100,000,000.

Each of these genocides was distinct and unique, for one reason or another, as were (and are) others that go unmentioned here. In one case the sheer numbers of people killed may make it unique. In another case, the percentage of people killed may make it unique. In still a different case, the greatly compressed time period in which the genocide took place may make it unique. In a further case, the greatly extended time period in which the genocide took place may make it unique. No doubt the targeting of a specific group or groups for extermination by a particular nation's official policy may mark a given genocide as unique. So too might another group's being unofficially (but unmistakably) targeted for elimination by the actions of a multinational phalanx bent on total extirpation. Certainly the chilling utilization of technological instruments of destruction, such as gas chambers, and its assembly-line, bureaucratic, systematic methods of destruction makes the Holocaust unique. On the other hand, the savage employment of non-technological instruments of destruction, such as the unleashing of trained and hungry dogs to devour infants, and the burning and crude hacking to death of the inhabitants of entire cities, also makes the Spanish anti-Indian genocide unique.

A list of distinctions marking the uniqueness of one or another group that has suffered from genocidal mass destruction or near (or total) extermination could go on at length. Additional problems emerge because of a looseness in the terminology commonly used to describe categories and communities of genocidal victims. A traditional Eurocentric bias that lumps undifferentiated masses of "Africans" into one single category and undifferentiated masses of "Indians" into another, while making fine distinctions among the different populations of Europe, permits the ignoring of cases in which genocide against Africans and American Indians has resulted in the *total* extermination—purposefully carried out—of entire cultural, social, religious, and ethnic groups.

A secondary tragedy of all these genocides, moreover, is that partisan representatives among the survivors of particular afflicted groups not uncommonly hold up their peoples' experience as so fundamentally different from the others that not only is scholarly comparison rejected out of hand, but mere cross-referencing or discussion of other genocidal events within the context of their own flatly is prohibited. It is almost as though the preemptive conclusion that one's own group has suffered more than others is something of a horrible award of distinction that will be diminished if the true extent of another group's suffering is acknowledged.

Compounding this secondary tragedy is the fact that such insistence on the incomparability of one's own historical suffering, by means of what Irving Louis Horowitz calls "moral bookkeeping," invariably pits one terribly injured group against another—as in the all too frequent contemporary disputes between Jews and African Americans, or the recent controversy over the U.S. Holocaust Memorial. In that particular struggle, involving the inclusion or exclusion of Gypsies from the Memorial program, tensions reached such a pitch that the celebrated Jewish Nazi hunter Simon Wiesenthal was driven to write to the Memorial Commission in protest over the omission of Gypsies from the program, arguing that they too deserved commemorative recognition since "the Gypsies had been murdered in a proportion similar to the Jews, about 80 percent of them in the area of the countries which were occupied by the Nazis."[10]

Although Wiesenthal's willingness to extend a hand of public recognition and commiseration to fellow victims of one of history's most monstrous events was typical of him (and today support solicitations for the Holocaust Memorial Museum point out that Jehovah's Witnesses, the physically and mentally handicapped, homosexuals, Gypsies, Soviet prisoners of war, and others also were targets of the Nazi extermination effort) it was an unusual act in the context of these sorts of controversies. Denial of massive death counts is common—and even readily understandable, if contemptible—among those whose forefathers were the perpetrators of the genocide. Such denials have at least two motives: first, protection of the moral reputations of those people and that country responsible for the genocidal activity (which seems the primary motive of those scholars and politicians who deny that massive genocide campaigns were carried out against American Indians); and second, on occasion, the desire to continue carrying out virulent racist assaults upon those who were the victims of the genocide in question (as seems to be the major purpose of the anti-Semitic so-called historical revisionists who claim that the Jewish Holocaust never happened or that its magnitude has been exaggerated). But for those who have themselves been victims of extermination campaigns to proclaim uniqueness for their experiences only as a way of denying recognition to others who also have suffered massive genocidal brutalities is to play into the hands of the brutalizers.[11] Rather, as Michael Berenbaum has wisely put it, "we should let our sufferings, however incommensurate, unite us in condemnation of inhumanity rather than divide us in a calculus of calamity."[12]

Noam Chomsky once observed that "if you take any two historical events and ask whether there are similarities and differences, the answer is always going to be both yes and no. At some sufficiently fine level of detail, there will be differences, and at some sufficiently abstract level, there will be similarities." The key question for most historical investigations, however, "is whether the level at which there are similarities is, in fact, a significant one." [13] Among all the cases of genocide mentioned above there were, we have noted, important differences. Indeed, in most technical particulars, the differences among them may well outweigh the similarities. But there were and are certain similarities of significance, and between the Jewish Holocaust and the Euro-American genocide against the Indians of the Americas one of those similarities involves the element of religion— where Des Pres's preference for the word "demonic" resides most appropriately. And here, in considering the role of religion in these genocides there is no better place to begin than with the words of Elie Wiesel, a fact that is not without some irony since for years Wiesel has argued passionately for the complete historical uniqueness of the Jewish Holocaust. In seeking at least a partial answer to the question posed at the start of this chapter—"what *are* these people?"—an observation of Wiesel's regarding the perpetrators of the Jewish Holocaust is an equally apt beginning for those who would seek to understand the motivations that ignited and fanned the flames of the mass destruction of the Americas' native peoples:

> All the killers were Christian. . . . The Nazi system was the consequence of a movement of ideas and followed a strict logic; it did not arise in a void but had its roots deep in a tradition that prophesied it, prepared for it, and brought it to maturity. That tradition was inseparable from the past of Christian, civilized Europe.[14]

Indeed, despite an often expressed contempt for Christianity, in *Mein Kampf* Hitler had written that his plan for a triumphant Nazism was modeled on the Catholic Church's traditional "tenacious adherence to dogma" and its "fanatical intolerance," particularly in the Church's past when, as Arno J. Mayer has noted, Hitler observed approvingly that in "building 'its own altar,' Christianity had not hesitated to 'destroy the altars of the heathen.' "[15] Had Hitler required supporting evidence for this contention he would have needed to look no further than the Puritans' godly justifications for exterminating New England's Indians in the seventeenth century or, before that, the sanctimonious Spanish legitimation of genocide, as ordained by Christian Truth, in fifteenth- and sixteenth-century Meso- and South America. (It is worth noting also that the Führer from time to time expressed admiration for the "efficiency" of the American genocide campaign against the Indians, viewing it as a forerunner for his own plans and programs.)[16] But the roots of the tradition run far deeper than that—back to the high Middle Ages and before—when at least part of the Christians' willingness to destroy the infidels who lived in what was considered to be a spiritual wilderness was rooted in a rabid need to kill the sinful wilderness that lived within themselves. To understand the horrors that were inflicted by Europeans and white Americans on the Indians of the Americas it is necessary to begin with a look at the core of European thought and culture—Christianity—and in particular its ideas on sex and race and violence.

II

Popular thought long has viewed pre-Christian Rome as a bacchanalian "Eden of the unrepressed," in one historian's words, and a similar impression often is held of ancient Greece as well. Neither view is correct. In Greece, virginity was treasured, and a young, unmarried woman discovered in the act of sex could legally be sold into slavery. "Given that this is the only situation in which Solonian law allows a free Athenian to be reduced to slavery," writes Giulia Sissa, "it is clear that premarital sexual activity constituted an extremely serious threat to the laws governing relationships within and among families."[17] Athena herself, it is worth recalling, was not only a goddess of war, but also a virgin—a symbolic juxtaposition of characteristics that, as we shall see, was destined to resonate through many centuries of Western culture. And in Rome, no less a light than Cicero observed that since "the great excellence of man's nature, above that of the brutes and all other creatures" is founded on the fact that brutes "are insensible to everything but pleasure, and they will risk everything to attain it,"

> from this we are to conclude, that the mere pursuits of sensual gratifications are unworthy the excellency of man's nature; and that they ought therefore to be despised and rejected; but that if a man shall have a small propensity for pleasure, he ought to be extremely cautious in what manner he indulges it. We, therefore, in the nourishment and dress of our bodies, ought to consult not our pleasure, but our health and our strength; and should we examine the excellency and dignity of our nature, we should then be made sensible how shameful man's life is, when it melts away in pleasure, in voluptuousness, and effeminacy; and how noble it is to live with abstinence, with modesty, with strictness, and sobriety.[18]

The idea is hardly a Christian invention, then, that immoderate enjoyment of the pleasures of the flesh belongs to the world of the brute, and that abstinence, modesty, strictness, and sobriety are to be treasured above all else. Still, it is understandable why subsequent European thought would regard Greece and Rome as realms of carnal indulgence, since subsequent

European thought was dominated by Christian ideology. And as the world of the Christian Fathers became the world of the Church Triumphant, while fluid and contested mythologies hardened into dogmatic theology, certain fundamental characteristics of Christianity, often derived from the teachings of Paul, came to express themselves in fanatical form. Not the least of these was the coming to dominance of an Augustinian notion of sex as sin (and sin as sexual) along with a larger sense, as Elaine Pagels puts it, that all of humanity was hopelessly "sick, suffering, and helpless." As late antiquity in Europe began falling under the moral control of Christians there occurred what historian Jacques le Goff has called *la déroute du corporal*—"the rout of the body." Not only was human flesh thenceforward to be regarded as corrupt, but so was the very nature of humankind and, indeed, so was nature itself; so corrupt, in fact, that only a rigid authoritarianism could be trusted to govern men and women who, since the fall of Adam and Eve, had been permanently poisoned with an inability to govern themselves in a fashion acceptable to God.[19]

At its heart, Christianity expressed a horror at the tainting of godliness with sexuality. Some early Christian Fathers, such as Origen, had taken literally the prophet Matthew's charge (19:11–12) that "there be eunuchs, which have made themselves eunuchs for the kingdom of heaven," and castrated themselves. Such self-mutilating behavior finally was condemned by the Church in the fourth century as being excessive and unnecessary; thenceforward celibacy would be sufficient. But then this too was carried to extremes. Saint Paul had written (Cor. 7:1,9) that "it is good for a man not to touch a woman. . . . But if they cannot contain, let them marry: for it is better to marry than to burn." Even marital sex invariably was infected with lust, however, so there developed in Christian culture the anachronistic institution of sexless so-called chaste marriage, and it endured with some popularity for nearly a thousand years.[20]

As Peter Brown has pointed out, however, perhaps the most remarkable thing about what he calls this *gran rifiuto,* or "great renunciation," was the way it quickly became the basis for male leadership in the Church. One key to understanding this phenomenon is located in the contrast between Judaism at the time and its radical offshoot of Christianity. For as Brown notes: "In the very centuries when the rabbinate rose to prominence in Judaism by accepting marriage as a near-compulsory criterion of the wise, the leaders of the Christian communities moved in the diametrically opposite direction: access to leadership became identified with near-compulsory celibacy." The Christian leader, then, stood apart from all others by making a public statement that in fact focused enormous attention on sexuality. Indeed, "sexuality became a highly charged symbolic marker" exactly because its dramatic removal as a central activity of life allowed the self-proclaimed saintly individual to present himself as "the ideal of the single-hearted person"—the person whose heart belonged only to God.[21]

Of course, such fanatically aggressive opposition to sex can only occur among people who are fanatically obsessed *with* sex, and nowhere was this more ostentatiously evident than in the lives of the early Christian hermits. Some time around the middle of the third century the holiest of Christian holy men decided that the only way to tame their despicable sexual desires was to remove themselves completely from the world of others. Moving to the desert, they literally declared war on their sexual selves, first by reducing their intake of food to near-starvation levels. "When one wants to take a town, one cuts off the supply of water and food," wrote a sainted monastic named John the Dwarf. The same military strategy, he continued, "applies to the passions of the flesh. If a man lives a life of fasting and hunger, the enemies of his soul are weakened."[22]

Weakened, perhaps; but never, it seems, defeated. On the contrary, the more these godly hermits tried to drive out thoughts of sex, the more they were tortured by desire. Thus, when one young monk, Palladius, reported to an older one, Pachon, that he was thinking of leaving the desert because, no matter what he did, "desire filled his thoughts night and day, and . . . he was increasingly tormented by visions of women," the old man replied that after forty years of exile and isolation in the desert he too "still suffered the same intolerable urges. He said that between the ages of fifty and seventy he had not spent a single night or day without desiring a woman."[23] But try he and the others did, with maniacal obsessiveness. Aline Rousselle provides a few examples:

Ammonius used to burn his body with a red-hot iron every time [he felt sexual desire]. Pachon shut himself in a hyena's den, hoping to die sooner than yield, and then he held an asp against his genital organs. Evagrius spent many nights in a frozen well. Philoromus wore irons. One hermit agreed one night to take in a woman who was lost in the desert. He left his light burning all night and burned his fingers on it to remind himself of eternal punishment. A monk who had treasured the memory of a very beautiful woman, when he heard that she was dead, went and dippled his coat in her decomposed body and lived with this smell to help him fight his constant thoughts of beauty.[24]

But let Saint Jerome describe for himself the masochistic joys of desert exile:

There I sat, solitary, full of bitterness; my disfigured limbs shuddered away from the sackcloth, my dirty skin was taking on the hue of the Ethiopian's flesh: every day tears, every day sighing: and if in spite of my struggles sleep would tower over and sink upon me, my battered body ached on the naked earth. Of food and drink I say nothing, since even a sick monk uses only cold water, and to take anything cooked is a wanton luxury. Yet that same I, who for fear of hell condemned myself to such a prison, I, the comrade of scorpions and wild beasts, was there, watching the maidens in their dances:

my face haggard with fasting, my mind burnt with desire in my frigid body, and the fires of lust alone leaped before a man prematurely dead. So, destitute of all aid, I used to lie at the feet of Christ, watering them with my tears, wiping them with my hair, struggling to subdue my rebellious flesh with seven days' fasting.[25]

Extreme though such thoughts and behavior may seem today, in the early centuries of Christianity, when the seeds of faith were being nurtured into dogma, such activities characterized the entire adult lives of thousands of the most saintly and honored men. During the fourth century about 5000 holy ascetics lived in the desert of Nitria, with thousands more tormenting themselves around Antinoe in the Thebiad, at Hermopolis, and elsewhere. Indeed, so popular did the life of the sex-denying hermit become among Christian men that in time it was difficult to find sufficient isolation to live the true hermit's life. They began to live in small groups, and then eventually in organized monasteries. Here, because of the closeness of other bodies, carnal temptation was more difficult to suppress. The institution did what it could to assist, however: rules were instituted prohibiting the locking of cell doors to discourage masturbation; it was forbidden for two monks to speak together in the dark, to ride a donkey together, or to approach any closer than an arm's length away; they were to avoid looking at each other as much as possible, they were required to keep their knees covered when sitting in a group, and they were admonished against lifting their tunics any higher than was absolutely necessary when washing their clothes.[26]

Although sex was at the core of such commitments to self-denial, it was not all that the saintly Christian rejected. Indeed, what distinguished the Christian saint from other men, said the early Church fathers, was the Christian's recognition of the categorical difference and fundamental opposition between things of the spirit and things of the world. The two realms were utterly incompatible, with the result, says the Epistle to Diognetus, that "the flesh hates the soul, and wages war upon it, though it has suffered no evil, because it is prevented from gratifying its pleasures, and the world hates the Christians though it has suffered no evil, because they are opposed to its pleasures."[27] In demonstrating their opposition to the world's proffered pleasures, some monks wrapped themselves in iron chains in order that they might never forget their proper humility, while others "adopted the life of animals," writes Henry Chadwick, "and fed on grass, living in the open air without shade from the sun and with the minimum of clothing." Still others, such as Saint Simeon Stylites, displayed his asceticism by living his life on top of a column; by so doing, he not only "won the deep reverence of the country people," but he also "inspired later imitators like Daniel (409–93) who spent thirty-three years on a column near Constantinople."[28]

During those same first centuries of the Church's existence some paragons of the faith took to literal extremes the scriptural charge to "love not the world, neither the things that are in the world," by flinging themselves into what Augustine was to call the "daily sport" of suicide and by searching for ways to become Ignatius's longed-for "fodder for wild beasts."[29] Suicide, like castration, in time was discouraged by the Church as at best institutionally counter-productive, but the idea of flesh as corruption and of the physical pleasures of the world as sin continued to evolve over the centuries, by the Middle Ages flourishing into a full-fledged ideology that came to be known as the *contemptus mundi* or "contempt for the world" tradition. All of life on earth was *properly* seen as a "vale of tears," as a "desert," an "exile." As one medieval saint, Jean de Fecamp, exclaimed, human life was and should be viewed as "miserable life, decrepit life, impure life sullied by humours, exhausted by grief, dried by heat, swollen by meats, mortified by fasts, dissolved by pranks, consumed by sadness, distressed by worries, blunted by security, bloated by riches, cast down by poverty."[30] The torment of life lay, therefore, not only in its pains, but equally (if perversely) in its pleasures that systematically had to be both resisted and condemned. Thus, an anonymous twelfth-century poet confronted himself with the riddle—"Evil life of this world then / Why do you please me so?"—and answered piously with the following litany:

Fugitive life,
more harmful than any beast.

Life which should be called death,
Which one should hate, not love

Worldly life, sickly thing
More fragile than the rose

Worldly life, source of labors,
Anguished, full of suffering

Worldly life, future death,
Permanent ruin,

Worldly life, evil thing
Never worthy of love

Worldly life, foul life
Pleasing only to the impious

Life, stupid thing
Accepted only by fools,

I reject you with all my heart
For you are full of filth.

With all my heart I reject you
I prefer to undergo death,
O life, rather than serve you.[31]

A century later the poet and Franciscan monk Giacomino di Verona expressed the matter of humanity's proper Christian understanding of itself in similar, if even more pithy terms:

In a very dirty and vile workroom
You were made out of slime,
So foul and so wretched
That my lips cannot bring themselves to tell you about it.
But if you have a bit of sense, you will know
That the fragile body in which you lived,

Where you were tormented eight months and more,
Was made of rotting and corrupt excrement . . .
You came out through a foul passage
And you fell into the world, poor and naked . . .
. . . Other creatures have some use:
Meat and bone, wool and leather;
But you, stinking man, you are worse than dung:
From you, man, comes only pus . . .
From you comes no virtue,
You are a sly and evil traitor;
Look in front of you and look behind,
For your life is like your shadow
Which quickly comes and quickly goes . . .[32]

In response to learned and saintly medieval urgings of this sort, the efforts of good Christians to purge themselves of worldly concerns and carnal impulses became something truly to behold, something that had its roots in the asceticism of the early Church Fathers of almost a thousand years earlier and something that would persist among the faithful for centuries yet to come. Norman Cohn has provided us with one vivid though not untypical example by quoting an account from the fourteenth century when, on a winter's night, a devout friar

shut himself up in his cell and stripped himself naked . . . and took his scourge with the sharp spikes, and beat himself on the body and on the arms and legs, till blood poured off him as from a man who has been cupped. One of the spikes on the scourge was bent crooked, like a hook, and whatever flesh it caught it tore off. He beat himself so hard that the scourge broke into three bits and the points flew against the wall. He stood there bleeding and gazed at himself. It was such a wretched sight that he was reminded in many ways of the appearance of the beloved Christ, when he was fearfully beaten. Out of pity for himself he began to weep bitterly. And he knelt down, naked and covered in blood, in the frosty air, and prayed to God to wipe out his sin from before his gentle eyes.[33]

Monks and other males were not the only devout souls of this time who tried to work their way to heaven with self-flagellation and other forms of personal abasement. In fact, if anything, women showed more originality than men in their undertakings of humiliation. In addition to the routine of self-flagellation and the commitment of themselves to crippling and sometimes fatal bouts of purposeful starvation, would-be female saints "drank pus or scabs from lepers' sores, eating and incorporating disease," reports a recent student of the subject, "and in the frenzy of trance or ecstasy, pious women sometimes mutilated themselves with knives." One such holy woman displayed her piety by sleeping on a bed of paving stones, whipping herself with chains, and wearing a crown of thorns. As Caroline Walker Bynum dryly remarks:

> Reading the lives of fourteenth- and fifteenth-century women saints greatly expands one's knowledge of Latin synonyms for whip, thong, flail, chain, etc. Ascetic practices commonly reported in these *vitae* include wearing hair shirts, binding the flesh tightly with twisted ropes, rubbing lice into self-inflicted wounds, denying oneself sleep, adulterating food and water with ashes or salt, performing thousands of genuflections, thrusting nettles into one's breasts, and praying barefoot in winter. Among the more bizarre female behaviors were rolling in broken glass, jumping into ovens, hanging from a gibbet, and praying upside down.[34]

Such behavior was motivated primarily by the now traditional Christian compulsion to deny and to rout the pleasures of the flesh and by so doing to accentuate the importance of the spirit, for by this time the sundering of the mundane from the spiritual, the profane from the sacred, was a well-established characteristic of European Christian culture. But by listening closely, Bynum has shown that the sounds of other promptings to asceticism can be discerned as well. These additional (not alternative) explanations for such extreme performances included straightforward efforts to escape the restrictions and menial activities dictated by life in authoritarian Christian families and communities. This was a motive particularly likely among women living in a harshly misogynist world, women who by becoming acknowledged saints and mystics were able to use the institution of chaste marriage to negotiate non-sexual relationships for themselves during an era when sexual marriage could be an extraordinarily brutal institution, and women who, when all else failed, sometimes were able "accidentally" to drop an unwanted infant into the fire during a trance of mystical ecstasy.[35]

To be sure, much as its priesthood fondly wanted it to be, Christianity never was able to become an entirely totalitarian religion. During the thirteenth and fourteenth centuries in particular, some citizens of Europe found for themselves cultural pockets of at least some sensual freedom. What these exceptions almost invariably demonstrate, however, is that once European sexual mores and attitudes toward the body had been shaped on the anvil of early Christian asceticism, whatever variations those mores and attitudes underwent during the course of time they always were variations that remained partially embedded in that repressive ideal. As a culture, the Christian West never was (and still is not) at ease with sexuality. Thus, even on those short-lived occasions when erotic repression relaxed for a time, the emerging liberatory impulse indulged in by a relative few invariably had about it an almost desperate quality of both flamboyance and risk.

When a few women of prominence in certain parts of Europe during the fourteenth century felt free for a time to express themselves sexually, for example—no doubt, as part of the breakdown in Christian morality that came in the aftermath of the Black Death—they did it by ostentatiously exposing their breasts, applying rouge or jewel-studded caps to their nipples, and sometimes piercing their nipples so as to hang gold chains from them. If this fashion was a bit extreme for some, an alternative was to cover as little as possible of one's breasts and then to push them up and out; the result, according to one observer, was to make "two . . . horns on their bosom, very high up and artificially projected toward the front, even when nature has not endowed them with such important advantages."[36] Such determinedly—or frantically—erotic fashion statements were never the rule for many, of course; and for those few who did indulge in them, the lifespan of the vogue was short. For constantly lurking everywhere was the dominant moral code of the Church. As John Bromyard, an approximate contemporary of those rouge-nippled fourteenth-century would-be libertines and their male companions, warned:

> In place of scented baths, their body shall have a narrow pit in the earth, and there they shall have a bath more foul than any bath of pitch and sulphur. In place of a soft couch, they shall have a bed more grievous and hard than all the nails and spikes in the world. . . . Instead of wives, they shall have toads; instead of a great retinue and a throng of followers, their body shall have a throng of worms and their soul a throng of demons.[37]

Bromyard's reference to scented baths is also telling. Inspired by the example of Muslims living in Spain during the twelfth and thirteenth centuries, public baths slowly spread throughout Europe during the course of the next two hundred years. By the turn of the fourteenth century, Paris, for instance, had about two dozen public baths. In some of them a visitor might encounter what the Italian writer Poggio did on a visit to Zurich in the early fifteenth century: partially clad men and women singing and drinking, and "young girls, already ripe for marriage, in the fullness of their nubile forms . . . standing and moving like goddesses . . . their garments form[ing] a floating train on the surface of the waters."[38]

By the end of the fifteenth century, however, the baths were being closed throughout Europe; within half a century more they were gone.[39] (The Spanish, in particular, had never supported regular bathing, public or otherwise, associating it with Islam and thus regarding it as "a mere cover for Mohammedan ritual and sexual promiscuity.")[40] Similarly, brothels had been tolerated and even given municipal institutional status in some European communities during the fourteenth and early fifteenth century. But, just as bath houses began being closed by authorities in the 1470s, so too were the brothels; like the public baths, open brothels effectively had disappeared by the mid-sixteenth century.[41] As for bare-breasted or other revealing fashions, they also quickly became a thing of the past. Spain led the way here as the fifteenth century was drawing to a close. Mantles or *mantos* for women became the approved attire, Hans Peter Duerr notes, and they

> completely enveloped the female figure, leaving only a small peephole. Black became the colour of choice, the expression of the face froze into a mask, bodices had iron staves sewed into them, even the hint of a bosom was shunned. Lead plates served to keep breasts flat and to impede their development.[42]

In other parts of Europe "there was even a return to the medieval caps and chin bands," Duerr writes, "revealing nothing of the hair beneath." Behind this shift back to traditional Christian denial of the body and rejection of things sexual, says Ioan P. Couliano, was the persistent ideology that

> woman is the blind instrument for seduction of nature, the symbol of temptation, sin, and evil. Besides her face, the principal baits of her allure are the signs of her fertility, hips and breasts. The face, alas, must stay exposed, but it is possible for it to wear a rigid and manly expression. The neck can be enveloped in a high lace collar. As to the bosom, the treatment dealt it closely resembles the traditional deformation of the feet of [Chinese] women, being no less painful and unhealthy. . . . Natural femininity, overflowing, voluptuous, and sinful is categorized as unlawful. Henceforth only witches will dare to have wide hips, prominent breasts, conspicuous buttocks, long hair.[43]

Couliano's passing reference to witches in this context is worth pausing over, for it is precisely here that Christianity—and in particular the Christianity that structured life, culture, and ideas at the time that Columbus was making ready his plans to sail to Cathay—located the only proper home in the contemporary world for nudity and eroticism. Both of the major texts on witchcraft produced at this time—Jakob Sprenger's famous *Malleus Maleficarum* in 1486, and Fray Martin de Castenega's *Tratado de las Supersticiones y Hechicherias* in 1529—observed that "all witchcraft comes from carnal lust." Indeed, "the literature and imagery relating to witchcraft border on the pornographic," Couliano says: "the inhibitions of an entire era of repression are poured into it. All possible and impossible perversions are ascribed to witches and their fiendish partners"—"perversions" both heterosexual and homosexual, for as Jeffrey Burton Russell has observed, one "commonplace" allegation that appears "again and again" in witchcraft trials was the charge of sodomy.[44]

The ritualized gatherings of witches in Europe during this time were known as "synagogues," and later as "sabbats"—both terms, of course, derived from Judaism, which was itself regarded as a form of devil worship. There are numerous supposed accounts of such gatherings (the so-called Great European Witch Hunt was building toward its peak by the end of the fifteenth century), but Norman Cohn has put together a representative collage of what Christians from this time believed took place during a typical witches' sabbat:

> The sabbat was presided over by the Devil, who now took on the shape not of a mere man but of a monstrous being, half man and half goat: a hideous black man with enormous horns, a goat's beard and goat's legs . . . . First the witches knelt down and prayed to the Devil, calling him Lord and God, and repeating their renunciation of the Christian faith; after which each in turn kissed him, often on his left foot, his genitals or his anus. Next delinquent witches reported for punishment, which usually consisted of whippings. . . . Then came the parody of divine service. Dressed in black vestments, with mitre and surplice, the Devil would preach a sermon, warning his followers against reverting to Christianity and promising them a far more blissful paradise than the Christian heaven. . . . The proceedings ended in a climax of profanity. Once more the witches adored the Devil and kissed his anus . . . . Finally, an orgiastic dance, to the sound of trumpets, drums and fifes. The witches would form a circle, facing outwards, and dance around a witch bent over, her head touching the ground, with a candle stuck in her anus to serve as illumination. The dance would become a frantic and erotic orgy, in which all things, including sodomy and incest, were permitted. At the height of the orgy the Devil would copulate with every man, woman and child present.[45]

Needless to say, sex with Satan—or even with one or more of the incubi or succubae who assisted him—was not something one easily forgot. Nicolas Remy, a sixteenth-century expert on these matters (he had made a fifteen-year study of approximately 900 witchcraft trials) reported to an eager Christian public the experiences, recounted in official testimony, of some witches who had endured the ordeal:

> Hennezel asserts that his Scuatzebourg (those were the names of succubae) gave him the impression of having a frozen hole (instead of a vagina) and that he had to withdraw before having an orgasm. As to witches, they declare that the virile organs of demons are so thick and hard that it is impossible to be penetrated by them without dreadful pain. Alice Drigée compared her demon's erect penis with a kitchen tool she pointed out to the assembly and gave the information that the former lacked scrotum and testicles. As to Claudine Fellée, she knew how to avoid the piercing pain of such intercourse by a rotary movement she often performed in order to introduce that erect mass, which no woman, of no matter what capacity, could have contained.

. . . And nevertheless, there are some who reach orgasm in this cold and loathsome embrace.[46]

It is not hard to imagine the effect—or, indeed, the function—of listening to this sort of thing, day in and day out, among people adamantly committed to intense sexual repression as the fundamental key to eternal salvation. In the event that verbal description might prove insufficient, however, artistic works abounded, depicting the disgustingly thrilling orgiastic rites and rituals that occurred during witches' sabbats. So too, of course, were visual representations readily available of the horrendous postmortem fate—including violent assaults by demons on the genitals—that was in store for ordinary mortals who might have succumbed to the temptations of lust and lechery.

There was, however, a third artistic genre in which sexual behavior was often central—depictions of the long, lost Golden Age. Thus, in the midst of the sixteenth century's culture of sexual denial, Agostino Carracci—among others—could openly depict explicit and voluptuous sensuality and eroticism so long as it was labeled *Love in the Golden Age* and contained appended verses with language like: "As the palm is a sign of victory, so the fruit of congenial love is that sweetness from which is produced the seed whence Nature and heaven are glorified."[47]

By definition, of course, the Golden Age belonged safely to the past—although there was always the very real possibility that displaced remnants of it existed, and could be found, in distant parts of the world that had not yet been explored. If somewhere on the earth's outer fringes there lay a land of demigods and milk and honey, however, there also lurked in distant realms demi-brutes who lived carnal and savage lives in a wilderness controlled by Satan. Which one, if either, of these a medieval or Renaissance explorer was likely to find, only time and experience would tell.

III

Contrary to a notion that has become fashionable among American historians, the concept of race was not invented in the late eighteenth or nineteenth century. Indeed, systems of categorical generalization that separated groups of people according to social constructions of race (sometimes based on skin color, sometimes with reference to other attributes) and ranked them as to disposition and intelligence, were in use in Europe at least a thousand years before Columbus set off across the Atlantic.[48] Even a thousand years earlier than that, says historian of ancient Greece Kurt von Fritz, since it was, he contends, during the time of Hippocrates in the fourth century B.C. "that race theory first raised its head." Others might argue for an earlier date still, but certainly it is true, as Fritz points out, that from Hippocrates to Callisthenes to Posidonius several centuries later, the concept was elaborated and refined until it was held that "not only the populations of different continents constituted different races, but every tribe or nation had its racial characteristics which were the product of hereditary factors, climate, diet, training and traditions." As a consequence of this, Posidonius contended, the behavior of individuals and groups was attributable to a variety of factors, one of which was their "racial character."[49] Moreover, as Orlando Patterson has shown, "strong racial antipathy was not uncommon in Rome," and in particular, "Negro features were not an asset in the slave-holding societies of the Greco-Roman world."[50]

Long before this era, however, at least as early as the late eighth century B.C., Homer and Hesiod and other Greek poets were describing a time, as A. Bartlett Giamatti puts it, "when Cronos reigned and the world was young, the age of the Golden race, and said it still existed to the north in the land of the Scythians and Hyperboreans." The poets were not alone in speaking and writing of these Fortunate Islands of delight, repose, and physical bliss, for "as poets sang of this happy place, ancient geographers and historians charted and described it—sight unseen, save with the mind's eye."[51]

Unseen, perhaps, but there was no doubt that the earthly paradise was an actual place situated in a distant realm, a group of islands or a peaceful plain at the end of the earth. As Menelaus was promised in the *Odyssey:*

> [I]t is not your fate to die in Argos, to meet your end in the grazing-land of horses. The Deathless Ones will waft you instead to the world's end, the Elysian fields where yellow-haired Rhadamanthus is. There indeed men live unlaborious days. Snow and tempest and thunderstorms never enter there, but for men's refreshment Ocean sends out continually the high-singing breezes of the west.[52]

In other traditions the Elysian Fields were in the Islands of the Blest where, according to Hesiod, there lived the fourth age of men, the "godly race of the heroes who are called demigods," to whom Zeus had "granted a life and home apart from men, and settled them at the ends of the earth." And still today, says Hesiod, there they "dwell with carefree heart in the Isles of the Blessed Ones, beside deep-swirling Oceanus: fortunate Heroes, for whom the grain-giving soil bears its honey-sweet fruits thrice a year."[53]

These were demigods because they were half god, half human, descended from unions between gods and mortal women. Their existence had been preceded by that of three other races. First, there were the "Golden race" of people who "lived like gods, with carefree heart, remote from toil and misery" and who, at the end of their reign, were transformed into "divine spirits . . . watchers over mortal men, bestowers of wealth." Then there followed the Silver race, "much inferior" to the Golden race, "but still they too have honour." The third race, the race of Bronze men, was "a terrible and fierce race," characterized by violence and a lack of agriculture—a clear sign of civilization's absence—a people who ate only meat and whatever grew wild. They were "unshapen hulks, with great strength and indescribable arms growing from their shoulders above their stalwart bodies." They did not have iron, or at least they did not know how to work it, and they now lived in "chill Hades' house of decay."[54]

The present is located in the fifth age, the age of the race of Iron men. In terms of moral character, the world of Hesiod's Iron race contemporaries seems to have been situated somewhere between that of the deformed and violent and primitive Bronze race and that of the demigods who lived in the Blessed Isles: although troubled with vice and selfishness and dishonesty, at least the Iron race is civilized, though in time it too is fated to be abandoned by the gods because of its insistent sinfulness. However, as Giamatti notes, Hesiod later introduces the notions of justice and morality as paths that mortal men and women can choose to follow and in which "a kind of Golden Age is open to [those] who deserve it by their just and virtuous lives."[55] Neither war, nor famine, nor blight will fall upon those whose communities select the path of virtue:

> For them Earth bears plentiful food, and on the mountains the oak carries acorns at its surface and bees at its centre. The fleecy sheep are laden down with wool; the womenfolk bear children that resemble their parents; they enjoy a continual sufficiency of good things. Nor do they ply on ships, but the grain-giving ploughland bears them fruit.[56]

This is about as close as humans are likely to get to a paradise on earth. For "those who occupy themselves with violence and wickedness and brutal deeds," however, godly retribution is in store: "disaster . . . famine and with it plague, and the people waste away. The womenfolk do not give birth, and households decline."[57]

The theme evolved from Greek to Roman thought and, as Giamatti observes, the "note of morality," of virtue and its reward as a choice humans could make, "rendered Golden Age places 'safe' for Christian adaptation." In time Christianity did indeed integrate the idea into its own ideology. Although in Christian legend the terrestrial paradise was linked to the Garden of Eden, as Giamatti says, "early Christian descriptions of the earthly paradise owed as much to ancient literature as to Christian Biblical literature, and finally the two strands became inseparable."[58] Whatever the variations imposed by the different European cultures that adopted it, the terrestrial paradise was always a place linked to the past, but still existing somewhere on the other side of the world in the present— a place of simplicity, innocence, harmony, love, and happiness, where the climate is balmy and the fruits of nature's bounty are found on the trees year round.

Other, less pleasant realms and their inhabitants existed in distant lands as well, however, for mixed in among the varied races of the world was a special category of being collectively known as the "monstrous races." They are described in the writings of Homer, Ctesias, Megasthenes, and others dating back at least as far as the eighth century B.C.—along with earlier parallels that can be found in the ancient Near East—but the first major compilation describing the appearance and character of the different monstrous races was that of Pliny the Elder in his first century A.D. *Natural History*. In thirty-six volumes Pliny soberly and seriously informs his readers about the existence of different peoples living in far off lands whose feet are turned backwards; whose upper or lower lips are so large that they curl them back over their heads to use as umbrellas; who walk upside down; who walk on all fours; who are covered with hair; who have no mouths and nourish themselves by smelling their food; who have neither heads nor necks and whose faces are embedded in their chests; who have one eye—or three, or four; who have the heads of dogs, and breathe flames; who have only one leg on which they nevertheless run very fast, a leg containing an enormous foot that they use to shield themselves from the sun; who are gigantic or miniature in size; who have six fingers or six hands; who have hooves instead of feet; whose ears are so long that they use them as blankets; and more. Other such alien races have women who conceive at age five and die by the time they are eight, or children who are born with white hair that gradually turns to black as they grow older.[59]

It is important to recognize that these creatures were truly believed to exist and to exist not in some supernatural or demonic realm, but within the larger context of humanity—if often on its outermost margins. Beyond the matter of gross difference in physical type and biological characteristics in general, the monstrous races were distinguishable by cultural patterns that varied from European ideals. They spoke strangely; "barbarians" were, after all, literally *barbaraphonoi*, or those whose speech sounded like "bar bar" to Greek ears. They ate and drank strange foods and potions, from insects to human flesh to dog's milk. They went about unclothed, or if clothed they usually were covered by animal skins. They used crude weapons of war, clubs or other wooden objects, or they were ignorant of weaponry altogether. And they lived in small communities, not urban environments—and thus were largely ungoverned by laws.

Once integrated into Christian thinking, the monstrous races came to be associated with the lineage of Cain; that is, they were actual creatures whose strangeness was part of their deserved suffering because of their progenitor's sin. Whether Greeks, Romans, or medieval Christians, moreover, the Europeans of all eras considered themselves to be "chosen" people, the inhabitants of the center and most civil domain of human life. The further removed from that center anything in nature was, the further it was removed from God, from virtue, and from the highest essence of humanity. Thus, the fact that the monstrous races were said to live on the distant extremes of the earthly realm was one crucial element in their radical otherness, and also in their being defined as fundamentally unvirtuous and base. So great was their alienation from the world of God's—or the gods'—most favored people, in fact, that well into late antiquity they commonly were denied the label of "men." [60]

This eventually became a problem for Christianity, eager as the faith was to convert all humanity to God's revealed truth. The classic statement of the early church on this matter was the work of Augustine who, in *The City of God,* affirmed that "whoever is born anywhere as a human being, that is, as a rational mortal creature, however strange he may appear to our senses in bodily form or colour or motion or utterance, or in any faculty, part or quality of his nature whatsoever, let no true believer have any doubt that such an individual is descended from the one man who was first created." Though often regarded as a fairly unambiguous statement of support for the humanity of distant peoples, Augustine's linking of humanity to "rationality" left open a large area for definitional disagreement. Nor did his closing words on the subject help: "Let me then tentatively and guardedly state my conclusion. Either the written accounts of certain races are completely unfounded or, if such races do exist, they are not human; or, if they are human, they are descended from Adam." [61] All that really can be concluded from this is that, for Augustine, someone who worships within the fold of Christianity certainly is rational and certainly is human, though there clearly are races that in some respects might seem to be human, but are not.

A great challenge was thus posed to the Church. It was met with avidity. Stories circulated throughout medieval Europe of creatures with hooves for feet, and with claws, who had been converted to the way of Christ; of people as small as seven-year old children, with horses the size of sheep, who had been brought to see the light. Even people with the heads of dogs and who ate human flesh were said to have been brought within Christianity's embrace. Indeed, in several accounts of the conversion of St. Christopher—for centuries one of the Church's most popular saints—the preconversion Christopher was a Cynocephalus, or dog-headed creature with "long hair, and eyes glittering like the morning star in his head, and [with] teeth like the tusks of a wild boar." [62] If, however—to some enthusiastic Christians, at least—physical appearance was no bar to conversion and even to sainthood, another less generous conclusion from this same premise was equally important, and equally linked with Augustine's earlier ambivalence on the subject: those creatures who made up the alien races in far flung lands and who were not "rational"—that is, unlike St. Christopher and others, those who were *incapable* of being converted—must be considered beyond the most charitable definition of personhood.

Gradually, during the later Middle Ages, interest in the great variety of monstrous races that Pliny and others laboriously had described began to fade. Concern increasingly focused on a single example of the type—the *sylvestres homines,* or wild man. As Richard Bernheimer, in the classic study of the subject, describes the wild man, it is a hairy creature

> curiously compounded of human and animal traits, without, however, sinking to the level of an ape. It exhibits upon its naked human anatomy a growth of fur, leaving bare only its face, feet, and hands, at times its knees and elbows, or the breasts of the female of the species. Frequently the creature is shown wielding a heavy club or mace, or the trunk of a tree; and, since its body is usually naked except for a shaggy covering, it may hide its nudity under a strand of twisted foliage worn around the loins.[63]

Hidden or not, however, the loins of the wild man and his female companion were of abiding interest to Christian Europeans. For, in direct opposition to ascetic Christian ideals, wild people were seen as voraciously sexual creatures, some of them, in Hayden White's phrase, "little more than ambulatory genitalia." Adds historian Jeffrey Russell: "The wild man, both brutal and erotic, was a perfect projection of the repressed libidinous impulses of medieval man. His counterpart, the wild woman, who was a murderess, child-eater, bloodsucker and occasionally a sex nymph, was a prototype of the witch."[64]

Wild men, like the other representatives of the earth's monstrous races, had inhabited the Near Eastern and Western imaginations for millennia. So too had the wild man's adversary, the heroic human adventurer. And from at least the time of the ancient *Epic of Gilgamesh,* with its numerous parallels in Old Testament ideas, one recurring characteristic of the wild man's brave antagonist was his avoidance of, and even flight from, sexuality and the world of women. In the Gilgamesh legend, for example—which was composed in about 2000 B.C. from tales that are older still—the first wild man encountered is Enkidu. Possessed of "titanic strength," Enkidu's "whole body is covered with hair; the hair of his head is long like that of a woman. . . . With the game of the field he ranges at large over the steppe, eats grass and drinks water from the drinking-places of the open country, and delights in the company of animals."[65] In time Enkidu acknowledges Gilgamesh, the story's hero, as his superior, but only after Gilgamesh has had Enkidu brought down by the wiles and seductions of a courtesan.

With Enkidu now in tow—indeed, having almost merged into a second self—Gilgamesh next encounters another wild man, a terrifying, forest-dwelling, and far less cooperative ogre named Humbaba, and together—with the help of the sun god—Enkidu and Gilgamesh destroy Humbaba and cut off his head. Impressed by Gilgamesh, Ishtar, the goddess of love, proposes marriage to him, along with all the riches and accompanying pleasures she can give him; but Gilgamesh rejects her, knowing of her reputation as a fickle consumer of men. After another sequence of events Gilgamesh proclaims himself "the most glorious among heroes . . . the most eminent among men" and receives the approving acclaim of multitudes. The spurned Ishtar has her revenge, however, and Enkidu is killed, leaving Gilgamesh to cry "bitterly like unto a wailing woman," for seven days and seven nights, before launching a quest for the secret of eternal life. At last he is given it, in the form of a thorny plant from the bottom of the sea—but before he can use it the plant is stolen from him by a serpent, and Gilgamesh returns home to live out his days condemned to the ultimate fate of all mankind.

There are, certainly, numerous themes in the Gilgamesh story that have worked their way into the patterns of subsequent Western literature, and certainly the quest for eternal life, whether in the form of the earthly paradise or the fountain of youth, is relevant to understanding the adventures of Columbus and many of the European explorers who followed him. Of more immediate concern, however, is that the world of the adventurer is not only a male world, but a world in which women are at best irrelevant or ineffectual, and at worst are harlots, castrators, or murderesses. As such, they must at all costs be avoided. Paul Zweig has shown how this is true not only in the obvious cases (as with Beowulf having to overcome both Grendel and Grendel's monstrous mother, or in Odysseus' various dealings with Calypso, Circe, Scylla, and Charybdis), but also in the genre that, of all male writings, seems most sympathetic to women—the medieval romance. For on the whole, Zweig observes:

> medieval romance follows an implicit pattern which enables the adventurer to triumph over his female adversary. Typically, the romance opens as the knight gratefully swears oaths of love and loyalty which bind him to the lady of his choice. Before the story even begins, he is "defeated," helplessly in love. All he desires, apparently, is to sit idly at the feet of his queen. What could be more painful than to leave the lady's presence? But that is precisely what he must do; because his lady requires proof—he encourages her to require proof—of his love. And so the knight is banished into the wandering, unattached life of adventure, proving his courage and improving his reputation, all for the greater glory of the lady, whom he may, in fact, never see again.[66]

But, of course, seeing her again is not the point. The point is to live a life of exploration and danger—though a properly chaste and Christian life of exploration and danger, fighting against devilish men and beasts of the woods—preferably in the company of one or more male companions. "What is done *for* the lady, need not be done *with* her," Zweig notes. Indeed, from Achilles and Patroclus in the *Iliad* to Cervantes's Don Quixote and Sancho Panza—to say nothing of numerous examples up to the present— the same motif "recurs in the literature of adventure":

> uprooting himself from women, the adventurer forms a masculine friendship so intimate, so passionate, that it reasserts, in male terms, the emotional bond which formerly anchored him within the world of the city. . . . The adventurer, in his desire to reinvent himself as a man, reinvents his emotions, so that they may be served wholly by male pleasures: the rooted society of women superseded by the mobile society of men.[67]

Such relationships, to modern observers, often are viewed in a homo-erotic light. Zweig is ambivalent on the point, and it is not of particular importance in the context of this discussion, except to the extent that in the Christian versions of this literature, at least, the *consciously* idealized life of the adventurer not only is adamantly non-homosexual, it is deter-minedly non-sexual in every possible respect. It is, and must be, *deter-minedly* so, however, because carnal temptation lurks externally at every bend in the road, as well as deep within the Christian's imperfect self. Indeed, once on the march against the beasts of the forest or the enemies of God and civilization, this most noble of the Church's non-ordained rep-resentatives constantly has to contend with the fact that the most abhor-rent (because salacious) characteristics of both the wild man and the devil— in whatever guises they may appear—are perpetually latent within the darkness of even the finest Christian's own heart.

In sum, the wild man and his female companion, at their unconstrained and sensual worst, symbolized everything the Christian's ascetic *contemp-tus mundi* tradition was determined to eradicate—even as that tradition also acknowledged that the wild man's very *same* carnal and uncivilized sinfulness gnawed at the soul of the holiest saint, and (more painful still) that it was ultimately ineradicable, no matter how fervent the effort. The fact that failure was inevitable in the quest to crush completely such fes-tering inner sinfulness was discouraging, of course, as we saw in the dra-matic testimonies of the Church's early ascetic hermits; but as those testi-monies also revealed, to the true Christian believer discouragement was only prelude to ever more zealous and aggressive action.

As Richard Bernheimer and others have shown, the very notion of wildness, to the European mind at this time, suggested "everything that eluded Christian norms and the established framework of Christian soci-ety, referring to what was uncanny, unruly, raw, unpredictable, foreign, uncultured, and uncultivated."[68] However, the wild man, in that sense, was only the outer personification of the beast-like baseness that existed within even the most holy of the Church's saints, the beast-like baseness that must be overcome—if need be, by excruciating rituals of self-torment or by terrifying campaigns of violence—were the Christian saint or the Christian soldier or adventurer to attain a proper state of holiness. Should such a wild man be on the right side of the indistinct boundary separating man and beast, of course, he was not necessarily beyond the reach of Christian taming and teaching, not necessarily beyond conversion. But before his potential virtue could be released from its dark imprisonment, as Frederick Turner correctly notes, the wild man, as wild man, "must cease to exist, must either be civilized or sacrificed to civilization—which amounts to the same thing."[69]

Determining whether a particular collection of wild people, or others who differed greatly from the European ethnocentric ideal, were actually human was no easy task. We have seen how Augustine wavered on the topic. So did innumerable others. That is because the framework, the organizing principle that guided such thinking, was deliberately ambiguous. The idea of the Great Chain of Being that categorized and ranked all the earth's living creatures was born among the Greeks, but like so much else of such provenance it became central as well to medieval Christian thought. As the fifteenth-century jurist Sir John Fortescue explained, in God's perfect ordering of things

> angel is set over angel, rank upon rank in the kingdom of heaven; man is set over man, beast over beast, bird over bird, and fish over fish, on the earth in the air and in the sea: so that there is no worm that crawls upon the ground, no bird that flies on high, no fish that swims in the depths, which the chain of this order does not bind in most harmonious concord. . . . God created as many different kinds of things as he did creatures, so that there is no creature which does not differ in some respect from all other creatures and by which it is in some respect superior or inferior to all the rest. So that from the highest angel down to the lowest of his kind there is absolutely not found an angel that has not a superior and inferior; nor from man down to the meanest worm is there any creature which is not in some respect superior to one creature and inferior to another.[70]

However, within that formal "hierarchy of nature," observes Anthony Pagden,

> the highest member of one species always approaches in form to the lowest of the next. . . . There might, therefore, be, in the interstices of these interlocking categories—in what Aquinas called the "connexio rerum," "the wonderful linkage of beings"—a place for a "man" who is so close to the border with the beast, that he is no longer fully recognisable by other men as a member of the same species.[71]

Indeed, as Aquinas's thirteenth-century teacher, Albertus Magnus, put it: "nature does not make [animal] kinds separate without making something intermediate between them; for nature does not pass from extreme to extreme *nisi per medium*." Or, in theologian Nicolaus Cusanus's words:

> All things, however different, are linked together. There is in the genera of things such a connection between the higher and the lower that they meet in a common point; such an order obtains among species that the highest species of one genus coincides with the lowest of the next higher genus, in order that the universe may be one, perfect, continuous.[72]

Somewhere in these murky zones of species overlap, such European thinkers were certain, there lived creatures who may have seemed bestial, but who were humans, with souls, and who even—as, again, with St. Christopher—might become the holiest of saints if treated with Christian care. However, in that same indistinct, borderline, substratum of life, there also existed human-like creatures whose function in God's scheme of things was to be nothing more than what Aquinas called "animated instruments of service" to civilized Christian humanity. That is, slaves. And finally, there were those residents of this dark and shadowy nether realm who may have been distant descendants of the children of Adam, but whose line of ancestry had become so corrupt and degenerate that, as Hayden White puts it, "they are men who have fallen below the condition of animality itself; every man's face is turned against them, and in general (Cain is a notable exception) they can be slain with impunity."[73]

The same ambiguity existed in the European mind regarding the homeland of the wild man, the wilderness itself. Although it has become commonplace in the past few decades for writers on Western attitudes toward the environment to assert that, with almost no important exceptions, Christians traditionally have regarded nature and the wilderness in negative terms, in fact, Christianity's view of untamed landscapes has always been acutely ambivalent.[74] On the one hand, as Ulrich Mauser has shown, the Old Testament language describing the wilderness into which the ancient Jews were driven does indeed combine "the notion of confusion and destruction with the image of the barren land."[75] Even more importantly, in this same vein, adds David R. Williams, for Jews and Christians alike the wilderness

> became a symbol of emptiness at the core of human consciousness, of the profound loneliness that seemed to open like a bottomless pit underneath the vanity of each of humankind. It became the symbol of a place located in the mind, a black hole of unknowing around which orbit all the temporary illusions of human self-confidence. . . . a realm of chaos that completely surrounded and undermined the vanities of human consciousness.[76]

From this perspective, the wilderness was, in fact, nothing less than an earthly representation of Hell. However, since a true Christian properly had to undergo a time of testing and trial prior to revelation, the image of the wilderness also carried with it, conversely, the sense of a place of repentance—even a place of sanctuary. As well as the preserve of dangerous and lurking beasts, then, in addition the wilderness was "the location of refuge, trial, temptation, and ultimate victory over Satan" for the truly soul-purifying holy person.[77] Thus, the would-be Christian—saint and soldier alike—was drawn to the wilderness, the wilderness both within and without, in part precisely because it was a place of terror and temptation, and therefore of trial, and in part because it provided the only true path to salvation. In sum, the wilderness and the carnal wild man within the wilderness—like the irrepressibly sensual wild man within the self—were there to be confronted by the Christian, confronted and converted, domesticated, or destroyed.

IV

Much of Christianity's success in establishing itself as the state religion of Europe was due to the exuberant intolerance of it adherents. In a sense, the faith itself was founded on the idea of war in the spiritual realm—the titanic war of Good against Evil, God against Satan. And within the faith non-belief was equivalent to anti-belief. To tolerate skepticism regarding Christianity's central tenets, therefore, was to diminish in power the source of the belief itself. Non-believers, in sum, were seen as willing the death of the Christians' God.[78]

During the first centuries of Christianity's existence, when the religion's faithful were subject to intense persecution, Christianity often was regarded by its critics as a cult of orgiastic devil worshipers who indulged in rituals of blood-consuming infanticide and cannibalism.[79] Once in a position of power, however, Christianity turned the tables and leveled precisely the same accusations against others—first against pagans whom they regarded as witches, magicians, and idolaters, and eventually against all non-Christians. And, of those who were near at hand, few were regarded as more non-Christian than Jews.

During the Middle Ages Europe's Jews lived a precarious existence, subject to constant harassment and accusation from Christian zealots. Charges against Jews ranged from the claim that they indulged in ritual murder of Christians (allegedly using the Christian victims' blood for the preparation of matzo, for circumcision rituals, for the anointing of rabbis, and for various medicinal purposes) to the imputation that Jews were engaged in conspiracies to buy or steal consecrated Hosts, intended for use in Catholic Communion ceremonies, in order to desecrate them and thereby to torture Christ.[80] The Jews, in the meantime, had their own popular ideas about Christianity, based in large measure on their *Ma'aseh Yeshû* ("Story of Jesus") or *Tôldôt Yeshû* ("History of Jesus") dating from the late second century. Created as a defense against Christian teaching and proselytizing, this work tells the story of Jesus' illegitimate birth nine months after his mother had been seduced during her menstrual period; from there it goes on to describe the young man's life as a blasphemous sorcerer, his execution by hanging, and the theft of his body from its grave—followed by the dragging of the corpse through the streets of Jerusalem, thereby putting to the lie any notions that he had not died or that he had been bodily resurrected.[81]

By the time of the high Middle Ages, in the Hebrew chronicles recounting the Christians' persecutions of the Jews, Jesus was being described as "an abhorred offshoot, a bastard, a son of a menstruating woman, a son of lechery, a trampled corpse, their [the Christians'] detestable thing, the desecrated and detestable hanged one, the son of whoredom," and more.[82] Modern Jewish historians long have been of two minds on the recounting of these invectives, some urging their suppression from the historical record so as not to encourage anti-Semitic responses, others arguing for their full discussion as examples of the understandable rage Jews felt as the victims of violent Christian persecution.[83] Recently, however, it has been shown that the invectives' principal historical value may reside in the sense they convey, not so much of rage, but of "the efforts of the Jews to keep their group together by consolidating their defenses against the forces threatening the continued existence of a corporate Jewish identity."[84] For if the Jewish resistance to Christian conversion efforts was extraordinary— and it was—the lengths to which Jews were forced to go in order to hold their communities together is a measure of the equally extraordinary pressures they were under.

As Raul Hilberg has noted, since the beginning of Christianity's engagement with Judaism as a separate religion it has presented Jews successively with three options from which to choose: convert to Christianity, suffer expulsion, or undergo annihilation. At first, writes Hilberg, "the missionaries of Christianity had said in effect: You have no right to live among us as Jews. The secular rulers who followed had proclaimed: You have no right to live among us. The German Nazis at last decreed: You have no right to live."[85] If anything, however, Hilberg's historical encapsulation is too benign, for Jews were being massacred by Christians even before the dawn of the twelfth century.

The first great slaughter of Europe's Jews by Christians began on May 3, 1096, in the town of Speyer, Germany. There, on that date, eleven Jews who refused to accept baptism and conversion to the despised faith of Christianity were murdered. The number of deaths would have been much higher, but for the intercession of the local bishop who understood the canon law's technical restrictions against forced conversion, and who protected the remaining local Jewish population within the confines of his castle. The legalistic niceties of canon proscription were lost, then as always, on most local priests and popular preachers, however, and in a matter of days the anti-Jewish blood lust spread to the town of Worms. With the Christian authorities in Worms less willing than the bishop in Speyer had been to protect the innocent Jews from assault, Christian enthusiasts sacked the local synagogue and looted the Jews' houses. All the town's adult Jews who refused to convert, and who did not commit suicide in acts of defiance—approximately eight hundred in all—were stripped naked, murdered, and buried *en masse*. Some among the Jewish children also were murdered. The rest were carted off to be baptized and raised as Christians.[86]

The worst was yet to come. In Mainz, a city just to the north of Worms, the archbishop briefly defended the Jews, but soon fled for his own life as the Christian mobs attacked. According to Solomon bar Simson's chronicle of the events that followed, the leader of the Christians in Mainz

> showed no mercy to the aged, or youths, or maidens, babes or sucklings—not even the sick. And he made the people of the Lord like dust to be trodden underfoot, killing their young men by the sword and disemboweling their pregnant women. . . . The enemy came into the chambers, they smashed the doors, and found the Jews still writhing and rolling in blood; and the enemy took their money, stripped them naked, and slew those still alive. . . . They threw them, naked, through the windows onto the ground, creating mounds upon mounds, heaps upon heaps, until they appeared as a high mountain. . . . On a single day—the third of Sivan, the third day of the week—one thousand and one hundred holy souls were killed and slaughtered, babes and sucklings who had not sinned or transgressed, the souls of innocent poor people.[87]

And still it was not over. From Mainz the killing spread to Trier. From there it moved on to Metz, and then to Cologne, and then to Regensburg, and then to Prague. By the time the killing stopped little more than a month was gone since it had begun in the town of Speyer, and as many as eight thousand Jews lay dead.[88]

It was not coincidence that the massacres of May and June 1096 occurred at the same time that the First Crusade of Pope Urban II was just getting under way. For the mass murderers of the Jews in Speyer and Worms and Mainz and Metz and Cologne and Regensburg and Prague were errant bands of Christian soldiers who had wandered from the overlong trail to Jerusalem, under the leadership of such pervervid souls as Peter the Hermit and Count Emicho of Leiningen, to search out and destroy heretical victims who were closer to home than were the Saracens of the Holy Land. Those Crusaders who fulfilled the charge to march all the way to Jerusalem, however, were no less faithful to the impulse of Christian blood lust.

The very earliest Christian leaders had been of differing minds on the matter of warfare in general, having themselves suffered from military oppression under Roman rule. Thus, the influential Church father Origen was outspokenly opposed to war, while other Christians were members of Marcus Aurelius' "thundering legion"; similarly, the New Testament contains passages that have been interpreted as supporting any number of positions on the matter, from pacifism to warlike zealotry.[89] The Old Testament, however, is unremitting: "And when the Lord thy God shall deliver [thy enemies] before thee," says Deuteronomy 7:2, 16, "though shalt smite them, and utterly destroy them; thou shalt make no covenant with them, nor shew mercy unto them. . . . Thou shalt consume all the people which the Lord thy God shall deliver thee; thine eye shall have no pity upon them." And later, in Deuteronomy 20:16–17 (the passage noted earlier that was cited so gleefully by Puritan John Mason as justification for the extermination of Indians): "Of the cities . . . which the Lord thy God doth give thee for an inheritance, thou shalt save alive nothing that breatheth. . . . But thou shalt utterly destroy them." This was "war commanded by God," writes James Turner Johnson, "a form of holy war. In such war not only was God conceived as commanding the conflict, but he was understood to be directly involved in the fighting, warring with the divinities of the enemy on the cosmic level even as the soldiers of Israel dealt with their human counterparts on the earthly level."[90]

When Augustine came to pronounce on these matters he uttered some words warning of excess in the violence one was properly to bring to bear on one's enemies, but his overall pronouncements were strongly in support of divinely inspired wrack and ruin. As Frederick H. Russell summarizes Augustine's views:

> Any violations of God's laws, and by easy extension, any violation of Christian doctrine, could be seen as an injustice warranting unlimited violent punishment. Further, the . . . guilt of the enemy merited punishment of the enemy population without regard to the distinction between soldiers and civilians. Motivated by righteous wrath, the just warriors could kill with impunity even those who were morally innocent.[91]

Following Augustine, the Church enthusiastically came to accept the idea of "just war," and from that developed the concept of "mission war" or Holy War—an idea similar in certain respects to the Islamic jihad.[92] This evolution of belief took on great importance during the last years of the eleventh century, when Europe was awash in disaster—flood, pestilence, drought, and famine—and had unemployed standing armies on hand in most countries, living off the peasantry. Belief in the Second Coming's imminence was encouraged by the turmoil in the land, and it was hardly diminished by a shower of comets—a clear sign from God—that appeared overhead in April of 1095. Before Christ could return, however, the Holy Land had to be liberated by the Christian faithful. Thus it was—or at least such was the rationale—that three years after the marauding Christian troops had laid waste the Jewish citizenry of Speyer and the other European towns and cities that lay in their path, Pope Urban's warriors for Christ found themselves surrounding Jerusalem, the Holy City.

Preparatory to their assault the soldiers of the Lord underwent a sequence of penitential rituals that later became routine procedure for crusading Christian armies. In the manner of the ascetics they fasted for three days, they confessed their sins, they received communion; and then they marched barefoot around the walls of the city, chanting psalms, some of them carrying crosses and relics, in abasement before the greater glory of God.[93] From within the city the commander of the Muslim garrison watched the Christians in astonishment—but with more astonishment still when they suddenly began hurling themselves against Jerusalem's walls "like madmen, without carrying a single ladder."[94] "Regardless of age or condition," wrote the Archbishop of Tyre regarding the Muslims and Jews whom the Christians destroyed upon entering Jerusalem,

> they laid low, without distinction, every enemy encountered. Everywhere was frightful carnage, everywhere lay heaps of severed heads, so that soon it was impossible to pass or to go from one place to another except over the bodies of the slain. . . . It was impossible to look upon the vast numbers of the slain without horror; everywhere lay fragments of human bodies, and the very ground was covered with the blood of the slain. It was not alone the spectacle of headless bodies and mutilated limbs strewn in all directions that roused the horror of all who looked upon them. Still more dreadful was it to gaze upon the victors themselves, dripping with blood from head to foot, an ominous sight which brought terror to all who met them. It is reported that within the Temple enclosure alone about ten thousand infidels perished.[95]

Other eyewitness accounts of the sacking of the Holy City were equally gruesome. "Piles of heads, hands, and feet were to be seen in the streets of the city," wrote the anonymous author of the *Gesta Francorum:* among other "wonderful sights" that testified to God's divine glory, said this observer, was the fact that the conquering Christians had "to pick [their] way over the bodies of men and horses" all throughout Jerusalem, while at the Temple of Solomon "men rode in blood up to their knees and bridle reins." Jews who had taken refuge in the city's synagogue were burned alive. Thousands of Muslims were chopped to death in al-Aqsa mosque. The old and the sick were the first among the infidels to meet their proper end, their bodies slashed open in search of gold coins they might have swallowed—for the Pope had decreed that any spoils of war were possessions the Christians could keep. Finally, the few living victims of the Cru-

saders' wrath were forced to drag the decomposing bodies of their countrymen beyond the gates of the city and to stack them into enormous funeral
pyres to inhibit the spread of disease. But not before the bodies were mutilated: "a whole cargo of noses and thumbs sliced from the Saracens"
was shipped home, writes religious historian Roland Bainton.[96] Once again,
Her Holy Mother the Church was triumphant, as she would be, repeatedly, for many great and grisly years to come.

But not always. Sometimes there were defeats. Never, however, were
defeats unexplainable: those crusaders who were beaten had failed because
they had sinned—and the sins they had committed invariably were sins of
pride and especially sins of carnality. God was on the Christians' side *unless* they succumbed to temptation. Example after example, the medieval
chronicles claimed, showed this to be so. From the Hungarian defeat of
Peter the Hermit's disciple Gottschalk to the failures of the Christians at
Antioch, "the lesson was plain," observes one historian: "the crusaders
were assured of victory in this life and salvation in the next, but only so
long as they avoided carnal sins."[97]

Because of this, women—including wives—constantly were driven from
the Crusaders' military encampments. And also because of this chaste ideal,
the Crusaders' non-Christian enemies were portrayed as lustful and licen-
tious beasts: the infidel males were said to be rapists who were "addicted
to lurid forms of sexual debauchery and [had] a special lust for the charms
of virtuous Christian women," while non-Christian women were viewed
as defiled and wanton whores and seductresses. Sexual contact between a
Christian crusader and a native woman was said to cause "an enormous
stench to rise to heaven," and the penalty for such transgressions was castration for the Crusader and facial mutilation for the woman. If they had
to have contact with a tainted native female, far better that it be of the
sort sardonically described by Fulcher of Chartres at the battles of Antioch
where the Christians "did no other harm to the women they found in [the
enemy's] tents—save that they ran their lances through their bellies."[98]

Such Christian ferocity was only to be expected, of course, since the
Muslims and Jews who refused to convert to Christianity were displaying
with their spiritual recalcitrance and their stubbornly non-Christian attitudes (including their offensively non-ascetic behavior regarding sex) an
anti-Christian pattern of behavior. As such they were viewed as effectively
at war with Christianity—that is, as engaged in a conspiracy with Antichrist to destroy everything that Christ and Christianity represented. Such
infidels thus became, in the popular Christian image, "demons in human
form," as Norman Cohn has put it, to whom were "attributed every quality which belonged to the Beast from the Abyss. . . . And the Saints knew
that it was their task to wipe that foul black host off the face of the earth,
for only an earth which had been so purified would be fit to carry the New
Jerusalem, the shining Kingdom of the Saints."[99]

If not wiped from the face of the earth, such foul hosts could, as an alternative, be enslaved. Slavery, of course, was an ancient tradition in the West. While no reliable figures exist regarding the number of slaves who were held throughout all of ancient Greece, there were as many as 100,000 slaves laboring in Athens during the fourth and fifth centuries B.C., or at least three or four slaves for each free household. This is a proportion of the population much larger than that of the slave states in America on the eve of the Civil War.[100] The practice continued in Rome, where slaves— who under Roman law were non-persons—were inspected and auctioned off in public marketplaces. During the late first and early second centuries A.D., between a third and nearly half the population of Italy were slaves. It has been estimated that in order to maintain the slave population at a stable level throughout the empire during this time—a level of 10,000,000 slaves in a total imperial population of about 50,000,000—more than 500,000 new slaves had to be added to the population every year.[101]

In the fourth century the first Christian emperor, Constantine, decreed that "anyone who picks up and nourishes at his own expense a little boy or girl cast out of the home of its father or lord with the latter's knowledge and consent may retain the child in the position for which he intended it when he took it in—that is, as child or slave, as he prefers." In view of the enormous numbers of children who were being abandoned by their parents in this era, Constantine's edict assured that there would be a vast supply of young slaves for owners to hire out as prostitutes and laborers, which they commonly did.[102] And when, in the eleventh century, England's William the Conqueror commissioned the famous Domesday Book, the most extensive population survey and analysis conducted during medieval times, it was determined that approximately one out of every ten citizens of Britain was a slave whose life was totally under the control of his or her owner. "Legally no more than chattel goods," writes David Brion Davis, "these people could apparently be killed by their owners without penalty."[103]

During the twelfth and thirteenth centuries slavery began to decline in northern Europe, but it persisted in the Continent's southern countries. The labor shortage that followed in the aftermath of the Black Death created a new boom in slavery throughout the Mediterranean world, but this time it was a boom in imported slaves, mostly Turks, Bulgarians, Armenians, Tatars, and Africans, because at the same time that the market for slaves was opening up, the Church—which always had supported the general principle of slavery—was beginning to impose more rigorous restrictions on the enslavement of persons who had been born as Christians. Italian, Spanish, and Portuguese cities thus became huge slave markets, dealing largely in chattel of infidel ancestry. As Davis points out, "between 1414 and 1423 no fewer than ten thousand bondsmen (mostly bondswomen) were sold in Venice alone."[104] And in Lisbon, in 1551, 10 percent of its 100,000 people were slaves, mostly Africans, Moors who had been captured in wars and raids, and a somewhat smaller percentage of Turks.[105] Indeed, writes John Boswell, "actual slavery (as opposed to feudal servitude or indenturing) became more common in the later Middle Ages than it had been at any time after the fall of Rome."[106]

"The Mediterranean, central to the development of human civilization and lovingly celebrated in Euro-American historiography," observes Orlando Patterson, "from the viewpoint of human oppression has been a veritable vortex of horror for all mankind, especially for the Slavic and African peoples." During the fifteenth century its waters were filled with sailing ships carrying legal and illegal loads of slaves from foreign lands, sometimes a few dozen in a single shipment, sometimes four hundred and more. "Cargoes of two hundred slaves at a time were not exceptional," Charles Verlinden once noted, adding elsewhere that many of these ships were "floating tombs . . . . [where] available space was quite restricted and epidemics rampant," and where death rates of 30 percent and more were not uncommon. But even for those foreign captives who survived the seaborne ordeal, there was little that could be looked forward to with optimism, for "in medieval Italy," writes Davis, "slaves were tortured by magistrates and whipped without restraint by masters; in Siena a man who damaged another's slave paid the same fine as if he had damaged a cow."[107]

Throughout the Middle Ages, then, war against the infidel in the holy land was a virtually perpetual Christian endeavor, while within Europe tens of thousands of captured Muslim men, women, and children were held as chattel—and Jews lived in a near-permanent state of crisis. Even otherwise innocuous Catholic theatrical productions in Europe's city streets commonly portrayed Jews as demons assisting Antichrist in his attempted destruction of Christianity. During and immediately after such performances the life of any Jew not safely under lock and key was in serious jeopardy. For the same reason, the slightest changes in fortune for the Christian community could result in violent assault on Jewish scapegoats, while major changes in fortune might lead the entire local Jewish population to the brink of extermination by simultaneously enraged and terrified self-styled Christian Soldiers—as indeed happened in the wake of the colossal Black Death epidemic of the mid-fourteenth century.

As early as 1215, in fact—more than a century before the Black Death burst upon the Continent—a papal directive was issued requiring both Muslims and Jews to wear distinctive attire. This was done in large measure to inhibit potential sexual liaisons between them and Christians. Punishment for such affairs ranged from public whipping while naked to burning at the stake. Buffeted about and expelled from various European countries, including England and France, throughout the Middle Ages, Jews living in Spain were tolerated—if barely—even in the years immediately following the Black Death, primarily because of their contributions to the economy. But popular preachers were relentless in their anti-Jewish propaganda and finally, in 1391, Christian hatred and rage exploded in riots that swept across Aragon, Catalonia, and Castile. Many Jews were murdered, their identification made easy by the brightly colored "badges of shame" that all Jews above the age of ten had been forced to display prominently on their outer clothing since the early part of the fourteenth century. Many others converted, simply to save their lives and those of their children. By the time the violence died down, of the Jews who remained in Spain as many may have converted to Christianity and become what were called *conversos* or *marranos* as remained outwardly true to their Jewish faith.[108]

Anti-Jewish sentiment remained high among the Spanish, erupting from time to time in further riots and persecutions. At such times all the ancient charges were hauled out, as in 1460, with the publication of the Franciscan Alonso de Espina's four-volume *Fortalitium Fidei,* or Fortress of the Faith. According to Espina, both Jews and most *marranos* (who in actuality, he said, remained "secret" Jews or "crypto" Jews) were guilty of stealing consecrated Hosts for profane rituals, of kidnapping and killing Christian children for their blood, and so on. Gradually, however, and quietly, more and more ostensibly converted Jews began returning to the ancestral fold. This disturbed not only the Catholic hierarchy and populace (whose feared sense of deception and treachery in their midst was thus vindicated, they thought), but it also troubled many *marranos,* because revelations of false conversions among others endangered the credibility of their own proclaimed loyalty to the Church—thereby putting their attained post-conversion social and economic positions at risk.

It was, then, not to persecute faithful Jews, but rather to investigate the *marranos* for possible falsity in their commitment to Christ that the Inquisition was instituted in Castile in 1483, finally spreading to Barcelona in 1487. Although some *marranos* who were true converts supported the Inquisition, all *marranos* now fell under suspicion. As a result, they were barred from holding various public and private offices, from attending universities, or from serving in Tomás de Torquemada's heretic burning "Militia of Christ," while those of their number who were physicians routinely were accused of secretly killing their Christian patients.[109]

Under the agony of the rack and other ingenious methods of torture many *marranos* confessed to being crypto-Jews and to performing the heinous acts the Church attributed to them. One case can serve as emblematic of hundreds. For a year, from December of 1490 to November of 1491, six Jews and five *marranos* were tried for using black magic in an effort to stop the Inquisition and eventually to destroy all Christians. The charge—as it was reported at the trial and circulated in different versions for decades in Spain—claimed that the accused Jews and *marranos* had kidnapped a Catholic child (named Christobalico) and forced him to drag a heavy cross up a hill and into a cave. There he supposedly received 6200 lashes, had a crown of thorns placed on his head, and was nailed to the cross he had carried. After reciting various curses mocking Christ—some of which (such as that Christ was "the bastard son of a perverse and adulterous woman") came straight from the *Tôldôt Yeshû*, discussed earlier— the child's heart allegedly was torn from his chest and was used, along with a stolen consecrated Host, to cast an evil spell on the inquisitors and on Christianity in general. All the accused, of course, were found guilty and were burned at the stake. Immediately, the place where Christobalico was said to be buried became a shrine that for years to come was visited by thousands of pilgrims, including such royalty as Charles V and Philip II.[110]

V

To most Europeans, as the fifteenth century was heading into its final decade, the world was not safe for the saintly so long as infidels remained camped at Christendom's gates, while Jews who refused to accept Christ remained a cancerous threat from within the autocratic body politic of the Church. Both groups were hated and spurned and persecuted by Christians because they were defined categorically as enemies of the faith and often were identified with Antichrist.

Still, neither Muslims nor Jews were unsalvageable. The Muslims inhabited the ancient cities of the Holy Land. In Europe they were famed for the culture, art, and architecture they had created in Toledo, Córdoba, and Seville. And the Jews were an ancient people, the very stock from which Christianity was born. They also were urban people and an integral part of European society. That is, both Jews and Muslims were human; they were "civilized"; their main offenses in Christian eyes were religious and cultural. And however craftily resistant they may have been to Christian proselytizing, they were *capable* of conversion. No doubt, on many occasions, individual packs of Christian zealots had been seized with sufficient blood lust that they would have exterminated every Jew or every Muslim had they only been given the chance. But for all its savage ferocity, Christian ideology did not encourage campaigns of extinction against human creatures who had souls that might be saved.

Important changes were in the air, however, even as Columbus was tramping about in search of someone to underwrite his voyage to Cathay—changes in the religious province of ideas as well as in the more mundane worlds of politics and money. These changes will be examined briefly here, and more extensively in the chapter to follow, because it is the particular conditions of a given time and place that bring on events of historical consequence. Of course, an exclusive focus on such particularities invariably results in historical nearsightedness and thus leads to superficial, contextless explanations. But the reverse is also true: examining only long-term and deeply imbedded cultural themes, as we have largely done thus far, places the burden of historical explanation solely on evolved collective consciousness, and collective consciousness by itself cannot explain why individual events occurred when and where they did. Moreover, certain of the institutions of Christian culture and society that we have canvassed here—slave-holding, for instance—were not unique to the European or the Christian world. For such individual social practices or cultural habits to become implicated in the emergence of specific historical events, the essential substance of the phenomena—in the case of slavery, the objectification and dehumanization of people—must fuse with other complementary social and cultural traits, and be activated and directed by events.

For an example of this we can turn to the matter with which the first part of this chapter concluded, the problem of explaining the Jewish Holocaust. Here we noted that Elie Wiesel has said that a key to that explanation is the fact that "all the killers were Christian," and that the Holocaust "did not arise in a void but had its roots deep in a tradition that prophesied it, prepared for it, and brought it to maturity." This no doubt is correct. Indeed, the characteristics of Christian tradition delineated in the immediately preceding pages that, we shall see, prophesied, prepared for, and brought to maturity a frame of mind that would allow to take place the genocide that was carried out against the native peoples of the Americas were in many cases the same religio-cultural traits that buttressed justifications for the Holocaust.

However, as Arno J. Mayer recently has shown, it was certain specific conditions and certain specific events—in addition to the larger historical context of Christian anti-Semitism—that triggered the actual mobilization of the "Final Solution" in twentieth-century Germany. By itself, Mayer points out, Christianity's age-old and collectively conscious "Judeophobia" was not sufficient to bring on the Nazi "Judeocide." Rather, he demonstrates, during the first few decades of the twentieth century "there was a constant interplay of ideology and contingency in which both played their respective but also partially indeterminate roles. Above all, this raging fusion of ideas and circumstances which produced the Judeocide was part of a single, larger historical confluence." The major elements in that confluence, Mayer believes, derived from the several decades of "cataclysmic upheaval" in Europe that preceded and enveloped the outbreak of the Second World War, combined with specific crises that erupted within Germany when war in the east—a "crusade," Mayer calls it, that was waged with "pseudoreligious furor"—began going badly.[111]

The historical backdrop of intense and ancient European anti-Semitism is, of course, an essential (if by itself insufficient) element in explaining the Nazi Judeocide, and of particular importance in that regard is the distinctly racial turn anti-Semitism began taking late in the nineteenth century. Further, as Stephan L. Chorover has shown, the Final Solution ideology that led to the destruction of two-thirds of Europe's Jews was itself "a logical extension of sociobiological ideas and eugenics doctrines which had nothing specifically to do with Jews and which flourished widely in Germany well before the era of the Third Reich." Indeed, drawing on a perverse interpretation of Darwinian theory, in 1933 the architects of the Nazi legal system devised and enacted a compulsory sterilization law—in the interests of "racial hygiene"—for individuals afflicted with genetic defects, and by the decade's end the wholesale killing of psychiatric patients, regardless of religion or ethnicity, had begun. These were people officially referred to by the Nazi regime as "life devoid of value," or as "useless eaters," and by the time the killing had ended at least 275,000 of them had been exterminated.[112]

Certainly there was much more than this to the engine of holocaust that thundered across Europe in the early 1940s. As Richard L. Rubenstein has argued, for instance, the combination of bureaucratic domination of German social thought and the Nazis' perception of excess and superfluous (and thus expendable) populations within their midst is a critical factor in accounting for Auschwitz and Birkenau.[113] But the point here is simply to show that explaining the Jewish Holocaust, to the extent that such monstrosities can ever adequately be explained, requires the understanding of an intertwined complex of phenomena—an understanding, at the very least, of the deep historical tradition of Christianity's persecution of Jews, of the modern evolution of "racial" anti-Semitism, of the Nazi eugenicists' attitudes toward non-Jewish "life devoid of value," and of specific political, economic, and military events that occurred during the early 1940s.

The same sort of multi-level historical, cultural, political, economic, and military exploration is necessary if we are to begin to understand the four centuries of genocide that took place in the Americas. For while specific parallels are crude at best, the final years of the fifteenth century in Europe were marked by a dynamism of ideas and circumstances involving religious, social, economic, and military backgrounds—and contemporary upheaval—that, while very different in content, cannot help but resonate disturbingly among readers familiar with the more horrendous and genocidal aspects of twentieth century history.

From the moment of its birth Christianity had envisioned the end of the world. Saints and theologians differed on many details about the end, but few disagreements were as intense as those concerned with the nature and timing of the events involved. There were those who believed that as the end drew near conditions on earth would grow progressively dire, evil would increase, love would diminish, the final tribulations would be unleashed—and then suddenly the Son of Man would appear: he would over-come Satan, judge mankind, and bring an end to history. Others had what is generally thought to be a more optimistic view: before reaching the final grand conclusion, they claimed, there would be a long reign of peace, jus-tice, abundance, and bliss; the Jews would be converted, while the heath-ens would be either converted or annihilated; and, in certain versions of the prophecy, this Messianic Age of Gold would be ushered in by a Last World Emperor—a human saviour—who would prepare the way for the final cataclysmic but glorious struggle between Good and Evil, whereupon history would end with the triumphant Second Coming.

Among the innumerable forecasters of the end of time who adopted a variation that combined elements of both versions of the prophecy was the twelfth-century Calabrian abbot Joachim of Fiore. Joachim's ideas became much more influential than most, however, largely because they were adopted and transmitted by the Spiritual branch of the Church's Francis-can Order during the thirteenth through the fifteenth century. He and his followers made calculations from evidence contained in Scriptural texts, calculations purporting to show that the sequence of events leading to the end of time would soon be—or perhaps already was—appearing. As word of these predictions spread, the most fundamental affairs of both Church and state were affected. And there had been no previous time in human history when ideas were able to circulate further or more rapidly, for it was in the late 1430s that Johann Gutenberg developed the technique of printing with movable type cast in molds. It has been estimated that as many as 20 million books—and an incalculable number of pamphlets and tracts—were produced and distributed in Europe between just 1450 and 1500.[114]

The fifteenth century in Italy was especially marked by presentiments that the end was near, as Marjorie Reeves has shown in exhaustive detail, with "general anxiety . . . building up to a peak in the 1480s and 1490s." Since at least the middle of the century, the streets of Florence, Rome, Milan, Siena, and other Italian cities—including Genoa, where Columbus was born and spent his youth—had been filled with wandering prophets, while popular tracts were being published and distributed by the tens of thousands, and "astrological prognostications were sweeping" the coun-try. "The significant point to grasp," Reeves demonstrates, "is that we are not dealing here with two opposed viewpoints or groups—optimistic hu-manists hailing the Age of Gold on the one hand, and medieval-style prophets and astrologers proclaiming 'Woe!' on the other." Rather, "foreboding and great hope lived side by side in the same people. . . . Thus the Jo-achimist marriage of woe and exaltation exactly fitted the mood of late fifteenth-century Italy, where the concept of a humanist Age of Gold had to be brought into relation with the ingrained expectation of Anti-christ."[115]

The political implications of this escalating fever of both disquietude and anticipation grew out of the fact that Joachim and those who were popularizing his ideas placed the final struggle between ultimate good and ultimate evil *after* the blissful Golden Age. Thus, "Joachim's central message remained his affirmation of a real—though incomplete—achievement of peace and beatitude *within* history," a belief that, in the minds of many, "was quickly vulgarized into dreams of world-wide empire."[116] Different European nations and their leaders, naturally, tried to claim this mantle—and with it the title of Messiah-Emperor—as their own. But a prominent follower of Joachim in the thirteenth and early fourteenth century, Arnold of Villanova, had prophesied that the man who would lead humanity to its glorious new day would come from Spain. As we shall see, Columbus knew of this prophecy (though he misidentified it with Joachim himself) and spoke and wrote of it, but he was not alone; for, in the words of Leonard I. Sweet, as the fifteenth century was drawing to a close the Joachimite scheme regarding the end of time "burst the bounds of Franciscan piety to submerge Spanish society in a messianic milieu."[117]

To a stranger visiting Europe during these years, optimism would seem the most improbable of attitudes. For quite some time the war with the infidel had been going rather badly; indeed, as one historian has remarked: "as late as 1490 it would have seemed that in the eight-centuries-old struggle between the Cross and the Crescent, the latter was on its way to final triumph. The future seemed to lie not with Christ but with the Prophet."[118] At the end of the thirteenth century Jaffa and Antioch and Tripoli and Acre, the last of the Christian strongholds in the Holy Land, had fallen to the Muslims, and in 1453 Constantinople had been taken by Sultan Muhammed II. Despite all the rivers of blood that had been shed since the days of the first Crusade, the influence of Christianity at this moment in time was confined once again to the restricted boundaries of Europe. And within those boundaries things were not going well, either.

Since the late fourteenth century, when John Wyclif and his followers in England had publicly attacked the Church's doctrine of transubstantiation and claimed that all godly authority resided in the Scriptures and not to any degree in the good offices of the Church, the rumblings of reformation had been evident. In the fifteenth century the criticism continued, from a variety of directions and on a variety of matters. On one side, for instance, there was John Huss, an advocate of some of Wyclif's views and a critic of papal infallibility and the practice of granting indulgences. For his troubles, in 1415 Huss was burned at the stake—after the Inquisitors first stripped him of his vestments, cut the shape of a cross in his hair, and placed on his head a conical paper hat painted with pictures of devils—following which war broke out between Hussites and Catholics, war in which politics and religion were inextricably intertwined, and war that continued throughout most of the fifteenth century.[119] From another direction criticism of the Church was emerging among Renaissance humanists such as Lorenzo Valla, who proved that the Donation of Constantine—an eighth-century document that granted great temporal powers to the papacy—was a forgery, and who, in the mid-fifteenth century, attacked both monasticism and chastity as ideals.

The papacy itself, meanwhile, recently had suffered through forty years of the so-called Great Schism, during which time there were two and even three rival claimants as Pope of the Roman Catholic Church. After the schism was ended at the Council of Constance in 1418, for the rest of the century the papacy's behavior and enduring legacy continued to be one of enormous extravagance and moral corruption. As many of the late Middle Ages' "most pious minds" long had feared, observes the great historian of the Inquisition, Henry Charles Lea, "Christianity was practically a failure. . . . The Church, instead of elevating man, had been dragged down to his level." [120] This, of course, only further fanned the hot embers of reformation which would burst into flame during the first decades of the century to follow.

On the level of everyday life, we saw in an earlier chapter the atrocious conditions under which most of the peoples of Europe were forced to live as the late Middle Ages crept forward. It was only a hundred years before Columbus's mid-fifteenth-century birth that the Black Death had shattered European society along with enormous masses of its population. Within short order millions had died—about one out of every three people across the entirety of Europe was killed by the pandemic—and recovery was achieved only with excruciating slowness. "Those few discreet folk who remained alive," recalled the Florentine historian Matteo Villani, "expected many things":

> They believed that those whom God's grace had saved from death, having beheld the destruction of their neighbours . . . would become better conditioned, humble, virtuous and Catholic; that they would guard themselves from iniquity and sin and would be full of love and charity towards one another. But no sooner had the plague ceased than we saw the contrary. . . . [People] gave themselves up to a more shameful and disordered life than they had led before. . . . Men thought that, by reason of the fewness of mankind, there should be abundance of all produce of the land; yet, on the contrary, by reason of men's ingratitude, everything came to unwonted scarcity and remained long thus; nay, in certain countries . . . there were grievous and unwonted famines. Again, men dreamed of wealth and abundance in garments . . . yet, in fact, things turned out widely different, for most commodities were more costly, by twice or more, than before the plague. And the price of labour and the work of all trades and crafts, rose in disorderly fashion beyond the double. Lawsuits and disputes and quarrels and riots rose elsewhere among citizens in every land.[121]

Modern historical analysis has, in general terms, confirmed Villani's description, with one important difference: it was far too sanguine. For example, although wages did increase in the century immediately following the explosion of the plague in the middle of the fourteenth century, after that time they spiraled drastically downward. The real wages of a typical English carpenter serve as a vivid point of illustration: between 1350 and 1450 his pay increased by about 64 percent; then his wages started falling precipitously throughout the entirety of the next two centuries, at last bottoming out at approximately half of what they had been at the outbreak of the plague in 1348, fully three centuries earlier. Meanwhile, during this same period, prices of foodstuffs and other commodities were soaring *upward* at an equivalent rate and more, ultimately achieving a 500 percent overall increase during the sixteenth century.[122]

The combination of simultaneously collapsing wages and escalating prices in an already devastated social environment was bad enough for an English carpenter, but English carpenters were by no means poorly off compared with other laborers in Europe—and other laborers were positively well off compared with the starving multitudes who had no work at all. At the same time that the Black Death was wiping out a third of Europe's population, and bouts of famine were destroying many thousands more with each incident, the Hundred Years War was raging; it began in 1337 and did not end until 1453. And while the war was on, marauding bands of discharged soldiers turned brigands and highwaymen—aptly named *écorcheurs* or "flayers"—were raping and pillaging the countryside. Finally, the requirements of a war economy forced governments to increase taxes. Immanuel Wallerstein explains how it all added up:

> The taxes, coming on top of already heavy feudal dues, were too much for the producers, creating a liquidity crisis which in turn led to a return to indirect taxes and taxes in kind. Thus started a downward cycle: The fiscal burden led to a reduction in consumption which led to a reduction in production and money circulation which increased further the liquidity difficulties which led to royal borrowing and eventually the insolvency of the limited royal treasuries, which in turn created a credit crisis, leading to hoarding of bullion, which in turn upset the pattern of international trade. A rapid rise in prices occurred, further reducing the margin of subsistence, and this began to take its toll in population.[123]

In sum, all the while that the popes and other elites were indulging themselves in profligacy and decadence, the basic political and economic frameworks of Europe—to say nothing of the entire social order—were in a state of near collapse. Certain states, of course, were worse off than others, and there are various ways in which such comparative misery can be assayed. One measure that we shall soon see has particular relevance for what happened in the aftermath of Columbus's voyages to the New World, is the balance and nature of intra-European trade. In England and northwestern Europe generally, legislative and other efforts during this time discouraged the export of raw materials, such as wool in the case of England, and encouraged the export of manufactured goods. Thus, by the close of the fifteenth century, Britain was exporting 50,000 bolts of cloth annually, rising to more than two and a half times that figure within the next five decades. Spain and Portugal, at the same time, remained exporters of raw materials (wool, iron ore, salt, oil, and other items) and importers of textiles, hardwares, and other manufactured products. The Iberian nations, with their backward and inflexible economic systems, were rapidly becoming economic dependencies of the expanding—if themselves still impoverished—early capitalist states of northwest Europe.[124]

This, then, was the Old World on the eve of Columbus's departure in 1492. For almost half a millennium Christians had been launching hideously destructive holy wars and massive enslavement campaigns against external enemies they viewed as carnal demons and described as infidels— all in an effort to recapture the Holy Land, and all of which, it now seemed to many, effectively had come to naught. During those same long centuries they had further expressed their ruthless intolerance of all persons and things that were non-Christian by conducting pogroms against the Jews who lived among them and whom they regarded as the embodiment of Antichrist—imposing torture, exile, and mass destruction on those who refused to succumb to evangelical persuasion. These great efforts, too, appeared to have largely failed. Hundreds of thousands of openly practicing Jews remained in the Europeans' midst, and even those who had converted were suspected of being the Devil's agents and spies, treacherously boring from within.

Dominated by a theocratic culture and world view that for a thousand years and more had been obsessed with things sensual and sexual, and had demonstrated its obsession in the only way its priesthood permitted—by intense and violent sensual and sexual repression and "purification"—the religious mood of Christendom's people at this moment was near the boiling point. At its head the Church was mired in corruption, while the ranks below were dispirited and increasingly disillusioned. These are the sorts of conditions that, given the proper spark, lend themselves to what anthropologists and historians describe as "millenarian" rebellion and upheaval, or "revitalization movements."[125] In point of fact, this historical moment, seen in retrospect, was the inception of the Reformation, which means that it truly was nothing less than the eve of a massive revolution. And when finally that revolution did explode, Catholic would kill Protestant and Protestant would kill Catholic with the same zeal and ferocity that their common Christian ancestors had reserved for Muslims and Jews.

"Don't let them live any longer, the evil-doers who turn us away from

God," the Protestant radical Thomas Muntzer soon would be crying to his followers. "For a godless man"—he was referring to Catholics—"has no right to live if he hinders the godly. . . . The sword is necessary to exterminate them. . . . If they resist, let them be slaughtered without mercy."[126] And, again and again, that is precisely what happened: Catholics were indeed slaughtered without mercy. The Church, of course, was more than eager to return such compliments, in deed as well as in word. Thus, for instance, Catholic vengeance against Calvinists in sixteenth-century France resulted in the killing of thousands. Infants were stabbed to death, women had their hands cut off to remove gold bracelets, publishers of "heretical" works were burned to death atop bonfires made from their books. The treatment of Gaspard de Coligny, a Protestant leader, was not atypical: after murdering him, the Catholic mob mutilated his body, "cutting off his head, his hands, and his genitals—and then dragged it through the streets, set fire to it, and dumped it in the river. . . . [B]ut then, deciding that it was not worthy of being food for the fish, they hauled it out again . . . [and] dragged what was left of the body to the gallows of Montfaucon, 'to be meat and carrion for maggots and crows.' "[127] Such furious rage continued well into the seventeenth century, as, for example, in the Catholic sacking of the Protestant city of Magdeburg, when at least 30,000 Protestants were slain: "In a single church fifty-three women were found beheaded," reported Friedrich Schiller, while elsewhere babies were stabbed and thrown into fires. "Horrible and revolting to humanity was the scene that presented itself," Schiller wrote, "the living crawling from under the dead, children wandering about with heart-rending cries, calling for their parents; and infants still sucking the breasts of their lifeless mothers."[128]

And this was Christian against Christian. European against European. "Civilized" against "civilized." There were, all Europeans knew, "wild" races, carnal and un-Christian and uncivilized, who lived in as-yet unexplored lands on the far distant margins of the earth. Some of them were beasts, some of them were human, and some of them hovered in the darkness in between. One day—perhaps one day soon—they would be encountered, and important decisions would then have to be made. If they possessed souls, if they were capable of understanding and embracing the holy faith, every effort would be made to convert them—just as every effort had always been made to convert Muslims and Jews. If they proved incapable of conversion, if they had no souls—if they were, that is, children of the Devil—they would be slain. God demanded as much.

For this era in the history of Christian Europe appeared to many to be the threshold of the end of time. Three of the Four Horsemen of the Apocalypse clearly were loose in the land: the rider on the red horse, who is war; the rider on the black horse, who is famine; and the rider on the pale horse, who is death. Only the rider on the white horse—who in most interpretations of the biblical allegory is Christ—had not yet made his presence known. And, although the signs were everywhere that the time of his return was not far off, it remained his godly children's responsibility to prepare the way for him.

Before Christ would return, all Christians knew, the gospel had to be spread throughout the entire world, and the entire world was not yet known. Spreading the gospel throughout the world meant acceptance of its message by all the world's people, once they had been located—and that in turn meant the total conversion or extermination of all non-Christians. It also meant the liberation of Zion, symbol of the Holy Land, and it likely meant the discovery of the earthly paradise as well.

Christopher Columbus knew all these things. Indeed, as we soon shall see, he was obsessed by them. In her own way, Isabella, the queen of Spain, shared his grandiose vision and his obsession. Still, in his first approach to the Spanish court in 1486, seeking support for his planned venture, he had been rebuffed. It was, in retrospect, understandable. Spain was at that moment engaged intensely in its war with the Moors in Granada. The Crown was impoverished. And Columbus offered a far from secure investment. Five years later, however, the king and queen relented. The reason for their change of heart in 1491 has never been made entirely clear, but Isabella's unquenchable thirst for victory over Islam almost certainly was part of the equation. "A successful voyage would bring Spain into contact with the nations of the East, whose help was needed in the struggle with the Turk," writes J.H. Elliott. "It might also, with luck, bring back Columbus by way of Jerusalem, opening up a route for attacking the Ottoman Empire in the rear. Isabella was naturally attracted, too, by the possibility of laying the foundations of a great Christian mission in the East. In the climate of intense religious excitement which characterized the last months of the Grenada campaign even the wildest projects suddenly seemed possible of accomplishment."[129]

And then, on January 2, 1492, the Muslims who controlled Granada surrendered. The first real victory of Christian over infidel in a very long time, clearly it was a sign that God looked favorably upon the decision to fund the enterprise of the man whose given name meant "Christ-bearer." On March 30th of that year the Jews of Spain were allowed four months to convert to Catholicism or suffer expulsion—an ultimatum the Moors also would be presented with before the following decade had ended. And on April 30th, one month later, a royal decree was issued suspending all judicial proceedings against any criminals who would agree to ship out with Columbus, because, the document stated, "it is said that it is necessary to grant safe-conduct to the persons who might join him, since under no other conditions would they be willing to sail with him on the said voyage."[130] With the exception of four men wanted for murder, no known felons accepted the offer. From what historians have been able to tell, the great majority of the crews of the *Niña,* the *Pinta,* and the *Santa María*—

together probably numbering a good deal fewer than a hundred—were not at that moment being pursued by the law, although, no doubt, they were a far from genteel lot.[131]

The three small ships left the harbor at Palos "half an hour before sunrise," Columbus noted in his journal of August 3rd, "and took the route for the Canary Islands," passing as they went the last Jewish stragglers who were being driven out of their homeland by way of the open sea.[132] This tiny ragtag fleet, representing a nation that was not much better than destitute and a Church that was in disgrace, was off on its imperial and holy mission. The world would never again be the same: before long, the bloodbath would begin.

6

C HRISTOPHER COLUMBUS VIEWED himself as a man of divine destiny in an age of apocalyptic promise. He was unequivocally sure of himself. And one thing of which he was especially certain was that the world was going to end in 150 years. He had made the calculations himself, but they were based on his careful reading of a work entitled *Imago Mundi,* by the Catholic Cardinal and late Chancellor of the University of Paris—and high priest at the Inquisition and execution of John Huss for heresy—Pierre d'Ailly. Written in 1410, though Columbus's copy was printed in Louvain around 1480, *Imago Mundi* was an encyclopedia of sorts for the instruction of lay people in the fields of Christianity-infused geography and cosmology.[1]

It was from this same book of compiled knowledge and ancient wisdom that Columbus had derived a potpouri of information (based on Aristotle, Seneca, Pliny, and others) allowing him to calculate that the distance across the Atlantic Ocean—known then as the Ocean Sea—was much shorter than it actually turned out to be. Long before he left on his famous voyage, more sophisticated navigators knew full well and told Columbus that his estimate was too short. That is a principal reason why the Portuguese Crown turned down his request for assistance in 1484. But Columbus pressed on. His stubborn unwillingness to be persuaded by superior evidence and logic ironically resulted in his beating the Portuguese to the islands of the Caribbean. That only deepened his conviction, of course, and to the end of his life he continued to believe the illusion that his original calculations had been correct.[2]

The *Imago Mundi* contained a wealth of equally dubious information on other matters that Columbus, like many in that era, readily took to heart. For what Columbus saw in the Cardinal's work, and what was intended by its author to be seen, was an outline of the history of the world—past, present, and future. By combining and folding together the ideas of such writers as Roger Bacon, the ninth-century Arabian astronomer Albumasar, and others, Pierre d'Ailly had laid out for his readers, writes Pauline Moffitt Watts, "the 'horoscopes' of the great religions and empires in much the same way that one would cast a personal horoscope." Once one has learned the proper techniques, believed all these writers and Columbus as well, one could "predict the future, for all events are imprinted on the present."[3]

Columbus read Ailly with the burning intensity of an autodidact who discovered in the Cardinal's writings nothing less than the divine path to truth. The margins of the Admiral's copy of *Imago Mundi,* which survives today in Seville's Biblioteca Colombina, are covered with almost 900 separate annotations by Columbus on matters of theology, geography, and history. Africa, he notes, is half the size of Europe—and south of the equator the days are only 12 hours long. Chinese people in small boats have drifted across the Atlantic to Europe, including a man and a woman who have turned up in Ireland. "Aristotle [says] between the end of Spain and the beginning of India is a small sea navigable in a few days." Other ancient authors are called upon who allegedly say the same or similar things, all of which indicate to Columbus that the earth is small and that India and China can be reached rather easily by sailing west. Alongside these temporal if fanciful observations are comments on Scripture, along with calculations for determining when the Muslims finally will be destroyed and when to expect the arrival of Antichrist.[4]

It was through the exploration of sources such as this, apparently in addition to lengthy conversations with Franciscan monks who were convinced that the end was near, that Columbus figured out to his satisfaction precisely when the Second Coming would occur. He did this through a kind of simplistic biblical numerology he had worked out, but he also knew it from the historical signs that were all around him.[5] Failure as well as success always has been absorbed easily into the all-embracing chiliastic logic of those convinced that the millennium is at hand; even contradictory evidence is interpreted so that it leads to the same desired conclusion. Thus, the obstinate resistance of the Jews to conversion, like the alarming successes of the Muslims in Turkey, were only part of God's great plan, his testing of the Christians—the inevitable dark before the dawn—Columbus thought. Conversely, the even more recent expulsion of the Jews from Spain (along with the baptism of those who repented), like the fall of the Muslims at Granada, were equally clear indications that a new and glorious day was arising.

What was present in Columbus's mind and marginal jottings before his departure in 1492 became a fully elaborated (if wildly confused and undisciplined) theory following the end of his third voyage in 1500, when he began compiling what he called his *Libro de las Profecías*—his Book of Prophecy: a scrapbook of hundreds of quotations from Scripture, from early Christian writers, and from classical authors, all purporting to demonstrate that the end of time was but a century and a half away, that the Jews and infidels and heathens throughout the entire world soon would be either destroyed or converted to Christ, and that before long the Holy Land would be recaptured. By the beginning of the sixteenth century Columbus had become certain that his voyages and discoveries had confirmed all this. Moreover, not only would each of these miraculous events soon be initiated, so the prophecies said, by the Messiah-Emperor from Spain, but the final conquests and the liberation of Jerusalem would be funded by vast quantities of gold that Columbus expected to discover either in those densely populated islands he had found lying off the coast of what he continued to think was Asia, or on the mainland of the continent itself. Indeed, for a time he thought he had discovered—with the Lord's guidance, of course—King Solomon's mines, and it was this gold that would launch the crusade that would bring on the end of the world. "Never was the popular image of the gold of the Indies more mystically spiritualized than on this occasion," writes John Leddy Phelan, adding: "The discovery and the conquest of America, among many other things, was the last crusade. If Columbus had had his way, this would have been literally so."[6]

But Columbus had read more than Ailly's *Imago Mundi* before embarking on his famous voyages. He also had read Plutarch and Marco Polo and several other works—including Pliny's *Natural History,* the earliest catalogue of the monstrous races that were said to live in distant realms, and John Mandeville's *Travels,* a largely plagiarized volume of supposed reports on the Holy Land and on the monstrous races of the East, a book that also happened to be the most popular prose work of the Middle Ages.[7] Columbus believed in and expected to encounter in his travels representatives of the monstrous races, just as he expected to find—and never stopped searching for—the fabled terrestrial paradise. Again, Columbus was far from alone in these assumptions. As he wrote in his letter to the king and queen while returning from his first voyage: "In these islands I have so far found no human monstrosities, as many expected," but elsewhere he wrote that within a few weeks of his first sighting of land he had been told by some Indians that on other islands "there were men with one eye, and others with dogs' heads who ate men and that in killing one they beheaded him and drank his blood and cut off his genitals."[8]

In fact, there was no real evidence of cannibalism (to say nothing of dog-headed people) anywhere in the Indies, despite widespread popular belief to the contrary that continues to exist today, belief largely based on the fact that Columbus said the alleged man-eaters were called Caribs. Through Spanish and English linguistic corruption that name evolved into "cannibal," and although both the more level-headed of Columbus's contemporaries and the consensus of modern scholarship have strenuously contradicted the charge, it has stuck as a truism in the Western imagination.[9] The important point here, however, is not the spuriousness of the claim that some of the natives ate human flesh, but only that Columbus and those who heard his report readily believed, indeed, *needed* to believe, that the charge was true. If no dog-headed people had yet actually been seen, or races without heads and with faces in their chests, or one-legged folk, or cyclopes, or other bizarre semi-human beasts, that did not mean they were not there. But for the time being rumors of some cannibals would do.

As for the terrestrial paradise Columbus knew to exist, he found it. At least he thought he did. It took awhile—six years and three long voyages—but in the autumn of 1498, while sailing along the coasts of Venezuela and Colombia and then on north to Honduras, the Admiral noticed (or so he wrote to his king and queen) that the people he observed were not as "dark" or "extremely black" as he claimed they were in other regions, "but are of very handsome build and whiter than any others I have seen in the Indies. . . . [and] are more intelligent and have more ability." At the same time he observed that he was in the vicinity of towering mountains and fabulously powerful rivers, including the one that we now know as the Orinoco, that rushed from the mountains in powerful currents down into the Gulf of Paria. Recalling no doubt that in some traditional accounts the earthly paradise had been located atop a high mountain, which allowed it to survive the great biblical flood, and noting that "Holy Scripture testifies that Our Lord created the Terrestrial Paradise and planted it in the tree of life, and that a fountain sprang up there, from which flow the four principal rivers of the world," the logical conclusion could not be ignored: "I say that if this river [the Orinoco] does not originate in the Terrestrial Paradise, it comes and flows from a land of infinite size to the south, of which we have no knowledge as yet. But I am completely persuaded in my own mind that the Terrestrial Paradise is in the place I have described."[10]

Indeed, so extraordinary was this insight that it caused Columbus to revise his entire vision of the shape of the earth. "I am compelled," he wrote to his royal patrons, "to come to this view of the world":

> I have found that it does not have the kind of sphericity described by the authorities, but that it has the shape of a pear, which is all very round, except at the stem, which is rather prominent, or that it is as if one had a very round ball, on one part of which something like a woman's teat were placed, this part with the stem being the uppermost and nearest to the sky. . . . So neither Ptolemy nor the others who wrote about the world had any

information about this half, for it was altogether unknown. They merely based their opinion on the hemisphere in which they lived, which is round, as I have said above.[11]

At this point, some modern observers have claimed, Columbus was demented, or at least had been at sea too long. Others have said that obviously he was looking at the island now known as Marguerite, lying at the mouth of the Orinoco, and that indeed there is on that island what Germán Arciniegas calls "the extraordinary mount that anyone today may see. . . . They call it María Guevara's Teats."[12] In any case, Columbus was convinced that he had seen paradise, at least from a distance, bulging out like a woman's breast and nipple at the top of the world. It was soon after this that he began compiling his *Book of Prophecies*. And when he died, just six years later, this man whose life has so aptly been described as "a curious combination of the celestial and the crass," was laid out in the garb of a Franciscan monk and was buried in a Carthusian monastery. As it turns out, he had been deeply involved with the Franciscans for years— as the Franciscans had been deeply involved with the Inquisition for years— perhaps even was a lay member of the order, and in 1497 and 1498, "while preparing for his third voyage," writes Leonard I. Sweet, "Columbus wore the habit of a Minorite friar, and was indistinguishable in the streets of Cadiz and Seville from his Franciscan friends."[13]

Apart from his navigational skills, what most set Columbus apart from other Europeans of his day were not the things that he believed, but the intensity with which he believed in them and the determination with which he acted upon those beliefs. If most Christians at that time did not walk around wearing the robes of Franciscan monks, as Columbus did, few would have denied that the conversion of the world to Christianity (and the destruction of those who resisted) was a necessary prerequisite to Christ's Second Coming—or that there were then present unmistakable signs that such mass conversions and mass destructions were imminent. Similarly, if most people did not cross the ocean in search of the terrestrial paradise or King Solomon's mines, as Columbus did, few would have denied that such places probably existed in some distant, hidden realm. And if most people did not take part in slaving voyages to the coast of Africa "many times," as Columbus acknowledged that he had done, few would have found any-thing morally improper in such activities.[14]

Columbus was, in most respects, merely an especially active and dra-matic embodiment of the European—and especially the Mediterranean— mind and soul of his time: a religious fanatic obsessed with the conversion, conquest, or liquidation of all non-Christians; a latter-day Crusader in search of personal wealth and fame, who expected the enormous and mysterious world he had found to be filled with monstrous races inhabiting wild forests, and with golden people living in Eden. He was also a man with sufficient intolerance and contempt for all who did not look or behave or believe as he did, that he thought nothing of enslaving or killing such people simply because they were not like him. He was, to repeat, a secular personification of what more than a thousand years of Christian culture had wrought. As such, the fact that he launched a campaign of horrific violence against the natives of Hispaniola is not something that should surprise anyone. Indeed, it would be surprising if he had *not* inaugurated such carnage.

But why did the firestorm of violence turn openly genocidal, and why did it continue for so long? Why did it take the grotesque forms that it did? Why was it morally justified in the terms that it was? And why, and in what ways, were the later British and American genocide campaigns different from those of the Spanish—if at least equally destructive in the long run? The answers to all these questions must be sought in the constant interplay of Western ideologies and material realities, beginning with the initial Spanish quest for gold and for glory, proceeding from there to evolving concepts of race along with traditional notions of divine providence and sin, and then back again to the hunger and thirst for wealth and for power, sought down different paths by different European peoples on the different American continents of the north and of the south.

II

Columbus drove a hard bargain with his royal patrons. Not only did he demand a substantial share of whatever treasure he might bring back from his journey across the Atlantic horizon, he also required of them, as he noted in the prologue to the journal of his first voyage, "that henceforth I might call myself *Don* and be Grand Admiral of the Ocean Sea and Viceroy and Perpetual Governor of all the islands and mainland that I should discover and win."[15] Since he thought he was sailing to China and India, these were not meager titles, were he to succeed in gaining them. For Columbus, like the conquistadors to follow, was driven by various forces in his quest to discover and conquer, but during this era when individualism was sharply ascendant in European culture, few if any motives were more important than what in Spanish is called *el afán de honra*—"an anxiety, a hunger for glory and for recognition," is the way one historian puts it.[16]

To Columbus, the Genoese ex-slave trader and would-be holy Crusader, returning to Spain with slaves and with gold and with tales of innumerable heathens waiting to be converted was the surest way to achieve such fame. Thus, within hours of landfall on the first inhabited island he encountered in the Caribbean, Columbus seized and carried off six native people who, he said, "ought to be good servants . . . . [and] would easily be made Christians, because it seemed to me that they belonged to no religion." Bereft of religion though he thought these "very handsome and . . . very well proportioned" people to be, the Admiral was certain that they possessed gold: "I was attentive and worked hard to know if there was any gold," he wrote during the second day of his visit, "and saw that some of them wore a little piece hanging from a thing like a needle case, which they have in the nose; and by signs I could understand that, going to the S, or doubling the island to the S, there was a king there who had great vessels of it and possessed a lot." This was likely the island of Cipango—or Japan—Columbus thought, the fabulous place Marco Polo had written about, and he set out the next day to find it.[17]

And so the man who now could call himself *Don* moved from island to island, snaring more natives for eventual servitude, and grilling them— incoherently—as to the whereabouts of the great deposits of gold. He thought he understood them to say that on one island the people "wore very big bracelets of gold on their legs and arms." They didn't, and Columbus bitterly but probably correctly noted later "that all they said was humbug in order to escape." But he pressed on, always believing that magnificent riches in gold and jewels lay just beyond the next landfall. Columbus continued to think he was quite close to the Asian mainland and that the people of "all these islands are at war with the Grand Khan" who presumably wanted from them what Columbus wanted: their precious metals and the wealth of their forced labor. Hearing what he wanted to hear in the words of a people whose language he did not understand, the Admiral "was the victim of the same psychological illusions," one writer has observed, "that lead us to hear sweet melodies in the chime of church-bells, or to discover in the clouds familiar features or impressive images of phantastic shapes."[18]

It is clear that Columbus had several purposes, none especially complex, for lusting after the gold of the Indies. Personal wealth and fame and power, of course; that is evident in everything he wrote. But there is no reason to believe he was not also sincere in his expressed desire to bring gold back to Spain in order to finance the last great crusade that would liberate the souls of all the world's infidels and heathens 'who were willing to convert, while at the same time crushing the bodies of those unwilling to cooperate. And, of course, there was the matter of financing the next transatlantic excursions. As Leonardo Olschki rightly puts it: "Gold represented the only profit immediately realizable of such costly enterprises, and provided the most direct means of financing an oceanic expedition in this critical epoch of Spain's economic life."[19]

There was little doubt in Columbus's mind that with sufficient manpower, both military and ecclesiastical, he would reap with ease a vast fortune in gold and souls. Both of these godly gifts to the Admiral and to his Spanish supporters were simply there for the taking. In a letter to the king and queen dated April 9, 1493, Columbus outlined his plans for the second voyage. Instead of the fewer than 100 men he had brought on the initial expedition, he recommended that he be allowed to transport twenty times that number "so that the country may be made more secure and so that it may be more expeditiously won and managed." So great was the supply of gold that awaited them, and so effortless would be its collection, he believed, that he urged the sovereigns to establish on the islands magistrates and notaries to oversee what he repeatedly referred to as the "gathering" of this fabulous wealth, all of which was to be "immediately melted and marked . . . and weighed" and placed in carefully guarded chests. He also proposed that "of all the gold which may be found, one percent be reserved for the erection of churches and their furniture and for the support of the priests or friars attached to them."[20] One percent may not appear to be much, but if the Admiral's estimate of how much gold awaited them had been even close to the truth, one percent could have paid for cathedrals.

Following the deduction for the Church's one percent of all the gold that was gathered, and a little something for the magistrates and notaries, Columbus recommended that during the first year of Hispaniola's colonization those who did the gathering be allowed to keep one-half of what they personally collected, the other half going to the Crown. After the first year this proportional division was to be reassessed, in light of the amount of treasure actually found. Considering the immensity of riches that awaited them, however, and "since, owing to the greed for gold, everyone will prefer to seek it rather than engage in other necessary occupations," Columbus suggested that "during a part of the year hunting for gold should be prohibited, so that there may be on the said island an opportunity for performing other tasks of importance to it."[21]

Between the time of his return from the first voyage and the date of embarkation for the second journey, word had spread everywhere in Spain of the gold and souls that Columbus had found. No longer would there be any need to enlist the services of wanted criminals or other lowlife to staff the ships of the enterprise to the Indies. The Admiral's enthusiasm was infectious, as was his avarice. The others aboard the ships that sailed with Columbus on this second voyage—and those who were to follow in years and decades to come—rarely were possessed by the array of motives that drove his quest for discovery and conquest. Some just wanted to save heathens. Far more just wanted to get rich. But operating in tandem, these two simple goals spelled disaster for the indigenous peoples who welcomed the shiploads—in time the floodtide—of Europeans who came as reapers of souls and of gold. That is because, initially at least, there were few souls wishing to be converted and very little gold to be had. Nor was either pursuit much helped by the furious epidemics that were unleashed by the Europeans soon after they came into contact with their native hosts.

The men aboard the Niña, the Pinta, and the Santa María almost certainly spread strange, new diseases among the people of the islands they visited during the first Spanish excursion through the Caribbean from October of 1492 through January of 1493. But, as we saw in an earlier chapter, it was with the landing of the ships of the second voyage, on the northern coast of Hispaniola in January of 1494, that the first known explosion of European epidemic disease occurred. Ferdinand and Isabella had instructed Columbus not to mistreat the Indians he encountered on this second voyage. That was their word. With their deed, however, they loaded his ships with hundreds of heavily armed and armored infantry and cavalrymen, many of them battle-hardened and fresh from victory over the hated Moors in Granada. As Hispaniola's natives retreated inland from the deadly epidemics that followed immediately upon the landing of the Spanish troops, they were pursued by these soldiers of fortune who had no time to waste.

Consulting his classical sources, Columbus determined that "according to Ptolemy there must be plenty of gold in the rivers" of this huge island. When one of the military parties he sent out returned with three pieces of gold that had been taken from an Indian settlement, Columbus "and all of us made merry," recalled one of the participants in the revelry, "not caring any longer about any sort of spicery but only of this blessed gold. Because of this," he continued, "the Lord Admiral wrote to the King that he was hoping to be able shortly to give him as much gold as the iron mines of Biscay gave him iron." [22] In this excited mood Columbus sent a number of ships back to Spain—and 500 troops inland to find the gold. Although "not too well fitted out with clothes," wrote Michele de Cuneo, they set out on their trek:

> [B]etween going, staying, and returning, we spent 29 days with terrible weather, bad food and worse drink; nevertheless, out of covetousness of that gold, we all kept strong and lusty. We crossed going and coming two very rapid rivers, as I have mentioned above, swimming; and those who did not know how to swim had two Indians who carried them swimming; the same, out of friendship and for a few trifles that we gave them, carried across on top of their heads our clothes, arms and everything else there was to be carried. [23]

The trip was a painful ordeal covering many miles through difficult country. And when they reached the place they were seeking they "built a fort of wood in the name of St. Thomas." There these hundreds of Spanish troops and adventurers frantically fished in the rivers that Ptolemy had said would be filled with treasure, "but," wrote Cuneo, "never was found by anyone a single grain of gold." He then added portentously: "For this reason we were very displeased with the local Indians." [24]

For months to follow, this pattern was repeated. Although there was gold on the island, and although the conquistadors ultimately found whatever was there—and forced the natives to mine it for them—never did the holdings of the Indians or the products of the island's mines and rivers produce riches of the sort the soldiers had been led to expect. Unable to believe what was apparent, that this was no King Solomon's mine, the troops convinced themselves that the Indians cared as much as the Spanish did for the precious metal and that they were hoarding it in secret caches. To these men whose profession was violence, only violence could be counted on to wrest from the natives what God and the Lord Admiral had promised them.

When the crossbow was invented centuries earlier the Church had decreed it to be such a terrifying weapon that it could be used only on infidels.[25] On Hispaniola, and then on Jamaica, and elsewhere in the Caribbean it was used routinely—along with the lance and the sword and the armored and hungry dog—to terrorize and subdue those natives who somehow were surviving the lethal pathogens that the invaders carried in their blood and their breath. Within a matter of months 50,000 Indians were dead, the proportional equivalent of 1,500,000 American deaths today. Europe at this time was still excited over the mysteriousness of these new-found lands and their handsome and innocent people, but the men on the front lines of the endeavor to strip the Indies of its gold had long since overcome their sense of wonder with their greed and their furious sadism.

Even the most educated and cultured and high-minded among the voyagers on this second expedition wasted no time in expressing their contempt for the native people. Cuneo, for example, the Italian nobleman and apparent boyhood friend of Columbus, repeatedly referred to the natives as "beasts" because he could not discern that they had any religion, because they slept on mats on the ground rather than in beds, because "they eat when they are hungry," and because they made love "openly whenever they feel like it."[26] This judgment comes, it will be recalled, from a man who took a fancy to a beautiful young native woman during this trip and, when she rebuffed his advances, thrashed her with a rope, raped her, and then boasted of what he had done.

Cuneo's opinion of the natives was echoed by Dr. Diego Alvarez Chanca, a physician on the voyage who later was singled out by the Crown for a special award in recognition of his humanitarianism. For various reasons, including his disapproval of the Indians' method of laying out their towns and the fact that they ate cooked iguana (which the Spanish themselves later came to regard as a delicacy), Dr. Chanca declared that the natives were barbarous and unintelligent creatures whose "degradation is greater than that of any beast in the world."[27] Cuneo and Chanca and other island visitors who recorded their thoughts for posterity probably had little influence on the lance- and sword- and crossbow-wielding conquistadors who accompanied them, but that is only because the conquistadors did not need the encouragement of their superiors to carry out what Las Casas called their "massacres and strange cruelties" against the native people.

Back in Europe, on the other hand, these reports were read with avidity. And before long a consistent picture began to emerge. The *lands* of the Indies were indeed as wondrous as Columbus originally had described them. Thus, Andrés Bernáldez—chaplain to the Archbishop of Seville, member of the Royal Council, and Grand Inquisitor—described for his faithful readers the delightful islands of Hispaniola and Cuba, "the most lovely that eyes have seen," whose "fields were such that they appeared to be the loveliest gardens in the world." The *people* of the islands, however—said this holy man who once had rejoiced in the burning of Jews and Moors "in living flames until they be no more"—were but "a brutish race . . . [who] take no pleasure in anything save eating and women."[28]

Even before his first voyage was complete, Columbus had written to Ferdinand and Isabella promising to bring back from subsequent expeditions "slaves, as many as [the Crown] shall order"—while assuring his king and queen that such Indian bondsmen "will be idolators," that is, non-Christians, which would make their trade legitimate in the supervisory view of the Church.[29] In the eyes of Hispaniola's Spanish invaders, however, hardly had the second voyage completed its minimal tasks ashore when the native "idolators" were turning into full-fledged beasts. To some, that helped explain why the natives were dying so quickly and in such huge numbers; but in any case, die though they might, there were millions of them who could still be enslaved, and there was work to be done— much gold remained to be seized.

It is by no means surprising, then, that in only the second printed chronicle from the New World (the first being Columbus's report to the Crown on his initial voyage), the Spanish nobleman Guillermo Coma of Aragon dwelt at great length and in minute detail on the allegedly "very dark and grim-visaged" cannibals of the Indies. "They customarily castrate their infant captives and boy slaves and fatten them like capons," was but one of his numerous imaginings. And with equal vividness and equal falsity he described the great quantities of gold that awaited the adventurous, who could gather nuggets almost like fruit from a tree. "In that region," he told his readers, there are "a large number of rivers and more than 24 streams,—a country of such bountifulness that it is marvellous to describe and unbelievable to hear about." He continued:

> Gold is collected by cutting away the river banks. First the water rushes in, frothing and somewhat muddy; then it becomes clear again and the heavy grains of gold which lie at the bottom are plainly revealed. They weigh a drachma [about 60 grains] more or less. . . . There is a very lovely tale, which I should have been ashamed to relate if I had not got it from a credible

witness, that a rock close to the mountain, when struck with a club, poured out a great quantity of gold and that gold splinters flashed all over with indescribable brightness.[30]

The story continues, reporting on other discoveries, such as that of a native goldsmith who supposedly crafted solid gold plates so large that no one man could lift them, and of rivers that flowed over beds that were thick with gold-bearing sand. And then Coma put all the pieces together, in homage to Columbus and the king and queen of Spain, linking the recent "memorable victory" over the infidel Moors in Granada, the expulsion of the Jews from Spain, and now the exploration of "the shores of the Orient," all events destined and intended "for the enhancement of the religion of Christ."[31]

Thus, the Indies: the most beautiful lands on earth, filled with more wealth than anyone could imagine, but also inhabited by "very dark and grim-visaged" cannibals and other uncivilized brutes who hoarded and hid the gold that the Spanish needed to fulfill the prophecies of the faith—the prophecies ordering them to convert or destroy the ungodly, be they Moors, Jews, or the beastly denizens of "the shores of the Orient," and to bring God's kingdom home. Such was the rationale, at least, for the carnage that already was well under way, and no doubt there were those who believed it. Others were less starry-eyed, such as the famed conquistador (and official historian of the Conquest) Gonzalo Fernández de Oviedo y Valdés, who advised would-be adventurers to mouth all the right words when applying for passage to the Indies, but who added that he knew as well as they "that the truth is just the opposite; you are going solely because you want to have a larger fortune than your father and your neighbors." It was this same sort of cynicism (later repeated by Cortés, Pizarro, and others) that allowed Oviedo elsewhere to write sardonically of the sanctity he felt when killing Indians: "Who can deny that the use of gunpowder against pagans is the burning of incense to Our Lord?"[32]

This is not to say that belief in the earthly paradise and its golden race of people disappeared. After all, Columbus sincerely continued to look for it—and thought he had found it when he encountered, as we saw earlier, people "whiter than any others I have seen in the Indies," and who, not incidentally, were "more intelligent and have more ability." But as time wore on the dominant European image of the New World's indigenous peoples was one that fit well with other very ancient Old World traditions: Columbus's story of "men with one eye, and others with dogs' noses," who ate men after decapitating them, castrating them, and finally drinking their blood soon became an article of faith among many Europeans; moreover, elsewhere in the Caribbean, it was said, there existed islands inhabited only by Amazons and others with people whose skin color was blue and whose heads were square.[33] And everywhere, whatever their physical appearance, the sins of the natives were the same—lust, gluttony, carnality, and all the other untamed and un-Christian pleasures of the flesh that long had been the distinguishing characteristics of wild men and the monstrous, beastly races.

Some of this had been heard before, of course, during the long centuries of holy war with the Muslims and the equally holy persecution of the Jews. But in associating the Indians with wild men and the monstrous races described in the works of Pliny and John Mandeville something new was being added—the question of race, the question of the native peoples' very humanity. For while those like Señor Coma of Aragon were drawing a parallel between darkness of flesh and commitment to cannibalism— while Columbus and others were expounding on an opposite relationship (but one with identical consequences) involving light skin, intelligence, and closeness to God—still more Spaniards were locating evidence for the Indians' alleged inferiority within their very biology, in what was said to be the "size and thickness of their skulls," writes J.H. Elliott, "which indicated a deformation in that part of the body which provided an index of a man's rational powers," and which could be used to support the increasingly popular idea that the Indians were made by God to be the "natural slaves" of the Spanish and, indeed, of all Europeans.[34]

In the preceding chapter we noted that race is an ancient Western concept and that skin color has long been one of the many characteristics with which it has been associated. ("It is significant," writes David Brion Davis, for example, that during the thirteenth-century slave trade "Sicilian officials qualified the general designation for 'Moor' or 'Saracen' with the Latin terms for 'white,' 'sallow,' and 'black.' " Adds Elena Lourie, also writing of the thirteenth century: "Only with great difficulty, after he had already been sold as a Muslim slave, did a 'very black man,' 'with thick features,' prove to the authorities that he was in fact a good Catholic.")[35] For most of the duration of this idea's existence, however, race was not seen as an immutable phenomenon. Skin color, for instance, commonly was viewed as environmentally changeable and, as we have seen, even semi-human monstrosities—such as the dog-headed beast who became St. Christopher—were susceptible to favorable transformation. Such permutability of human essence was thoroughly compatible during Christianity's reign in Europe with the Church's fervent crusade to bring all the world's people under its heavenly wing. However, a little more than a century before Columbus put to sea on his journey that would shake the world, cracks began to appear in the edifice of Christianity's racial ecumenism. The cause of the problem was slavery.

The booming slave trade in the fourteenth-century Mediterranean was at least a two-way operation. That is, while Christian Europeans were buying shiploads of captured infidels, Muslims were doing the same thing—except that many of their purchased slaves were Christians. This greatly upset the Church and led to various methods of discouraging trade in Christian captives, including efforts to cut off all trade of any sort with Muslim countries and the excommunication of Christians caught buying or selling their religious brethren as bondsmen. (At that time it generally was agreed that free Christians could not be enslaved by other Christians except as punishment for certain crimes.) However, since the Church remained devoted to its evangelical mission *and* to supporting the slave trade in general, a difficulty of potentially major proportions soon developed: what to do with the legally enslaved infidel who saw the light and converted to Catholicism? To order the manumission of such a person might rapidly undermine the lucrative trade in captive infidels, but to fail to free him or her would be to condone the enslavement of Christians. It was on the horns of this dilemma, writes David Brion Davis, that the Church made an ominous decision:

> In 1366 the Priors of Florence, who had previously given their sanction to the import and sale of infidel slaves, explained that by "infidel" they had meant "all slaves of infidel *origin,* even if at the time of their arrival they belong to the Catholic faith"; and "infidel origin" meant simply "from the land and race of the infidels." With this subtle change in definition the Priors of Florence by-passed the dilemma of baptism by shifting the basis of slavery from religious difference to ethnic origin.[36]

It may have been a subtle change in definition, but the larger meaning of this declaration would signal an alteration in consciousness containing enormous and far-reaching implications. From this point forward the "race of the infidels" would be sufficient to justify their enslavement, and no transformations of any sort—including conversion to the faith of Christ—would have any bearing on their worldly condition. Less than a century later a functionally similar declaration was imposed upon Spain's Jews. In the wake of the anti-Jewish riots of 1449 in Toledo, Jews were barred from holding public office in the city; only those citizens who could demonstrate Christian "purity of blood," said the first decree of *limpieza de sangre,* were eligible for such positions. Conversion to Catholicism would no longer suffice, for oneself or even for one's descendants. Blood—in effect, race—was now the fundamental criterion.

The conceptual underpinnings for this ominous shift in consciousness had been building for a very long time. As early as the ninth century in Aragon and Castile the general term for nobility, *caballero hidalgo,* was reserved for those of specified "blood" and lineage; achieved economic or other influence was insufficient to overcome the genetic exclusivity of the institution. At issue was the nobleman's allegedly unique possession of *verguenza*—the sense of honor—that was bestowed solely through genealogical inheritance. As Alfonso X of Castile explained:

In ancient times, in order to create knights, men chose hunters in the mountains who were men of great endurance, and carpenters and smiths and masons because they were accustomed to giving blows and their hands are strong. Also butchers, because they were used to killing live things and shedding their blood. Such men are well formed, strong and lithe. The Ancients chose knights in this manner for a very long time. But when they saw that in many cases their proteges, lacking *verguenza,* forgot the reasons for their elevation and instead of defeating their enemies were defeated themselves, men knowledgeable in these matters looked for knights who, *by their nature,* possessed *verguenza.* . . . For they held a weak man with the will to endure far preferable to a strong one who easily fled. Because of this the authorities saw to it that knights should be men of good lineage.[37]

The *limpieza de sangre* was, in effect, a particularly crude and malignant revision of this long-held exclusionary principle, and during the late fifteenth century and for all of the sixteenth it became a mania throughout Spain. Specialists in genealogy known as *linajudo* checked and scrutinized bloodlines and pedigrees. Neither fame nor even death provided escape for those accused of being tainted. Thus, the remains of the celebrated pioneer in medicine, Garcia d'Orta, were exhumed in 1580 "and solemnly burned in an auto-da-fé held at Goa, in accordance with the posthumous punishment inflicted on crypto-Jews who had escaped the stake in their lifetime." Catholic Spaniards with distant Jewish ancestors changed their names and falsified their genealogies to avoid the ruination of their reputations or the loss of their access to professions and education. For even the most humble peasant of "pure" Christian ancestry now could proudly regard himself as superior to the wealthiest *marrano.* It was all just a matter of blood.[38]

Historically, then, it was within this evolving context of ethnic and racial discrimination that there emerged in Europe the idea that the people of the Indies might be a separate, distinct, and naturally subordinate race. By 1520 the popular Swiss physician and philosopher Paracelsus, whose eventual burial place became a Catholic shrine, was arguing that Africans, Indians, and other non-Christian peoples of color were not even descended from Adam and Eve, but from separate and inferior progenitors.[39] Paracelsus advanced this thesis less than thirty years after Columbus's first contact with the people of the Caribbean, although in that short time the Indies' many millions of native peoples—whose ancestry in those islands long predated even that of the Vandals and Visigoths in Spain—had effectively been exterminated. But the assault on Mexico and the rest of Meso- and South America was at that moment only beginning.

Paracelsus's notion of separate and unequal human creations was an early version of what in time would become known as "polygenesis," one of the staples of nineteenth-century pseudoscientific racism. Even before the Swiss writer committed this idea to print, however, there was in circulation a complementary suggestion, put forward in 1512 by Spaniards

Bernardo de Mesa (later Bishop of Cuba) and Gil Gregorio, and in 1519 by a Scotsman named John Mair (Johannes Major), that the Indians might be a special race created by God to fulfill a destiny of enslavement to Christian Europeans. Drawing on both Aristotle and Aquinas, the Spaniards—who were meeting at the king's behest—placed the matter in the context of "natural law," with Gregorio contending that since it was apparent that these creatures were "idle, vicious, and without charity," it was a violation of the natural order to permit them to remain free. Mair, at the time a member of the Collège de Montaigu in Paris, first pointed out what by then was commonly accepted by most Europeans—that the recently discovered people of the New World "live like beasts" and indeed, in some locales, are truly "wild men." Neither these facts, nor the late success of the Europeans in conquering these creatures, should be cause for surprise, Mair thought, since "as the Philosopher [Aristotle] says in the third and fourth chapters of the first book of the *Politics,* it is clear that some men are by nature slaves, others by nature free. . . . On this account the Philosopher says in the first chapter of the aforementioned book that this is the reason why the Greeks should be masters over the barbarians because, by nature, the barbarians and slaves are the same." [40]

Few notions could have been sweeter to the minds of early sixteenth-century Spanish thinkers, and they lost no time in adopting it. From the time of that first royal *junta* in 1512, at which Mesa and Gregorio had used natural law to justify enslavement of the Indians, throughout the 1520s and 1530s and 1540s—while the indigenous peoples of Middle and South America were being consumed by the millions in the same inferno of disease and fiery carnage that had turned the Caribbean's natives to ash—Spain's philosophers and theologians debated among themselves whether the Indians were men or monkeys, whether they were mere brutes or were capable of rational thought, and whether or not God intended them to be permanent slaves of their European overlords. By the time these discussions reached their famous apogee in the confrontation between Bartolomé de Las Casas and Juan Ginés de Sepúlveda at Valladolid, in the summer of 1550, more native people of the Americas had been consumed in the combined conflagrations of pestilence and genocide than the mind can comprehend.

Called before the so-called Council of Fourteen by Charles V—the Holy Roman Emperor and the most powerful man in Europe—to argue whether the natives of the Americas should be considered natural slaves because, as Sepulveda claimed, they were mere *"homunculi* [contemptible little people] in whom you will scarcely find even vestiges of humanity," Las Casas and Sepúlveda publicly argued back and forth for about a month. Even Las Casas—the most passionate and humane European advocate for the Indians of his own time and for many years to come—felt forced to acknowledge that the Indians "may be completely barbaric." However, he contended, they were not *so* low in the order of things that they were totally "irrational or natural slaves or unfit for government." To Sepúlveda and others, on the contrary, as Las Casas rightly said, the native peoples of the Americas were indeed so barbarically inhuman "that the wise may hunt [them] down . . . in the same way as they would wild animals."[41] As if to anticipate and underscore this point, only a few months earlier the conquistador Pedro de Valdivia proudly announced to Charles V that he and his men had just concluded a massacre against a large community of Indians in Chile: "some 1500 or 2000 were killed and many others lanced," he wrote; among the survivors whom he had taken prisoner, Valdivia saw to it that "two hundred had their hands and noses cut off for their contumacy"—that is, for not heeding the conquistadors' demands that they behave in a sufficiently obsequious way, consistent with that of the natural slave.[42]

After the debate ended, the members of the Council of Fourteen, selected by Charles as the best minds in Spain, fell to arguing among themselves and never rendered a collective verdict—although Sepúlveda later claimed, and there is some reason to believe him, that in the end all but one of the Council supported his position that the Indians were indeed divinely created beasts of burden for their conquerors.[43] In any case, if the men considered by the Holy Roman Emperor to be the most learned in the realm could not agree on this matter among themselves, the same could not be said for the Spanish masses. As Bernardino de Minaya wrote, a decade and a half before the great debate at Valladolid, "the common people" had long "regarded as wise men" those who were convinced that "the American Indians were not true men, but a third species of animal between man and monkey created by God for the better service of man."[44] Or, as Oviedo had written, with widespread popular approval:

[The Indians are] naturally lazy and vicious, melancholic, cowardly, and in general a lying, shiftless, people. Their marriages are not a sacrament but a sacrilege. They are idolatrous, libidinous, and commit sodomy. Their chief desire is to eat, drink, worship heathen idols, and commit bestial obscenities. What could one expect from a people whose skulls are so thick and hard that the Spaniards had to take care in fighting not to strike on the head lest their swords be blunted?[45]

If that was popular opinion early in the sixteenth century, it doubtless was even more widespread after the Valladolid debate was over. For on at least one topic virtually all historians of this subject agree: as the sixteenth century wore on Spanish opinion regarding the Indians was marked by a decided "decline of sympathy and . . . narrowing of vision," in J.H. Elliott's words.[46] Elliott uses as an illustrative example a series of meetings held by the Spanish clergy stationed in Mexico between 1532 and 1585, during which verbal depictions of the region's native people drastically deteriorated. An even more vivid example of this transformation involved the fabled Tupinamba people of Brazil.

When first contacted by Europeans in the early years of exploration the Tupinamba were described as the most handsome and best-proportioned people in the world, virtually creatures of perfection. They were, said Pedro Vaz de Caminha in 1500, people of "fine bodies and good faces as to good men," and a kind and generous people of "innocence" and "pure simplicity" to boot. An imaginative Portuguese painting of the Adoration of the Magi from this time even replaced one of the traditional wise men with a young and handsome representative of these Brazilian natives, replete with distinctive feather headdress and gold earrings, bracelets, and anklets. At almost this same time, however, woodcut illustrations began appearing in other parts of Europe depicting the Brazilians as cannibals and sexual libertines. And by the 1550s, when Brazil was in the process of being denuded of its native people by European slavery, violence, and imported diseases, those very same gold and feather Tupinamba decorations could be found adorning the head and body of Satan in another Portuguese painting, a grotesque and horrific portrait of the Devil's Inferno. Meanwhile, in concert with the change in visual representation, European writers had now taken to calling these lately dubbed Brazilian paragons of pure virtue and simplicity "beasts in human form," to quote Nicolas Durand de Villegagnon.[47]

Such ideological transformation did not occur, of course, without a social context or without serving a larger political function. The same was true of the earlier intellectual innovations we have noted. The Priors of Florence had declared as acceptable the traffic in Christian slaves who were "of infidel origin" because to fail to do so might have undermined the slave trade, with which the Church was so profitably involved. And the *limpieza de sangre,* although initially inspired by religious hatred, soon became a valuable weapon of class struggle with which low-born Spanish Catholics could push their way into positions of authority that might otherwise be held by high-born persons of Jewish ancestry. As Elliott demonstrates in his discussion of the *limpieza,* the doctrine functioned as a "compensating code" for commoners "which might effectively challenge the code of the aristocracy." After all, they would argue, "was it not preferable to be born of humble, but pure Christian parentage, than to be a *caballero* of suspicious racial antecedents?"[48]

In neither of these cases, certainly, was the social or political or economic function of the race discrimination in question the sole and sufficient motivation for its being institutionalized. Each one drew for its authorization on a deep well of centuries-old and symbolically embedded antipathy for its targeted victims. Once in operation, however, the racially oppressive institution justified, reinforced, and thus exacerbated the negative racial stereotypes that had made the institution permissible in the first place—which, in turn, further sanctified the institution itself.

In late fifteenth- and early sixteenth-century Spain and Spanish America, the primary economic context within which anti-Indian racial ideologies were cultivated and institutionalized was the feverish hunt for gold. Then later, as the sixteenth century wore on, the context changed to the mining of silver, which was available in much greater volume. Spain at this time, as noted earlier, was a nation with effectively no manufactured items to export. It was an exporter of raw materials and an importer of finished goods. Even within its own borders Spain was plagued by a stagnating economy, with most local production intended for local consumption. With its broad and mountainous terrain, whatever goods were moved around were carried by pack mules. And despite the presence of perhaps 400,000 such primitive beasts of burden, as an exchange economy the nation was dormant.[49] One consequence of this was both very small productive volume and a great deal of duplication, along with a steady outflow of capital to those other European countries on which Spain was economically dependent.

In contrast with its state of commercial impoverishment, however, fifteenth-century advances in ship design, primarily of Portuguese inspiration, along with developments in pilotage, navigation, and cartography—and the persistence of Christopher Columbus—allowed Spain, with its ideal geographic location, to lead the way in exploration of the Indies. Thus, it came about that one of the European nations that could least afford to finance colonization abroad—and that had a sudden over-abundance of experienced military men within its midst, due to the recent defeat of the Moors in Granada—was given first entry into the New World.

The stories of indescribable wealth available in the Indies to those who could seize it—of riverbeds filled with nuggets and of boulders that shattered and poured forth gold when struck with a club—fired the imaginations of individual adventurers, of course, but it did the same for religious and financial collectivities as well. The Church now envisioned the wealth of the Indies, both in gold and in souls to harvest, as the means for launching the final Crusades, while wealthy nobles and merchants knew that the Crown was in no position to direct the conquest and exploitation of the islands without deriving virtually all its financial backing from private sources.

For about a dozen years, from the launching of Columbus's second voyage in 1493 to the eve of the conquests of Cuba, Jamaica, and Puerto Rico after 1506, the capital behind the provisioning of ships and stores and mercenary soldiers was raised by merchant and noble partnerships within Spain. From 1506 forward, however, the conquest of the rest of the Caribbean was financed by the gold that was taken from Hispaniola. (In 1499—after the great majority of the island's millions of people had

been destroyed—the long dreamed-of gold mine was discovered on Hispaniola, producing for a time between three and six tons of gold per year.)[50]
"Similarly," writes Ralph Davis, "while the first attempts to settle the
mainland coast were organized from Spain, the series of expeditions after
1516 which culminated in Cortés's conquest of Mexico were backed by
Cuban resources; and the wealth of Mexico paid for the northward and
southward extension of exploration and gave some backing to the colonization of the Panama isthmus and, a decade later, to the conquest of Peru."
Thus, one after another, Caribbean and American locales were raided and
drained of their wealth, a portion of which was divided among the Crown,
the conquistadors, and those who provided the conquistadors' financial
support, while the rest was used to mount further depredations. By and
large the Spanish were uninterested in building New World colonial societies, but rather in draining the New World of its wealth. "Indeed," notes
Davis, "by the 1570s the investment movement had been reversed and
returning colonists were investing capital accumulated in America in entirely Spanish financial and industrial enterprises."[51]

The first waves of Spanish violence denuded the Caribbean of its wealth
in gold and, as we saw earlier, of its wealth in people as well. Once the
islands were thus made barren, the Spanish found goals to pursue elsewhere, and moved on. There were about 8000 Spaniards living on Hispaniola in 1509, for instance, forcing the few surviving Indians to produce the
remaining dregs of gold that the white men hungered for, but within a
decade only a few hundred Spaniards remained to begin slowly building
sugar plantations on the backs of growing numbers of imported African
slaves. Not only had the island's gold supply been depleted and its millions
of native people effectively exterminated by then, but most of those who
had done the exterminating had left for richer fields of exploitation. Davis
describes well the pattern that was repeated for decades still to come:

Many of the early conquerors shared in the gold finds, from the small ones
in the islands to the hoard in the treasure house of Atahualpa that astounded
Pizarro's followers in 1533. Yet these hoards were quickly distributed and
when the king's share and the leaders' big portions had been taken out few
rank-and-file soldiers secured enough to take them home to the longed-for
life of luxurious idleness in Castile. . . . The followers and hangers-on of
the conquerors, restless, unreliable material for permanent colonial settlements, were therefore constantly on the move to seek fresh opportunities of
fortune. The opening of Cuba rapidly drained Española of most of its Spanish population after 1513; news of the entry to the mainland accelerated this
exodus after 1517 and it turned into a stampede from all the island settlements when Cortés secured a firm grip on the Aztec Empire in 1521. But the
palace and temple hoards of Tenochtitlán were not adequate to satisfy the
cravings of all the Spaniards who followed Cortés. Large numbers of them
pushed on, under other leaders; into the jungles that separated Mexico from

the little colony on the Panama isthmus, over vast desert plateaus towards California, south to Colombia where gold mines were found by Quesada in 1537, and above all, after 1532, to the new bonanza in Peru. Every township established by the Spaniards in Mexico, with the exception of Mexico City and perhaps Vera Cruz, lost most of its Spanish population within a few years of its foundation.[52]

During these years—and especially after the Incas' fabulous "silver mountain" of Potosí was discovered by the Spanish and converted, through the importation of forced Indian mine labor, into the most populous "city" in the entire Spanish empire—vast sums of wealth flowed back to Spain from the Americas. At the beginning of the sixteenth century, between 1503 and 1505, Spain imported 445,266 ducats' worth of treasure from the New World; by 1536–40 that amount had increased more than ten-fold to 4,725,470 ducats; by 1571–75 it had more than tripled again to 14,287,931 ducats; and by the end of the century, between 1596 and 1600, it had almost tripled again to 41,314,201 ducats—nearly 100 times what it had been a century earlier.[53] But as quickly as those riches flowed back to Spain they also flowed out of Spain's primitive and dependent economy into the pockets of the country's European creditors. As the century wore on this bad situation steadily deteriorated, exacerbated in large measure by the imperial vision—and the pauper's purse, once all the debts were paid—of Charles V and his successor, Philip II.

Within Spain, during the sixteenth century, tax increase followed upon tax increase—at one point the tax load tripled in just two decades—in an effort to sustain the empire's overextended growth, but still when Philip took the Crown at mid-century he inherited a debt of 70,000,000 ducats. By the time his reign was ending two-thirds of the Crown's revenues were earmarked for interest payments alone, and on a number of occasions Philip was forced to convert short-term indebtedness to long-term debt because he simply was unable to pay his obligations.[54] Immanuel Wallerstein has put it simply and well: "Spain was an empire," he writes, "when what was needed in the sixteenth century was a medium-size state."[55]

Much historiographical debate has taken place regarding the ultimate centrality of New World gold and silver to Spain's economy in the sixteenth century, some scholars declaring it to have been much more important than others. What is beyond debate, however, is that Spain at the time *perceived* the wealth of the Indies and the Americas as absolutely essential to its economic health and pursued it with the cupidity of the crudest and greediest conquistador.

The conquistadors, meanwhile, were plying their lethal trade not only in the Americas. No doubt, that was where most Spanish soldiers would have liked to be spending their time—especially after stories began circulating in Spain of people like Gaspar de Espinosa, who was said to have returned home in 1522, after eight years in Panama, with the huge fortune of a million gold pesos—but there was fighting to be done within Europe as well. Indeed, during most of the sixteenth century the Old World was awash in what military historian Robert L. O'Connell calls a "harvest of blood," as European killed European with an extraordinary unleashing of passion. And, of course, Spain was in the thick of it.[56]

In 1568, to cite but one example among many, Philip ordered the duke of Alva—"probably the finest soldier of his day," says O'Connell, "and certainly the cruelest"—to the Netherlands, where Philip was using the Inquisition to root out and persecute Protestants. The duke promptly passed a death sentence upon the entire population of the Netherlands: "he would have utter submission or genocide," O'Connell writes, "and the veterans of Spain stood ready to enforce his will." Massacre followed upon massacre, on one occasion leading to the mass drowning of 6000 to 7000 Netherlanders, "a disaster which the burghers of Emden first realized when several thousand broad-brimmed Dutch hats floated by."[57]

As with most of his other debts, Philip did not pay his soldiers on time, if at all, which created ruptures in discipline and converted the Spanish troops into angry marauders who compensated themselves with whatever they could take. As O'Connell notes:

> Gradually, it came to be understood that should the Spanish succeed in taking a town, the population and its possessions would constitute, in essence, the rewards. So it was that, as the [Netherlands] revolt dragged on, predatory behavior reinforced by economic self-interest came to assume a very pure form. Thus, in addition to plunder, not only did the slaughter of adult males and ritual rape of females increasingly become routine, but other more esoteric acts began to crop up. Repeatedly, according to John Motley, Spanish troops took to drinking the blood of their victims . . . .[58]

If this was the sort of thing that became routine within Europe—as a consequence of "predatory behavior reinforced by economic self-interest" on the part of the Spanish troops—little other than unremitting genocide could be expected from those very same troops when they were loosed upon native peoples in the Caribbean and Meso- and South America— peoples considered by the soldiers, as by most of their priestly and secular betters, to be racially inferior, un-Christian, carnal beasts, or, at best, in Bernardino de Minaya's words quoted earlier, "a third species of animal between man and monkey" that was created by God specifically to provide slave labor for Christian *caballeros* and their designated representatives. Indeed, ferocious and savage though Spanish violence in Europe was during the sixteenth century, European contemporaries of the conquistadors well recognized that by "serving as an outlet for the energies of the unruly," in J.H. Elliott's words, the New World saved Europe, and Spain itself, from even worse carnage. "It is an established fact," the sixteenth-century Frenchman Henri de la Popelinière wrote with dry understatement, "that if the Spaniard had not sent to the Indies discovered by Columbus all the rogues in his realm, and especially those who refused to return to their ordinary employment after the wars of Granada against the Moors, these would have stirred up the country or given rise to certain novelties in Spain."[59]

To the front-line Spanish troops, then, once they had conquered and stolen from the Indians all the treasure the natives had accumulated for themselves, the remaining indigenous population represented only an immense and bestial labor force to be used by the Christians to pry gold and silver from the earth. Moreover, so enormous was the native population—at least during the early years of each successive stage in the overall conquest—that the terrorism of torture, mutilation, and mass murder was the simplest means for motivating the Indians to work; and for the same reason—the seemingly endless supply of otherwise superfluous population—the cheapest way of maximizing their profits was for the conquistadors to work their Indian slaves until they dropped. Replacing the dead with new captives, who themselves could be worked to death, was far cheaper than feeding and caring for a long-term resident slave population.

To be sure, there were those who protested this monstrous treatment of the native people. Las Casas was the most outspoken, the most vigorous, and the most famous, although he was not alone in his efforts. However, he and his supporters were far from a majority, even within the religious fellowship. Here, for example, is what the pious Dominican Tomás Ortiz wrote to the Council of the Indies early in the sixteenth century regarding the New World's peoples:

> On the mainland they eat human flesh. They are more given to sodomy than any other nation. There is no justice among them. They go naked. They have no respect either for love or for virginity. They are stupid and silly. They have no respect for truth, save when it is to their advantage. They are unstable. They have no knowledge of what foresight means. They are ungrateful and changeable. . . . They are brutal. They delight in exaggerating their defects. There is no obedience among them, or deference on the part of the young for the old, nor of the son for the father. They are incapable of learning. Punishments have no effect on them. . . . They eat fleas, spiders, and worms raw, whenever they find them. They exercise none of the human arts or industries. When taught the mysteries of our religion, they say that these things may suit Castilians, but not them, and they do not wish to change their customs. . . . I may therefore affirm that God has never created a race more full of vice and composed without the least mixture of kindness or culture. . . . The Indians are more stupid than asses, and refuse to improve in anything.[60]

The only thing demonstrably true in this litany of Christian hate was that the Indians often were understandably reluctant to give up the faiths of their forefathers and adopt the foreign religious beliefs of the people who had come to kill and torture and enslave them. In addition, many of those who appeared to have undergone conversion turned out to be backsliders, or false conversions in the first place. The Spanish, of course, had a tried and true answer to problems of this sort: the Inquisition. So they instituted among the natives Inquisitorial proceedings to locate and punish those Indians who had given false witness or who had returned to "idolatry" after claiming to have seen the light. Thus, the friars joined the conquistadors in burning Indians at the stake.[61]

If the assertions of Ortiz and others regarding the habits of the Indians were fabrications, they were not fabrications without design. From the Spaniards' enumerations of what they claimed were the disgusting food customs of the Indians (including cannibalism, but also the consumption of insects and other items regarded as unfit for human diets) to the Indians' supposed nakedness and absence of agriculture, their sexual deviance and licentiousness, their brutish ignorance, their lack of advanced weaponry and iron, and their irremediable idolatry, the conquering Europeans were purposefully and systematically dehumanizing the people they were exterminating. For the specific *categories* of behavior chosen for these accusations were openly derived from traditional Christian and earlier Roman and Greek ideas regarding the characteristics of fundamentally evil and non-rational creatures, from Hesiod's Bronze race to the medieval era's wild men and witches. Thus, time and again, the enslavement and terroristic mass slaughter of Indians by the Spanish was justified by pointing to the natives' supposed ignorance or their allegedly despicable and animalistic behavior—as, for example, when Balboa's troops murdered hundreds of native people in one locale, hacking them to death and feeding them to the dogs, because Balboa claimed that some of their chiefs were addicted to the "nefarious and dirty sin [of] sodomy."[62]

All this, of course—from the miraculous discovery of the Indies to the destruction of the heathenish Incas—was part of God's master plan. Indeed, the very priest who had persuaded Las Casas to become a friar, Father Domingo de Betanzos, had widely and influentially proclaimed a prophecy during the early years of the conquest that "the Indians were beasts and that God had condemned the whole race to perish for the horrible sins that they had committed in their paganism." Although Betanzos eventually repudiated the prophecy just before dying while on a pilgrimage to the Holy Land—several decades after pronouncing it, and apparently under pressure from some of his gentler Dominican brothers—by then it was commonly accepted truth by those of both high and low station, within the sacred as well as the secular communities. In fact, no sooner was Betanzos dead than his repudiated prophecy quickly was edited, revised, and recirculated by the Dominican chronicler Dávila Padilla.[63]

Some explanation, after all, had to be given for the apparent ease with which the Indians went to their graves, whether from the storms of European epidemic disease (from which, said one Spaniard, the Indians "died in heaps, like bedbugs") or from the blades of Spanish rapiers.[64] Since, to the minds of Europeans at that time, such extraordinary events did not occur except by divine intent, what could God's purpose be in permitting—or directing—the mass destruction of the native peoples?

The Spanish friars were divided on this question. Some of them argued, in line with Fathers Betanzos and Ortiz, that the Indians had such a terrible history of ungodliness—and especially of indulgence in sins of the flesh—that God was punishing them by exterminating them, and the Spanish were merely the means of carrying out his holy will. (As noted above, such ideas were rooted not only in early Christian thought but in Western classical tradition as well: it was about 800 years before the rise of Christianity, for instance, that Greek wisdom had described famine, plague, and infertility—the crushing burdens now being imposed on the Indians—as the divinely ordered and inevitable just due of those societies that behaved "wickedly.")[65] Others, such as the distinguished Franciscan monk and historian Gerónimo de Mendieta, contended that, on the contrary, the massive Indian die-off was God's punishment to the *Spanish* for their horrendous mistreatment of the natives. Because of their great evil in oppressing the Indians, Mendieta concluded, God had decided to deprive the Spanish of their seemingly inexhaustible supply of slaves and forced labor. "Once the Indians are exterminated," he wrote in his *Historia eclesiástica indiana* from Mexico in the later sixteenth century, "I do not know what is going to happen in this land except that the Spaniards will then rob and kill each other." He continued: "And concerning the plagues that we see among [the Indians] I cannot help but feel that God is telling us: 'You [the Spaniards] are hastening to exterminate this race. I shall help you to wipe them out more quickly. You shall soon find yourselves without them, a prospect that you desire so ardently.' "[66]

In sum, whether God was punishing the Indians for their sins or the Spanish for their cruelties, both sides in this ecclesiastical debate were agreed that God wanted the Indians dead. The conquistadors were only too happy to oblige their Lord and be his holy instrument. If the divinely ordered immolation of these creatures—whom the wisest men in Spain, after all, had long since declared to be mere beasts and natural slaves—was in the end intended to be a punishment for the conquistadors' brutality, they could worry about that in the future, while counting their gold and silver. But the Crown and the merchants who were funding the New World enterprise wanted their share of the treasure now. Moreover, apart from the diseases that God was using to kill off the native people, should anyone express concern over the massive killings that took place in the mines that were supplying all that treasure, the appeal to Aristotle—now enhanced with an insidious element of outright racism—was readily available, and ever more widely employed with every passing year.

The Spanish magistrate Juan de Matienzo provides just one example among many. Writing of the native people of the Andes in his 1567 *Government of Peru,* following six years of service in the viceroyalty there, Matienzo declared that "men of this type or complexion are, according to Aristotle, very fearful, weak, and stupid. . . . It is clear that this is their complexion from the colour of their faces, which is the same in all of them." In addition to the color of their skin, the distinguished jurist wrote, there was the evidence from the strength and shape of their bodies: "It can be known that they were born for this [forced labor in the service of the Spanish] because, as Aristotle says, such types were created by nature with strong bodies and were given less intelligence, while free men have less physical strength and more intelligence." In sum, the Spanish were justified in working the Indians to death, and in killing outright those who were reluctant to serve their natural masters, because these brute creatures were nothing more than "animals who do not even feel reason, but are ruled by their passions."[67] Within a few years after Matienzo's words appeared in print, the huge tide of silver pouring into Europe from the death-camp mines of Peru—silver now worth at least 8,000,000 ducats each year—reached its enormous all-time high. Meanwhile, upwards of 8,000,000 Peruvian natives had been turned into corpses by the Spanish, with barely 1,000,000 remaining alive. And before long, most of those survivors would be destroyed as well.[68]

Some years ago a debate took place among historians of early America concerning the priority of racism or slavery in what both sides agreed was the ultimately racist enslavement of African Americans. Some contended that, of the two, racism was the primary phenomenon, since without it racial slavery of the sort that emerged in the Americas could not have come into being. Others claimed that true racism actually followed on the heels of black slavery in the Americas, forming into a system of thought in large part as rationalization for an otherwise morally indefensible institution. Although the first of these assertions clearly is correct, so too, in a more limited sense, is the second: while sixteenth- and seventeenth-century Western thought was thick with anti-African racist stereotypes, as black slavery as an economic institution took hold and grew so also did elaborate racist justifications for its moral propriety—justifications which then further encouraged the continuing expansion of the institution itself.[69]

This dialectic of ongoing mutual reinforcement between ideology and institution is what historian Winthrop Jordan has called the "cycle of degradation" that continually fueled the "engine of oppression" that wearied and broke the bodies of captive African Americans for two and a half long centuries.[70] And that ideological-institutional cycle of degradation is precisely the dynamic that also emerged early on among the Spanish regarding the native peoples of the Indies and Meso- and South America.

Just as social thought does not bloom in a political vacuum, however, neither do institutions come into being and sustain themselves without the inspiration of economic or political necessity. In sixteenth-century Spain, as we have seen, that necessity was created by an impoverished and financially dependent small nation that made itself into an empire, an empire that engaged in ambitious wars of expansion (and vicious Inquisitorial repression of suspected non-believers within), but an empire with a huge and gaping hole in its treasury: no sooner were gold or silver deposited than they drained away to creditors. The only remedy for this, since control of expenditures did not fit with imperial visions, was to accelerate the appropriation of wealth. And this demanded the theft and mining of more and more New World gold and silver.

The Spanish possessed neither the manpower nor the inclination for mining America's vast store of precious metals themselves. But, along with all those riches, God had provided more laborers than could be imagined—tens upon tens of millions—so many, in fact, that the first Portuguese governor of Brazil claimed it would be impossible to exhaust the supply even if the Europeans were to cut the natives up in slaughterhouses. There was, however, nothing to be gained from the wholesale butchery of Indians for mere entertainment—although that commonly did occur at the hands of enthusiastic conquistadors—while a great deal was to be achieved from working them until they collapsed. So enormous was the reservoir of native muscle and flesh that no rational slave driver would spend good money on caring for these beasts (and beasts they were, and natural slaves, so the wisest of wise men had come to agree); it was more efficient simply to use them up and then replace them.

Mass murder and torture and mutilation had their place, of course, as instruments of terror to recruit reluctant natives and to be sure they stayed in line. But the extermination of entire communities and cultures, though commonplace, was rarely the Spaniards' declared end goal, since to do so meant a large expenditure of energy with no financial return. As with Hispaniola, Tenochtitlán, Cuzco, and elsewhere, the Spaniards' mammoth destruction of whole societies generally was a by-product of conquest and native enslavement, a genocidal means to an economic end, not an end in itself. And therein lies the central difference between the genocide committed by the Spanish and that of the Anglo-Americans: in British America extermination *was* the primary goal, and it was so precisely because it made economic sense.

III

By the close of the sixteenth century bullion, primarily silver, made up more than 95 percent of all exports leaving Spanish America for Europe. Nearly that same percentage of the indigenous population had been destroyed in the process of seizing those riches. In its insatiable hunger, Spain was devouring all that was of most value in its conquered New World territories—the fabulous wealth in people, culture, and precious metals that had so excited the European imagination in the heady era that immediately followed Columbus's return from his first voyage. The number of indigenous people in the Caribbean and Meso- and South America in 1492 probably had been at least equal to that of all Europe, including Russia, at the time. Not much more than a century later it was barely equal to that of England. Entire rich and elaborate and ancient cultures had been erased from the face of the earth. And by 1650 the amount of silver coming out of the Americas was down to far less than half of what it was only fifty years earlier, while gold output had fallen below 10 percent of what it had been.[71] For a century and more the Spanish presence in the Americas had been the equivalent of a horde of ravenous locusts, leaving little but barrenness behind them.

And still, despite so many years of such incredible plunder, Spain itself remained an economic disaster. The treasure it had imported from the Indies, Mexico, and Peru only paid brief visits to the Iberian peninsula before ending up in the coffers of Spain's northerly European creditors. In retrospect, the foundations thus were laid for the "underdevelopment" of Latin America as a modern Third World region. The pattern was the same in other places: wherever the path of Western conquest led, if there were vast available natural and human resources that easily could be taken and used, they were—but the end result was, at best, short-term economic *growth* in the area of colonization, as opposed to long-term economic *development*.[72]

The story of British conquest and colonization in North America is, in economic terms, almost precisely the opposite of Spain's experience to the south. In the north, without a cornucopia of treasure to devour and people to exploit, the English were forced to engage in endeavors that led to long-term development rather than short-term growth, particularly in New England. Far fewer native people greeted the British explorers and colonists than had welcomed the Spanish, in part because the population of the continent north of Mexico had always been smaller and less densely settled, and in part because by the time British colonists arrived European diseases had had more time to spread and destroy large numbers of Indians in Virginia, New England, and beyond. These regions also contained nothing even remotely comparable to the exportable mineral wealth the Spanish had found in the areas they invaded. The most the northern climes had to offer in this regard was fish. To be sure, in the sixteenth and seventeenth centuries the English imported huge amounts of cod from America's North Atlantic waters, and later tobacco and furs were brought in.[73] But fish, tobacco, and furs were not the same as gold or silver.

Nevertheless, despite the very dissimilar economic and native demographic situations they found, the British wasted little time in exterminating the indigenous people. The English and later the Americans, in fact, destroyed at least as high a percentage of the Indians they encountered as earlier had the Spanish, probably higher; it was only their means and motivation that contrasted with those of the conquistadors. To understand both the savagery of the Anglo-American genocide against the North American natives, and the characteristics that made it different from the earlier Spanish genocide, requires a brief glance at the political economy of Britain when its first New World explorations and settlements were being launched, then a look at Anglo-American religious and racial attitudes, and finally a return to the economic realities not of England, but of the colonies themselves.

While Spain in the sixteenth century was overextending its primitive economy with expensive imperial adventures, thereby driving itself to financial ruin, England was developing into one of what Immanuel Wallerstein has called "the strong core states" of northwest Europe that in time would become "the economic heartland of the European world-economy." Unlike Spain, England during this time had a strong export trade in manufactured goods, and although it ran a net deficit in its economic relationship with France, this was more than made up for by a favorable balance of trade elsewhere.[74] It was a time of relative political stability and low taxation, including no personal taxes at all. One historian has made clear the contrast between late sixteenth-century Spain and England with a single telling statistic: "While in Spain Philip II may have absorbed 10 percent of Castile's national income to pay for his wars in the 1580s and 1590s," Ralph Davis writes, "it is doubtful whether in the same years Elizabeth I, at her wits' end to meet war expenses, took more than 3 percent of the national income for them."[75]

For better or for worse—and it was both—England's population was growing rapidly at this time as well. From approximately 2,500,000 at the time of Columbus's birth in the mid-1400s, it had doubled to about 5,000,000 by 1620, when the first permanent British colony was being founded in New England. Although the overall economy was comparatively healthy, the nation contained large masses of desperately poor and potentially dangerous people. The government's response included the passage of poor laws—which drove the poor out of the towns and cities and into marginal rural areas—and the encouragement of migration out of the country altogether. Private individuals, like the famous advocate of exploration Richard Hakluyt, joined in the call to settle England's poor and criminal classes outside the realm, where their conditions and habits might find "hope of amendement."[76]

The first significant move of imperial expansion by the British at this time was into Ireland. Here, the intent of the English was in some ways similar—if on a far smaller scale—to that of the Spanish in the Indies: to convert and "civilize" the natives, while stripping the land bare of its wealth. In the case of Ireland that wealth was not in gold or silver, but in timber, and in just one century the English despoliation reduced the amount of Ireland's rich timberland from an area covering about 12 percent of its territory to practically zero.[77] As we saw in a previous chapter, the English also imitated the Spanish in one other way during their invasion of Ireland—they tortured and killed huge numbers of Irish people.

The English treatment of Ireland's native people provides important insight into understanding the way the British later would treat the indigenous people of North America—not only because it reveals the extent to which the English would go in defining non-Englishmen as savages and destroying them in the process of seizing their land, but also because it shows how far they would *not* go when the native people in question were white. For while it is true that the English demolished large portions of the Irish population in the sixteenth century—massacring the people of Ireland in the same way their forebears had mass-murdered Muslims—the example of the Irish does not equate with that of American Indians. On the contrary, it actually serves to demonstrate how *differently* the British treated people they regarded as lesser than themselves—but lesser in varying degrees, and different precisely because of the rapidly evolving European ideology of race.

First, in their depredations and colonizing campaigns in Ireland, the English clearly distinguished between those natives who were Gaelic Irish and those—though certainly Irish—who were known as "Old English" because they were descendants of earlier Anglo-Norman conquerors. Although both groups were regarded as barbaric by the English, even those British who most vociferously denounced all things Irish tended to make favorable exceptions for the Old English since they were believed to have *fallen* into barbarism as a result of their long-term association with the Gaelic Irish. In contrast, as genealogically non-Anglo-Norman, the Gaelic Irish (like the American Indians) were considered *always* to have been barbaric. Further, in what might seem a paradox only to those innocent of the workings of the racist mind, the British sustained this invidious distinction even when they were arguing that the Old English could be more dangerous and treacherous opponents than were the more barbarous Gaelic Irish. As the Irish historian Nicholas Canny has shown, the British considered the Old English to be more formidable in these ways because they combined "the perverse obstinacy of the *authentic* barbarian" (i.e., the Gaelic Irish) with "the knowledge and expertise of civil people."[78]

"Authentic" barbarians though they may have been in English eyes, nevertheless, the Gaelic Irish still were not so savage as the darker-skinned people the British at that same time were encountering on the huge continents of Africa and the Americas. As a result, whether living among the Gaelic Irish or the Old English populations, the British never set up segregated enclaves—as those Englishmen who moved to North America did—and, despite the terrible levels of violence perpetrated by the English against the Irish, the English were always determined that in time they would assimilate *all* the Irish within English culture and society. "Thus," writes Canny, "while the establishment of British authority in Ireland was closely identified with war, brutality, and the confiscation of property, those on both sides who survived that ordeal learned how to live and associate with each other on the same territory."[79] This did not prevent enormous violence, not only in the sixteenth century, but during the Irish rising of 1641–42 and long after, when tens of thousands of Irish died. However, the English all the while persisted in their efforts to meld the Irish into the British world. As Canny writes:

> More thought was given by Englishmen to this effort at the assimilation of a foreign population into an English-style polity than to any other overseas venture upon which they were then engaged. . . . It will become immediately apparent that whatever the analogies drawn between the Irish and the American Indians, the reality was that English and Scots settlers of the seventeenth century encountered little difficulty in living in close proximity to the Irish and that it seemed, for a time, that the different elements of the population would come together to constitute a single people.[80]

Without minimizing, then, the carnage the English were willing to call down upon their Irish neighbors, such devastation—like that wrought by Europeans upon other Europeans during the Thirty Years War—was of the sort that Frantz Fanon once described as, in the long run, a "family quarrel."[81] For even when such quarrels culminated in multiple and often horrendous instances of mass fratricide, rarely did the rhetoric or action lead to all-out efforts of extermination—as they did in America, repeatedly, when the struggle was an actual race war.

From the start, the English explorers' presuppositions about the human and moral worth of America's native peoples were little different from those of the Spanish, because in large measure they were based directly on Spanish writings and reports. Throughout the sixteenth century, English publishers of travel literature on the Americas studiously avoided reprintings of or references to Las Casas (with the exception of a single small edition of his *Brévissima Relación* in 1583), or to any other Spaniard with even marginally favorable views on the Indians. Rather, they drew almost exclusively on the writings of Gonzalo Fernández de Oviedo y Valdés, Francisco López de Gómara, and other Spanish adventurers and writers who, as Loren E. Pennington puts it, "presented a nearly unrelieved picture of native savagery."[82] Indeed, the very first book on America that was published in the English language appeared in 1511, a decade before Cortés had even laid eyes upon Tenochtitlán; it described the Indians as "lyke bestes without any resonablenes. . . . And they ete also on[e] a nother. The man etethe his wyf his chyldern . . . they hange also the bodyes or persons fleeshe in the smoke as men do with us swynes fleshe."[83] As for how such savages should be treated, notes Pennington, "far from being repelled by Spanish repression of the natives," the earliest English propagandists writing about the New World "looked upon [such repression] as the model to be followed by their own countrymen."[84]

To citizens of Britain and the lands of northern Europe, as with the Spanish and Portuguese to the south, wild men and other creatures of half-human pedigree were as real in the sixteenth and seventeenth centuries as they had been in the Middle Ages. As always, such odd and dangerous species were given their place on the outer fringes of humanity within the Great Chain of Being. John Locke believed in the existence of hybrid species that encompassed characteristics of the human and animal—and even the plant and animal—kingdoms, and so did most other intellectuals, such as the great seventeenth- and eighteenth-century philosopher Gottfried Leibniz. As Leibniz wrote, in the midst of a long peroration on the subject:

> All the orders of natural beings form but a single chain, in which the various classes, like so many rings, are so closely linked one to another that it is impossible for the senses or the imagination to determine precisely the point at which one ends and the next begins—all the species which, so to say, lie near to or upon the borderlands being equivocal, and endowed with characters which might equally well be assigned to either of the neighboring species. Thus there is nothing monstrous in the existence of zoophytes, or plant-animals, as Budaeus calls them; on the contrary, it is wholly in keeping with the order of nature that they should exist.[85]

Added Locke:

> In all the visible corporeal world we see no chasms or gaps. All quite down from us the descent is by easy steps, and a continued series that in each remove differ very little one from the other. There are fishes that have wings and are not strangers to the airy region; and there are some birds that are inhabitants of the water, whose blood is as cold as fishes. . . . There are animals so near of kin both to birds and beasts that they are in the middle between both. Amphibious animals link the terrestrial and aquatic together; . . . not to mention what is confidently reported of mermaids or sea-men. There are some brutes that seem to have as much reason and knowledge as some that are called men; and the animal and vegetable kingdoms are so nearly joined, that if you will take the lowest of one and the highest of the other, there will scarce be perceived any great difference between them.[86]

Until well into the eighteenth century others of the finest minds in Europe believed in, along with the principle of overlapping species continuity in the Great Chain of Being, the existence of half man/half beast creatures who were the product of cross-species mating. As Keith Thomas has pointed out, even Linnaeus, in his famous eighteenth-century classificatory system, "found room for the wild man *(homo ferus)*, 'four-footed, mute and hairy,' and cited ten examples encountered over the previous two centuries." In the popular mind, as in medieval days, Thomas writes, "the early modern period swarmed with missing links, half-man, half-animal." [87] An example of especial relevance to the present discussion is the illustration of an "Acephal"—a headless creature with his face in his chest—among the depictions of America's native peoples in the Jesuit Joseph François Lafitau's highly respected *Customs of the American Indians,* published in 1724. [88]

It is, therefore, far from surprising to find sixteenth-century English sea captains, adventurers, and soldiers of fortune—all of whom had heard the most negative Spanish descriptions of the native peoples of the New World—solemnly performing inspections of captured Indians to see (as we noted earlier in the case of Martin Frobisher) if they had cloven feet or other marks of the Devil. To some Englishmen there also remained, for a time, the possibility that the New World natives were of some sort of Golden Age ancestry. Both these expectations can be found in the earliest writings of the British in America. Thus, for example, Arthur Barlowe—after landing in Virginia in 1584 and "tak[ing] possession of [the land] in the right of the queen's most excellent Majesty . . . under her Highness' Great Seal"—recalled that upon encountering the Indians,

> we were entertained with all love and kindness and with as much bounty, after their manner, as they could possibly devise. We found the people most gentle loving and faithfull, void of all guile and treason, and such as lived after the manner of the Golden Age. . . . a more kind and loving people, there can not be found in the world, as farre as we have hitherto had triall. [89]

There is probably no more favorable description of the Indians of North America in the annals of the early explorers. This did not, however, prevent these very same Englishmen from attacking these very same Indians at the slightest provocation: "we burnt, and spoyled their corne, and Towne, all the people" (those "gentle loving and faithfull" people) "beeing fledde." [90] For, on the other hand, these same Virginia Indians were soon after described by the likes of Robert Gray as

> wild beasts, and unreasonable creatures, or . . . brutish savages, which by reason of their godles ignorance, and blasphemous Idolatrie, are worse than those beasts which are of most wilde and savage nature. . . . [They are] incredibly rude, they worship the divell, offer their young children in sacrifice unto him, wander up and downe like beasts, and in manners and conditions, differ very little from beasts. [91]

Any number of commentators can be summoned to support either of these contrasting views of the Indians, and still more can be called upon to provide judgments of the Indians ranging variously between these two extremes. As had been the case earlier with the Spanish, however, the more negative views very quickly came to dominate. And they were not infrequently expressed by drawing direct parallels between the experiences of the British in Virginia or New England and the Spanish in Mexico and the Caribbean. Thus, in an early treatise on the Virginia Company's progress in the New World, the company's secretary, Edward Waterhouse, discussed at length the Spanish experience with the natives of the Indies and approvingly quoted the Indian-hating and genocide-supporting conquistador Fernández de Oviedo to the effect that those Indians were "by nature sloathful and idle, vicious, melancholy, slovenly, of bad conditions, lyers, of small memory, of no constancy or trust. . . . lesse capable than children of sixe or seaven yeares old, and lesse apt and ingenious." Oviedo's description of the Indies' indigenous inhabitants was offered the reader, Waterhouse said, "that you may compare and see in what, and how farre, it agrees with that of the Natives of Virginia." Indeed, so closely did it agree, he contended, that the proper response of the British against this "Viperous brood . . . of Pagan Infidels" should be the same as that meted out by the Spanish: extermination.[92] This conclusion was reached, it should be noted, at a time when there were barely 2000 Englishmen living in all of North America, and nearly a decade before Britain's Massachusetts Bay Company would be sending settlers into New England.

There are other ways in which we now can see, retrospectively, how the evolution of British racial thought in North America paralleled what had happened previously among the Spanish and Portuguese. We noted earlier, for instance, how changing Portuguese attitudes toward the Indians of Brazil were illustrated dramatically in an early sixteenth-century painting of the Gift of the Magi that used a depiction of a Brazilian Indian in place of one of the wise men calling on the Christ child, followed by a mid-sixteenth-century painting that used a feather-bedecked Indian of the same region to illustrate a depiction of Satan in his lair of Hell. A similar transformation in the Europeans' moral perceptions of Virginia's Indians is traceable in the famous illustrations of Theodor de Bry and his sons, throughout the thirty volumes of pictorial representations they published between 1590 and 1634. From initial imagery suggestive of Virginia as a place inhabited by people, in Barlowe's words, who "lived after the manner of the Golden Age," iconographic evolution soon converted that world into a place of monstrously deformed and diseased savages. To the European artists, as to Europeans in general, notes Bernadette Bucher in her structural analysis of the de Brys illustrations, there was from the start a categorical ambiguity surrounding the New World's native peoples. Citing the work of anthropologist Mary Douglas, Bucher notes that beings and things that participate in two or more categories as fixed by a given culture appear ambiguous and monstrous for that reason, and become instantly burdened with interdictions, horror and disgust. . . . At first, the Amerindian, by his very existence on a previously unknown continent and the mystery surrounding his origins, introduced chaos into the order of things such as the Europeans imagined it in their own cosmogony, moral code, and ideas on the origin of man.[93]

But before long, as Bucher says, the Europeans became fairly settled in their opinion that while the Indians were likely human, they were not so in an unambiguous sense—for if they were men, they were "men *without* God, *without* law, *without* breeches." These final two words presumably are an unattributed reference to the closing sentence of Michel de Montaigne's famous ironic essay, "Of Cannibals," in which Montaigne—writing in the late 1570s—favorably compares the life and culture and dignity of the American Indian to that of the "real savages" of Europe, only to conclude sarcastically, "but what of it? They don't wear breeches."[94] If Montaigne and Bucher were being pointedly lighthearted, however, many other Europeans saw nothing amusing in the stories of the Indians' near-nakedness and what it represented in terms of the allegedly libidinous and bestial nature of these people of the fearsome wilderness. And there is no doubt that that is how Europe was coming to regard the New World peoples. Indeed, as John Higham recently has demonstrated, artistic conventions of the time personified each of the world's continents as female, but in distinct and individually stereotyped ways:

> To differentiate America from Africa and Asia, artists relied chiefly on her partial or complete nudity. Asia was always fully clothed, often sumptuously so. Africa, attired in sometimes revealing but always elegant dress, was supposed to look Moorish, since Europeans were most familiar with the Mediterranean littoral. America alone was a savage.[95]

In recent years some historians have begun pointing out that the British colonists in Virginia and New England greatly intensified their hostility toward and their barbarous treatment of the Indians as time wore on. One of the principal causes of this change in temperament, according to these scholars, was the Europeans' realization that the native people were going to persist in their reluctance to adopt English religious and cultural habits, no matter how intense the British efforts to convert them. No doubt they are correct in this interpretation—a notion that is not at all at odds with Bucher's structural analysis of the de Brys iconography, with the earlier Spanish experience, or with the traditional Christian suspicion, at least since Augustine, that stubborn resistance to conversion by those living beyond the margins of civilization was a sign that they were less than rational and thus less than human—but this increased antipathy and violence was a matter of escalating degree, not (as some of these writers imply) a wholesale change in consciousness.[96] For as we have seen at some length in the preceding pages, the Europeans' predisposition to racist enmity regarding the Indians had long been both deeply embedded in Western thought and was intimately entwined with attitudes toward nature, sensuality, and the body. That there were some Europeans who appreciated and even idealized native cultural values—and some settlers who ran off to live with the Indians because they found their lifeways preferable to their own—is undeniable. But these were rarities, and rarities with little influence, within a steadily rising floodtide of racist opinion to the contrary.[97]

What in fact was happening in those initial years of contact between the British and America's native peoples was a classic case of self-fulfilling prophecy, though one with genocidal consequences. Beginning with a false prejudgment of the Indians as somehow other than conventionally human in European terms (whether describing them as living "after the manner of the Golden Age" or as "wild beasts and unreasonable creatures"), everything the Indians did that marked them as incorrigibly non-European and non-Christian—and therefore as *permanently* non-civilized in British eyes—enhanced their definitionally less-than-human status. Treating them according to this false definition naturally brought on a resentful response from the Indians—one which only "proved" (albeit spuriously) that the definition had been valid from the start. In his famous study of this phenomenon Robert K. Merton—after quoting the sociological dictum that "if men define situations as real, they are real in their consequences"— pointed out that "the specious validity of the self-fulfilling prophecy perpetuates a reign of error."[98] In the early and subsequent years of British-Indian contact, however, it produced and perpetuated a reign of terror because it was bound up with an English lust for power, land, and wealth, and because the specific characteristics that the English found problematic in the Indians were attributes that fit closely with ancient but persistently held ideas about the anti-Christian hallmarks of infidels, witches, and wild men.

It was only to be expected, therefore, that when the witchcraft crisis at Salem broke out as the seventeenth century was ending, it would be blamed by New England's foremost clergyman on "the Indians, whose chief Sagamores are well known unto some our Captives, to have been horrid Sorcerers, and hellish Conjurers, and such as Conversed with Daemons."[99] Indeed, as Richard Slotkin has shown, the fusion of the satanic and the native in the minds of the English settlers by this time had become so self-evident as to require no argument. Thus, when a young woman named Mercy Short became possessed by the Devil, she described the beast who had visited her as "a wretch no taller than an ordinary Walking-Staff; hee was not of a Negro, but of a Tawney, or an Indian colour; he wore a high-crowned Hat, with straight Hair; and had one Cloven-foot." Observes Slotkin: "He was, in fact, a figure out of the American Puritan nightmare . . . Indian-colored, dressed in a Christian's hat, with a beast's foot—a kind of Indian-Puritan, man-animal half-breed."[100]

In the preceding chapter we explored at some length Catholic doctrines of asceticism, purity, and religious self-righteousness and intolerance—as well as the Church's murderous treatment of those it regarded as unchaste and impure non-believers. But Protestantism deserves some scrutiny in its own right. For even though most of England's Protestants had shunted aside asceticism of the specifically *contemptus mundi* variety (the anti-Roman elements of the faith condemned monastic withdrawal from the world and insisted that Saints partake—albeit in moderation—of the earthly gifts that God had provided for men and women), asceticism in the larger sense remained alive and well for centuries. Indeed, probably never before in Christian history had the idea that humankind was naturally corrupt and debased reached and influenced the daily lives of a larger proportion of the lay community than during New England's seventeenth and early eighteenth centuries. New England Congregationalist Susanna Anthony was only one among many thousands of Protestant divines who as late as the 1760s delighted in examining her soul and—in phrases reminiscent of her saintly Catholic sisters from four and five centuries earlier—discovering

the sinfulness of my nature, the corrupt fountain from whence proceeded every sinful act. . . . My heart has looked like a sink of sin, more loathsome than the most offensive carrion that swarms with hateful vermin! My understanding dark and ignorant; my will stubborn; my affections carnal, corrupt and disordered; every faculty depraved and vitiated; my whole soul deformed and polluted, filled with pride, enmity, carnality, hypocrisy, self-confidence, and all manner of sins. . . . Woe is me, because of the leprosy of sin, by which I am so defiled, that I pollute all I touch! . . . Good God, what a leprous soul is this! How polluted, how defiled! What a running sore, that pollutes all I touch!"[101]

Unlike her medieval Catholic forebears, Miss Anthony did not (as far as we know) accompany this torrent of self-hatred with self-inflicted physical abuse. But like them before her, the more she expressed her loathing for the rottenness of her heart and will and all her sensual affections, the more admirable and godly a person she was in her own eyes and in those of others. Such sanctification of what one commentator has described as the "furtive gratifications of an ascetic sadism" was, after all, the evangelical way. And as Philip Greven clearly has shown, in the fanatical and obsessive efforts of people like Miss Anthony and her spiritual kin "to placate implacable consciences and in their systematic efforts to mortify and subdue the body and the self," along with their consequently heightened perception of the world "as a dangerous and seductive place," the early New England settlers of evangelical Puritan character "often saw evidence of anger and hostility in *other* people which they denied within themselves." And in no people did they see such things so clearly as in the indigenous people of the territory they were invading who became the unwilling victims of the Protestants' "unending . . . warfare with the unregenerate world in which they lived."[102]

This also is why what David Brion Davis once said about the belated emergence of the antislavery movement was equally true regarding the unlikelihood of any semblance of humanitarian concern for the Indians gaining serious support during this time: it could not and would not happen so long as Christians "continued to believe that natural man was totally corrupt, that suffering and subordination were necessary parts of life, and that the only true freedom lay in salvation from the world."[103] For a core principle of the saintly Puritan's belief system was that the "natural" condition of the hearts of all humans prior to their conversion to Christ—even the hearts of the holiest and most innocent of Christian infants—was, in the esteemed New England minister Benjamin Wadsworth's words, "a meer nest, root, fountain of Sin, and wickedness."[104] By defining the Indians as bestial *and* as hopelessly beyond conversion, then, the colonists were declaring flatly that these very same words aptly described the natives' *permanent* racial condition. And to tolerate known sin and wickedness in their midst would be to commit sin and wickedness themselves.

Moreover—and ominously—from the earliest days of settlement the British colonists repeatedly expressed a haunting fear that they would be "contaminated" by the presence of the Indians, a contamination that must be avoided lest it become the beginning of a terrifying downward slide toward their own bestial degeneration. Thus, unlike the Spanish before them, British men in the colonies from the Carolinas to New England rarely engaged in sexual relations with the Indians, even during those times when there were few if any English women available. Legislation was passed that "banished forever" such mixed race couples, referring to their offspring in animalistic terms as "abominable mixture and spurious issue," though even without formal prohibitions such intimate encounters were commonly "reckoned a horrid crime with us," in the words of one colonial Pennsylvanian.[105] It is little wonder, then, that Mercy Short described the creature that possessed her as both a demon and, in Slotkin's words, "a kind of Indian-Puritan, man-animal half-breed," for this was the ultimate and fated consequence of racial contamination.

Again, however, such theological, psychological, and legislative preoccupations did not proceed to the rationalization of genocide without a social foundation and impetus. And if a possessive and tightly constricted attitude toward sex, an abhorrence of racial intermixture, and a belief in humankind's innate depravity had for centuries been hallmarks of Christianity, and therefore of the West's definition of civilization, by the time the British exploration and settlement of America had begun, the very essence of humanity also was coming to be associated in European thought with a similarly possessive, exclusive, and constricted attitude toward property. For it is precisely of this time that R.H. Tawney was writing when he observed the movement away from the earlier medieval belief that "private property is a necessary institution, at least in a fallen world . . . but it is to be tolerated as a concession to human frailty, not applauded as desirable in itself," to the notion that "the individual is absolute master of his own, and, within the limits set by positive law, may exploit it with a single eye to his pecuniary advantage, unrestrained by any obligation to postpone his own profit to the well-being of his neighbors, or to give account of his actions to a higher authority."[106]

The concept of private property as a positive good and even an insignia of civilization took hold among both Catholics and Protestants during the sixteenth century. Thus, for example, in Spain, Juan Ginés de Sepúlveda argued that the absence of private property was one of the characteristics of people lacking "even vestiges of humanity," and in Germany at the same time Martin Luther was contending "that the possession of private property was an essential difference between men and beasts."[107] In England, meanwhile, Sir Thomas More was proclaiming that land justifiably could be taken from "any people [who] holdeth a piece of ground void and vacant to no good or profitable use," an idea that also was being independently advanced in other countries by Calvin, Melanchthon, and others. Typically, though, none was as churlish as Luther, who pointed out that the Catholic St. Francis had urged his followers to get rid of their property and give it to the poor: "I do not maintain that St. Francis was simply wicked," wrote Luther, "but his works show that he was a weak-minded and freakish man, or to say the truth, a fool."[108]

The idea that failure to put property to "good or profitable use" was grounds for seizing it became especially popular with Protestants, who thereby advocated confiscating the lands owned by Catholic monks. As Richard Schlatter explains:

> The monks were condemned, not for owning property, but because they did not use that property in an economically productive fashion. At best they used it to produce prayers. Luther and the other Reformation leaders insisted that it should be used, not to relieve men from the necessity of working, but as a tool for making more goods. The attitude of the Reformation was practically, "not prayers, but production." And production, not for consumption, but for more production.[109]

The idea of production for the sake of production, of course, was one of the central components of what Max Weber was to call the Protestant Ethic. But it also was essential to what C.B. Macpherson has termed the

ideology of "possessive individualism." And at the heart of that ideology
was a political theory of appropriation that was given its fullest elaboration in the second of John Locke's *Two Treatises of Government*. In addition to the property of his own person, Locke argued, all men have a
right to their own labor and to the fruits of that labor. When a person's
private labor is put to the task of gathering provisions from the common
realm, the provisions thus gathered become the private property of the one
who labored to gather them, so long as there are more goods left in the
common realm for others to gather with their labor. But beyond the right
to the goods of the land, Locke argued, was the right to "the Earth it self."
It is, he says, "plain" that the same logic holds with the land itself as with
the products of the land: "As much Land as a Man Tills, Plants, Improves,
Cultivates, and can use the Product of, so much is his Property. He by his
Labour does, as it were, inclose it from the Common."[110]

Only through the ability to exercise such individual acquisitiveness,
thought Locke, does a man become fully and truly human. However, notes
Macpherson, concealed within this celebration of grasping and exclusive
individualism was the equally essential notion that "full individuality for
some was produced by consuming the individuality of others." Thus, "the
greatness of seventeenth-century liberalism was its assertion of the free
rational individual as the criterion of the good society; its tragedy was that
this very assertion was necessarily a denial of individualism to half the
nation."[111] Indeed, more than a denial of individualism, Locke's proposals
for how to treat the landless poor of his own country—whom he considered a morally depraved lot—were draconian: they were to be placed
into workhouses and forced to perform hard labor, as were all their children above the age of three. As Edmund S. Morgan observes, this proposal
"stopped a little short of enslavement, though it may require a certain
refinement of mind to discern the difference."[112]

Locke's work, of course, post-dates the era of early British colonization
in North America, but the kernels of at least these aspects of his thought
were present and articulated prior to the founding of the English colonies
in the work of Luther, Calvin, More, Melanchthon, and other British and
Continental thinkers.[113] An obvious conclusion derivable from such an
ideology was that those without a Western sense of private property were,
by definition, not putting their land to "good or profitable use," as More
phrased it, and that therefore they deserved to be dispossessed of it. Thus,
in More's *Utopia,* first published in Latin in 1516 and in English in 1551,
he envisions the founding of a colony "wherever the natives have much
unoccupied and uncultivated land"; should the natives object to this taking of their property or should they "refuse to live according to their [the
settlers'] laws," the settlers are justified in driving the natives "from the
territory which they carve out for themselves. If they resist, they wage war
against them."[114] In practice this became known as the principle of *vac-*

uum domicilium, and the British colonists in New England appealed to it enthusiastically as they seized the shared common lands of the Indians.[115]

One of the first formal expressions of this justification for expropriation by a British colonist was published in London in 1622 as part of a work entitled *Mourt's Relation, or a Journal of the Plantation of Plymouth.* The author of this piece describes "the lawfulness of removing out of England into parts of America" as deriving, first, from the singular fact that "our land is full . . . [and] their land is empty." He then continues:

> This then is a sufficient reason to prove our going thither to live lawful: their land is spacious and void, and they are few and do but run over the grass, as do also the foxes and wild beasts. They are not industrious, neither have [they] art, science, skill or faculty to use either the land or the commodities of it; but all spoils, rots, and is marred for want of manuring, gathering, ordering, etc. As the ancient patriarchs therefore removed from straiter places into more roomy [ones], where the land lay idle and wasted and none used it, though there dwelt inhabitants by them . . . so is it lawful now to take a land which none useth and make use of it.[116]

The most well known and more sophisticated statement on the matter, however, came from the pen of the first governor of the Massachusetts Bay Colony, John Winthrop. While still in England, on the eve of joining what became known as the Great Migration to Massachusetts in the 1630s, Winthrop compiled a manuscript "justifieinge the undertakeres of the intended Plantation in New England," and answering specific questions that might be raised against the enterprise. The first justification, as with Columbus nearly a century and a half earlier, was spiritual: "to carry the Gospell into those parts of the world, to helpe on the comminge of the fullnesse of the Gentiles, and to raise a Bulworke against the kingdome of Ante-Christ," an understandable reason for a people who believed the world was likely to come to an end during their lifetime.[117] Very quickly, however, Winthrop got to the possible charge that "we have noe warrant to enter upon that Land which hath beene soe longe possessed by others." He answered:

> That which lies common, and hath never beene replenished or subdued is free to any that possesse and improve it: For God hath given to the sonnes of men a double right to the earth; theire is a naturall right, and a Civill Right. The first right was naturall when men held the earth in common every man sowing and feeding where he pleased: then as men and theire Cattell encreased they appropriated certaine parcells of Grownde by inclosing and peculiar manuerance, and this in time gatte them a Civill right. . . . As for the Natives in New England, they inclose noe Land, neither have any setled habytation, nor any tame Cattell to improve the Land by, and soe have noe

other but a Naturall Right to those Countries, soe as if we leave them sufficient for their use, we may lawfully take the rest, there being more than
enough for them and us.[118]

In point of fact, the Indians had thoroughly "improved" the land—
that is, cultivated it—for centuries. They also possessed carefully structured and elaborated concepts of land use and of the limits of political
dominion, and they were, as Roger Williams observed in 1643, "very ex-
act and punctuall in the bounds of their Land, belonging to this or that
Prince or People."[119] This was, however, not private "ownership" as the
English defined the term, and it is true that probably no native people
anywhere in the Western Hemisphere would have countenanced a land use
system that, to return to Tawney's language, allowed a private individual
to "exploit [the land] with a single eye to his pecuniary advantage, unrestrained by any obligation to postpone his own profit to the well-being of
his neighbors." And thus, in the view of the English, were the Indian nations "savage."

For unlike the majority of the Spanish before them—who, in Las Casas's words, "kill[ed] and destroy[ed] such an infinite number of souls"
only "to acquire gold, and to swell themselves with riches in a very brief
time and thus rise to a high estate disproportionate to their merits"—all
that the English wanted was the land. To that end, the Indians were merely
an impediment. Unlike the situation in New Spain, the natives living in
what were to become the English colonies had, in effect, no "use value."
With the exception of the earliest British explorers in the sixteenth century,
England's adventurers and colonists in the New World had few illusions
of finding gold or of capturing Indians for large-scale enslavement. Nor
did they have an impoverished European homeland, like Spain, that was
desperate for precious goods that might be found or stolen or wrenched
from American soil (with forced native labor) in order to sustain its imperial expansion. They did, however, have a homeland that seemed to be
bursting at the seams with Englishmen, and they felt they needed what in
another language in another time became known as *Lebensraum*. And so,
during the first century of successful British settlement in North America
approximately twice as many English men and women moved to the New
World as had relocated from Spain to New Spain during the previous
hundred years. And unlike the vast majority of the Spanish, the British
came with families, and they came to stay.[120]

To that flood of British colonists the Indians were, at best, a superfluous population—at least once they had taught the English how to survive.
In Virginia, true plantation agriculture did not begin until after most of
the Indians had been exterminated, whereupon African slaves were imported to carry out the heavy work, while in New England the colonists
would do most of the agricultural tasks themselves, with the help of British

indentured servants, but they required open land to settle and to cultivate. A simple comparison between the inducements that were given the early Spanish and the early British New World settlers reveals the fundamental difference between the two invasions: the Spanish, with the *repartimiento*, were awarded not land but large numbers of native people to enslave and do with what they wished; the English, with the "headright," were provided not with native people but with fifty acres of land for themselves and fifty acres more for each additional settler whose transatlantic transportation costs they paid.

These differences in what material things they sought had deep effects as well on how the Spanish and the English would interpret their respective American environments and the native peoples they encountered there. Thus, however much they slaughtered the natives who fell within their orbit, the Spanish endlessly debated the ethical aspects of what it was that they were doing, forcing upon themselves elaborate, if often contorted and contradictory, rationalizations for the genocide they were committing. As we saw earlier, for example, Franciscans and Dominicans in Latin America argued strenuously over what God's purpose was in sending plagues to kill the Indians, some of them contending that he was punishing the natives for their sins, while others claimed he was chastening the Spanish for their cruelties by depriving them of their slaves. Additionally, throughout the first century of conquest Spanish scholars were embroiled in seemingly endless debates over the ethical and legal propriety of seizing and appropriating Indian lands, disputes that continued to haunt independence struggles in Spanish America well into the nineteenth century.[121] No such disputation took place among the Anglo-American colonists or ministers, however, because they had little doubt as to why God was killing off the Indians or to whom the land rightfully belonged. It is, in short, no accident that the British did not produce their own Las Casas.

As early as the first explorations at Roanoke, Thomas Hariot had observed that whenever the English visited an Indian village, "within a few days after our departure . . . the people began to die very fast, and many in a short space: in some towns about twenty, in some forty, in some sixty, and in one six score, which in truth was very many in respect of their numbers." As usual, the British were unaffected by these mysterious plagues. In initial explanation, Hariot could only report that "some astrologers, knowing of the Eclipse of the Sun, which we saw the same year before on our voyage thitherward," thought that might have some bearing on the matter. But such events as solar eclipses and comets (which Hariot also mentions as possibly having some relevance) were, like the epidemics themselves, the work of God. No other interpretation was possible. And that was why, before long, Hariot also was reporting that there seemed to be a divinely drawn pattern to the diseases: miraculously, he said, they affected only those Indian communities "where we had any subtle device practiced against us." [122] In other words, the Lord was selectively punishing only those Indians who plotted against the English.

Needless to say, the reverse of that logic was equally satisfying—that is, that only those Indians who went *un*punished were *not* evil. And if virtually all were punished? The answer was obvious. As William Bradford was to conclude some years later when epidemics almost totally destroyed the Indian population of Plymouth Colony, without affecting the English: "It pleased God to visit these Indians with a great sickness and such a mortality that of a thousand, above nine and a half hundred of them died, and many of them did rot above the ground for want of burial." All followers of the Lord could only give thanks to "the marvelous goodness and providence of God," Bradford concluded. It was a refrain that soon would be heard throughout the land. After all, prior to the Europeans' arrival, the New World had been but "a hideous and desolate wilderness," Bradford said elsewhere, a land "full of wild beasts and wild men." [123] In killing the Indians in massive numbers, then, the English were only doing their sacred duty, working hand in hand with the God who was protecting them.

For nothing else, only divine intervention, could account for the "prodigious Pestilence" that repeatedly swept the land of nineteen out of every twenty Indian inhabitants, wrote Cotton Mather, "so that the Woods were almost cleared of these pernicious Creatures, to make room for a better Growth." Often this teamwork of God and man seemed to be perfection itself, as in King Philip's War. Mather recalled that in one battle of that war the English attacked the native people with such ferocity that "their city was laid in ashes. Above twenty of their chief captains were killed; a proportionable desolation cut off the interior salvages; mortal sickness, and horrid famine pursu'd the remainders of 'em, so we can hardly tell where any of 'em are left alive upon the face of the earth." [124]

Thus the militant agencies of God and his chosen people became as one. Mather believed, with many others, that at some time in the distant past the "miserable salvages" known as Indians had been "decoyed" by the Devil to live in isolation in America "in hopes that the gospel of the Lord Jesus Christ would never come here to destroy or disturb his absolute empire over them." [125] But God had located the evil brutes and sent his holiest Christian warriors over from England where—with the help of some divinely sprinkled plagues—they joyously had "Irradiated an Indian wilderness." [126] It truly was, as another New England saint entitled his own history of the holy settlement, a "wonder-working providence."

IV

Again and again the explanatory circle closed upon itself. Although they carried with them the same thousand years and more of repressed, intolerant, and violent history that earlier had guided the conquistadors, in their explorations and settlements the English both left behind and confronted before them very different material worlds than had the Spanish. For those who were their victims it didn't matter very much. In addition to being un-Christian, the Indians were uncivilized and perhaps not even fully human. The English had been told that by the Spanish, but there were many other proofs of it; one was the simple fact (untrue, but that was immaterial) that the natives "roamed" the woods like wild beasts, with no understanding of private property holdings or the need to make "improvements" on the land. In their generosity the Christian English would bring to these benighted creatures the word of Christ and guidance out of the dark forest of their barbarism. For these great gifts the English only demanded in return—it was, after all, their God-given right—whatever land they felt they needed, to bound and fence at will, and quick capitulation to their religious ways.

In fact, no serious effort ever was made by the British colonists or their ministers to convert the Indians to the Christian faith. Nor were the Indians especially receptive to the token gestures that were proffered: they were quite content with their peoples' ancient ways.[127] In addition, it was not long before the English had outworn their welcome with demands for more and more of the natives' ancestral lands. Failure of the Indians to capitulate in either the sacred or the secular realms, however, was to the English all the evidence they needed—indeed, all that they were seeking—to prove that in their dangerous and possibly contaminating bestiality the natives were an incorrigible and inferior race. But God was making a place for his Christian children in this wilderness by slaying the Indians with plagues of such destructive power that only in the Bible could precedents for them be found. His divine message was too plain for misinterpretation. And the fact that it fit so closely with the settlers' material desires only made it all the more compelling. There was little hope for these devil's helpers of the forest. God's desire, proved by his unleashing wave upon wave of horrendous pestilence—and pestilence that killed selectively only Indians—was a command to the saints to join his holy war.

Writing of New England's Puritans (though the observation holds true as well for most other Anglo-American settlers), Sacvan Bercovitch makes clear an essential point:

> The Puritans, despite their missionary pretenses, regarded the country as *theirs* and its natives as an obstacle to *their* destiny as Americans. They could remove that obstacle either by conversion (followed by "confinement"), or else by extermination; and since the former course proved insecure, they had recourse to the latter. The Spanish, for all their rhetoric of conquest, regarded the country as the Indians' and native recruitment as essential to their design of colonization.[128]

Given that difference, Bercovitch continues, the Iberian "colonists saw themselves as Spaniards in an inferior culture. By that prerogative, they converted, coerced, educated, enslaved, reorganized communities, and established an intricate caste system, bound by a distinctly Spanish mixture of feudal and Renaissance customs." The Anglo-American colonists, in contrast, simply obliterated the natives they encountered, for they considered themselves, almost from the start, as "new men," in Crèvecoeur's famous phrase, in a new land, and not as expatriates in a foreign place. Bercovitch illustrates what he calls the subsequent New World Spaniards' "profound identity crisis" as *Americanos* by citing Simón Bolívar's Jamaica Letter of 1815, following the outbreak of revolution against Spain: we were "not prepared to secede from the mother country," Bolívar wrote, "we were left orphans . . . uncertain of our destiny. . . . [W]e scarcely retain a vestige of what once was; we are, moreover, neither Indian nor European, but an intermediate species between the legitimate owners of this country and the Spanish usurpers." [129]

The point is further sharpened if we compare Bolívar's lament—after more than three centuries of Spanish rule in Latin America—with the boastful and self-confident words of Thomas Jefferson's first inaugural address, delivered more than a dozen years before Bolívar's letter and less than two centuries since the founding of the first permanent English colonies:

> A rising nation, spread over a wide and fruitful land, traversing all the seas with the rich productions of their industry, engaged in commerce with nations who feel power and forget right, advancing rapidly to destinies beyond the reach of the mortal eye—when I contemplate these transcendent objects, and see the honor, the happiness, and the hopes of this beloved country committed to the issue, and the auspices of this day, I shrink from the contemplation, and humble myself before the magnitude of the undertaking. [130]

It was in pursuit of these and other grand visions that Jefferson later would write of the remaining Indians in America that the government was obliged "now to pursue them to extermination, or drive them to new seats beyond our reach." For the native peoples of Jefferson's "rising nation," of his "beloved country"—far from being Bolívar's "legitimate owners"— were in truth, most Americans believed, little more than dangerous wolves. Andrew Jackson said this plainly in urging American troops to root out from their "dens" and kill Indian women and their "whelps," adding in his second annual message to Congress that while some people tended to grow "melancholy" over the Indians' being driven by white Americans to their "tomb," an understanding of "true philanthropy reconciles the mind to these vicissitudes as it does to the extinction of one generation to make room for another." [131]

Before either Jefferson or Jackson, George Washington, the father of the country, had said much the same thing: the Indians were wolves and beasts who deserved nothing from the whites but "total ruin."[132] And Washington himself was only repeating what by then was a very traditional observation. Less than a decade after the founding of the Massachusetts Bay Colony in 1630, for example, it was made illegal to "shoot off a gun on any unnecessary occasion, or at any game except an Indian or a wolf." As Barry Lopez has noted, this was far from a single-incident comparison. So alike did Indians and wolves appear to even the earliest land-hungry New England colonist that the colonist "fell to dealing with them in similar ways":

> He set out poisoned meat for the wolf and gave the Indian blankets infected with smallpox. He raided the wolf's den to dig out and destroy the pups, and stole the Indian's children . . . . When he was accused of butchery for killing wolves and Indians, he spun tales of Mohawk cruelty and of wolves who ate fawns while they were still alive. . . . Indians and wolves who later came into areas where there were no more of either were called renegades. Wolves that lay around among the buffalo herds were called loafer wolves and Indians that hung around the forts were called loafer Indians.[133]

As is so often the case, it was New England's religious elite who made the point more graphically than anyone. Referring to some Indians who had given offense to the colonists, the Reverend Cotton Mather wrote: "Once you have but got the Track of those Ravenous howling Wolves, then pursue them vigourously; *Turn not back till they are consumed. . . .* Beat them small as the *Dust before the Wind.*" Lest this be regarded as mere rhetoric, empty of literal intent, consider that another of New England's most esteemed religious leaders, the Reverend Solomon Stoddard, as late as 1703 formally proposed to the Massachusetts Governor that the colonists be given the financial wherewithal to purchase and train large packs of dogs "to hunt Indians as they do bears." There were relatively few Indians remaining alive in New England by this time, but those few were too many for the likes of Mather and Stoddard. "The dogs would be an extreme terror to the Indians," Stoddard wrote, adding that such "dogs would do a great deal of execution upon the enemy and catch many an Indian that would be too light of foot for us." Then, turning from his equating of native men and women and children with bears deserving to be hunted down and destroyed, Stoddard became more conventional in his imagery: "if the Indians were as other people," he acknowledged, ". . . it might be looked upon as inhumane to pursue them in such a manner"; but, in fact, the Indians were wolves, he said, "and are to be dealt withal as wolves."[134] For two hundred years to come Washington, Jefferson, Jackson, and other leaders, representing the wishes of virtually the entire white nation, followed these ministers' genocidal instructions with great care. It was their Christian duty as well as their destiny.

. . .

In sum, when in 1492 the seal was broken on the membrane that for tens of thousands of years had kept the residents of North and South America isolated from the inhabitants of the earth's other inhabited continents, the European adventurers and colonists who rushed through the breach were representatives of a religious culture that was as theologically arrogant and violence-justifying as any the world had ever seen. Nourished by a moral history that despised the self and that regarded the body and things sensual as evil, repulsive, and bestial, it was a culture whose holiest exemplars not only sought out pain and degradation as the foundation of their faith, but who simultaneously both feared and pursued what they regarded as the dark terrors of the wilderness—the wilderness in the world outside as well as the wilderness of the soul within. It was a faith that considered all humanity in its natural state to be "sick, suffering, and helpless" because its earliest mythical progenitors—who for a time had been the unclothed inhabitants of an innocent Earthly Paradise—had succumbed to a sensual temptation that was prohibited by a jealous and angry god, thereby committing an "original sin" that thenceforth polluted the very essence of every infant who had the poor luck to be born. Ghastly and disgusting as the things of this world—including their own persons—were to these people, they were certain of at least one thing: that their beliefs were absolute truth, and that those who persisted in believing otherwise could not be tolerated. For to tolerate evil was to encourage evil, and no sin was greater than that. Moreover, if the flame of intolerance that these Christian saints lit to purge humanity of those who persisted down a path of error became a sacred conflagration in the form of a crusade or holy war—that was only so much the better. Such holocausts themselves were part of God's divine plan, after all, and perhaps even were harbingers of his Son's imminent Second Coming.

It is impossible to know today how many of the very worldly men who first crossed the Atlantic divide were piously ardent advocates of this worldview, and how many merely unthinkingly accepted it as the religious frame within which they pursued their avaricious quests for land and wealth and power. Some were seeking souls. Most were craving treasure, or land on which to settle. But whatever their individual levels of theological consciousness, they encountered in this New World astonishing numbers of beings who at first seemed to be the guardians of a latter-day Eden, but who soon became for them the very picture of Satanic corruption.

And through it all, as with their treatment of Europe's Jews for the preceding half-millennium—and as with their response to wildness and wilderness since the earliest dawning of their faith—the Christian Europeans continued to display a seemingly antithetical set of tendencies: revulsion from the terror of pagan or heretical pollution and, simultaneously, eagerness to make all the world's repulsive heretics and pagans into followers of Christ. In its most benign racial manifestation, this was the same inner prompting that drove missionaries to the ends of the earth to Christianize people of color, but to insist that their new converts worship in segregated churches. Beginning in the late eighteenth century in America, this conflict of racial abhorrence and mission—and along with it a redefined concept of holy war—became secularized in the form of an internally contradictory political ideology. In the same way that the Protestant Ethic was transformed into the Spirit of Capitalism, while the Christian right to private property became justifiable in wholly secular terms, America as Redeemer Nation became Imperial America, fulfilling its irresistible and manifest destiny.

During the country's early national period this took the form of declarations that America should withdraw from world affairs into moral isolation (to preserve the chaste new nation from the depravities of the Old World and the miserable lands beyond) that was uttered in the same breath as the call to export the "Rising Glory of America," to bring democracy and American-style civilization to less fortunate corners of the earth.[135] Less than a century later, during the peak era of American imperialism, the same contradictory mission presented itself again: while those Americans who most opposed expansion into the Philippines shared the imperialists' belief in the nation's predestined right to rule the world, they resisted efforts to annex a nation of "inferior" dark-skinned people largely because of fears they had of racial contamination. Charles Francis Adams, Jr., said it most straightforwardly when he referred to America's virulent treatment of the Indians as the lesson to recall in all such cases, because, harsh though he admitted such treatment was, it had "saved the Anglo-Saxon stock from being a nation of half-breeds."[136] In these few words were both a terrible echo of past warrants for genocidal race war and a chilling anticipation of eugenic justifications for genocide yet to come, for to this famous scion of America's proudest family, the would-be extermination of an entire race of people was preferable to the "pollution" of racial intermixture.

It was long before this time, however, that the notion of the deserved and fated extermination of America's native peoples had become a commonplace and secularized ideology. In 1784 a British visitor to America observed that "white Americans have the most rancorous antipathy to the whole race of Indians; nothing is more common than to hear them talk of extirpating them totally from the face of the earth, men, women, and children."[137] And this visitor was not speaking only of the opinion of those whites who lived on the frontier. Wrote the distinguished early nineteenth-century scientist, Samuel G. Morton: "The benevolent mind may regret the inaptitude of the Indian for civilization," but the fact of the matter was that the "structure of [the Indian's] mind appears to be different from that of the white man, nor can the two harmonize in the social relations except on the most limited scale."[138] "Thenceforth," added Francis Parkman, the most honored American historian of his time, the natives—whom he described as "man, wolf, and devil all in one"—"were destined to melt and vanish before the advancing waves of Anglo-American power, which now rolled westward unchecked and unopposed." The Indian, he wrote, was in fact responsible for his own destruction, for he "will not learn the arts of civilization, and he and his forest must perish together." [139]

But by this time it was not just the native peoples of America who were being identified as the inevitable and proper victims of genocidal providence and progress. In Australia, whose aboriginal population had been in steep decline (from mass murder and disease) ever since the arrival of the white man, it commonly was being said in scientific and scholarly publications, that

> to the Aryan . . . apparently belong the destinies of the future. The races whose institutions and inventions are despotism, fetishism, and cannibalism—the races who rest content in . . . placid sensuality and unprogressive decrepitude, can hardly hope to contend permanently in the great struggle for existence with the noblest division of the human species. . . . The survival of the fittest means that might—wisely used—is right. And thus we invoke and remorselessly fulfil the inexorable law of natural selection when exterminating the inferior Australian. [140]

Meanwhile, by the 1860s, with only a remnant of America's indigenous people still alive, in Hawai'i the Reverend Rufus Anderson surveyed the carnage that by then had reduced those islands' native population by 90 percent or more, and he declined to see it as a tragedy; the expected total die-off of the Hawaiian people was only natural, this missionary said, somewhat equivalent to "the amputation of diseased members of the body." [141] Two decades later, in New Zealand, whose native Maori people also had suffered a huge population collapse from introduced disease and warfare with invading British armies, one A.K. Newman spoke for many whites in that country when he observed that "taking all things into consideration, the disappearance of the race is scarcely subject for much regret. They are dying out in a quick, easy way, and are being supplanted by a superior race." [142]

Returning to America, the famed Harvard physician and social commentator Oliver Wendell Holmes observed in 1855 that Indians were nothing more than a "half-filled outline of humanity" whose "extermination" was the necessary "solution of the problem of his relation to the white race." Describing native peoples as "a sketch in red crayons of a rudimental manhood," he added that it was only natural for the white man to "hate" the Indian and to "hunt him down like the wild beasts of the forest, and so the red-crayon sketch is rubbed out, and the canvas is ready for a picture of manhood a little more like God's own image." [143]

Two decades later, on the occasion of the nation's 1876 centennial celebration, the country's leading literary intellectual took time out in an essay expressing his "thrill of patriotic pride" flatly to advocate "the extermination of the red savages of the plains." Wrote William Dean Howells to the influential readers of the *Atlantic Monthly:*

> The red man, as he appears in effigy and in photograph in this collection [at the Philadelphia Centennial Exposition], is a hideous demon, whose malign traits can hardly inspire any emotion softer than abhorrence. In blaming our Indian agents for malfeasance in office, perhaps we do not sufficiently account for the demoralizing influence of merely beholding those false and pitiless savage faces; moldy flour and corrupt beef must seem altogether too good for them.[144]

Not to be outdone by the most eminent historians, scientists, and cultural critics of the previous generation, several decades later still, America's leading psychologist and educator, G. Stanley Hall, imperiously surveyed the human wreckage that Western exploration and colonization had created across the globe, and wrote:

> Never, perhaps, were lower races being extirpated as weeds in the human garden, both by conscious and organic processes, so rapidly as to-day. In many minds this is inevitable and not without justification. Pity and sympathy, says Nietzsche, are now a disease, and we are summoned to rise above morals and clear the world's stage for the survival of those who are fittest because strongest. . . . The world will soon be overcrowded, and we must begin to take selective agencies into our own hands. Primitive races are either hopelessly decadent and moribund, or at best have demonstrated their inability to domesticate or civilize themselves.[145]

And not to be outdone by the exalted likes of Morton, Parkman, Holmes, Howells, Adams, or Hall, the man who became America's first truly twentieth century President, Theodore Roosevelt, added his opinion that the extermination of the American Indians and the expropriation of their lands "was as ultimately beneficial as it was inevitable. Such conquests," he continued, "are sure to come when a masterful people, still in its raw barbarian prime, finds itself face to face with the weaker and wholly alien race which holds a coveted prize in its feeble grasp." It is perhaps not surprising, then, that this beloved American hero and Nobel Peace Prize recipient (who once happily remarked that "I don't go so far as to think that the only good Indians are dead Indians, but I believe nine out of ten are, and I shouldn't like to inquire too closely into the case of the tenth") also believed that "degenerates" as well as "criminals . . . and feeble-minded persons [should] be forbidden to leave offspring behind them." The better classes of white Americans were being overwhelmed, he feared, by "the unrestricted breeding" of inferior racial stocks, the "utterly shiftless," and the "worthless."[146]

These were sentiments, applied to others, that the world would hear much of during the 1930s and 1940s. (Indeed, one well-known scholar of the history of race and racism, Pierre L. van den Berghe, places Roosevelt within an unholy triumvirate of the modern world's leading racist statesmen; the other two, according to van den Berghe, are Adolf Hitler and Hendrik Verwoerd, South Africa's original architect of apartheid.)[147] For the "extirpation" of the "lower races" that Hall and Roosevelt were celebrating drew its justification from the same updated version of the Great Chain of Being that eventually inspired Nazi pseudoscience. Nothing could be more evident than the fundamental agreement of both these men (and countless others who preceded them) with the central moral principle underlying that pseudoscience, as expressed by the man who has been called Germany's "major prophet of political biology," Ernst Haeckel, when he wrote that the "lower races"—Sepúlveda's *"homunculi"* with few "vestiges of humanity"; Mather's "ravenous howling wolves"; Holmes's "half-filled outline of humanity"; Howells's "hideous demons"; Hall's "weeds in the human garden"; Roosevelt's "weaker and wholly alien races"—were so fundamentally different from the "civilized Europeans [that] we must, therefore, assign a totally different value to their lives."[148] Nor could anything be clearer, as Robert Jay Lifton has pointed out in his exhaustive study of the psychology of genocide, than that such thinking was nothing less than the "harsh, apocalyptic, deadly rationality" that drove forward the perverse holy war of the Nazi extermination campaign.[149]

The first Europeans to visit the continents of North and South America and the islands of the Caribbean, like the Nazis in Europe after them, produced many volumes of grandiloquently racist apologia for the genocidal holocaust they carried out. Not only were the "lower races" they encountered in the New World dark and sinful, carnal and exotic, proud, inhuman, un-Christian inhabitants of the nether territories of humanity—contact with whom, by civilized people, threatened morally fatal contamination—but God, as always, was on the Christians' side. And God's desire, which became the Christians' marching orders, was that such dangerous beasts and brutes must be annihilated.

Elie Wiesel is right: the road to Auschwitz *was* being paved in the earliest days of Christendom. But another conclusion now is equally evident: on the way to Auschwitz the road's pathway led straight through the heart of the Indies and of North and South America.

EPILOGUE

It is unlikely to have escaped notice that this book is being published to coincide with the Columbian Quincentennial—the 500th anniversary of the beginning of the genocide that nearly expunged the Western Hemisphere of its people. It is, however, less probable that many readers will know that 1992 also is the 50th anniversary of the Nazis' conversion of Auschwitz from a prisoner of war and concentration camp into a chamber of unspeakable horrors, designed to exterminate systematically as many as possible of Europe's Jews, Gypsies, and other Nazi-characterized "useless lives."

As we have seen, one of the preconditions for the Spanish and Anglo-American genocides against the native peoples of the Americas was a public definition of the natives as inherently and permanently—that is, as racially—inferior beings. To the conquering Spanish, the Indians more specifically were defined as natural slaves, as subhuman beasts of burden, because that fit the use to which the Spanish wished to put them, and because such a definition was explicable by appeal to ancient Christian and European truths—through Aquinas and on back to Aristotle. Since the colonizing British, and subsequently the Americans, had little use for Indian servitude, but only wanted Indian land, they appealed to other Christian and European sources of wisdom to justify their genocide: the Indians were Satan's helpers, they were lascivious and murderous wild men of the forest, they were bears, they were wolves, they were vermin. Allegedly having shown themselves to be beyond conversion to Christian or to civil life—and with little British or American need for them as slaves—in this case, straightforward mass killing of the Indians was deemed the only thing to do.

Native peoples, however, are not alone as objects of Christianity's disdain. During most of the past millennium of European history—since at least the first pogrom in Germany in the year 1096—Jews have lived in wary knowledge of their own precarious existence. Entire volumes exist that detail Christian Europe's long-entrenched and pathological hatred of Jews and all things Jewish. There is neither room nor need to recount again that bitter history here. But one example will make a necessary point. In a lengthy tract of 1543 entitled *On the Jews and Their Lies,* Martin Luther referred to Jews as "a plague, a pestilence," as "venomous, bitter worms," as "a desperate, thoroughly evil, poisonous, and devilish lot," as "useless, evil, pernicious people," as "tricky serpents, assassins, and children of the devil," as a "brood of vipers," and as "mad dogs." With his characteristically crude eloquence Luther, of course, was only speaking the thoughts that countless Christian saints and saintly aspirants had held and expressed regarding Jews for centuries. So, too, was he representing the ideas of Christian masses when he offered his "sincere advice":

to set fire to their synagogues or schools and to bury and cover with dirt whatever will not burn, so that no man will ever again see a stone or cinder of them. . . . I [also] advise that their houses be razed and destroyed. . . . I advise that all their prayer books and Talmudic writings, in which such idolatry, lies, cursing, and blasphemy are taught, be taken from them. . . . that their rabbis be forbidden to teach henceforth on pain of loss of life and limb. . . . that safe-conduct on the highways be abolished completely for the Jews. . . . that all cash and treasure of silver and gold be taken from them and put aside for safekeeping. . . . I [also] recommend putting a flail, an ax, a hoe, a spade, a distaff, or a spindle into the hands of young, strong Jews and Jewesses and letting them earn their bread in the sweat of their brow. . . . But if the authorities are reluctant to use force and restrain the Jews' devilish wantonness, the latter should, as we said, be expelled from the country and be told to return to their land and their possessions in Jerusalem, where they may lie, curse, blaspheme, defame, murder, steal, rob, practice usury, mock, and indulge in all those infamous abominations which they practice among us, and leave us our government, our country, our life, and our property, much more leave our Lord the Messiah, our faith, and our church undefiled and uncontaminated with their devilish tyranny and malice.[1]

Even to someone possessed of Luther's towering ferocity and hate, however, Jews in that time were not yet considered a separate category of being. Indeed, after almost 200 pages of vituperative screed such as that extracted out above, Luther closes his diatribe by saying: "May Christ, our dear Lord, *convert them mercifully* and preserve us steadfastly and immovably in the knowledge of him, which is eternal life. Amen."[2]

In sum, for all their allegedly despicable traits, Jews still had souls, they still were human—and it still was possible that they might be saved. Time, of course, would change that perception, at least for some later Christians of Teutonic ancestry. It took a long while for this shift in perception to work toward its hideously logical conclusion—although in Spain, during the time that Luther was writing, the doctrine of *limpieza de sangre* was doing its part in laying the essential groundwork—but three centuries later an otherwise insignificant German writer and Jew-hater named Wilhelm Marr publicly proposed that Jews were a separate and degenerate and dangerously polluting race. The idea was picked up by others who churned out their own variations on the theme.[3]

"In these works the Jews are shown not simply as evil," Norman Cohn has observed, "but as irremediably evil, the source of their depravity lies no longer simply in their religion but in their very blood."[4] Among those more influential than Marr who elaborated on his slander was a devout Christian of puritanically ascetic sexual pretension, an Englishman-turned-German named Houston Stewart Chamberlain. To Chamberlain a fight to the death—a holy war—between Jews and Aryans was inevitable, and once the Jewish " 'race' was decisively defeated," writes Cohn of Chamberlain's grand design, "the Germanic 'race' would be free to realize its own divinely appointed destiny—which was to create a new, radiant world, transfused with a noble spirituality and mysteriously combining modern technology and science with the rural, hierarchical culture of earlier times."[5] If that is a dream of manifest destiny that sounds disturbingly familiar to students of early American history—with echoes in the writings of John Winthrop, Thomas Jefferson, and others—Chamberlain once made an arresting historical connection of his own: upon meeting Hitler, he wrote, he thought of Martin Luther.[6]

Chamberlain's intuition wasn't wrong. And therein, at first, appears to be a paradox. For we have suggested that Luther's Judeophobia, hateful though it was, was separated from Judeocide—from the Holocaust—by the absence in Luther's thought of a "racial" definition of the Jews, a definition that was essential to Hitlerian genocidal ideology. It is a distinction that should not be minimized. But neither should something else be forgotten: for all that Hitler held Christianity in low regard, central to his thinking, as well as to that of the Christian Fathers (and to Luther), was an intense concern with human depravity, with pollution, with defilement—and with cleansing, purity, and purgation—as well as an absolute and violent animosity for all who disagreed with him.[7]

It is, of course, only coincidental, but during the summer of 1924, while Hitler was imprisoned outside Munich and was dictating to Rudolf Hess the contents of *Mein Kampf,* the author Joseph Conrad died of a heart attack near Canterbury, England. On the surface, there was almost nothing that the two men had in common. Among his numerous crimes against humanity, for instance, Hitler was to become the architect of Operation Barbarossa, the furious invasion of the Soviet Union that killed more than three million Soviet troops during just the first three months of fighting, while Conrad had condemned all European imperialism, and especially the exploitation of Africa, as "the vilest scramble for loot that ever disfigured the history of human conscience and geographical exploration."[8] But just as Hitler had nothing but scorn and hatred for altruistic behavior (brutality, he liked to say, was the sole basis for whatever advances humans had achieved), so Conrad was filled with a more genteel contempt for human promise. Thus, the day after reading a life of Saint Teresa, he wrote to his close friend Cunninghame Graham:

> The mysteries of the universe made of drops of fire and clods of mud do not concern us in the least. The fate of humanity condemned ultimately to perish from cold is not worth troubling about. If you take it to heart it becomes an unendurable tragedy. If you believe in improvement you must weep, for the attained perfection must end in cold, darkness and silence.[9]

It would be of small consequence what Joseph Conrad thought about such matters if he were not generally considered, in Albert J. Guerard's words, "the most philosophical and, as a psychologist, the most complex of English novelists," and the author of two of "the half-dozen greatest short novels in the English language."[10] One of those short novels, the one for which Conrad is most famous—and which "is today perhaps the most commonly prescribed novel in twentieth-century literature courses in English departments of American universities" as it is "read by practically every freshman as an introduction to great fiction"—is *Heart of Darkness*.[11]

There exist few, if any, superior fictional portrayals of the Christian West's obsession with the immersion of the self in its own alleged vileness, or of Christian culture's irresistible attraction to and simultaneous terror in the face of savagery and wilderness and wildness and the dark. As in the didactic stories of the early Christian hermits, who wandered in the barren desert and tormented themselves with everyday reminders of the disgusting filth that lurked within their bodies and their souls, *Heart of Darkness* is an exploration of the bleak and ghastly horror that much of Western thought has long believed resides in the core of every person as well as in the savage wilds beyond the far horizon. What has been remarked upon too little by Western readers of this work, however, is how infused it is with the malignancy of Conrad's own racist vision. Indeed, it is telling that after what shortly will be a century of critical praise for *Heart of Darkness,* it took Chinua Achebe—a distinguished Nigerian novelist and man of letters—to demonstrate most clearly that while "Conrad saw and condemned the evil of imperial exploitation [he] was strangely unaware of the racism on which it sharpened its iron tooth." And unaware because Conrad was himself "a thoroughgoing racist." [12]

For Conrad, as for all those many millions who have read his work without revulsion, it is African humanity that intuitively serves to symbolize the worst—the most bestial and most ugly—of mankind's inner essence. Conrad knew his Western readers would understand without instruction, and he was right. No argument is necessary, description is enough:

> [S]uddenly, as we struggled round a bend, there would be a glimpse of rush walls, of peaked grass-roofs, a burst of yells, a whirl of black limbs, a mass of hands clapping, of feet stamping, of bodies swaying, of eyes rolling, under the droop of heavy and motionless foliage. The steamer toiled along slowly on the edge of the black and incomprehensible frenzy. The prehistoric man was cursing us, praying to us, welcoming us—who could tell? We were cut off from the comprehension of our surroundings; we glided past like phantoms, wondering and secretly appalled, as sane men would be before an enthusiastic outbreak in a madhouse. . . . We are accustomed to look upon the shackled form of a conquered monster, but there—there you could look at a thing monstrous and free. It was unearthly, and the men were—No, they were not inhuman. Well, you know, that was the worst of it—this suspicion of their not being inhuman. It would come slowly to one. They howled and leaped, and spun, and made horrid faces; but what thrilled you was just the thought of their humanity—like yours—the thought of your remote kinship with this wild and passionate uproar. Ugly. Yes, it was ugly enough; but if you were man enough you would admit to yourself that there was in you just the faintest trace of a response to the terrible frankness of that noise, a dim suspicion of there being a meaning in it which you—you so remote from the night of first ages—could comprehend. [13]

"Well, you know, that was the worst of it—this *suspicion* of their not being inhuman"—for surely the purpose of this passage is to demonstrate as powerfully as possible just how *absolutely* inhuman the Africans truly seemed, and how close to the murky borderland of the animal world they really were; thus the impact of the European's haunting sense "that there was in you just the faintest trace of a response" to—and a "remote kinship with"—such brutal, monstrous beings. As Achebe says in a different essay: "In confronting the black man, the white man has a simple choice: either to accept the black man's humanity and the equality that flows from it, or to reject it and see him as a beast of burden. No middle course exists except as an intellectual quibble." [14] In fact, however, it is precisely that "intellectual quibble" that has poisoned Western thought, not only about Africans, but about all peoples of non-European ancestry, for centuries long past and likely for a good while yet to come. And therein lies the true heart of Western darkness. For the line that separates Martin Luther's anti-

Jewish fulminations from those of Adolf Hitler is a line of great importance, but it also is a line that is frighteningly thin. And once crossed, as it was not only in Germany in the early twentieth century, but in the Indies and the Americas four centuries before, genocide is but a step away.

From time to time during the past half-century Americans have edged across that line, if only temporarily, under conditions of foreign war. Thus, as John W. Dower has demonstrated, the eruption of war in the Pacific in the 1940s caused a crucial shift in American perceptions of the Japanese from a prewar attitude of racial disdain and dismissiveness (the curator of the Smithsonian Institution's Division of Anthropology had advised the President that the Japanese skull was "some 2,000 years less developed than ours," while it was widely believed by Western military experts that the Japanese were incompetent pilots who "could not shoot straight because their eyes were slanted") to a wartime view of them as super-competent warriors, but morally subhuman beasts. This transformation became a license for American military men to torture and mutilate Japanese troops with impunity—just as the Japanese did to Americans, but in their own ways, following the cultural reshaping of their own racial images of Americans. As one American war correspondent in the Pacific recalled in an *Atlantic Monthly* article:

> We shot prisoners in cold blood, wiped out hospitals, strafed lifeboats, killed or mistreated enemy civilians, finished off the enemy wounded, tossed the dying into a hole with the dead, and in the Pacific boiled the flesh off enemy skulls to make table ornaments for sweethearts, or carved their bones into letter openers.[15]

Dower provides other examples of what he calls the "fetish" of "collecting grisly battlefield trophies from the Japanese dead or near dead, in the form of gold teeth, ears, bones, scalps, and skulls"—practices receiving sufficient approval on the home front that in 1944 *Life* magazine published a "human interest" story along with "a full-page photograph of an attractive blonde posing with a Japanese skull she had been sent by her fiancé in the Pacific."[16] (Following the Battle of Horse Shoe Bend in 1814, Andrew Jackson oversaw not only the stripping away of dead Indians' flesh for manufacture into bridle reins, but he saw to it that souvenirs from the corpses were distributed "to the ladies of Tennessee.")[17]

A little more than two decades after that *Life* photograph and article appeared, General William C. Westmoreland was describing the people of Vietnam as "termites," as he explained the need to limit the number of American troops in that country:

> If you crowd in too many termite killers, each using a screwdriver to kill the termites, you risk collapsing the floors or the foundation. In this war we're

using screwdrivers to kill termites because it's a guerrilla war and we cannot use bigger weapons. We have to get the right balance of termite killers to get rid of the termites without wrecking the house.[18]

Taking their cue from the general's dehumanization of the Southeast Asian "gooks" and "slopes" and "dinks," in a war that reduced the human dead on the enemy side to "body counts," American troops in Vietnam removed and saved Vietnamese body parts as keepsakes of their tours of duty, just as their fathers had done in World War Two. Vietnam, the soldiers said, was "Indian Country" (General Maxwell Taylor himself referred to the Vietnamese opposition as "Indians" in his Congressional testimony on the war), and the people who lived in Indian country "infested" it, according to official government language. The Vietnamese may have been human, but as the U.S. Embassy's Public Affairs Officer, John Mecklin, put it, their minds were the equivalent of "the shriveled leg of a polio victim," their "power of reason . . . only slightly beyond the level of an American six-year old."[19] Gonzalo Fernández de Oviedo y Valdés could not have said it better.

And then, another two decades later still, in another part of the world, as American tanks by the hundreds rolled over and buried alive any humans that were in their path, the approved term for dead Iraqi women and children became "collateral damage." Even well before the war with Iraq broke out, the U.S. Air Force's 77th Tactical Fighter Squadron produced and distributed a songbook describing what they planned to do on their inevitable Middle East assignments. Here is the only sample that is publishable:

> Phantom flyers in the sky,
> Persian-pukes prepare to die,
> Rolling in with snake and nape,
> Allah creates but we cremate.[20]

The rest of the book's verses are a melange of sadism and obscenity, most of them employing personifications of entire Arabic and Islamic peoples as racially inferior, maggot-infested women whose mass destruction by the Americans is equated with brutal, violent sex. During the brief duration of the war itself, American pilots referred to the killing of unarmed, retreating enemy soldiers as a "turkey shoot," and compared the Iraqi people—otherwise known as "ragheads"—to "cockroaches" running for cover when allied planes appeared overhead. Graffiti on bombs slung under the wings of American aircraft labeled them as "Mrs. Saddam's sex toy" and "a suppository for Saddam," while the American field commander subsequently admitted in a television interview that he wished he had been able to complete his job: "We could have completely closed the door and made it a battle of annihilation," he said; it was "literally about to become the battle of Cannae, a battle of annihilation" before—to his disappointment—the general was called off.[21]

It should be noted that the third century B.C. battle of Cannae, during which Carthaginian troops under the command of Hannibal almost completely exterminated a group of 80,000 to 90,000 Romans, is still regarded as an exemplar of total destructiveness to military historians. Even today, Italians living in the region where the attack took place refer to the site of the massacre as *Campo di Sangue,* or "Field of Blood." In his own words, this is what General Norman Schwarzkopf had hoped to create in Iraq. And when confronted by the press with evidence that appeared to demonstrate the American government's lack of concern for innocent civilians (including as many as 55,000 children) who died as a direct consequence of the war—and with a United States medical team's estimate that hundreds of thousands more Iraqi children were likely to die of disease and starvation caused by the bombing of civilian facilities—the Pentagon's response either was silence, evasion, or a curt "war is hell."[22]

Indeed it is. The purpose of this brief tour across several recent battlegrounds is not simply to condemn what is so easily condemnable, however, but rather to illustrate how close to the surface of everyday life is the capacity for racist dehumanization and consequently massive devastation. For among the many things that warfare does is temporarily define the entire enemy population as superfluous, as expendable—a redefinition that must take place before most non-psychopaths can massacre innocent people and remain shielded from self-condemnation. And nothing is more helpful to that political and psychological transformation than the availability of a deep well of national and cultural consciousness that consigns whole categories of people to the distant outback of humanity.

But even the worst wars end. Military defeat leads to political surrender, for it is politics that most wars are about. Genocide is different. The *purpose* of genocide is to do away with an entire people, or to indiscriminately consume them, either by outright mass murder or by creating conditions that lead to their oblivion. Thus, the slave labor projects that worked people to death in the synthetic rubber factory at Auschwitz, or in the nearby coal mines, were no less genocidal than the gas chambers there and in other camps. Moreover, although Arno J. Mayer may well be correct in contending that "from 1942 to 1945, certainly at Auschwitz, but probably overall, more Jews [in the camps] were killed by so-called "natural" causes than by "unnatural" ones—"natural" causes being "sickness, disease, undernourishment, [and] hyperexploitation," as opposed to "unnatural" causes such as "shooting, hanging, phenol injection, or gassing"—there can be no denying, as Mayer himself insists, that those who died "naturally" were no less victims of genocide than others who were murdered outright.[23]

Indeed, it is insufficient to stop even here. For as Michael R. Marrus rightly states:

> It is clearly wrong to separate from the essence of the Holocaust those Jews who never survived long enough to reach the camps, or who were shot down by the Einsatzgruppen in the Soviet Union, or who starved in the ghettos of eastern Europe, or who were wasted by disease because of malnutrition and neglect, or who were killed in reprisal in the west, or who died in any of the countless other, terrible ways—no less a part of the Holocaust because their final agonies do not meet some artificial standard of uniqueness.[24]

The same is true of the anti-Indian genocide in the Americas. Just as those Jews and others who died of exploitation and disease and malnutrition and neglect and in "countless other, terrible ways"—other, that is, than straightforward cold-blooded butchery—would not have died when and where they did, but for the genocide campaign that was swirling furiously all about them, so too in the Indies and the Americas: the natives of Hispaniola and Mexico and Peru and Florida and Virginia and Massachusetts and Georgia and Colorado and California and elsewhere who died from forced labor, from introduced disease, from malnutrition, from death marches, from exposure, and from despair were as much victims of the Euro-American genocidal race war as were those burned or stabbed or hacked or shot to death, or devoured by hungry dogs.

To some, the question now is: Can it happen again? To others, as we said in this book's opening pages, the question is, now as always: Can it be stopped? For in the time it has taken to read these pages, throughout Central and South America Indian men and women and children have been murdered by agents of the government that controls them, simply because they were Indians; native girls and boys have been sold on open slave markets; whole families have died in forced labor, while others have starved to death in concentration camps.[25] More will be enslaved and more will die in the same brutal ways that their ancestors did, tomorrow, and every day for the foreseeable future. The killers, meanwhile, will continue to receive aid and comfort and support from the United States government, the same government that oversees and encourages the ongoing dissolution of Native American families within its own political purview— itself a violation of the U.N. Genocide Convention—through its willful refusal to deal adequately with the life-destroying poverty, ill health, malnutrition, inadequate housing, and despair that is imposed upon most American Indians who survive today.[26]

That is why, when the press reported in 1988 that the United States Senate finally had ratified the United Nations Genocide Convention—after forty years of inaction, while more than a hundred other nations had long since agreed to its terms—Leo Kuper, one of the world's foremost experts on genocide wondered in print whether "the long delay, and the obvious reluctance of the United States to ratify the Genocide Convention" derived from "fear that it might be held responsible, retrospectively, for the annihilation of Indians in the United States, or its role in the slave trade, or its contemporary support for tyrannical governments engaging in mass murder." Still, Kuper said he was delighted that at last the Americans had agreed to the terms of the Convention.[27]

Others were less pleased—including the governments of Denmark, Finland, Ireland, Italy, the Netherlands, Norway, Spain, Sweden, and the United Kingdom, who filed formal objections with the United Nations regarding the U.S. action. For what the United States had done, unlike the other nations of the world, was approve and file with the U.N. a self-servingly *conditional* instrument of ratification. Whatever the objections of the rest of the world's nations, however, it now seems clear that the United States is unlikely ever to do what those other countries have done—ratify unconditionally the Genocide Convention.[28]

For more than forty years another nation with a shameful past, Poland, refused to acknowledge officially what had transpired in the death camps—including Auschwitz, Sobibor, and Treblinka—that had been located on Polish soil. But in the spring of 1991 Poland's President, Lech Walesa, traveled to Jerusalem and addressed the Israeli Parliament, saying in part: "Here in Israel, the land of your culture and revival, I ask for your forgiveness."[29] At almost precisely that same moment, in Washington, angry members of the U.S. Senate were threatening to cut off or drastically reduce financial support for the Smithsonian Institution because a film project with which it was marginally involved had dared use the word "genocide" to describe the destruction of America's native peoples. In that instant contrast of ethical principles, in the chasm of moral difference that separated the Polish President and the American Senators, the seamy underside of America's entire history was briefly but brightly illuminated.

Illuminated as well at that moment was the persistence in American thinking of what has been termed the syndrome—the racist syndrome—of "worthy and unworthy victims."[30] For at the same time that almost all Americans would properly applaud President Walesa's long-overdue acknowledgment of and apology for the horrors that were perpetrated against Jewish and other European "worthy" victims in Poland's Nazi extermination centers during forty ghastly months in the 1940s, they by and large continue to turn their backs on the even more massive genocide that for four grisly centuries was perpetrated against what their apathy implicitly defines as the "unworthy" natives of the Americas.

Moreover, the suffering has far from stopped. The poverty rate on American Indian reservations in the United States, for example, is almost four times the national average, and on some reservations, such as Pine

Ridge in South Dakota and Tohono O'Odham in Arizona (where more than 60 percent of homes are without adequate plumbing, compared with barely 2 percent for the rest of the country) the poverty rate is nearly five times greater than for the nation at large. The destitution and ill health and general squalor that are the norm on many reservations today are no different from conditions that prevail throughout much of the indigent Third World. Indeed, so desperate and demoralizing are life conditions on most reservations that the suicide rate for young Indian males and females aged 15 to 24 years is around 200 percent above the overall national rate for the same age group, while the rate for alcohol-caused mortality—itself a form of suicide—is more than 900 percent higher than the national figure among 15 to 24 year-old Indian males and nearly 1300 percent higher than the comparable national figure among 15 to 24 year-old Indian females.[31]

Meanwhile, the reservations themselves—the last chance for the survival of ancient and cherished cultural traditions and lifeways, however viciously deprived of resources they are by the overseeing state and federal governments—remain under relentless assault, at the same time that the United States with much fanfare about human rights is encouraging ethnic and national sovereignty movements in Eastern Europe and the former Soviet Union. Today, American Indian tribal lands total in size less than half of what they were in 1890, following the massacre at Wounded Knee and the supposed end of the euphemistically-named Indian wars.[32] And much of the tribal land that still exists, constituting a little more than 2 percent of what commonly is the most inhospitable acreage in the United States, is in perpetual jeopardy of political disentitlement. Most of the Western Shoshoni people's land, for example, was long ago confiscated for underground nuclear testing, while individual states routinely drive Indians off their land by denying tribes access to traditional water supplies and other necessary resources. The states are free to carry out such policies of confiscation because the federal government, in the disingenuous guise of granting Indians "self-determination," steadfastly continues to abdicate its legal responsibility for defending tribes against state encroachment. Thus, the Indians' ongoing struggle for a modicum of independence and cultural freedom is turned against them in a classic governmental maneuver of blaming the victim, while the campaign to terminate tribal sovereignty once and for all continues.

Greatly varied though the specific details of individual cases may be, throughout the Americas today indigenous peoples continue to be faced with one form or another of a five-centuries-old dilemma. At the dawn of the fifteenth century, Spanish conquistadors and priests presented the Indians they encountered with a choice: either give up your religion and culture and land and independence, swearing allegiance "as vassals" to the Catholic Church and the Spanish Crown, or suffer "all the mischief and damage" that the European invaders choose to inflict upon you. It was called the *requerimiento*. The deadly predicament that now confronts native peoples is simply a modern *requerimiento:* surrender all hope of continued cultural integrity and effectively cease to exist as autonomous peoples, or endure as independent peoples the torment and deprivation we select as your fate.

In Guatemala, where Indians constitute about 60 percent of the population—as elsewhere in Central and South America—the modern *requerimiento* calls upon native peoples either to accept governmental expropriation of their lands and the consignment of their families to forced labor under *criollo* and *ladino* overlords, or be subjected to the violence of military death squads.[33] In South Dakota, where Indians constitute about 6 percent of the population—as elsewhere in North America—the effort to destroy what remains of indigenous cultural life involves a greater degree of what Alexis de Tocqueville described as America's "chaste affection for legal formalities." Here, the modern *requerimiento* pressures Indians either to leave the reservation and enter an American society where they will be bereft and cultureless people in a land where poor people of color suffer systematic oppression and an ever-worsening condition of merciless inequality, or remain on the reservation and attempt to preserve their culture amidst the wreckage of governmentally imposed poverty, hunger, ill health, despondency, and the endless attempts of the federal and state governments at land and resource usurpation.[34]

The Columbian Quincentennial celebrations have encouraged scholars worldwide to pore over the Admiral's life and work, to investigate every rumor about his ancestry and to analyze every jotting in the margins of his books. Perhaps the most revealing insight into the man, as into the enduring Western civilization that he represented, however, is a bland and simple sentence that rarely is noticed in his letter to the Spanish sovereigns, written on the way home from his initial voyage to the Indies. After searching the coasts of all the islands he had encountered for signs of wealth and princes and great cities, Columbus says he decided to send "two men upcountry" to see what they could see. "They traveled for three days," he wrote, "and found an infinite number of small villages and people without number, but nothing of importance."[35]

People without number—but nothing of importance. It would become a motto for the ages.

APPENDIXES

APPENDIX I
On Pre-Columbian Settlement and Population

Until the 1930s, it generally was believed that the earliest human inhabitants of the Americas had moved from the Alaskan portion of Berengia to what is now known as North America no more than 6000 years ago. Following the development of radioactive carbon dating techniques in the 1940s and 1950s, this date was pushed back an additional 6000 years to the end of the Wisconsin Ice Age, around 12,000 years ago. During this time the most recent interstadial, or regional dissipation of the massive continent-wide glaciers that previously had blocked passage to the south, opened up an inland migratory corridor. Once settled in what is now the upper midwestern United States, it was supposed, these migrants branched out and very slowly made their way overland, down through North, Central, and South America to the Southern Andes and Tierra del Fuego at the southernmost tip of the southern continent.

Some scholars had long suspected that even this projected date of first arrival was too recent, but it wasn't until the latter 1950s and early 1960s that they began being taken seriously.[1] For it was then, slowly but steadily, that human habitation dates of 12,000 B.C. and earlier from the most *southerly* parts of the hemisphere began turning up in the archaeological record. In addition, dates of 20,000 to 30,000 B.C. were being placed on sites to the north of these, while more problematic dates of 30,000 B.C. in Chile and Brazil and 40,000 to 50,000 B.C. for skeletal remains discovered in southern California were being claimed.[2] By the late 1970s it was becoming clear to many archaeologists that regions throughout all of North and South America were inhabited thousands of years earlier than traditionally had been believed, with some scholars suggesting a date of 70,000 B.C. as the possible time of first human entry into the hemisphere.[3]

Skeptics remained unconvinced, however. Then Monte Verde was discovered—a human habitation site in a remote Chilean forest with unambiguous evidence (including a preserved human footprint) of a complex human community at least 13,000 years old. The excavated site revealed a dozen wooden structures made of planks and small tree trunks, the bones of butchered mammals, clay-lined hearths, mortars and grinding stones, and a variety of plant remains, some of which had been carried or traded from a locale 15 miles distant, that the community's inhabitants had cultivated and used for nutritional and medicinal purposes.[4] Clearly, since no scientists seriously doubt that the first human passage into the Americas was by way of Berengia, this meant that humans must have entered areas to the north of Chile thousands of years earlier, a fact that was at the same time being confirmed by reported datings of 27,000 to 37,000 B.C. from animal remains butchered by humans in Old Crow Basin and Bluefish Caves in the Yukon, of 17,000 to 19,000 B.C. for human habitation in the Meadowcroft Rock Shelter in Pennsylvania, of 13,000 to 16,000 B.C. for a site in Missouri, of 11,000 B.C. for human activity at Warm Mineral Springs in southwestern Florida, and elsewhere.[5]

Then, a few years later, at Monte Verde in Chile again, archaeologist Tom D. Dillehay discovered definite human artifacts that dated to at least 30,000 B.C.—an age that corresponds closely to dated charcoal remains from what are believed to have been human hearths at Pedra Furada in northeast Brazil.[6] Since it is a truism of archaeological research that the earliest sites discovered today are always unlikely to be anything temporally close to the first sites that actually were inhabited—both because of the degradation of ancient materials and a site discovery process that makes finding a needle in a haystack a comparatively easy task—there increasingly is little doubt from the archaeological evidence that the northerly parts of the Americas had to have been inhabited by humans at least 40,000 years ago, and probably earlier.[7]

A welcome recent trend in this research is the attention scholars from a variety of other disciplines, including linguistics and genetics, have been paying to data in their fields regarding the first human occupation of North America. As a result, the earliest dates suggested by the archaeological evidence are now receiving independent confirmation. At present the most intense controversies regarding the early settlement of the Americas in these fields surround work that is being done on DNA linkages and language analysis. Geneticists and biochemists who have studied mitochondrial DNA samples from widely separated native American peoples today have come to equally widely separated conclusions: one group of scientists finds a high level of shared heritage, suggesting that the great majority of American Indians are descended from a single population that migrated from Asia up to 30,000 years ago; another group, studying the same type of data from different sources, contends that their findings point to at least thirty different major population movements, by different peoples, extending back about 50,000 years.

A similarly structured debate exists among the linguists. It commonly is agreed that the people living in the Americas prior to 1492 spoke at least 1500 to 2000 different languages, and probably hundreds more that have been lost without a trace. These languages derived from a cluster of more than 150 language families—each of them as different from the others as Indo-European is from Sino-Tibetan.[8] (By comparison, there are only 40–odd language families ancestral to Europe and the Middle East.) Some linguists claim, however, to have located a trio of language families, or "proto-languages," from which that great variety of languages developed: Amerind, Na-Dene, and Eskimo-Aleut. Others contend that these three proto-languages can be further reduced to a single language that was spoken by one ancestral group that entered North America about 50,000 years ago—while still others argue that the multitude of Indian languages cannot be traced to fewer than the 150 known language families, and that there is no way convincingly to link that knowledge to estimates of the earliest human entry into North America.[9]

Beyond these specific controversies, however, at least one recent study, building on these data and combining language and geographic research, clearly shows that there already was enormous language and geo-cultural diversity in North America south of the glacial mass during the apex of the last Ice Age—that is, between 14,000 and 18,000 years ago. Language isolates only emerge after very long stretches of time, of course, when a once unified people have been divided and separated for a sufficient duration to erase any linguistic common denominator between them. And we now have linguistic maps of North America showing the existence of scores of independent and mutually unintelligible language groups across the entire continent even before the glaciers of the Wisconsin Ice Age began to retreat. Indeed, although the general direction of American Indian migration was from north to south and from west to east, it appears that certain long established, language-identified peoples—such as some Siouan, Caddoan, Algonquian, and Iroquoian speakers—moved north following the glacier ice as it receded. For as the huge frigid barrier slowly melted, invitingly large glacial lakes emerged, their clear waters trapped between the ice to the north and the southerly high ground, while thick, broadleaf deciduous forests spread northward in the wake of the glaciers' retreat.[10]

By at least 15,000 B.C., then, native American peoples on the Pacific coast, in the northern plains, and in the woodlands east of the Rocky Mountains, were living in what by then were age-old hunting and gathering societies that sustained themselves on herds of caribou, musk oxen, bison, moose, mammoths, and mastodons, as well as a large variety of fish and plant life. At the same time, more than 5000 miles to the south—separated by deserts, jungles, and mountains, many of them seemingly impassable by foot even today—distant relatives of those northern coast, plains, and woodland peoples had already become well established and long-settled hunters of South American elephants, horses, camelids, deer, and huge ground sloths, and there is even evidence that by this time gardening cultures had emerged as far south as Chile and Peru. Between these two extremes south of the glacial ice, innumerable other linguistically and culturally distinct peoples had fanned out over millions of square miles of North American, Central American, and South American land and by then had been pursuing their independent lives and cultures for generations beyond memory.

For such linguistic and cultural diversity to have been extant among the native peoples of the Americas at this early date, many different culturally unique Indian communities must have existed throughout both the northern and southern continents for previous untold millennia. And for that sort of widespread migration, elaborate social fissioning, and cultural and linguistic evolution to have taken place, the date of first human entry into the Western Hemisphere has to be placed tens of thousands of years before the end of the Wisconsin Ice Age. Indeed, there are only two good reasons for categorical skepticism regarding an entry date prior to 40,000 or 50,000 B.C.: first, the absence of archaeological evidence for human populations in far eastern Siberia at that early date, the assumption being that this was the area that fed the migration to Berengia; and second, the fact that no skeletons other than those of modern humans have ever been found in the Americas, and modern humans did not emerge and replace Neanderthals, it long has been believed, until about 40,000 or 50,000 years ago. Neither of these, however, are incontestable arguments.

As for the first contention, the failure thus far to locate archaeological evidence for sites older than 40,000 B.C. in such a forbidding landscape as that of Siberia does not mean that they do not—or did not—exist. As archaeologist Fumiko Ikawa-Smith has pointed out, given the weather conditions in this region early inhabitants "may have preferred the milder climates close to the shore, and their remains may have been obliterated by subsequent marine transgressions"—as indeed has happened to early human habitation sites throughout the island Pacific.[11] Moreover, far eastern Siberia was not necessarily the sole source of the early Berengian migration: during peak glacial eras Berengia extended well to the south and may first have been populated by emigrants from the cave dwelling communities of Pekin.[12] The second assertion has similar problems, particularly since it is now known with certainty (as Louis Leakey long ago claimed, but without definitive evidence) that modern humans did not evolve around 40,000 or 50,000 B.C., but rather came into existence at least 100,000 to 130,000 years ago—while some very recent DNA research puts the date of modern humans' emergence closer to 200,000 B.C. and even earlier.[13] Although no archaeological evidence has yet been uncovered that would indicate the presence of modern humans in the icy realms of northeastern

Asia earlier than 40,000 or so B.C., the entire history of the field of archaeology is testament to the truism that absence of evidence for the existence of a phenomenon is not sufficient grounds for categorically declaring it to be or to have been non-existent; site degradation and loss is a very serious problem in regions such as this—and there is always a new discovery to be made. This is an especially relevant consideration when the temporal gap between archaeological evidence for modern humans in northeastern Asia and in other parts of the world has now yawned open to a range of between 60,000 and 90,000—and possibly as much as 150,000—years.

In sum, there is no necessary barrier to the possibility that humans—whether of modern or pre-modern type—entered the Western Hemisphere as early as 60,000 or 70,000 years ago, although the best scientific evidence to date, drawing on coalescent findings from several disciplines, suggests a more prudent estimate would be for an entry date of around 40,000 B.C., or perhaps a little earlier.

In mapping the pre-Columbian native languages of North America, an extraordinarily dense collection of different tongues are found along the western seaboard, especially between present-day southern British Columbia and San Francisco. (California alone was home to at least 500 distinct cultural communities prior to European contact.) Unless the post-Columbian disease holocaust in the Eastern part of the continent was immensely greater than most scholars now believe, resulting in the extinction of many scores of entire language groups before they could be separated out and distinguished by early European explorers and settlers, the especially thick concentration of different languages along the west coast suggests that to have been the path of earliest human dispersal and settlement.

Whether the earliest southward-moving exodus from Berengia, over the course of many thousands of years, was carried out primarily on land or on sea—or whether the path of the earliest population movements down through North America toward Mexico was along the west coast or through a temporary ice-free corridor in what is now America's northern midwest—are still other controversies that remain unsettled. Traditionally, it has been held that the earliest migrants south from Alaska had to wait for temporary melts to open inland passageways through the glaciers that blocked their way. Such ice-free interstadials occurred at least five times during the Wisconsin era, each one lasting for thousands of years, with the mid-point of the most temporally distant one located about 75,000 years ago. It now appears increasingly likely, however, that early Alaska inhabitants might not have had to follow an inland path, but rather may have made their way south along the Pacific coastline, either overland, along a narrow, unglaciated, but exposed part of the continental shelf, or by sea, in coast-hugging wooden dugouts or skin boats.[14]

Since it is known that the first human inhabitants of New Guinea and Australia (which, during the Wisconsin glaciation, was a single land mass) had to carry out at least part of their journey to those lands across a sea gap in eastern Indonesia—and since the initial settlement of New Guinea and Australia occurred at least 50,000 years ago, and probably much earlier—it certainly is possible, perhaps likely, that America's first people had the technological skills to make seaborne, stepping-stone migrations down the western coastline tens of thousands of years before the end of the last Ice Age.[15] Moreover, if that was the primary path of migration, it now is forever hidden from archaeological inquiry, because any coastal settlements or villages that may have existed forty, fifty, or sixty thousand years ago were located on the continental shelf that, like the homeland of Berengia, presently is hundreds of feet beneath the ocean's waves.[16]

If the evolving scholarly estimates of the date when humans first entered the Western Hemisphere seem dramatic—changing within the past half-century from about 4000 B.C. to around 40,000 B.C., and perhaps even earlier—the proportionate change is at least equally striking for advances in knowledge during that same time regarding the magnitude of human population in the Americas prior to European contact.

The earliest recorded estimates of New World population came from the first Spanish intruders in the late fifteenth and early sixteenth century. While they of course could make no estimates for lands they had not seen, they did produce figures for the areas in which they had traveled. Bartholomé de Las Casas, for example, put the figure for the island of Hispaniola at between 3,000,000 and 4,000,000 at the time of the Spanish arrival, although Las Casas himself did not visit the island until ten years after Columbus's first voyage, by which time the population was only a fraction—perhaps 10 percent—of what it had been prior to European contact. Gonzalo Fernández de Oviedo, who arrived in the Americas a decade later than Las Casas, claimed that Panama and the adjacent portion of southern Central America originally held around 2,000,000 indigenous people. And even as late as the eighteenth century Francisco Javier Clavijero claimed that Mexico had an abundance of 30,000,000 people prior to the Spanish conquest.[17]

Because the post-conquest native population collapses in these and other regions were so massive and so sudden, many later writers found these first estimates—and their implications for an originally enormous hemispheric population—impossible to believe. As a result, by the 1920s there was general scholarly agreement that the combined population of North and South America in 1492 was probably no more than 40,000,000 to 50,000,000 people.[18] Within a decade, however, prevailing opinion had dropped even those reduced numbers down to less than 14,000,000—and in 1939 anthropologist Alfred L. Kroeber published a highly influential report suggesting that the population of the entire Western Hemisphere in 1492 was only about 8,400,000—with North America accounting for less than 1,000,000 of that total.[19]

Recognizing that all these estimates were founded upon a great deal of speculation and very little knowledge of local conditions, Kroeber suggested that work begin on detailed region-by-region analyses. The charge was accepted, particularly by a group of scholars from various disciplines at Kroeber's own University of California at Berkeley, most notably Carl Sauer, Sherburne F. Cook, and Woodrow Borah. The result was a pathbreaking revolution in historical demographic technique that in time became known as the "Berkeley School." Examining enormous amounts of data from a great variety of sources—ranging from church and government archives listing tribute, baptismal, and marriage records, to the environmental carrying capacities of known cultivated lands and much more—these researchers concentrated their efforts at first on California and central Mexico, extending their inquiries later to regions as diverse as New England, the Yucatán, and the island of Hispaniola.[20]

The results of these efforts were the most detailed and methodologically sophisticated population estimates ever conducted for the pre-European Americas. And the figures they turned up were astonishing: 25,000,000 people for central Mexico alone and 8,000,000 people for Hispaniola are just two of the more striking re-calculations by members of the Berkeley School. By the early 1960s the accumulated body of such studies was sufficient to allow Woodrow Borah to assert that the pre-Columbian population of the Americas was probably "upwards of one hundred million." Soon after, anthropologist Henry F. Dobyns published a famous watershed analysis of all the major studies that had been conducted up to that time. His conclusion was that North and South America contained between 90,000,000 and more than 112,000,000 people before the coming of the Spanish.[21] Comparative figures for selected other parts of the world at this same time put the population of Europe at 60,000,000 to 70,000,000; Russia at 10,000,000 to 18,000,000; and Africa at 40,000,000 to 72,000,000.[22]

Subsequently, since the mid-1960s, scores of scholars from around the world have published new pre-Columbian population estimates of unprecedented sophistication for nations, tribes, and regions from northernmost Canada to southern Chile—and for most other major habitation sites lying in between. One after another they have confirmed the general principle that the populations of individual locales were much higher in pre-Columbian times than heretofore suspected. Conservative-minded historical demographers have been reluctant to extrapolate from these findings to overall hemispheric projections, but even the more cautious among them generally now concede that the total population of the Americas prior to 1492 was in the neighborhood of 75,000,000 persons, about 10 percent of whom lived north of Mexico. Others—including Dobyns—have begun to suspect that Dobyns's earlier maximum of more than 112,000,000 may have been too low and that a figure of about 145,000,000 would be a closer approximation of the true number for the hemisphere, with 18,000,000 or so the best estimate for the region that presently constitutes the United States and Canada.[23]

Among the reasons for some researchers to have concluded recently that *all* estimates to date have been too low, is the increasingly acknowledged likelihood that European diseases, once introduced into the virgin soil environments of the Americas, often raced ahead of their foreign carriers and spread disastrously into native population centers long before the European explorers and settlers themselves arrived. In other instances, some Europeans may have been on the scene when the initial epidemics occurred, but these people generally were soldiers more interested in conquest than in studying those they were killing. New archaeological studies in particular locales have demonstrated that this previously "invisible" population loss may have been widespread—a phenomenon that also is now being uncovered among post-European contact indigenous peoples as far away from the Americas as New Zealand, the Pacific islands of Fiji, and Hawai'i.[24] If this did indeed happen on a large scale throughout the Americas, as Dobyns and others now contend that it did, even the higher range of current hemispheric population estimates may be too low. This is because the historical consequence of such archaeological research findings is the discovery that time and again the first European observers and recorders in an area arrived only well after it was totally bereft of its long-established human inhabitants, or at the very least that such observers and recorders found—and incorrectly took to be the norm prior to their arrival—only residual populations so small and demoralized that they provided no hint of true previous population magnitude or cultural vitality.[25]

Even if certain plagues, such as smallpox, did not always precede the appearance of the European disease carriers themselves into certain regions, however, those who still disagree with Dobyns and his supporters on this point acknowledge that population loss among native societies routinely reached and exceeded 95 percent—a rate of decline more than sufficient to account for a pre-Columbian hemispheric population in the neighborhood of 100,000,000 and more.[26] Comparative research in South America and Hawai'i has shown, moreover, that cultural and biological outgrowths of military assault and epidemic disease, such as severe psychological disorientation and high levels of pathogen- and stress-induced infertility, can by themselves be primary agents in population losses of near-extermination magnitude.[27] In sum, while debate continues as to the *actual* population of the Americas prior to the arrival of Europeans at the end of the fifteenth century, few informed scholars any longer contend that it was not at least within the general range of 75 to 100,000,000 persons, with roughly 8,000,000 to 12,000,000 living north of Mexico—while some of the more outstanding scholars in the field have begun to suspect that the true figure was even higher than the highest end of this range.

APPENDIX II
On Racism and Genocide

In the preceding pages I have referred repeatedly to European and white American attitudes toward the native peoples of the Americas as "racist" and to the Euro-Americans' furious destruction of the native peoples of the Americas as "genocide." The definitions of both these terms have been subject to discussion in recent years. Some readers may have wished to see in the text reference to those discussions, but to do so would have necessitated lengthy digressions that other readers might have found more distracting than enlightening. Therefore, I have added as an appendix the following remarks.

There are various ways in which cultures can construct ideologies of degradation, and such ideologies can be, and are, attached to any number of characteristics that serve to socially transform a collection of individuals within a culture into a group—gender, nationality, age, sexual preference, social and economic class, religion, and much else, including race. It is race that is the issue here. And the question, as it has been posed (and answered in opposing ways) in recent years is this: Did those Europeans and early American white colonists treat Indians and Africans as they did at least in part because of a racist ideology that long had been in place—or was Euro-American racism in the Americas a later development, even a product of white *versus* Indian and white *versus* black conflict? In short, which came first, the carrying out of terrible and systematic damage to others or the ideology of degradation?

To some, understandably, this may seem an academic question, in the worst sense of that term. After all, to the American native woman having her breasts cut off by sadistically gleeful Spanish conquistadors, or watching her infant thrown to a pack of dogs—or to the native man about to be impaled on a sword of European manufacture, or watching his village and his family being burned to cinders by Puritans who boasted that "our Mouth [was] filled with Laughter, and our Tongues with Singing" while they attempted to exterminate an entire people from the earth—it no doubt mattered little whether the genocidal racism of their tormentors had preceded or followed from the first meetings of their societies.[1] If such questions concern us now, for reasons other than academic curiosity, they do so in order that we may better understand how such horrors could have been perpetrated and how—perhaps—they may be anticipated and avoided in the future. Moreover, like many other matters of ivory tower pedigree, this one carries with it an inner element of real world political contentiousness. This is why, for many years, addressing it has caused such scholarly disagreement. That the answer to this question matters can best be seen by reviewing the ways historians have approached the issue first as it pertains to African Americans and then to Indians.

Until well into the twentieth century most white American historians spent little time arguing over the chronological priority of racism or slavery in the historical mistreatment of Africans in America. This was so for a reason that by itself is revealing: it was not a subject that lent itself to disagreement because those historians' *own* low regard for blacks was so second nature to them that they simply assumed it to be a natural, justified, and nearly universal attitude, and one that thereby must have long predated the formal enslavement of Africans. And the formal enslavement of blacks in America, they assumed, certainly began immediately upon the involuntary arrival in the colonies of the first Africans in 1619.

Although there were some earlier historians who raised questions that had bearing on this matter, it was not until the 1950s that they began to propose, in numbers and with some vigor, the thesis that slavery had preceded racism in America.[2] Working within a social climate to which they could not have been immune, a climate that was registering a rising chorus of insistent claims by African Americans for equal access to the social and political benefits of American life, these historians contended that slavery emerged gradually as an institution, following the first arrivals of blacks in North America, and that racism emerged still later, in part as a *rationale* for the maintenance of what by then had become a racially defined slave society.[3] Although this was an argument not without some documentary support, it also was an argument suited to the politics of academic liberals who then were coming to agree with historian Kenneth Stampp that "innately Negroes *are,* after all, only white men with black skins, nothing more, nothing less."[4]

From this political and ethical perspective—in the midst of a civil rights movement that was attempting to make such integrationist ideals conform with reality—the liberal historian's notion that racism was, in Winthrop

Jordan's words, "scarcely more than an appurtenance of slavery . . . . squared nicely with the hopes of those even more directly concerned with the problem of contemporary race relations. . . . For if prejudice was natural there would be little one could do to wipe it out. Prejudice must have followed enslavement, not vice versa, else any liberal program of action would be badly compromised."[5]

There was, of course, another benefit not mentioned by Jordan that was gained from such a reading of the historical record. The moral core of Western culture in general, and American culture in particular, appeared far more favorable in the light of an interpretation that found racism to be an aberration, rather than a constant, in Western history. Thus, not only did the slavery-begot-racism scenario encourage a more optimistic belief in the possibility of curtailing racism in the present, it also gave support to a relatively cheerful interpretation of the American and European cultural past.

Not everyone was convinced, however. In 1959 Carl N. Degler published an article, "Slavery and the Genesis of American Race Prejudice," strongly arguing that slavery took root very early in American colonial society and that it did so in large part because of the white colonists' pre-existing racist attitudes—attitudes visible, among other places, in Elizabethan literature, including Shakespeare's *Othello* and *Titus Andronicus,* but also evident in the relative prices of black and white servants, discriminatory court decisions, and more.[6] The ensuing flurry of debate on the issue had a number of internal problems, not the least of which was a tendency to assume that the general attitudes and behaviors of the white colonists were very nearly monolithic. Thus, whenever one partisan found an exception to the other's body of data he or she was likely to hold it up as a refutation of the other's entire thesis. Some writers, for example, pointed to a 1640 law prohibiting blacks in Virginia from bearing arms, and cited this as evidence of racially based discrimination, while critics of this interpretation noted the presence in Virginia during this same time of a black former slave who had gained his freedom and purchased a slave himself, and they used this as evidence that blacks were *not* treated with special unfairness. Within a few years, however, Degler's general contention was given an able assist by Winthrop Jordan, first in an article of his own, then in 1968 with his massive and justly celebrated study, *White Over Black: American Attitudes Toward the Negro, 1550–1812.*[7]

Examining materials ranging from biblical passages to sixteenth-century poetry, travelers' tales, and more, Jordan concluded in *White Over Black* that European antipathy for Africans had long pre-dated the enslavement of blacks in America, or for that matter, the arrival of Europeans to the Western Hemisphere. "From the first," he wrote, "Englishmen tended to set Negroes over against themselves, to stress what they conceived to be radically contrasting qualities of color, religion, and style of life, as well as animality and a peculiarly potent sexuality."[8] In short, virtually all the elements that would go into the full blown eighteenth- and nineteenth-century ideology of anti-black racism were present in European thought long before the arrival of the first blacks in Virginia in 1619.

But although racial antipathy preceded enslavement, Jordan cautioned against too simplistic a cause-and-effect model. A predisposition to invidious racial distinctions was not in itself sufficient to explain the wholesale enslavement and the horrendously systematic degradation of Africans that emerged in eighteenth- and nineteenth-century North America. Rather, Jordan suggested that "both slavery and prejudice [were] species of a general debasement of the Negro," each of them—once they were joined—"constantly reacting upon each other" in a dynamic "cycle of degradation" that created a unique "engine of oppression."[9] (It will be recalled that I quoted these phrases in my text and adopted the same ideological-institutional dynamic in pursuit of an explanation for genocide against the Americas' native peoples.)

In this conclusion Jordan actually was delivering heavily documented support to an insight first expressed by Alexis de Tocqueville more than a century earlier. Since the age of the ancients, Tocqueville had said, a scornful attitude toward the enslaved had followed upon their enforced servitude, a scornful attitude that remained for a time after the abolition of slavery, but one that eventually dissipated. However, in America, he wrote, "the insubstantial and ephemeral fact of servitude is most fatally combined with the physical and permanent fact of difference in race. Memories of slavery disgrace the race, and race perpetuates memories of slavery." Added to this, Tocqueville noted, was the fact that for whites in general, including himself:

> This man born in degradation, this stranger brought by slavery into our midst, is hardly recognized as sharing the common features of humanity. His face appears to us hideous, his intelligence limited, and his tastes low; we almost take him for some being intermediate between beast and man. . . . To induce the whites to abandon the opinion they have conceived of the intellectual and moral inferiority of their former slaves, the Negroes must change, but they cannot change so long as this opinion persists.[10]

In sum, as Jordan later picked up the argument, while the roots of a racist antipathy among whites toward blacks did indeed clearly precede the rise of the institution of slavery in America, this is a less important independent phenomenon than some may have thought, since once the attitude and the institution became fused—and they did so at a very early date—they reinforced one another, strengthening and deepening the white commitment to both of them. The idea of racism as deeply imbedded in Western consciousness was still a very troubling notion to many, however, and resistance to it remained strong among historians, despite Jordan's rich documentation and subtlety of analysis. The form this resistance subsequently would take was established by George M. Fredrickson in a highly influential article that appeared only three years after *White Over Black* was published.

It is necessary, Fredrickson contended, to distinguish between what he called "ideological" racism and "societal" racism. Ideological racism is "the *explicit* and *rationalized* racism that can be discerned in nineteenth- and twentieth-century thought and ideology" while societal racism can be observed in "one racial group [acting] *as if* another were inherently inferior . . . despite the fact that such a group may not have developed or preserved a conscious and consistent rationale for its behavior." This "dual definition of racism," Fredrickson claimed, made it possible to identify the differences between "genuinely racist societies and other inegalitarian societies where there may be manifestations of racial prejudice and discrimination but which nevertheless cannot be described as racist in their basic character." In a given society, according to this logic, as long as some reason *other than race* can be found to justify and rationalize the degradation—and, presumably, even the enslavement and mass murder—of people who are of a different race from that of their oppressors, that society "is not racist in the full sense of the word," Fredrickson claimed. Moreover,

> if the discrimination for reasons of color is not *consistently and universally* applied to individual members of what is, in a statistical sense, the socially inferior group [and] if some members of this group can, despite their physical characteristics, achieve high status because of such attributes as wealth, education, and aristocratic culture, there is evidence of the overriding importance of *nonracial* status criteria. In such a situation, race becomes only one factor in determining status, an attribute which can be outweighed or neutralized by other factors.[11]

By joining this definitional statement with the same sort of historical data produced by those historians who, twenty years earlier, had argued that American racism was essentially a product of slavery—for example, that along with slaves there were free blacks in seventeenth-century Virginia, some of whom enjoyed legal and economic rights—Fredrickson concluded that "America . . . was not born racist; it became so gradually as the result of a series of crimes against black humanity that stemmed primarily from selfishness, greed and the pursuit of privilege."[12] This judgment served to undergird Fredrickson's subsequent work and clearly influenced most of the other prominent discussions of the subject that would appear in the later 1970s and 1980s.[13]

There are, however, some problems with Fredrickson's analysis. The first of these is his use of the word "ideological" when "biological" would have been more precise in describing the nature of the formal structures of racist thought that emerged in the nineteenth century. Prior to the rise of the biological and zoological pseudosciences that served as the underpinnings for what Fredrickson calls "ideological" racism, and after the decline of those pseudosciences in the twentieth century, there existed and continues to exist in America a widespread, systematic, and ideologically justified degradation of entire categories of people who are readily identifiable by characteristics that commonly are associated with race.[14] The fact that in pre-pseudoscience days the categorical justifications drew heavily (though, as we saw in the text, not exclusively) on religious and philosophical structures of thought, while in post-pseudoscience days most justifications tend to draw on historical and environmental principles—such as the "culture of poverty" or the black American family's alleged "tangle of pathology"—does not make these systems of discrimination any less "ideological" (or any less racist) than those biological fictions that dominated racist thinking in the nineteenth century and part of the twentieth. Biology certainly can become ideological—but ideology is not necessarily based on biology.

As for the idea that racism proper did not and could not emerge until the rise of an "explicit and rationalized" pseudoscientific ideology regarding the term "race" itself, as Richard Drinnon has remarked, this "is roughly equivalent to saying—though the parallel is more benign—that the practice of birth control waited upon Margaret Sanger to coin the term."[15] In addition, since traditional pseudoscientific racism is no longer in vogue—and, indeed, since the very idea of "race" has long been scientifically discredited as a valid way of categorizing humans—by Fredrickson's definition, racism "in the full sense of the word" does not and can not exist today.[16] That will be news to its victims.

If these difficulties with Fredrickson's (and many other recent historians') definition of racism necessarily result in the dubious conclusion that, to use Fredrickson's terms, "genuine" or "explicit" racism was a momentary aberration in human history, arising in the early nineteenth century and dying out around the middle of the twentieth century, an additional problem with his definition is that one logical consequence of it leads to the remarkable discovery that true racism has, in fact, *never* existed, at least in America. For Fredrickson and most other historians writing on the topic continue to assert that for racism proper to exist—to quote again the passage in Fredrickson cited above—it must be "*universally* applied to individual members of what is, in a statistical sense, the socially inferior group." Should any exceptions to such categorical "discrimination for reasons of color" exist in an otherwise seemingly racist time and place, the exceptions serve as "evidence of the overriding importance of nonracial status criteria" and as sufficient documentation to establish that such a society cannot correctly be labeled racist.

It is by appealing to this definition that Fredrickson and others continue to assert that the existence of free blacks in seventeenth-century Virginia—and particularly of someone like Anthony Johnson, who arrived in Virginia as a slave from Africa and somehow became a freeman, a land owner, and the owner of a slave—proves that seventeenth-century Virginia was not a racist society, that racism only emerged in later years.[17] Again, not only can this criterion be used to argue that racism is not a serious and tenacious problem today (since some blacks and other people of color, in theory at least, may escape its tentacles), but in addition it speciously serves to establish that even the deep South in the middle of the nineteenth century was not ideologically or "explicitly" racist. For if Anthony Johnson, with his small plot of land and single slave is a sufficient example to show that seventeenth century Virginia was not racist, what are we to make of William Ellison, a black former slave who lived in South Carolina from the 1790s until the outbreak of the Civil War, acquiring in that time a 900-acre plantation, more than sixty slaves, and more wealth than 95 percent of the South's white men? And at least half a dozen other southern blacks at this time—among the more than 3600 African Americans who then possessed over 12,000 slaves—were wealthier and owned more slaves than Ellison.[18]

If ever a region in America could properly be described as racist, it was the deep South in the decades immediately preceding the Civil War. Thus, we are left with a choice between one of two conclusions: either the existence of Ellison and other wealthy, slave-owning southern blacks at this time proves that the deep South was not then a truly racist society, in which case, no locale in America, at any time, can ever have been categorically and "explicitly" racist; or the criteria used by Fredrickson and others are inappropriate and ineffective for use in locating and defining a racist society. It should not be necessary to point out that only the latter choice makes any sense at all.

It might also be noted that the same criteria used to demonstrate that the seventeenth-century slave-holding colonies were not "genuinely" racist can be used with equal veracity (which is to say none) to show that the German Nazi Party in the 1930s was not "genuinely" anti-Semitic, since a large proportion of its membership, when surveyed, expressed no anti-Semitic attitudes.[19] None of this should be taken to mean, however, that a formalized and widely believed pseudoscientific theory of racial inequality is not *different* from lower-level and more diffuse racist thinking. They are different, but they both are thoroughly racist.

There is a certain paradoxical quality to the fact that while the rest of informed society has come to recognize the existence of subtler and more complex forms of racism—such as "institutional" racism (or Joel Kovel's more psychologically grounded "metaracism") as forms of oppression that clearly are racist but do not depend for their existence on an openly artic-ulated and formal racial theory—many of the historians who have in re-cent years devoted their professional lives to studying the phenomenon have seemed determined to define racism almost out of existence.[20] Indeed, confusion on racism as a historical phenomenon has grown to the point that Jane Tompkins, the author of an article in a journal of avant-garde scholarly repute, has gone so far as to make the fanciful assertion—directly *contra* Fredrickson, but equally illogical—that racism could not have ex-isted in early American colonial society because white people at that time were *unanimous* in their racist opinions! In short, according to Tompkins (who, like Fredrickson, is not alone in her conviction), unanimity of opin-ion is indication of a cultural norm, of people simply "look[ing] at other cultures in the way their own culture had taught them to see one an-other."[21] Thus, on the one hand we have Fredrickson arguing that only if *every* member of an oppressed racial group in a society is oppressed for explicitly racial reasons can that society be characterized as racist—and on the other hand there is Tompkins contending that if there is unanimity of racist opinion among the oppressor group in a society, that society, by definition, is *non*-racist.

This is the sort of thing that gives professors a bad name. And, al-though thus far we have been looking largely at writings on early white American attitudes toward African Americans (the exception is Tomp-kins), the very same lines of argument have been and continue to be played out regarding sixteenth- and seventeenth-century Euro-American attitudes toward Indians. During the 1960s it had been customary for scholars, such as Alden T. Vaughan, who were studying Indian-white conflict in the American colonies, to assert that even during the ferocious extermination campaigns of the English against the native peoples of Virginia as well as against the Pequots and Narragansetts and Wampanoags of New England, the behavior of the British was not "determined by any fundamental dis-tinction of race," nor by "deep-seated bias" of any kind.[22] In *White Over Black,* Jordan inadvertently had provided further fuel for this argument, by comparing blatant assertions of racial antipathy of the English for Af-ricans with what he viewed as their more benign attitude toward Indian racial characteristics. His perspective was then used to underpin unin-formed claims by later historians that whites did not harbor racist atti-tudes toward Indians even centuries after their first proudly proclaimed attempts to exterminate them.[23]

In their denial of racial motivation as part of the driving force behind the colonists' efforts to eradicate the Indians, most of these historians' writings also were unblushing apologies for the genocide that had taken place. Thus, Vaughan, for example, dismissed mass murder as "some misunderstandings and injustices [that] occurred" while the British were only trying "to convert, civilize, and educate [the Indian] as quickly as possible."[24] During the 1970s and early 1980s, however, a series of books by historians taking a second look at these matters reached very different conclusions. Wilbur R. Jacobs, Francis Jennings, Richard Drinnon, and Neal Salisbury were only four among many during this time who rang down the curtain on the view that the colonists in their dealings with the Indians were kind and gentle souls.[25] Following their work, there remained little doubt that the colonists were driven by a racist zeal to eliminate the Indians—at least once the major colonist-Indian wars had gotten under way. But remaining to be addressed was the same question that had for so long entangled historians studying white minds and black slavery: Did the adventurers and colonists bring *with* them racist attitudes that predisposed them to such inhumane treatment of people of color, or did those attitudes emerge *after* and derive from their experience with the people they later enslaved and destroyed?

It should be clear from the discussion in Chapter Six of this book that Spanish, English, and other European attitudes toward the native peoples of the Americas were virulently racist long before the settlement of the first British colony in North America. Although European mistreatment of people because of a perception of them as racially different is a very ancient practice, a dramatic shift to a rigid European attitude toward race in general was becoming evident in the fourteenth century with the Church's authorization of the enslavement of Christians if their ancestry was non-European, and it escalated from that point forward with an able assist from the Spanish doctrine of *limpieza de sangre* and the other sixteenth-century European pseudobiological and religious rationales discussed earlier. It is impossible to read the voluminous Spanish justifications for the enslavement and mass murder of the Americas' native peoples—as well as the sixteenth- and early seventeenth-century statements of the British on the same subjects—without recognizing their deeply racist content. Impossible, that is, unless you carefully define racism so narrowly that it is certain not to be found.

And that is what has begun to happen in recent years. Race, of course, is a social construct that different societies create in different ways, drawing on supposedly "natural" characteristics in people that are held to be congenital; racism is the ideological use of such a construct to subordinate and dominate another group. Nevertheless, in scholarly imitation of the man who searches for his lost keys under a lamp post because the light is better there—even though he knows he dropped his keys a block away—Alden T. Vaughan has now invented the idea that racism cannot exist in the absence of negative statements about another group's *skin color*. Not surprisingly, in the light cast by this particular lamp post, he has found little explicit Anglo-American disparagement of Indians' skin color in the early years of settlement—those years when Indian men, women, and children were being butchered, burned alive, enslaved, poisoned en masse, and referred to as "wild beasts," "brutish savages," and "viperous broods"—and so, according to Vaughan's *ad hoc* definition, the British did not then think of the Indians they were systematically liquidating as "inherently inferior."[26]

As with Fredrickson's impossibly narrow definition of racism, so with Vaughan it needs to be pointed out that neither skin color distinctions nor pseudoscientific ideas of biological determinism are *necessary* criteria for the categorization and degradation of people under the rubric of "race." Even a glance at the standard etymologies of the word ("the outward race and stocke of Abraham"; "to be the Race of Satan"; "the British race"; "that Pygmean Race"—to cite some sixteenth- and seventeenth-century examples) clearly shows that the term "race" was in widespread use in Britain to denote groups of people and classes of things marked by characteristics *other* than color well before it was used exclusively in that way, and centuries before it had grafted upon it the elaborate apparatus of biological and zoological pseudoscience. Indeed, a sense of "racial" superiority—sometimes having to do with color and sometimes not—had been imbedded in English consciousness at least since the appearance in the twelfth century of Geoffrey of Monmouth's *History of the Kings of Britain,* the great elaboration of the Arthurian legend.[27]

It is true, as noted several times in Chapter Six of this book, that racist thought and behavior by whites toward Indians intensified during the course of the sixteenth and seventeenth centuries, but after the first few decades of the sixteenth century—at the very latest—the escalation of racism was a change in degree, not type (as Vaughan claims), of prejudice and oppression. In sum, there is little doubt that the dominant sixteenth- and seventeenth-century ecclesiastical, literary, and popular opinion in Spain and Britain and Europe's American colonies regarding the native peoples of North and South America was that they were a racially degraded and inferior lot—borderline humans as far as most whites were concerned. Although there was, even at that early date, beginning to emerge in Europe various detailed theories of racist pseudoscience, anyone who has ever been on the receiving end of racist aggression knows that such endeavors do not require of their perpetrators the presence of formal scientific or other doctrine; as W.E.B. DuBois once observed: "the chief fact [in my life] has been race—not so much scientific race, as that deep conviction of myriads of men that congenital differences among the main masses of human beings absolutely condition the individual destiny of every member of a group."[28] Most people of color today, as well as for centuries past, would have understood what DuBois was saying—even if some modern white historians apparently do not.

. . .

The definition of genocide, though also a subject of debate for many years, will take much less time to discuss. That is because most of the controversy over the term—such as whether victims of mass murder whose only common denominator is political belief are truly victims of genocide—is not relevant to the subject of this book. All that is relevant is whether the Spanish and Anglo-American destruction of the culturally and ethnically and racially defined peoples of the Americas constituted genocide.

The term "genocide" was coined by Raphael Lemkin in his book *Axis Rule in Occupied Europe,* published in 1944. Frank Chalk and Kurt Jonassohn summarize Lemkin's pioneering thinking:

> Under Lemkin's definition, genocide was the coordinated and planned annihilation of a national, religious, or racial group by a variety of actions aimed at undermining the foundations essential to the survival of the group as a group. Lemkin conceived of genocide as "a composite of different acts of persecution or destruction." His definition included attacks on political and social institutions, culture, language, national feelings, religion, and the economic existence of the group. Even nonlethal acts that undermined the liberty, dignity, and personal security of members of a group constituted genocide if they contributed to weakening the viability of the group. Under Lemkin's definition, acts of ethnocide—a term coined by the French after the war to cover the destruction of a culture without the killing of its bearers—also qualified as genocide.[29]

Two years after the publication of Lemkin's book—and thanks to his constant lobbying efforts—the United Nations General Assembly passed the following resolution:

> Genocide is the denial of the right of existence to entire human groups, as homicide is the denial of the right to live of individual human beings; such denial of the right of existence shocks the conscience of mankind, results in great losses to humanity in the form of cultural and other contributions represented by these groups, and is contrary to moral law and to the spirit and aims of the United Nations. Many instances of such crimes of genocide have occurred, when racial, religious, political and other groups have been destroyed, entirely or in part. The punishment of the crime of genocide is a matter of international concern. The General Assembly Therefore, Affirms that genocide is a crime under international law which the civilized world condemns, and for the commission of which principals and accomplices— whether private individuals, public officials or statesmen, and whether the crime is committed on religious, racial, political or any other grounds—are punishable.

Finally, in 1948, the Genocide Convention of the United Nations was adopted unanimously and without abstentions:

UNITED NATIONS CONVENTION ON THE PREVENTION AND PUNISHMENT OF THE CRIME OF GENOCIDE

TEXT OF THE CONVENTION

The Contracting Parties,

Having considered the declaration made by the General Assembly of the United Nations in its resolution 96 (I) dated 11 December 1946 that genocide is a crime under international law, contrary to the spirit and aims of the United Nations and condemned by the civilized world;

Recognizing that at all periods of history genocide has inflicted great losses on humanity; and

Being convinced that, in order to liberate mankind from such an odious scourge, international co-operation is required:

Hereby agree as hereinafter provided:

ARTICLE I

The Contracting Parties confirm that genocide, whether committed in time of peace or in time of war, is a crime under international law which they undertake to prevent and to punish.

ARTICLE II

In the present Convention, genocide means any of the following acts committed with intent to destroy, in whole or in part, a national, ethnical, racial, or religious group, as such:

(a) Killing members of the group;
(b) Causing serious bodily or mental harm to members of the group;
(c) Deliberately inflicting on the group conditions of life calculated to bring about its physical destruction in whole or in part;
(d) Imposing measures intended to prevent births within the group;
(e) Forcibly transferring children of the group to another group.

ARTICLE III

The following acts shall be punishable:

(a) Genocide;
(b) Conspiracy to commit genocide;
(c) Direct and public incitement to commit genocide;
(d) Attempt to commit genocide;
(e) Complicity in genocide.

ARTICLE IV

Persons committing genocide or any of the acts enumerated in Article III shall be punished, whether they are constitutionally responsible rulers, public officials, or private individuals.[30]

It is almost half a century since the Genocide Convention was passed, and in that time countless numbers of individuals have argued that the Convention's definition is too narrow (because, as a result of pressure brought by Soviet and Eastern bloc delegates, it does not include political groups as potential victims) or too broad (because "causing serious bodily or mental harm to members of the group" can be made applicable to cases that clearly are not genocidal), among other criticisms. However, the Convention's definition remains the most widely used definition of genocide throughout the world—and, indeed, in all the world there probably is no other word, in any language, whose definition has been more carefully discussed or more universally accepted. In light of the U.N. language—even putting aside some of its looser constructions—it is impossible to know what transpired in the Americas during the sixteenth, seventeenth, eighteenth, and nineteenth centuries and not conclude that it was genocide.

ACKNOWLEDGMENTS

During the course of researching and writing this book I have benefited from the generosity of a number of institutions and individuals. Some years ago, while conducting research on a different project under the auspices of a fellowship from the John Simon Guggenheim Memorial Foundation, I began reading and thinking about the historical fictions the First World routinely imposes on indigenous and Third World peoples in the process of retrospectively justifying genocidal aggression against them. A few years later the American Council of Learned Societies provided me with fellowship support for the initial phase of research that has led to this and other publications, some now in print, others still in preparation. The University of Hawai'i's Social Science Research Institute and its Director, Donald M. Topping, have unfailingly responded favorably to numerous requests for assistance from me, as has the beleaguered staff of the Thomas H. Hamilton Library. Also at the University of Hawai'i, the Center for Arts and Humanities has been most helpful.

Emanuel J. Drechsel and Catherine Vandemoer pointed me in the right direction on several technical points, while in various important ways Annette Mente and Nipa Rahim have helped assure that this book would indeed be published in 1992. Richard Drinnon and Peter T. Manicas carefully read and pointedly commented on an early draft of the entire manuscript; the kindness of their prompt assistance and the keenness of their criticisms were consistent with the example of their own vigorous and discerning scholarship.

This is my third book with Oxford University Press. As in the past, the experience has been rewarding. Sheldon Meyer was unreservedly supportive and patient and fair in his counsel, as well as astute in his insight, while Leona Capeless edited the manuscript with a subtle but certain touch. In addition, Karen Wolny, Scott Lenz, and Laura Brown at Oxford were most helpful at critical moments when the manuscript was being turned into a book.

The research and writing of a book such as this is at times an emotionally draining experience. No one is more aware of that fact than my companion throughout the ordeal—and for most of the preceding decade—Haunani-Kay Trask. A politically engaged scholar on the subjects of feminist theory, colonialism, and the contemporary struggles of indigenous peoples, as well as a native woman whose own people were almost rendered extinct within a century following their first contact with the West, her critical readings of the manuscript were of course invaluable. But more than that, the examples of her and her people's ongoing resistance to postcolonial oppression—and the innumerable hours of conversation we have shared on and around the general topic of this book—have been its primary and deepest inspiration.

NOTES

Prologue

1. The official American estimate for the number of people killed by the Hiroshima blast is less than 80,000, but the Japanese have long disputed this figure and the best current estimate ranges from at least 130,000 immediately following the bombing to about 200,000 total dead from the blast and its aftereffects within five years. See Committee for the Compilation of Materials on Damage Caused by the Atomic Bombs in Hiroshima and Nagasaki, *Hiroshima and Nagasaki: The Physical, Medical, and Social Effects of the Atomic Bombings,* translated by Eisei Ishikawa and David L. Swain (New York: Basic Books, 1981), pp. 363–69.

2. See Sherburne F. Cook and Woodrow Borah, "The Aboriginal Population of Hispaniola" in Cook and Borah, *Essays in Population History, Volume One: Mexico and the Caribbean* (Berkeley: University of California Press, 1971), pp. 376–410.

3. Richard Slotkin, *Regeneration Through Violence: The Mythology of the American Frontier, 1600–1860* (Middletown, Conn.: Wesleyan University Press, 1973), p. 565. On the matter of comparative survivorship ratios, according to recent adjustments in the 1990 U.S. census the national ethnic breakdown is as follows: whites—74.2 percent; blacks—12.5 percent; Hispanics—9.5 percent; Asians and others—3.8 percent. Thus, since whites and blacks combined total 86.7 percent of the population, if all whites and blacks were killed, the survivorship ratio for Americans would be significantly better than 1:10 (actually, about 1:7.5), compared with the estimated overall 1:20 survivorship ratio for the native peoples of the Americas.

4. The cited observer is Gonzalo Fernández de Oviedo y Valdés, from his *Historia Natural y General de las Indias,* quoted in Carl Ortwin Sauer, *The Early Spanish Main* (Berkeley: University of California Press, 1966), pp. 252–53.

5. Tzvetan Todorov, *The Conquest of America: The Question of the Other* (New York: Harper & Row, 1984).

6. From the testimony of Major Scott J. Anthony, First Colorado Cavalry, before United States Congress, House of Representatives: "Massacre of Cheyenne Indians," in *Report on the Conduct of the War* (38th Congress, Second Session, 1865), p. 27.

7. Alfred W. Crosby, Jr., *The Columbian Exchange: Biological and Cultural Consequences of 1492* (Westport, Conn.: Greenwood Press, 1972), p. 31.

8. For a recent example, in brief, of the common assertion that the Native American population collapse was an "unintended consequence" of native contact with Europeans who, in this version of the fiction, actually wanted to "preserve and increase"—as well as exploit—the native people, see Marvin Harris, "Depopulation and Cultural Evolution: A Cultural Materialist Perspective," in David Hurst Thomas, ed., *Columbian Consequences, Volume Three: The Spanish Borderlands in Pan-American Perspective* (Washington, D.C.: Smithsonian Institution Press, 1991), p. 584. Harris here is objecting specifically to my use of the word "holocaust" to describe the native population decline in the Americas in "The Consequences of Contact: Toward an Interdisciplinary Theory of Native Responses to Biological and Cultural Invasion," ibid., pp. 519–39. See also the recent assertion that "the first European colonists . . . did not want the Amerindians to die," but unfortunately the Indians simply "did not wear well," in Alfred W. Crosby, "Infectious Disease and the Demography of the Atlantic Peoples," *Journal of World History*, 2 (1991), 122, 124.

9. Alexander Saxton, *The Rise and Fall of the White Republic: Class Politics and Mass Culture in Nineteenth-Century America* (London: Verso Books, 1991), p. 153.

10. In Sylvia Rothchild, ed., *Voices from the Holocaust* (New York: New American Library, 1981), p. 4.

11. The dispute over the site of Columbus's first landing is discussed in John Noble Wilford, *The Mysterious History of Columbus: An Exploration of the Man, the Myth, the Legacy* (New York: Alfred A. Knopf, 1991), pp. 129–46.

12. On the number of deaths and disappearances in Guatemala between 1970 and 1985, see Robert M. Carmack, ed., *Harvest of Violence: The Maya Indians and the Guatemalan Crisis* (Norman: University of Oklahoma Press, 1988), p. 295. According to the U.S. Defense Department the number of battle deaths in those wars mentioned in the text was as follows: Civil War—274,235; World War One—53,402; World War Two—291,557; Korean War—33,629; Vietnam War—47,382.

13. For the percentage of rain forest destroyed, see *Cultural Survival Quarterly*, 14 (1990), 86. On the politics and ecology of rain forest destruction, focused on the Amazon but relevant to tropical forests throughout the Americas, see Susanna Hecht and Alexander Cockburn, *The Fate of the Forest: Developers, Destroyers, and Defenders of the Amazon* (New York: Verso Books, 1989).

14. This quotation and the one preceding it are from Vanderbilt University anthropologist Duncan M. Earle's report, "Mayas Aiding Mayas: Guatemalan Refugees in Chiapas, Mexico," in Carmack, ed., *Harvest of Violence*, pp. 263, 269. The rest of this volume of contemporary anthropological accounts from Guatemala makes overwhelmingly clear how devastating is the Guatemalan government's ongoing slaughter of its native Maya peoples—with the United States government's consent and financial support. For more detailed discussion of U.S.

involvement in and support for such activities, see Susanne Jonas, *The Battle for Guatemala: Rebels, Death Squads, and U.S. Power* (Boulder: Westview Press, 1991).

15. Quoted in Jonas, *Battle for Guatemala,* p. 145.

16. Ibid., pp. 148–49; Carmack, ed., *Harvest of Violence,* p. 11.

17. Bernal Díaz del Castillo, *The Discovery and Conquest of Mexico, 1517–1521,* translated by A.P. Maudslay (London: George Routledge & Sons, 1928), p. 409.

Chapter One

1. Woodrow Borah and Sherburne F. Cook, *The Aboriginal Population of Central Mexico on the Eve of the Spanish Conquest,* Ibero-Americana, Number 45 (Berkeley: University of California Press, 1963); Michael Coe, Dean Snow, and Elizabeth Benson, *Atlas of Ancient America* (New York: Facts on File Publications, 1986), p. 145.

2. Rudolph van Zantwijk, *The Aztec Arrangement: The Social History of Pre-Spanish Mexico* (Norman: University of Oklahoma Press, 1985), p. 281, is one of many recent writers who puts the figure at 350,000. More cautious scholars are likely to accept the general range of 250,000 to 400,000 proposed almost thirty years ago by Charles Gibson, although as Gibson notes, informed sixteenth-century estimates ranged as high as 1,000,000 and more. See Charles Gibson, *The Aztecs Under Spanish Rule: A History of the Indians of the Valley of Mexico, 1519–1810* (Stanford: Stanford University Press, 1964), pp. 377–78. For the population of London in 1500 see Lawrence Stone, *The Family, Sex and Marriage in England, 1500–1800* (New York: Harper & Row, 1977), p. 147; for Seville, see J.H. Elliott, *Imperial Spain, 1469–1716* (New York: St. Martin's Press, 1964), p. 177.

3. Bernal Díaz del Castillo, *The Discovery and Conquest of Mexico, 1517–1521,* translated by A.P. Maudslay (London: George Routledge & Sons, 1928), pp. 269–70. All subsequent references to and citations of Bernal Díaz in this chapter come from this same volume, pp. 269–302.

4. Hernan Cortés, *Letters From Mexico,* translated and edited by A.R. Pagden (New York: Grossman Publishers, 1971), p. 107. All subsequent references to and citations of Cortés in this chapter come from this same volume, pp. 100–113.

5. Diego Durán, *The Aztecs: The History of the Indies of New Spain,* translated by Doris Hayden Fernando Horcasitas (New York: Union Press, 1964), p. 183; J. Soustelle, *Daily Life of the Aztecs* (Stanford: Stanford University Press, 1970), pp. 32–33.

6. Venice, even in the middle of the sixteenth century, still had barely half the population of Tenochtitlán before the conquest. See the discussion of Venice's population in Fernand Braudel, *The Mediterranean and the Mediterranean World in the Age of Philip II* (New York: Harper & Row, 1972), Volume One, p. 414.

7. Bernard R. Ortiz de Montellano, *Aztec Medicine, Health, and Nutrition* (New Brunswick: Rutgers University Press, 1990), pp. 127–28.

8. Quoted in Lewis Hanke, *Aristotle and the American Indians: A Study in Race Prejudice in the Modern World* (Bloomington: Indiana University Press, 1959), p. 49.

9. For discussion of these matters among Europeans up through the eight-

eenth century, see Lee H. Huddleston, *Origins of the American Indians: European Concepts, 1492–1729* (Austin: University of Texas Press, 1969).

10. For general discussions of Berengia, see David M. Hopkins, ed., *The Bering Land Bridge* (Stanford: Stanford University Press, 1967); and David M. Hopkins, et al., *Paleoecology of Berengia* (New York: Academic Press, 1982).

11. The arguments for and against significant post-Ice Age, but pre-Columbian ocean contacts between the peoples of the Americas and peoples from other continents or archipelagoes is bound up with debate between two schools of thought—the "diffusionists," who believe that cultural evolution in the Americas was shaped importantly by outside influences, and the "independent inventionists," who hold to the more conventional (and more evidence-supported) view that the cultures evolved independent of such influences. For good overviews of the diffusionist perspective by one of its more responsible adherents, see Stephen C. Jett, "Diffusion versus Independent Invention: The Bases of Controversy," in Carroll L. Riley, et al., *Man Across the Sea: Problems of Pre-Columbian Contacts* (Austin: University of Texas Press, 1971), pp. 5–53; and Stephen C. Jett, "Precolumbian Transoceanic Contacts," in Jesse D. Jennings, ed., *Ancient North Americans* (New York: W.H. Freeman and Company, 1983), pp. 557–613.

12. See detailed discussion in Appendix I, pp. 261–66.

13. Ibid., pp. 266–68.

14. Ibid., p. 263.

15. Ali A. Mazrui, *The Africans: A Triple Heritage* (Boston: Little, Brown and Company, 1986), pp. 23–24, 30–31.

16. W. George Lovell, *Conquest and Survival in Colonial Guatemala: A Historical Geography of the Cuchumatan Highlands, 1500–1821* (Montreal: McGill-Queen's University Press, 1985), p. xii.

17. For a critical compilation of these and many more such descriptions from scholarly works and textbooks during the past decade or so, see James H. Merrell, "Some Thoughts on Colonial Historians and American Indians," *William and Mary Quarterly*, 46 (1989), 94–119.

18. Oscar and Lilian Handlin, *Liberty and Power, 1600–1760* (New York: Harper and Row, 1986); Bernard Bailyn, *The Peopling of British North America: An Introduction* (New York: Alfred A. Knopf, 1986); Bernard Bailyn, *Voyagers to the West: A Passage in the Peopling of America on the Eve of the Revolution* (New York: Alfred A. Knopf, 1986). For commentary on these works, see David E. Stannard, "The Invisible People of Early American History," *American Quarterly*, 39 (1987), 649–55; and Merrell, "Some Thoughts on Colonial Historians and American Indians."

19. Samuel Eliot Morison, *The European Discovery of America: The Southern Voyages, 1492–1616* (New York: Oxford University Press, 1974), p. 737; Samuel Eliot Morison, "Introduction," in Douglas Edward Leach, *Flintlock and Tomahawk: New England in King Philip's War* (New York: W.W. Norton, 1966), p. ix.

20. Hugh Trevor-Roper, *The Rise of Christian Europe* (New York: Harcourt, Brace & World, 1965), p. 9.

21. Leonard Thompson, *The Political Mythology of Apartheid* (New Haven: Yale University Press, 1985), p. 1.

22. Ibid., p. 70.

23. Francis Jennings, *The Invasion of America: Indians, Colonialism, and the Cant of Conquest* (Chapel Hill: University of North Carolina Press, 1975), p. 15.

24. Robert F. Berkhofer, Jr., *The White Man's Indian: Images of the American Indian from Columbus to the Present* (New York: Alfred A. Knopf, 1978), p. 119.

25. Edward W. Said, *The Question of Palestine* (New York: Times Books, 1979), pp. 18–23; Paul Carter, *The Road to Botany Bay: An Exploration of Landscape and History* (New York: Alfred A. Knopf, 1988), p. 335. Carter's specific reference here is to writings about Australia's native peoples, but it is equally applicable throughout the colonized regions of the globe. For a related piece on anthropology as traditionally "a partner in domination and hegemony," see Edward W. Said, "Representing the Colonized: Anthropology's Interlocutors," *Critical Inquiry,* 15 (1989), 205–25. For all its colonial underpinnings, however, anthropology always has been a more politically self-critical discipline than history. See, for example, Talal Asad, ed., *Anthropology and the Colonial Encounter* (New York: Humanities Press, 1973); and W. Arens, *The Man-Eating Myth: Anthropology and Anthropophagy* (New York: Oxford University Press, 1979), esp. pp. 165–85. On history, among several recent works that have begun to join historiographical analysis with anthropological critique, see Robert Young, *White Mythologies: Writing History and the West* (London: Routledge, 1990).

26. Frantz Fanon, "Mr. Debre's Desperate Endeavors" [1959], in *Toward the African Revolution* (New York: Grove Press, 1969), p. 159.

Chapter Two

1. Although much more recent research has been done on the Adena, one of the best general surveys remains William S. Webb and Charles E. Snow, *The Adena People* (Knoxville: University of Tennessee Press, 1974).

2. The physiological distinctiveness of peoples living in different cultural and geographic realms during the centuries of Adena and Hopewell social dominance in northeastern North America has long been recognized. See, for example, Charles E. Snow, "Adena Portraiture," in William S. Webb and Raymond S. Baby, eds., *The Adena People, Number Two* (Columbus: Ohio Historical Society, 1957), pp. 47–53.

3. James B. Griffin, "The Midlands," in Jesse D. Jennings, ed., *Ancient North Americans,* (New York: W.H. Freeman and Company, 1983), pp. 254–67. For recent discussion of the delicately incised copper, mica, obsidian, pearl, and silver jewelry and artifacts from Hopewell culture, see N'omi B. Greber and Katharine C. Ruhl, *The Hopewell Site: A Contemporary Analysis Based on the Work of Charles C. Willoughby* (Boulder: Westview Press, 1989).

4. George Gaylord Simpson, *Horses: The Story of the Horse Family in the Modern World and Through Sixty Million Years of History* (New York: Oxford University Press, 1951), esp. pp. 142–50; Peter Nabokov and Robert Easton, *Native American Architecture* (New York: Oxford University Press, 1989), p. 150.

5. See Barry Kaye and D.W. Moodie, "The Psoralea Food Resource of the Northern Plains," *Plains Anthropologist,* 23 (1978), 329–36.

6. Robert McGhee, *Canadian Arctic Prehistory* (Toronto: Van Nostrand Reinhold, 1978); cited in Barry Lopez, *Arctic Dreams: Imagination and Desire in*

a Northern Landscape (New York: Charles Scribner's Sons, 1986), pp. 181, 184. On the varied domestic architecture of the Arctic and Subarctic regions, see Nabokov and Easton, *Native American Architecture,* pp. 189–207.

7. Richard K. Nelson, *Make Prayers to the Raven: A Koyukon View of the Northern Forest* (Chicago: University of Chicago Press, 1983), pp. 245–46.

8. Lopez, *Arctic Dreams,* p. 265.

9. Noble David Cook, *Demographic Collapse: Indian Peru, 1520–1620* (Cambridge: Cambridge University Press, 1981), p. 108; Henry F. Dobyns, *Their Number Become Thinned: Native American Population Dynamics in Eastern North America* (Knoxville: University of Tennessee Press, 1983), p. 38.

10. Thomas Blackburn, "Ceremonial Integration and Social Interaction in Aboriginal California," in Lowell John Bean and Thomas F. King, eds., *'Antap: California Indian Political and Economic Organization* (Los Altos, Calif.: Ballena Press, 1974), pp. 93–110.

11. Dorothy Lee, *Freedom and Culture* (Englewood Cliffs: Prentice-Hall, 1959), p. 8; see also, pp. 43–44, 80–82, 172.

12. Malcolm Margolin, *The Ohlone Way: Indian Life in the San Francisco-Monterey Bay Area* (Berkeley: Heyday Books, 1978), p. 40.

13. Ibid., p. 57.

14. Juan Rodríguez Cabrillo, "Relation of the Voyage of Juan Rodríguez Cabrillo, 1542–1543," in Herbert Eugene Bolton, ed., *Spanish Exploration in the Southwest, 1542–1706,* (New York: Charles Scribner's Sons, 1916), pp. 13–39.

15. Sherburne F. Cook, *The Population of the California Indians, 1769–1970* (Berkeley: University of California Press, 1976), pp. 69–71; Stephen Powers, *Tribes of California* [Contributions to North American Ethnology, Volume 3] (Washington, D.C.: Department of the Interior, 1877), p. 416.

16. Cabrillo, "Relation of the Voyage," p. 14; on sixteenth- and seventeenth-century disease episodes in California, see, for example, Phillip L. Walker, Patricia Lambert, and Michael J. DeNiro, "The Effects of European Contact on the Health of Alta California Indians," in David Hurst Thomas, ed., *Columbian Consequences, Volume One: Archaeological and Historical Perspectives on the Spanish Borderlands West* (Washington, D.C.: Smithsonian Institution Press, 1989), p. 351.

17. See Carl Waldman, *Atlas of the North American Indian* (New York: Facts on File Publications, 1985), p. 223.

18. It has long been thought that agriculture in the southwest began even earlier—up to 6000 years ago—but recent research on the radiocarbon datings obtained from agricultural sites in the region put the earliest date at about 1200 B.C. See Alan Simmons, "New Evidence for the Early Use of Cultigens in the American Southwest," *American Antiquity,* 51 (1986), 73–88; and Steadman Upham, Richard S. MacNeish, Walton C. Galinat, and Christopher M. Stevenson, "Evidence Concerning the Origin of Maize de Ocho," *American Anthropologist,* 89 (1987), 410–19.

19. Emil W. Haury, *The Hohokam: Desert Farmers and Craftsmen* (Tucson: University of Arizona Press, 1976), pp. 120–51. Paul R. Fish, "The Hohokam: 1,000 Years of Prehistory in the Sonoran Desert," in Linda S. Cordell and George J. Gumerman, eds., *Dynamics of Southwest Prehistory* (Washington, D.C.: Smithsonian Institution Press, 1989), pp. 19–63.

20. For good overviews, among many works on the subject, see William A.

Longacre, ed., *Reconstructing Prehistoric Pueblo Societies* (Albuquerque: University of New Mexico Press, 1970), esp. pp. 59–83; and Robert H. and Florence C. Lister, *Chaco Canyon: Archaeology and Archaeologists* (Albuquerque: University of New Mexico Press, 1981).

21. See R. Gwinn Vivian, "Conservation and Diversion: Water Control Systems in the Anasazi Southwest," in T.E. Downing and M. Gibson, eds., *Irrigation's Impact on Society* (Tucson: Anthropological Papers of the University of Arizona, 1974), pp. 95–111.

22. Nabokov and Easton, *Native American Architecture*, p. 363.

23. For general studies, see Stephen H. LeBlanc, "Aspects of Southwestern Prehistory, A.D. 900–1400," in F.J. Mathien and R.H. McGuire, eds., *Ripples in the Chichimec Sea: New Considerations of Southwestern-Mesoamerican Interactions* (Carbondale: Southern Illinois University Press, 1986), pp. 105–34; and W. James Judge, "Chaco Canyon-San Juan Basin," in Cordell and Gumerman, eds., *Dynamics of Southwest Prehistory*, pp. 209–61. The most detailed studies of the ancient road systems are Gretchen Obenauf, "The Chacoan Roadway System" (M.A. Thesis, University of New Mexico, 1980) and Chris Kincaid, ed., *Chaco Roads Project: Phase I* (Albuquerque: Bureau of Land Management, 1983). For comment on how little of the Grand Canyon has thus far been studied, see Barry Lopez, "Searching for Ancestors," in his *Crossing Open Ground* (New York: Charles Scribner's Sons, 1988), pp. 176–77.

24. These and other early Spanish commentators' remarks on Pueblo egalitarianism and reciprocity are discussed in Ramón A. Gutiérrez, *When Jesus Came, the Corn Mothers Went Away: Marriage, Sexuality, and Power in New Mexico, 1500–1846* (Stanford: Stanford University Press, 1991), pp. 8–15.

25. Quoted in Lee, *Freedom and Culture*, p. 13.

26. For good introductions to these matters, see James M. Crawford, *Studies in Southeastern Indian Languages* (Athens: University of Georgia Press, 1975); Charles M. Hudson, *The Southeastern Indians* (Knoxville: University of Tennessee Press, 1976); and J. Leitch Wright, Jr., *The Only Land They Knew: The Tragic Story of the American Indians of the Old South* (New York: Free Press, 1981).

27. Wright, *The Only Land They Knew*, pp. 1–26.

28. Ibid., p. 24. See also the excellent discussion in William H. Marquardt, "Politics and Production Among the Calusa of South Florida," in Tim Ingold, David Riches, and James Woodburn, eds., *Hunters and Gatherers: History, Evolution, and Social Change* (Oxford: Berg Publishers, 1988), Volume One, pp. 161–88.

29. Marquardt, "Politics and Production Among the Calusa," p. 165.

30. See tables and discussion in Dean R. Snow, *The Archaeology of New England* (New York: Academic Press, 1980), pp. 31–42. See also, William A. Starna, "Mohawk Iroquois Populations: A Revision," *Ethnohistory*, 27 (1980), esp. 376–77. On the population of the Atlantic coastal plain, see Dobyns, *Their Number Become Thinned*, p. 41.

31. For recent comments on the debate, see Elisabeth Tooker, "The United States Constitution and the Iroquois League," *Ethnohistory*, 35 (1988), 305–37; Bruce E. Johansen, "Native American Societies and the Evolution of Democracy in America," *Ethnohistory*, 37 (1990), 279–90; Rejoinder to Johansen by Tooker, ibid., 291–97; and Bruce E. Johansen and Donald A. Grinde, Jr., "The Debate

Regarding Native American Precedents for Democracy: A Recent Historiography," *American Indian Culture and Research Journal*, 14 (1990), 61–88.

32. See, for a variety of approaches, William Brandon, *New Worlds for Old: Reports from the New World and Their Effect on the Development of Social Thought in Europe, 1500–1800* (Athens: Ohio University Press, 1986); Germán Arciniegas, *America in Europe: A History of the New World in Reverse,* translated by Gabriela Arciniegas and R. Victoria Arana (New York: Harcourt Brace Jovanovich, 1986), esp. pp. 49–71; and Jack M. Weatherford, *Indian Givers: The Continuing Impact of the Discovered Americas on the World* (New York: Crown Publishers, 1988).

33. Quoted in Tooker, "United States Consitution and the Iroquois League," 329.

34. Arthur C. Parker, *The Constitution of the Five Nations* (Albany: New York State Museum Bulletin, Number 184, 1916), p. 42.

35. Peggy Reeves Sanday, *Female Power and Male Dominance: On the Origins of Sexual Inequality* (Cambridge: Cambridge University Press, 1982), p. 28. For representative further discussion of female power among the Iroquois and other indigenous peoples of North America, see the following: Judith K. Brown, "Iroquois Women: An Ethnohistoric Note," in Rayna Rapp Reiter, ed., *Toward an Anthropology of Women* (New York: Monthly Review Press, 1978), pp. 235–51; M. Kay Martin and Barbara Voorhies, *Female of the Species* (New York: Columbia University Press, 1975), esp. pp. 225–29; and Jean L. Briggs, "Eskimo Women: Makers of Men," in Carolyn J. Matthiasson, ed., *Many Sisters: Women in Cross-Cultural Perspective* (New York: Macmillan, 1974), pp. 261–304.

36. Sanday, *Female Power and Male Dominance*, pp. 117–18. See also, John Witthoft, "Eastern Woodlands Community Typology and Acculturation," in W. Fenton and J. Gulick, eds., *Symposium on Cherokee and Iroquois Culture* (Washington, D.C.: Smithsonian Institution Press, 1961), pp. 67–76.

37. Pierre de Charlevoix, *Journal of a Voyage to North America* (London, 1761), excerpted in James Axtell, ed., *The Indian Peoples of Eastern America: A Documentary History of the Sexes* (New York: Oxford University Press, 1981), pp. 33–34.

38. Ibid., p. 34.

39. From Reuben Gold Thwaites, ed., *The Jesuit Relations and Allied Documents,* excerpted in Axtell, *Indian Peoples of Eastern America*, pp. 143–48.

40. Charlevoix, "Journal of a Voyage," in Axtell, *Indian Peoples of Eastern America*, p. 153.

41. See, for example, the comments of one Englishman, who had ventured deep into the Shenandoah Valley, on the impressive "judgement and eloquence" of the Indian people he encountered: John Lederer, *The Discoveries of John Lederer, in Three Several Marches from Virginia to the West of Carolina* (London, 1672), p. 5.

42. Joseph François Lafiteau, *Customs of the American Indians Compared with the Customs of Primitive Times,* translated and edited by William N. Fenton and Elizabeth L. Moore (Toronto: The Champlain Society, 1977),Volume Two, p. 61. On the population of the southern Great Lakes area, see Dobyns, *Their Number Become Thinned*, p. 41.

43. Waldman, *Atlas of the North American Indian*, p. 223.

44. Robert Silverberg, *Mound Builders of Ancient America: The Archaeology of a Myth* (Greenwich, Conn.: New York Graphic Society, 1968), p. 312.

45. M.L. Gregg, "A Population Estimate for Cahokia," in *Perspectives in Cahokia Archaeology: Illinois Archaeological Survey Bulletin,* 10 (1975), pp. 126–36; Fiedel, *Prehistory of the Americas,* p. 249.

46. Carl O. Sauer, "The March of Agriculture Across the Western World," in Sauer, *Selected Essays 1963–1975* (Berkeley: Turtle Island Foundation, 1981), pp. 46–47.

47. Russell Thornton, *American Indian Holocaust and Survival: A Population History Since 1492* (Norman: University of Oklahoma Press, 1987), p. 32; Dobyns, *Their Number Become Thinned* , pp. 42, 298.

48. The best introduction to the formative village phase of pre-Olmec culture in the Valley of Oaxaca is Kent V. Flannery, ed., *The Early Mesoamerican Village* (New York: Academic Press, 1976). For early examples of different viewpoints regarding the Olmecs as the single initiators of Mesoamerican civilization, see Michael Coe, *Mexico* (New York: Praeger, 1962); and Kent V. Flannery, "The Olmec and the Valley of Oaxaca: A Model for Interregional Interaction in Formative Times," in E.P. Benson, ed., *Dumbarton Oaks Conference on the Olmec* (Washington: Dumbarton Oaks Research Library and Collection, 1968), pp. 79–110. There no longer is any doubt, however, that complex societies existed in southeastern Mesoamerica prior to the rise of Olmec civilization; see, for example, John E. Clark, "The Beginnings of Mesoamerica: Apologia for the Soconusco Early Formative," and Michael Blake, "An Emerging Early Formative Chiefdom at Paso de la Amada," both in William R. Fowler, Jr., ed., *The Formation of Complex Society in Southeastern Mesoamerica* (Boca Raton: CRC Press, 1991), pp. 13–26, 27–46.

49. Michael D. Coe, *Mexico,* revised and enlarged edition (London: Thames and Hudson, 1984), p. 68.

50. See René Millon, *Urbanization at Teotihuacan, Mexico* (Austin: University of Texas Press, 1973); George L. Cowgill, "Quantitative Studies of Urbanization at Teotihuacan," in Norman Hammond, ed., *Mesoamerican Archaeology: New Approaches* (Austin: University of Texas Press, 1974), pp. 363–96.

51. Coe, *Mexico,* rev. ed., p. 93.

52. Ibid., p. 101.

53. This interpretation of Monte Albán's political status remains controversial. See Richard E. Blanton, *Monte Albán: Settlement Patterns at the Ancient Zapotec Capital* (New York: Academic Press, 1978), and Gordon R. Willey, "The Concept of the 'Disembedded Capital' in Comparative Perspective," *Journal of Anthropological Research,* 35 (1979), 123–37.

54. S.A. Kowalewski, "Population-Resource Balances in Period I of Oaxaca, Mexico," *American Antiquity,* 45 (1980), 151–65.

55. See Virginia Morell, "New Light on Writing in the Americas," *Science,* 251 (1991), 268–70.

56. Sylvanus G. Morley, *The Ancient Maya,* Third Revised Edition (Stanford: Stanford University Press, 1956); see discussion in Sherburne F. Cook and Woodrow Borah, "The Population of Yucatán," in their *Essays in Population History: Mexico and the Caribbean,* (Berkeley: University of California Press, 1974), Volume Two, pp. 22–23.

57. On this, with particular reference to the city of Tikal, see William A. Haviland, "Tikal, Guatemala, and Mesoamerican Urbanism," *World Archaeology,* 2 (1970), 186–97. On Tikal's reservoir system, see Vernon L. Scarborough and Gary G. Gallopin, "A Water Storage Adaptation in the Maya Lowlands," *Science,* 251 (1991), 658–62. On population densities, see Robert S. Santley, Thomas W. Killion, and Mark T. Lycett, "On the Maya Collapse," *Journal of Anthropological Research,* 42 (1986), 123–59.

58. T. Patrick Culbert, Laura J. Kosakowsky, Robert E. Fry, and William A. Haviland, "The Population of Tikal, Guatemala," in T. Patrick Culbert and Don S. Rice, eds., *Precolumbian Population History in the Maya Lowlands,* (Albuquerque: University of New Mexico Press, 1990), pp. 116–17. See also, in general, T. Patrick Culbert, *Classic Maya Political History: Hieroglyphic and Archaeological Evidence* (Cambridge: Cambridge University Press, 1989).

59. Anthony Aveni, *Empires of Time: Calendars, Clocks, and Cultures* (New York: Basic Books, 1989), pp. 233–45.

60. Ibid., p. 252.

61. Linda Newson, *The Cost of Conquest: Indian Decline in Honduras Under Spanish Rule* (Boulder: Westview Press, 1986), p. 91.

62. Linda A. Newson, *Indian Survival in Colonial Nicaragua* (Norman: University of Oklahoma Press, 1987), p. 88.

63. Cf. William M. Denevan, "Epilogue," in William M. Denevan, ed., *The Native Population of the Americas* (Madison: University of Wisconsin Press, 1976), p. 291; and Henry F. Dobyns, "Estimating Aboriginal American Population: An Appraisal of Techniques with a New Hemispheric Estimate," *Current Anthropology,* 7 (1966), 415.

64. Evan S. Connell, *A Long Desire* (New York: Holt, Rinehart and Winston, 1979), p. 162.

65. Richard L. Burger, "Concluding Remarks," in Christopher B. Donnan, ed., *Early Ceremonial Architecture in the Andes* (Washington, D.C.: Dumbarton Oaks Research Library and Collection, 1985), p. 273.

66. The earliest excavations and descriptions of El Paraíso were the work of F.A. Engel, "Le Complexe Preceramique d'El Paraíso (Perou)," *Journal de la Societe des Americanistes,* 55 (1966), 43–95; for the most recent work, see Jeffrey Quilter, Bernardino Ojeda E., Deborah M. Pearsall, Daniel H. Sandweiss, John G. Jones, and Elizabeth S. Wing, "Subsistence Economy of El Paraíso, an Early Peruvian Site", *Science,* 251 (1991), 277–85.

67. On the languages of the Incas, both before and after the Spanish conquest, see Bruce Mannheim, *The Language of the Inka Since the European Invasion* (Austin: University of Texas Press, 1991).

68. On the desert etchings of the Nazca peoples the best discussions are in *The Lines of Nazca,* ed. Anthony Aveni (Philadelphia: American Philosophical Society, 1990). For an evocative description of one man's encounter with a small scale North American example of this phenomenon, see Barry Lopez's essay, "The Stone Horse," in his *Crossing Open Ground,* pp. 1–17.

69. Pedro de Cieza de León, *The Incas,* translated by Harriet de Onis (Norman: University of Oklahoma Press, 1959), p. 203.

70. John Hemming, *The Conquest of the Incas* (New York: Harcourt Brace Jovanovich, 1970), p. 121.

71. For this and more see the chapter on Cuzco in Hemming, *Conquest of the Incas*, pp. 118–36. Garcilaso de la Vega is quoted in Graziano Gasparini and Louise Margolies, *Inca Architecture*, translated by Patricia J. Lyon (Bloomington: Indiana University Press, 1980), p. 198.

72. Cook, *Demographic Collapse*, pp. 39, 219.

73. Ibid., p. 200.

74. Ibid.

75. Cieza de León, *The Incas*, p. 318.

76. Ibid., pp. 328, 305.

77. See John Hyslop, *The Inka Road System* (New York: Academic Press, 1984), pp. 323–31.

78. Pedro Sancho, *Relacion para S.M. de lo sucedido en la conquesta y pacification de estas provincias de la Nueva Castilla y de la calidad de la tierra*, quoted (as is the preceding quotation from Pizarro) in Hemming, *Conquest of the Incas*, p. 101.

79. Ibid., pp. 123–24.

80. José de Acosta, *Historia Natural y Moral de las Indias* (Seville, 1590); cited in Brandon, *New Worlds for Old*, p. 12.

81. Sabine MacCormack, "Demons, Imagination, and the Incas," *Representations*, 33 (1991), 134. For a concentrated look at the religious worlds of North America's native peoples, showing how varied their spiritual lives were, while at the same time demonstrating how those lives were always logically connected with the specific nature of the immediately surrounding environment, see Ake Hultkrantz, *Native Religions of North America: The Power of Visions and Fertility* (New York: Harper & Row, 1987).

82. Quoted in Brandon, *New Worlds for Old*, p. 13.

83. John Hemming, *Red Gold: The Conquest of the Brazilian Indians, 1500–1760* (Cambridge: Harvard University Press, 1978), p. 46.

84. Jean de Léry, *Histoire d'un voyage faict en la terre du Bresil, autrement dite Amerique* (La Rochelle, 1578); quoted in Brandon, *New Worlds for Old*, p. 13.

85. On the varied languages of the Amazonian peoples, see Doris L. Payne, ed., *Amazonian Linguistics: Studies in Lowland South American Languages* (Austin: University of Texas Press, 1990). The discovery of 7000- to 8000–year-old pottery in the Amazon lowlands is discussed in A.C. Roosevelt, R.A. Housely, M. Imazio da Silveira, S. Maranca, and R. Johnson, "Eighth Millennium Pottery from a Prehistoric Shell Midden in the Brazilian Amazon," *Science*, 254 (1991), 1621–24. For general discussion, see J. Brochado and D.W. Lathrap, *Amazonia* (Urbana: University of Illinois Press, 1982); A.C. Roosevelt, *The Developmental Sequence at Santarém on the Lower Amazon, Brazil* (Washington, D.C.: National Endowment for the Humanities, 1990); and A.C. Roosevelt, *Moundbuilders of the Amazon: Geophysical Archaeology on Marajo Island, Brazil* (New York: Academic Press, 1991).

86. William Denevan has estimated the Amazon basin population at between 5.1 million and 6.8 million in "The Aboriginal Population of Amazonia," in Denevan, ed., *Native Population of the Americas*, pp. 205–34; Clastres's estimate for the Guaraní appears in his *Society Against the State: The Leader as Servant and the Humane Uses of Power Among the Indians of the Americas* (New York: Urizen Books, 1977), pp. 64–82.

87. Marshall Sahlins, "The Original Affluent Society," in Sahlins, *Stone Age Economics* (London: Tavistock Publications, 1974), pp. 1–39.

88. Junius B. Bird, "The Archaeology of Patagonia," in *Handbook of South American Indians* (Washington, D.C.: Bureau of American Ethnology Bulletin Number 143, 1946), pp. 17–24.

89. On the Timucuan language evidence, see Joseph H. Greenberg, *Language in the Americas*(Stanford: Stanford University Press, 1988), pp. 106–7, 336.

90. Irving Rouse, "On the Meaning of the Term 'Arawak'," in Fred Olsen, *On the Trail of the Arawaks* (Norman: University of Oklahoma Press, 1974), p. xv.

91. Bartolomé de las Casas, *Apologetica historia de las Indias* (Madrid: Marcelino Menendez y Pelayo, 1909), ch. 43; quoted in Carl Ortwin Sauer, *The Early Spanish Main* (Berkeley: University of California Press, 1966), p. 63.

92. Sauer, *Early Spanish Main,* pp. 51–53.

93. Olsen, *On the Trail of the Arawaks,* p. 342.

94. Sauer, *Early Spanish Main,* pp. 58–59; Robert S. Weddle, *Spanish Sea: The Gulf of Mexico in North American Discovery, 1500–1685* (College Station: Texas A&M University Press, 1985), p. 28.

95. Sauer, *Early Spanish Main,* p. 69.

96. J.H. Elliott, "The Discovery of America and the Discovery of Man," *Proceedings of the British Academy,* 58 (1972), 119.

97. Quoted in Brandon, *New Worlds for Old,* p. 60.

98. Edmund S. Morgan, *American Slavery, American Freedom: The Ordeal of Colonial Virginia* (New York: W.W. Norton & Company, 1975), p. 39.

99. Ibid., p. 40.

100. John C. Super, *Food, Conquest, and Colonization in Sixteenth-Century Spanish America* (Albuquerque: University of New Mexico Press, 1988), pp. 79–88.

101. Quoted in John S. Milloy, *The Plains Cree: Trade, Diplomacy, and War, 1790 to 1870* (Winnipeg: University of Manitoba Press, 1988), p. 71.

102. Jane E. Buikstra, ed., *Prehistoric Tuberculosis in the Americas* (Evanston: Northwestern University Archaeological Program, Scientific Papers Number 5, 1981), p. 18; Brenda J. Baker and George J. Armelagos, "The Origin and Antiquity of Syphilis," *Current Anthropology,* 29 (1988), 703–20; but see also the commentaries following the Baker and Armelagos article and Henry F. Dobyns, "On Issues in Treponemal Epidemiology," *Current Anthropology,* 30 (1989), 342–43.

103. See, for example, Mary Lucas Powell, *Status and Health in Prehistory: A Case Study of the Moundville Chiefdom* (Washington, D.C.: Smithsonian Institution Press, 1988), pp. 152–82.

104. George W. Gill, "Human Skeletal Remains on the Northwestern Plains," in George C. Frison, ed., *Prehistoric Hunters of the High Plains,* Second Edition (New York: Academic Press, 1991), pp. 442–43. An illustrative example of human longevity in this region is the Late Plains Archaic (approximately 1000 B.C. to 500 A.D.) skeleton of a man recently discovered at Iron Jaw Creek, Montana. Of greatly advanced years, having lost all his teeth long before his death and exhibiting a frame far too decrepit and infirm to have allowed him to contribute materially to the well-being of others in the community, he apparently was well cared for and fed a special soft diet to sustain him in his waning years. See George W. Gill and

Gerald R. Clark, "A Late Plains Archaic Burial from Iron Jaw Creek, Southeastern Montana," *Plains Anthropologist*, 28 (1983), 191–98; and George W. Gill, "Additional Comment and Illustration Relating to the Iron Jaw Skeleton," *Plains Anthropologist*, 28 (1983), 335–36.

105. The only evidence at all suggestive that this picture of exceptionally good health might be flawed derives from paleodemographic analyses based on osteological studies of pre-Columbian Indian skeletons that have found a short life expectancy in certain locales—about the same life expectancy as that historically recorded for eighteenth-century Europeans. Analyses of this sort are fraught with difficulties, however, and they are at their weakest in determining age at death—where there is a strong methodological bias toward underestimation. Although not well known outside the discipline, this has been recognized within the field as a serious problem for almost 20 years. See Kenneth M. Weiss, *Demographic Models for Anthropology* (Society for American Archaeology Memoir Number 27, 1973), p. 59; and the devastating critique of the field on this and other points in Jean-Pierre Bocquet-Appel and Claude Masset, "Farewell to Paleodemography," *Journal of Human Evolution*, 11 (1982), 321–33. Even the most ardent defenders of the field, subsequent to the critique by Bocquet-Appel and Masset, have conceded that the age estimates for older individuals studied by these techniques are invariably far too low. See, for example, Jane E. Buikstra and Lyle W. Koningsberg, "Paleodemography: Critiques and Controversies," *American Anthropologist*, 87 (1985), 316–33.

Chapter Three

1. Andrew B. Appleby, "The Disappearance of Plague: A Continuing Puzzle," *The Economic History Review*, Second Series, 33 (1980), 161–62.

2. R.P.R. Mols, "Population in Europe, 1500–1700," in C.M. Cipolla, ed., *The Fontana Economic History of Europe* (London: Fontana, 1973), p. 49.

3. J.H. Elliott, *Imperial Spain, 1469–1716* (New York: St. Martin's Press, 1964), p. 306.

4. David R. Weir, "Markets and Mortality in France, 1600–1789," in John Walter and Roger Schofield, eds., *Famine, Disease, and the Social Order in Early Modern Society* (Cambridge: Cambridge University Press, 1989), p. 229.

5. Quoted in Fernand Braudel, *The Mediterranean and the Mediterranean World in the Age of Philip II* (New York: Harper & Row, 1972), Volume One, p. 519.

6. Micheline Baulant, "Le prix des grains à Paris," *Annales*, 3 (1968), 538. The relationship between famine and disease, while profound, is not quite so simple as this comment suggests. For an example of more nuanced analysis of the interaction between nutritional deficiency and infection in European history, see John D. Post, "The Mortality Crises of the Early 1770s and European Demographic Trends," *Journal of Interdisciplinary History*, 21 (1990), 29–62.

7. See, for example, material in Angus MacKay, "Pogroms in Fifteenth Century Castille," *Past and Present*, 55 (1972), 33–67.

8. For one example of a historical effort to sort out deaths from disease and deaths from famine that demonstrates just how difficult a task it is, see Andrew B.

Appleby, "Disease or Famine? Mortality in Cumberland and Westmorland, 1580–1640," *The Economic History Review,* Second Series, 26 (1973), 403–31.

9. Lawrence Stone, *The Family, Sex and Marriage in England, 1500–1800* (New York: Harper & Row, 1977), pp. 77–78.

10. Ibid., p. 487.

11. See Norbert Elias, *The Civilizing Process: The History of Manners,* translated by Edmund Jephcott (New York: Urizen Books, 1978), pp. 191–205, for this and more on the "violent manners [and] brutality of passions" that characterized urban Europe at this time. (The quotations in the text from Elias and Huizinga are on pp. 195 and 203.) Incidentally, the famous essay by Robert Darnton, "Workers Revolt: The Great Cat Massacre of the Rue Saint-Severin," in Darnton's *The Great Cat Massacre and Other Episodes in French Cultural History* (New York: Basic Books, 1984), pp. 75–104, refers to an incident that occurred in Paris three centuries or so after the time we are discussing here, but a time when "the torture of animals, especially cats, was [still] a popular amusement" (p. 90). For some cogent recent comments on this article itself, see Harold Mah, "Suppressing the Text: The Metaphysics of Ethnographic History in Darnton's Great Cat Massacre," *History Workshop,* 31 (1991), 1–20.

12. Quoted in Jacques Boulanger, *The Seventeenth Century in France* (New York: Capricorn Books, 1963), p. 354.

13. Stone, *Family, Sex and Marriage,* pp. 98–99; H.C. Eric Midelfort, *Witch-Hunting in Southwestern Germany* (Stanford: Stanford University Press, 1972), p. 137; Norman Cohn, *Europe's Inner Demons: An Inquiry Inspired by the Great Witch-Hunt* (New York: Basic Books, 1975), p. 254.

14. Olwen H. Hufton, *The Poor of Eighteenth-Century France, 1750–1789* (Oxford: Clarendon Press, 1974), pp. 18, 20.

15. Ibid., 21–24.

16. Fernand Braudel, *Capitalism and Material Life, 1400–1800* (London: Weidenfeld and Nicolson, 1973), pp. 205, 216–17; Braudel, *The Mediterranean,* Volume One, pp. 258–59.

17. Michael W. Flinn, *The European Demographic System, 1500–1820* (Baltimore: The Johns Hopkins University Press, 1981), pp. 16–17.

18. By the eighteenth and nineteenth centuries these practices had become so epidemic that foundling hospitals were created in European cities, but they then became little more than dumping grounds for hundreds of thousands of infants, from which few children ever emerged alive. There is a large literature on this, but see especially: Thomas R. Forbes, "Deadly Parents: Child Homicide in Eighteenth and Nineteenth Century England," *The Journal of the History of Medicine and Allied Sciences,* 41 (1986), 175–99; Ruth K. McClure, *Coram's Children: The London Foundling Hospital in the Eighteenth Century* (New Haven: Yale University Press, 1981); Rachel Fuchs, *Abandoned Children: Foundlings and Child Welfare in Nineteenth Century France* (Albany: State University of New York Press, 1984); and David I. Kertzer, "Gender Ideology and Infant Abandonment in Nineteenth Century Italy," *Journal of Interdisciplinary History,* 22 (1991), esp. 5–9.

19. Letter of Piero Benintendi, "News from Genoa," in Robert S. Lopez and Irving W. Raymond, eds., *Medieval Trade in the Mediterranean World: Illustrative Documents* (New York: Columbia University Press, 1955), pp. 401, 402–403.

20. John Boswell, *The Kindness of Strangers: The Abandonment of Children*

in Western Europe from Late Antiquity to the Renaissance (New York: Pantheon Books, 1988), p. 407, note 27. Boswell also quotes here from different portions of the above-cited letter.

21. Louis B. Wright, *Gold, Glory, and the Gospel: The Adventurous Lives and Times of the Renaissance Explorers* (New York: Atheneum, 1970), pp. 16–17; Braudel, *The Mediterranean*, Volume One, p. 462.

22. Anthony Pagden, *The Fall of Natural Man: The American Indian and the Origins of Comparative Ethnology*, Revised Edition (Cambridge: Cambridge University Press, 1986), p. 84.

23. See, for example, Cohn, *Europe's Inner Demons*, passim; and R. Po-Chia Hsia, *The Myth of Ritual Murder: Jews and Magic in Reformation Germany* (New Haven: Yale University Press, 1988).

24. Bartholomew Senarega, *De Rubus Genuensibus, 1388–1514*, quoted in Boswell, *Kindness of Strangers*, p. 406.

25. The matter of starvation caused by inadequate supplies of grain perhaps deserves a brief digression. The French historian Pierre Chaunu has argued that the failing agricultural system of Europe, which was unable regularly to feed all but the well-to-do, acted as a spur to post-Columbian European expansion. He no doubt is correct in this, at least in part, and such New World foods as potatoes, beans, and maize have contributed greatly to European diets since the sixteenth century. But in the wake of that expansion, as gold and silver flowed in from forced-labor mines in Mexico and Peru, a terrible irony occurred: the price of grain in Europe, like everything else, spiraled upward with inflation—and the European poor continued to starve. Pierre Chaunu, *European Expansion in the Later Middle Ages*, translated by Katharine Bertram (Amsterdam: North-Holland Publishing Company, 1969), pp. 283–88; on the importance of American foodstuffs to Old World diets, see Alfred W. Crosby, Jr., *The Columbian Exchange: Biological and Cultural Consequences of 1492* (Westport, Conn.: Greenwood Press, 1972), pp. 165–207; on the sixteenth century rise in prices, see Braudel, *The Mediterranean*, Volume One, pp. 516–42.

26. "Columbus's Letter to the Sovereigns on His First Voyage, 15 February—4 March, 1493," in Samuel Eliot Morison, ed., *Journals and Other Documents on the Life and Voyages of Christopher Columbus* (New York: The Heritage Press, 1963), pp. 182–83.

27. Ibid., p. 183.

28. Frank E. Manuel and Fritzie P. Manuel, "Sketch for a Natural History of Paradise," in Clifford Geertz, ed., *Myth, Symbol, and Culture* (New York: W.W. Norton & Company, 1971), p. 119.

29. Despite his legendary sailing skills, Columbus has been roundly criticized on this point by several writers, most recently and most harshly by Kirkpatrick Sale in *The Conquest of Paradise: Christopher Columbus and the Columbian Legacy* (New York: Alfred A. Knopf, 1990), pp. 209–11 and 381–82.

30. Lewis Hanke, *Aristotle and the American Indians: A Study in Race Prejudice in the Modern World* (Bloomington: Indiana University Press, 1959), p. 6.

31. Ibid., p. 47.

32. Morison, ed., *Journals and Other Documents*, pp. 96, 105.

33. Arthur Helps, *The Spanish Conquest in America* (London: John Lane, 1900), Volume One, pp. 264–67.

34. Quoted in Tzvetan Todorov, *The Conquest of America: The Question of the Other* (New York: Harper & Row, 1984), p.148.

35. Morison, ed., *Journals and Other Documents*, p. 93.

36. Ibid., p. 226.

37. Ibid., p. 227.

38. Michele de Cuneo, "Letter on the Second Voyage," in Morison, ed., *Journals and Other Documents*, pp. 213–14.

39. Carl Ortwin Sauer, *The Early Spanish Main* (Berkeley: University of California Press, 1966), p. 76: Samuel Eliot Morison, *The European Discovery of America: The Southern Voyages, A.D. 1492–1616* (New York: Oxford University Press, 1974), p. 118; Sale, *Conquest of Paradise*, p. 149.

40. Frederick L. Dunn, "On the Antiquity of Malaria in the Western Hemisphere," *Human Biology*, 37 (1965), 385–93; Saul Jarcho, "Some Observations on Disease in Prehistoric North America," *Bulletin of the History of Medicine*, 38 (1964), 1–19.

41. On yellow fever, see Kenneth F. Kiple and Virginia Himmelsteib King, *Another Dimension to the Black Diaspora: Diet, Disease, and Racism* (Cambridge: Cambridge University Press, 1981), pp. 31–35. On smallpox in the Americas generally, as well as on this point, see Dauril Alden and Joseph C. Miller, "Unwanted Cargoes: The Origins and Dissemination of Smallpox via the Slave Trade from Africa to Brazil, c. 1560–1830," in Kenneth F. Kiple, ed., *The African Exchange: Toward a Biological History of Black People* (Durham: Duke University Press, 1987), pp. 35–109.

42. Francisco Guerra, "The Earliest American Epidemic: The Influenza of 1493," *Social Science History*, 12 (1988), 305–25.

43. Alfred W. Crosby, "Virgin Soil Epidemics as a Factor in the Aboriginal Depopulation in America," *William and Mary Quarterly*, 3rd Series, 33 (1976), 293–94; Henry F. Dobyns, *Their Number Become Thinned: Native American Population Dynamics in Eastern North America* (Knoxville: University of Tennessee Press, 1983), p. 18. For a discussion of zoonotic diseases from wildlife on this question, see Calvin Martin, "Wildlife Diseases as a Factor in the Depopulation of the North American Indian," *The Western Historical Quarterly*, 7 (1976), 47–62. There are some nagging problems with Guerra's thesis that need to be addressed. Key among them concern the relatively short incubation period for influenza, which makes it unlikely that the virus could have survived the lengthy ocean voyage (unless it was kept active by passing from host to host), and the difficulty of explaining how the virus was so well contained among the sows, even if they were stored below deck, and did not spread to the shipboard humans until the ships' arrival at the future site of Isabela. An answer to at least one of these problems may emerge from some new research on influenza suggesting that, in addition to direct host-to-victim transferral of the virus, many cases may be spread by symptomless year-round carriers of the disease in whom contagion is triggered by an unknown mechanism during so-called "flu seasons." See R.E. Hope-Simpson and D.B. Golubev, "A New Concept of the Epidemic Process of Influenza A Virus," *Epidemiology and Infection*, 99 (1987), 5–54. I have discussed this elsewhere in *Before the Horror: The Population of Hawai'i on the Eve of Western Contact* (Honolulu: Social Science Research Institute and University of Hawai'i Press, 1989), pp. 74–75, and

in a symposium on that book published in *Pacific Studies,* 13 (1990), esp. 292–94.

44. Quoted in Guerra, "Earliest American Epidemic," 312–13.

45. Morison, ed., *Journals and Other Documents,* p. 65.

46. Fernando Colón, *The Life of the Admiral Christopher Columbus by His Son Ferdinand,* translated by Benjamin Keen (New Brunswick: Rutgers University Press, 1959), p. 170. For another instance, in which the Spanish provoked the natives to throw rocks at them, causing a Spanish retaliation that casually killed a couple of dozen Indians, see the report by Cuneo in Morison, *Journals and Other Documents,* p. 222.

47. Bartolomé de Las Casas, *The Devastation of the Indies: A Brief Account* [1542], translated by Herma Briffault (New York: Seabury Press, 1974), pp. 54–55.

48. Carl Ortwin Sauer, *The Early Spanish Main* (Berkeley: University of California Press, 1966), pp. 86–87.

49. Bartolomé de Las Casas *History of the Indies,* translated and edited by Andree Collard (New York: Harper & Row, 1971), p. 94.

50. Quoted in Todorov, *Conquest of America,* pp. 139–40.

51. Ibid., p. 139.

52. Las Casas, *History of the Indies,* p. 121.

53. Sauer, *Early Spanish Main,* p. 89.

54. Sherburne F. Cook and Woodrow Borah, "The Aboriginal Population of Hispaniola," in Cook and Borah, *Essays in Population History: Mexico and the Caribbean,* (Berkeley: University of California Press, 1971), Volume One, pp. 402–403.

55. Linda Newson, *The Cost of Conquest: Indian Decline in Honduras Under Spanish Rule* (Boulder, Colorado: Westview Press, 1986), pp. 107–108.

56. Saver, *Early Spanish Main,* p. 101.

57. Las Casas, *History of the Indies,* p. 111.

58. Ibid., pp. 112, 114.

59. Quoted in John Boyd Thatcher, *Christopher Columbus: His Life, His Work, His Remains* (New York: Putnam's, 1903), Volume Two, pp. 348–49.

60. Las Casas, *History of the Indies,* p. 110.

61. Cook and Borah, "Aboriginal Population of Hispaniola," p. 401.

62. For a list of these and other twentieth-century genocides, including estimates of numbers killed, see Barbara Harff, "The Etiology of Genocides," in Isidor Wallimann and Michael N. Dobkowski, eds., *Genocide and the Modern Age: Etiology and Case Studies of Mass Death* (Westport, Conn.: Greenwood Press, 1987), p. 46, Table 3.1.

63. Inga Clendinnen, "The Cost of Courage in Aztec Society," *Past and Present,* 107 (1985), 44–89.

64. Ross Hassig, *Aztec Warfare: Imperial Expansion and Political Control* (Norman: University of Oklahoma Press, 1988), p. 237.

65. Ibid., pp. 241–42.

66. Hernan Cortés, *Letters from Mexico,* translated and edited by A.R. Pagden (New York: Grossman Publishers, 1971), p. 249.

67. Inga Clendinnen, " 'Fierce and Unnatural Cruelty': Cortes and the Con-

quest of Mexico," *Representations*, 33 (1991), 70, 78; Hassig, *Aztec Warfare*, pp. 242–43.

68. Bernardino de Sahagún, *Conquest of New Spain*, [1585 edition] translated by Howard F. Cline (Salt Lake City: University of Utah Press, 1989), pp. 76–77.

69. Ibid., pp. 78–89.

70. David Henige, "When Did Smallpox Reach the New World (And Why Does It Matter)?" in Paul E. Lovejoy, ed., *Africans in Bondage: Studies in Slavery and the Slave Trade* (Madison: University of Wisconsin African Studies Program, 1986), pp. 11–26.

71. Francisco López de Gómara, *Cortés: The Life of the Conquerer by His Secretary*, translated and edited by Lesley Byrd Simpson (Berkeley: University of California Press, 1965), pp. 204–205.

72. On the impact of smallpox in the struggle for Tenochtitlán, see Alfred W. Crosby, *The Columbian Exchange: Biological and Cultural Consequences of 1492* (Westport, Conn.: Greenwood Press, 1972), pp. 35–63.

73. Clendinnen, " 'Fierce and Unnatural Cruelty,' " 83.

74. See Victor Davis Hanson, *The Western Way of War: Infantry Battle in Classical Greece* (New York: Alfred A. Knopf, 1989).

75. Bernal Díaz del Castillo, *The Discovery and Conquest of Mexico, 1517–1521*, translated by A.P. Maudslay (London: George Routledge & Sons, 1928), p. 545.

76. Cortés, *Letters from Mexico*, pp. 252–53.

77. Ibid., pp. 257–62.

78. Ibid., p. 263.

79. Pedro de Cieza de León, *The Incas*, translated by Harriet de Onis (Norman: University of Oklahoma Press, 1959), p. 180.

80. Quoted in William Brandon, *New Worlds for Old: Reports from the New World and Their Effect on the Development of Social Thought in Europe, 1500–1800* (Athens, Ohio: Ohio University Press, 1986), p. 159. See also Brandon's brief further comments, pp. 159, 205. For some recent discussion on exaggerated estimates of human sacrifice in the New World, in India, and in Africa, see Inga Clendinnen, *Ambivalent Conquests: Maya and Spaniard in Yucatán, 1517–1570* (Cambridge: Cambridge University Press, 1987); Nigel Davies, "Human Sacrifice in the Old World and the New: Some Similarities and Differences," in Elizabeth H. Boone, ed., *Ritual Human Sacrifice in Mesoamerica* (Washington, D.C.: Dumbarton Oaks Research Library, 1984), pp. 220–22; James D. Graham, "The Slave Trade, Depopulation, and Human Sacrifice in Benin History," *Cahiers d'Etudes Africaines*, 5 (1965), 317–34; and Philip A. Igbafe, *Benin Under British Administration* (London: Longman, 1979), esp. pp. 40–49, 70–72.

81. Miguel Leon-Portilla, ed., *The Broken Spears: The Aztec Account of the Conquest of Mexico* (Boston: Beacon Press, 1962), p. 140.

82. Cortés, *Letters from Mexico*, pp. 265–66.

83. France V. Scholes, "The Spanish Conqueror as a Business Man: A Chapter in the History of Fernando Cortés," *New Mexico Quarterly*, 28 (1958), pp. 11, 16, 18, 21. Scholes calculated Cortés's net worth after the conquest of Tenochtitlán to have been "at least $2,500,000" in 1958 currency; according to the U.S.

Bureau of Labor Statistics, that is the equivalent of more than $10,000,000 in 1990.

84. Quoted in Pedro de Alvarado, *An Account of the Conquest of Guatemala in 1524*, ed. Sedley J. Mackie (Boston: Milford House, 1972), pp. 126–32.

85. For these and other enumerations, see Daniel T. Reff, *Disease, Depopulation, and Culture Change in Northwestern New Spain, 1518–1764* (Salt Lake City: University of Utah Press, 1991), pp. 194–242.

86. Crosby, *Columbian Exchange*, p. 50; Newson, *The Cost of Conquest*, pp. 109–110, 127.

87. Diego de Landa and Lorenzo de Bienvenida are quoted in Grant D. Jones, *Maya Resistance to Spanish Rule: Time and History on a Colonial Frontier* (Albuquerque: University of New Mexico Press, 1989), pp. 42–43.

88. Alonzo de Zorita, *Life and Labor in Ancient Mexico: The Brief and Summary Relation of the Lords of New Spain*, translated by Benjamin Keen (New Brunswick, N.J.: Rutgers University Press, 1963), p. 210.

89. There is a photograph of this façade in Robert S. Weddle, *Spanish Sea: The Gulf of Mexico in North American Discovery, 1500–1685* (College Station: Texas A & M University Press, 1985), between pages 158 and 159.

90. This handful of examples, from a seemingly endless library of such tales, comes from William L. Sherman, *Forced Native Labor in Sixteenth Century Central America* (Lincoln: University of Nebraska Press, 1979), pp. 44–45, 61, 268; Zorita, *Life and Labor in Ancient Mexico*, p. 210; Jones, *Maya Resistance to Spanish Rule*, pp. 42–43; and Alvarado, *An Account of the Conquest of Guatemala*, p. 129.

91. John Grier Varner and Jeannette Johnson Varner, *Dogs of the Conquest* (Norman: University of Oklahoma Press, 1983), pp. 192–93.

92. Ibid., pp. 36–39.

93. Peter Martyr, quoted in Todorov, *Conquest of America*, p. 141.

94. Sherman, *Forced Native Labor*, pp. 64–65. On repeated branding as slaves were passed from one owner to another, see Donald E. Chipman, *Nuño de Guzmán and the Province of Panuco in New Spain, 1518–1533* (Glendale, Calif.: Arthur H. Clark, 1967), p. 210.

95. In Morison, ed., *Journals and Other Documents*, p. 212.

96. Quoted in Todorov, *Conquest of America*, p. 139.

97. Sherman, *Forced Native Labor*, p. 311.

98. Ibid., pp. 315–16.

99. Ibid., p. 316.

100. For the examples cited, see Sherburne F. Cook and Woodrow Borah, *The Indian Population of Central Mexico, 1531–1610*, Ibero-Americana, Number 44 (Berkeley: University of California Press, 1960); Woodrow Borah and Sherburne F. Cook, *The Aboriginal Population of Central Mexico on the Eve of the Spanish Conquest*, Ibero-Americana, Number 45 (Berkeley: University of California Press, 1963); Peter Gerhard, *A Guide to the Historical Geography of New Spain* (Princeton: Princeton University Press, 1972), pp. 22–25; Peter Gerhard, *The Southeast Frontier of New Spain* (Princeton: Princeton University Press, 1979), p. 25; Peter Gerhard, *The North Frontier of New Spain* (Princeton: Princeton University Press, 1982), pp. 23–25; Clinton R. Edwards, "Quintana Roo: Mexico's Empty Quarter"

(Master's Thesis, University of California at Berkeley, 1957), pp. 128, 132; W. George Lovell, *Conquest and Survival in Colonial Guatemala: A Historical Geography of the Cuchumatan Highlands, 1500–1821* (Montreal: McGill-Queen's University Press, 1985), p. 145; David R. Radell, "The Indian Slave Trade and Population of Nicaragua During the Sixteenth Century," in William M. Denevan, ed., *The Native Population of the Americas* (Madison: University of Wisconsin Press, 1976), pp. 67–76; Newson, *The Cost of Conquest*, p. 330; and Patrick J. Carroll, *Blacks in Colonial Veracruz: Race, Ethnicity, and Regional Development* (Austin: University of Texas Press, 1991), p. 95.

101. Leon-Portilla, ed., *The Broken Spears*, pp. 137–38.

102. Quoted in Nathan Wachtel, *The Vision of the Vanquished: The Spanish Conquest of Peru Through Indian Eyes, 1530–1570,* translated by Ben and Sian Reynolds (Sussex: The Harvester Press, 1977), p. 31.

103. Noble David Cook, *Demographic Collapse: Indian Peru, 1520–1620* (Cambridge: Cambridge University Press, 1981), p. 114.

104. Quoted in John Hemming, *The Conquest of the Incas* (New York: Harcourt Brace Jovanovich, 1970), p. 359.

105. Pedro de Cieza de León, *The Incas,* translated by Harriet de Onis (Norman: University of Oklahoma Press, 1959), p. 62.

106. Ibid., pp. lviii-lix.

107. Hemming, *Conquest of the Incas,* p. 351.

108. Ibid., pp. 363–64.

109. Ibid., pp. 368–69.

110. Ibid., p. 372.

111. Raul Hilberg, *The Destruction of the European Jews* (Chicago: Quadrangle Books, 1961), p. 596.

112. Hemming, *Conquest of the Incas,* p. 348.

113. Quoted in Salvador de Madariaga, *The Rise of the Spanish American Empire* (New York: Macmillan, 1947), pp. 90–91.

114. Quoted in Cook, *Demographic Collapse,* p. 199. For detailed discussion of some of the matters mentioned in the preceding paragraph, see the same volume, pp. 199–210.

115. Ibid., p. 207.

116. Quoted in John Hemming, *Red Gold: The Conquest of the Brazilian Indians, 1500–1760* (Cambridge: Harvard University Press, 1978), p. 139.

117. All citations in this paragraph are from Hemming, *Red Gold,* pp. 139–41.

118. For maps and a history of the captaincies, see Lyle N. McAlister, *Spain and Portugal in the New World, 1492–1700* (Minneapolis: University of Minnesota Press, 1984), pp. 260–66.

119. Paul Slack, *The Impact of Plague in Tudor and Stuart England* (London: Routledge and Kegan Paul, 1985), p. 7. For a close and revealing look at plague in the country with Europe's best-organized system of public health—and in which 50 to 60 percent of infected individuals died—see Carlo M. Cipolla, *Cristofano and the Plague: A Study in the History of Public Health in the Age of Galileo* (London: William Collins Sons & Co., 1973).

120. Quoted in Hemming, *Red Gold,* p. 142.

121. Ibid., p. 143. See also, Alden and Miller, "Unwanted Cargoes," pp. 42–43.

122. Hemming, *Red Gold*, pp. 143–44; Stuart B. Schwartz, "Indian Labor and New World Plantations: European Demands and Indian Responses in Northeastern Brazil," *American Historical Review*, 83 (1978), 51.

123. Schwartz, "Indian Labor and New World Plantations," 55–56, 76.

124. Jones, *Maya Resistance to Spanish Rule*, p. 276.

125. Varner and Varner, *Dogs of the Conquest*, pp. 87, 178.

126. See J. Eric S. Thompson, *Maya History and Religion* (Norman: University of Oklahoma Press, 1970), pp. 48–83; and Sherburne F. Cook and Woodrow Borah, "The Population of Yucatán, 1517–1960" in their *Essays in Population History: Mexico and the Caribbean* (Berkeley: University of California Press, 1974), Volume Two, pp. 1–179. The mere fact of Maya survival is testament to their resiliency; that so much of their culture and their forms of social organization continue to thrive, despite nearly five centuries of genocide that persists to this day, is a mark of truly astonishing cultural strength. In Guatemala today, for example—despite ongoing genocidal warfare against them—the native people continue to speak at least twenty-two distinct dialects of their ancestral Maya tongue. For discussion of a range of social and cultural continuities in this region, see Robert M. Hill and John Monaghan, *Continuities in Highland Maya Social Organization: Ethnohistory in Sacapulas, Guatemala* (Philadelphia: University of Pennsylvania Press, 1987).

127. J.H. Elliott has estimated that about 118,000 Spaniards had settled in the New World by 1570; at that rate more than 150,000 would have been in place by the turn of the century. Elliott, *Imperial Spain*, p. 176. More recent estimates put the figure at closer to 200,000 and perhaps a bit more, although there also was a very heavy traffic in returnees to Spain. See Peter Boyd-Bowman, *Patterns of Spanish Emigration to the New World, 1493–1580* (Buffalo: State University of New York Council on International Studies, 1973), p. 2; and Magnus Mörner, "Spanish Migration to the New World Prior to 1810: A Report on the State of Research," in Fredi Chiappelli, ed., *First Images of America: The Impact of the New World on the Old* (Berkeley: University of California Press, 1976), Volume Two, pp. 737–82. The estimate of Indian dead is calculated from pre-Columbian population estimates for these regions of between 65,000,000 and 90,000,000. The former figure is the most recent estimate, that of Russell Thornton; the latter is the midpoint of the most widely quoted range of figures, that calculated by Henry Dobyns. See Russell Thornton, *American Indian Holocaust and Survival: A Population History Since 1492* (Norman: University of Oklahoma Press, 1987), pp. 22–32; and Henry F. Dobyns, "Estimating Aboriginal American Population: An Appraisal of Techniques with a New Hemispheric Estimate," *Current Anthropology*, 7 (1966), 395–416. This range of estimated native dead may be too conservative, however, for two reasons. First, Dobyns may be correct in now believing that his original estimates were too low, as discussed in Appendix One. And second, this calculation is based on approximately 90 percent decline rather than the more conventional 95 percent and more over the span of a century or so. This was done to account for native peoples not contacted until after the beginning of the seventeenth century, although all the major population centers—which accounted for

the bulk of the Mesoamerican and South American populations, and which were the hardest hit both by genocidal violence and disease—were contacted, and collapsed, within the first few decades of the conquest.

Chapter Four

1. Pedro Simon, *The Expedition of Pedro de Ursúa and Lope de Aguirre in Search of El Dorado and Omagua in 1560–1561,* translated by William Bollaert (London: Hakluyt Society, 1861), p. 228.

2. Louis B. Wright, *Gold, Glory and the Gospel: The Adventurous Lives and Times of the Renaissance Explorers* (New York: Atheneum, 1970), pp. 264–66.

3. See Charles Gibson, *The Black Legend: Anti-Spanish Attitudes in the Old World and the New* (New York: Alfred A. Knopf, 1971), pp. 1–27.

4. For detailed analyses and bibliography on these points, see Benjamin Keen, "Introduction: Approaches to Las Casas, 1535–1970," Manuel M. Martínez, "Las Casas on the Conquest of America," and Juan Comas, "Historical Reality and the Detractors of Father Las Casas," in Juan Friede and Benjamin Keen, eds., *Bartolomé de Las Casas in History: Toward an Understanding of the Man and His Work* (DeKalb: Northern Illinois University Press, 1971), pp. 3–63, 309–49, and 487–537.

5. Bruce B. Solnick, "After Columbus: Castile in the Caribbean," *Terrae Incognitae,* 4 (1972), 124.

6. Philip Wayne Powell, *Tree of Hate: Propaganda and Prejudice Affecting United States Relations with the Hispanic World* (New York: Basic Books, 1971), p. 27. This particular author's determination to protect the fifteenth and sixteenth century Spanish from criticism is so extreme that he even defends the Inquisition as a reasonable affair brought on by traitorous Jews who were "enemies of the state" and who themselves taught the supposedly tolerant Spanish in the ways and wiles of intolerance. For this latter claim, Powell cites Salvador de Madariaga, "certainly one who could not fairly be tarred with the epithet 'antisemitic,' " he says—failing to note that, among other examples, Madariaga claimed that Columbus was a Jew, based on the "evidence" that the admiral was "greedy," that he had a strong "bargaining sense," and a "typically Jewish mobility." On Madariaga and Columbus, see the brief but telling discussion in Leonardo Olschki, "What Columbus Saw on Landing in the West Indies," *Proceedings of the American Philosophical Society,* 84 (1941), 654–55.

7. Lawrence Stone, *The Family, Sex and Marriage in England, 1500–1800* (New York: Harper & Row, 1977), pp. 64, 68.

8. A.D.J. Macfarlane, *Witchcraft in Tudor and Stuart England* (New York: Harper & Row, 1970), pp. 60–61.

9. Quoted in Howard Mumford Jones, *O Strange New World: American Culture—the Formative Years* (London: Chatto and Windus, Ltd., 1964), p. 169.

10. Nicholas P. Canny, "The Ideology of English Colonization: From Ireland to America," *William and Mary Quarterly,* Third Series, 30 (1973), 582.

11. Ibid.

12. Ibid., 593–95.

13. From the account of the voyage by Dionise Settle in Richard Hakluyt, *The*

Principal Navigations, Voyages, Traffiques & Discoveries of the English Nation, Volume Five (London: J.M. Dent & Sons, Ltd., 1907), pp. 144–45.

14. Richard Collinson, *The Three Voyages of Martin Frobisher* (London: Hakluyt Society, 1867), pp. 144–45.

15. Ibid., p. 145.

16. "Postmortem Report of Dr. Edward Dodding," in Collinson, *Three Voyages,* pp. 189–91.

17. Henry F. Dobyns, *Their Number Become Thinned: Native American Population Dynamics in Eastern North America* (Knoxville: University of Tennessee Press, 1983), p. 292.

18. Paul E. Hoffman, *A New Andalucia and a Way to the Orient: The American Southeast During the Sixteenth Century* (Baton Rouge: Louisiana State University Press, 1990), pp. 10–17. For a higher estimate of the number of slaves seized during this raid, see Garcilaso de la Vega, *The Florida of the Inca,* translated by John G. Varner and Jeannette J. Varner (Austin: University of Texas Press, 1951), p. 10.

19. Hoffman, *A New Andalucia,* p. 91. Among the dogs the Spanish brought with them was a greyhound named Bruto, the favorite of de Soto, and a dog celebrated among the Spanish for his ability to track down Indians and tear them to pieces. See the discussion in John Grier Varner and Jeannette Johnson Varner, *Dogs of the Conquest* (Norman: University of Oklahoma Press, 1983), pp. 104–110.

20. Letter of Juan Rogel to Francis Borgia (28 August 1572) in Clifford M. Lewis and Albert J. Loomie, eds., *The Spanish Jesuit Mission in Virginia, 1570–1572* (Chapel Hill: University of North Carolina Press for the Virginia Historical Society, 1953), p. 111.

21. Sir Walter Cope to Lord Salisbury (12 August 1607) in Philip L. Barbour, ed., *The Jamestown Voyages Under the First Charter, 1606–1609* (Cambridge: Hakluyt Society, 1969), Volume One, p. 108; Anonymous [Gabriel Archer?] description of Virginia and her people (May-June 1607) in ibid., p. 104.

22. Dobyns, *Their Number Become Thinned,* pp. 275–76.

23. Letter of Luís de Quirós and Jean Baptista de Segura to Juan de Hinistrosa (12 September 1570), in Lewis and Loomie, eds., *The Spanish Jesuit Mission in Virginia,* pp. 89–90.

24. John Smith, et al., *A Map of Virginia, With a Description of the Countrey, the Commodities, People, Government and Religion* (Oxford, 1612), reprinted in Barbour, ed., *Jamestown Voyages,* Volume Two, p. 426.

25. Karen Ordahl Kupperman, *Settling with the Indians: The Meeting of English and American Cultures in America, 1580–1640* (Totowa, New Jersey: Rowman and Littlefield, 1980), p. 51.

26. Quoted in James Axtell, *The Invasion Within: The Contest of Cultures in Colonial North America* (New York: Oxford University Press, 1985), p. 303. On favorable early British attitudes toward the Indians, and the reality of those perceptions, see Kupperman, *Settling With the Indians,* esp. pp. 141–58. See also, Richard Drinnon, *White Savage: The Case of John Dunn Hunter* (New York: Schocken Books, 1972).

27. Axtell, *Invasion Within,* p. 303.

28. Ibid., p. 327.

29. Edward Arber and A.G. Bradley, eds. *Travels and Works of Captain John Smith, President of Virginia and Admiral of New England, 1580–1631* (Edinburgh: John Grant, 1910), Volume One, pp. 65, 75.

30. Jones, *O Strange New World*, pp. 170–71.

31. See, for example, Ralph Lane, "An Account of the Particularities of the Imployments of the Englishmen Left in Virginia," in David B. Quinn, ed., *The Roanoke Voyages, 1584–1590* (Cambridge: Hakluyt Society, 1955), Volume One, p. 262.

32. George Percy, "A Trewe Relacyon of the Procedeinges and Occurrentes of Momente which have hapned in Virginia," *Tyler's Quarterly Historical and Genealogical Magazine,* 3 (1922), 280.

33. On this, and on the Roanoke settlement in general, see Edmund S. Morgan, *American Slavery—American Freedom: The Ordeal of Colonial Virginia* (New York: W.W. Norton, 1975), pp. 25–43.

34. Percy, "A Trewe Relacyon," 271.

35. Ibid., 272–73.

36. Morgan, *American Slavery—American Freedom*, p. 99.

37. Edward Waterhouse, *A Declaration of the State of the Colony and Affaires in Virginia* (London, 1622), p. 23.

38. James Axtell, "The Rise and Fall of the Powhatan Empire," in Axtell, *After Columbus, Essays in the Ethnohistory of Colonial North America* (New York: Oxford University Press, 1988) pp. 218–19. For an example of colonists poisoning the Indians—in this case killing about 200 people in a single incident—see Robert Bennett to Edward Bennett, "Bennetes Welcome," [9 June 1623], *William and Mary Quarterly,* 2nd Series, 13 (1933), 122.

39. Ibid., pp. 219, 221.

40. The number of Indians under Powhatan's control in 1607 comes from Axtell, "Rise and Fall of the Powhatan Empire," p. 190. The reference to a population of more than 100,000 prior to European contact is in J. Leitch Wright, Jr., *The Only Land They Knew: The Tragic Story of the Indians in the Old South* (New York: Free Press, 1981), p. 60. The colonist population at the end of the seventeenth century—estimated at 62,800—is from Morgan, *American Slavery—American Freedom*, p. 404. The number of Powhatan people at the century's close is based on a multiplier of four times the number of Powhatan bowmen estimated in Robert Beverley, *The History and Present State of Virginia* [1705], ed. Louis B. Wright (Chapel Hill: University of North Carolina Press, 1947), pp. 232–33.

41. Morgan, *American Slavery—American Freedom*, p. 233; Gwenda Morgan, "The Hegemony of the Law: Richmond County, 1692–1776" (Doctoral dissertation, Johns Hopkins University, 1980), Chapter One.

42. Sherburne F. Cook, "The Significance of Disease in the Extinction of the New England Indians," *Human Biology,* 45 (1973), 485–508; Alfred W. Crosby, "Virgin Soil Epidemics as a Factor in the Aboriginal Depopulation in America," *William and Mary Quarterly,* 3rd Series, 33 (1976), 289–99. For a study that uses death rates of 50 and 60 percent as the norm for single epidemics, see William A. Starna, "Mohawk Iroquois Population: A Review," *Ethnohistory,* 27 (1980), 376–77. Long-running controversies regarding the total European death rate from the Black Death now seem reasonably settled around an overall mortality of about

one-third; see William H. McNeill, *Plagues and Peoples* (New York: Doubleday, 1976), p. 168.

43. William Bradford, *Of Plymouth Plantation,* ed. Samuel Eliot Morison (New York: Modern Library, 1967), pp. 270–71.

44. Thomas Morton, *New English Canaan* (Boston: Prince Society, 1883), p. 133.

45. John Winthrop to Sir Nathaniel Rich, May 22, 1634, in Everett Emerson, ed., *Letters from New England* (Amherst: University of Massachusetts Press, 1976), pp. 115–16.

46. Thomas Budd, *Good Order Established in Pennsylvania & New Jersey in America* (London, 1685), p. 33.

47. Adam J. Hirsch, "The Collision of Military Cultures in Seventeenth Century New England," *Journal of American History,* 74 (1988), 1190.

48. Ruth Benedict, *Patterns of Culture* (Boston: Houghton Mifflin Company, 1934), pp. 30–32.

49. George Bird Grinnell, "Coup and Scalp Among the Plains Indians," *American Anthropologist,* 12 (1910), 216–17.

50. Stanley Diamond, *In Search of the Primitive: A Critique of Civilization* (New Brunswick, N.J.: Transaction Books, 1974), pp.156–57. Las Casas had said much the same thing of the wars waged among themselves by the peoples of the Indies, describing them as "little more than games played by children." Bartolomé de Las Casas, *The Devastation of the Indies: A Brief Account,* translated by Herma Briffault (New York: Seabury Press, 1974), p. 43. There are, of course, exceptions to this as to other generalizations. It is worth noting, therefore, that warfare in the Great Plains area could on occasion be highly destructive, as is evident in the remains from an early fourteenth-century battle that took place in what is now south-central South Dakota. The archaeological and osteological data on those remains are most thoroughly discussed in P. Willey, *Prehistoric Warfare on the Great Plains: Skeletal Analysis of the Crow Creek Massacre Victims* (New York: Garland Publishing, 1990).

51. John Underhill, *Newes from America; or, A New and Experimentall Discoverie of New England* (London, 1638), p. 40; Henry Spelman, "Relation of Virginea" (London, 1613), in Arber and Bradley, eds., *Travels and Works of John Smith,* Volume One, p. cxiv.

52. Hirsch, "Collision of Military Cultures," 1191.

53. John Mason, *A Brief History of the Pequot War* (Boston: Kneeland & Green, 1736), p. 21.

54. On the smallpox epidemic, see John Winthrop, *Winthrop's Journal,* ed. James Kendall Hosmer (New York: Charles Scribner's Sons, 1908), Volume One, pp. 118–19.

55. Richard Drinnon, *Facing West: The Metaphysics of Indian Hating and Empire Building* (Minneapolis: University of Minnesota Press, 1980), pp. 35–45, provides a concise and powerful description of the Pequot War. My account is drawn from Drinnon and from that of Francis Jennings, *The Invasion of America: Indians, Colonialism, and the Cant of Conquest* (Chapel Hill: University of North Carolina Press, 1975), pp. 202–27. Another account, with some provocative interpretations, is in Ann Kibbey, *The Interpretation of Material Shapes in Puritanism: A Study of Rhetoric, Prejudice, and Violence* (Cambridge: Cambridge University

Press, 1986), pp. 92–120. For differing views on Oldham's reputation, compare Drinnon, p. 37 and Jennings, p. 206.

56. Jennings, *Invasion of America*, p. 210.

57. Underhill, *Newes from America*, p. 7.

58. Ibid., p. 9.

59. Jennings, *Invasion of America*, p. 212.

60. Mason, *Brief History*, p. 7.

61. Ibid., p. 8.

62. Ibid., pp. 9–10.

63. Jennings, *Invasion of America*, p. 222.

64. Underhill, *Newes from America*, pp. 39–40.

65. Bradford, *Of Plymouth Plantation*, p. 296.

66. Cotton Mather, *Magnalia Christi Americana; or, The Ecclesiastic History of New-England* [1702] (New York: Russell & Russell, 1967), Volume Two, p. 558; Mason, *Brief History*, p. 10.

67. Underhill, *Newes from America*, p. 43.

68. Drinnon, *Facing West*, p. 45.

69. Ibid., p. 47.

70. Ronald Sanders, *Lost Tribes and Promised Lands: The Origins of American Racism* (Boston: Little, Brown and Company, 1978), pp. 339–40. For a stimulating analysis of the complex relationship between imperialism and place-naming, see Paul Carter, *The Road to Botany Bay: An Exploration of Landscape and History* (New York: Alfred A. Knopf, 1988), passim, but esp. pp. 63–68, 326–31.

71. So close to totality was the colonists' mass murder of Pequot men, women, and children that it is now popularly believed that all the Pequots in fact were exterminated. Some, however, found their way to live among neighboring tribes, and in time to resurrect themselves as Pequots. For discussion of these matters, including the state of the Pequot nation today, see Laurence M. Hauptman and James D. Wherry, eds., *The Pequots in Southern New England: The Fall and Rise of an American Indian Nation* (Norman: University of Oklahoma Press, 1990).

72. Drinnon, *Facing West*, pp. 46–47.

73. Richard Slotkin and James K. Folsom, eds., *So Dreadful a Judgment: Puritan Responses to King Philip's War, 1676–1677* (Middletown, Conn.: Wesleyan University Press, 1978), p. 381.

74. *A True Account of the Most Considerable Occurrences that have Hapned in the Warre Between the English and the Indians in New England* (London, 1676), pp. 3–4.

75. Jennings, *Invasion of America*, p. 227.

76. Douglas Edward Leach, *Flintlock and Tomahawk: New England in King Philip's War* (New York: W.W. Norton & Company, 1958), p. 237.

77. *A True Account*, pp. 7–9.

78. Ibid., p. 6.

79. "John Easton's Relacion," in Charles H. Lincoln, ed., *Narratives of the Indian Wars, 1675–1699* (New York: Charles Scribner's Sons, 1913), pp. 14, 16. Spelling in text is modernized.

80. Increase Mather, *A Brief History of the Warr With the Indians in New-England* (Boston, 1676), reprinted in Slotkin and Folsom, *So Dreadful a Judgment*, p. 142.

81. Leach, *Flintlock and Tomahawk,* pp. 226–27.

82. Cotton Mather, *Fair Weather* (Boston, 1692), p. 86.

83. Sarah Kemble Knight, *The Journal of Madam Knight* (Boston: David R. Godine, 1972), pp. 21–22.

84. Dean R. Snow and Kim M. Lamphear, "European Contact and Indian Depopulation in the Northeast: The Timing of the First Epidemics," *Ethnohistory,* 35 (1988), p. 24, Table 1.

85. Colin G. Calloway, *The Western Abenaki of Vermont, 1600–1800: War, Migration, and the Survival of an Indian People* (Norman: University of Oklahoma Press, 1990), pp. 129–30. Calloway, it should be noted, thinks the contemporary report on some of these peoples' lower numbers should be increased: instead of 25 Norridgewocks in 1726, he thinks there may have been 40; instead of 7 Pigwackets, he thinks there may have been 24.

86. Martin Middlebrook, *The First Day of the Somme* (New York: W.W. Norton, 1972); John Keegan, *The Face of Battle* (New York: Viking Press, 1976), pp. 255, 280.

87. Peter R. Cox, *Demography,* Fourth Edition (Cambridge: Cambridge University Press, 1970), pp. 319, 361.

88. Donald J. Bogue, *Principles of Demography* (New York: John Wiley & Sons, 1969), p. 34; Paul R. Ehrlich, Anne H. Ehrlich, and John P. Holdren, *Ecoscience: Population, Resources, Environment* (San Francisco: W.H. Freeman and Company, 1977), p. 199.

89. Quoted in Drinnon, *Facing West,* pp. 331–32, 65.

90. Ibid., p. 332; Peter S. Schmalz, *The Ojibwa of Southern Ontario* (Toronto: University of Toronto Press, 1991), p. 99; Anthony F.C. Wallace, *The Death and Rebirth of the Seneca* (New York: Alfred A. Knopf, 1970), pp. 141–44.

91. Drinnon, *Facing West,* pp. 96, 98, 116; Ronald T. Takaki, *Iron Cages: Race and Culture in 19th-Century America* (New York: Alfred A. Knopf, 1979), pp. 61–65.

92. For the 1685 to 1790 figures, see Peter H. Wood, "The Changing Population of the Colonial South: An Overview by Race and Region, 1685–1790," in Peter H. Wood, Gregory A. Waselkov, and M. Thomas Hatley, eds., *Powhatan's Mantle: Indians in the Colonial Southeast* (Lincoln: University of Nebraska Press, 1989), p. 38.

93. Ibid.

94. James M. O'Donnell, *Southern Indians in the American Revolution* (Knoxville: University of Tennesse Press, 1973), p. 52.

95. James Mooney, *Historical Sketch of the Cherokee* [1900] (Chicago: Aldine Publishers, 1975), p. 51.

96. Takaki, *Iron Cages,* pp. 96, 102.

97. Michael Paul Rogin, *Fathers and Children: Andrew Jackson and the Subjugation of the American Indian* (New York: Alfred A. Knopf, 1975), pp. 132, 218–19, 355.

98. Ibid., pp. 219–20.

99. Quoted, ibid., p. 227.

100. Alexis de Tocqueville, *Democracy in America,* translated by George Lawrence, ed. J.P. Mayer (New York: Anchor Books, 1969), Volume One, p. 339.

101. Of the 10,000 or so Americans who were victims of the Bataan Death

March, 4000 survived to the end of the war, meaning that about 6000, or 60 percent, died on the march or during the subsequent three years of imprisonment. As noted in the text, about 8000 of the approximately 17,000 Cherokee who began that death march died on the Trail of Tears and in the immediate aftermath— about 47 percent. The comparison is incomplete, however, because, unlike the Bataan situation, no one knows how many Cherokee died during the next three years of reservation imprisonment—and also because, again, unlike the Bataan death march, the Cherokee death march included many thousands of women and children. For Bataan, see Donald Knox, *Death March: The Survivors of Bataan* (New York: Harcourt Brace Jovanovich, 1981).

102. Mooney, *Historical Sketch of the Cherokee*, p. 124.

103. In Grant Foreman, *Indian Removal: The Emigration of the Five Civilized Tribes of Indians* (Norman: University of Oklahoma Press, 1932), pp. 305–306.

104. Russell Thornton, "Cherokee Population Losses During the 'Trail of Tears': A New Perspective and a New Estimate," *Ethnohistory*, 31 (1984), 289–300.

105. Peter Calvocoressi, Guy Wint, and John Pritchard, *Total War: Causes and Courses of the Second World War*, Revised Second Edition (New York: Pantheon Books, 1989), p. 523; Raul Hilberg, *The Destruction of the European Jews* (Chicago: Quadrangle Books, 1961), p. 670.

106. "Log of John Boit," quoted in Erna Gunther, *Indian Life on the Northwest Coast of North America as Seen by the Early Explorers and Fur Traders During the Last Decades of the Eighteenth Century* (Chicago: University of Chicago Press, 1972), p. 74.

107. Quoted in Schmalz, *The Ojibwa of Southern Ontario*, pp. 99–100.

108. *Aberdeen Saturday Pioneer*, Aberdeen, South Dakota, December 20, 1891; quoted in Elliott J. Gorn, Randy Roberts, and Terry D. Bilhartz, *Constructing the American Past: A Source Book of a People's History* (New York: HarperCollins, 1991), p. 99.

109. Charles A. Eastman, *From the Deep Woods to Civilization* (Boston: Little, Brown and Company, 1916), pp. 111–12.

110. James Mooney, "The Ghost Dance Religion and the Sioux Outbreak of 1890," in *Fourteenth Annual Report of the United States Bureau of Ethnology* (Washington, D.C.: U.S. Government Printing Office, 1896), Part Two, p. 877.

111. Ibid., p. 885.

112. Quoted in Gorn, Roberts, and Bilhartz, *Constructing the American Past*, p. 99.

113. Eastman, *From the Deep Woods*, p. 113.

114. Kit Miniclier, "Lost Bird Comes Home to Wounded Knee," *Denver Post*, July 14, 1991, pp. 1C, 6C. The account in Colby's home town newspaper, *The Beatrice [Nebraska] Republican*, is quoted in part in Richard E. Jensen, R. Eli Paul, and John E. Carter, *Eyewitness at Wounded Knee* (Lincoln: University of Nebraska Press, 1991), p. 135.

115. In H.R. Schoolcraft, *Historical and Statistical Information Respecting the History, Condition, and Prospects of the Indian Tribes of the United States* (Philadelphia: Lippincott, Grambo & Co., 1851), Volume Two, p. 258.

116. Russell Thornton, *American Indian Holocaust and Survival: A Population History Since 1492* (Norman: University of Oklahoma Press, 1987), pp. 86–89, 124–25, 126–27; Robert T. Boyd, "Another Look at the 'Fever and Ague' of

Western Oregon," *Ethnohistory,* 22 (1975), 135–54 (for data on the Kalapuyan not covered in Thornton); Harry Kelsey, "European Impact on the California Indians, 1530–1830," *The Americas,* 41 (1985), 510; Russell Thornton, "Social Organization and the Demographic Survival of the Tolowa," *Ethnohistory,* 31 (1984), 191–92; Daniel T. Reff, "Old World Diseases and the Dynamics of Indian and Jesuit Relations in Northwestern New Spain, 1520–1660," in N. Ross Crumrine and Phil C. Weigand, eds., *Ejidos and Regions of Refuge in Northwestern Mexico* (Tucson: University of Arizona Press, 1987), p. 89; Steadman Upham, *Polities and Power: An Economic and Political History of the Western Pueblo* (New York: Academic Press, 1982), pp. 39–43; Robert S. Grumet, "A New Ethnohistorical Model for North American Indian Demography," *North American Archaeologist,* 11, (1990), 29–41; Francis Jennings, *The Ambiguous Iroquois Empire* (New York: W.W. Norton & Company, 1984), p. 88. John C. Ewers, "The Influence of Epidemics on the Indian Populations and Cultures of Texas," *Plains Anthropologist,* 18 (1973), 104, 109; Robert Fortuine, *Chills and Fever: Health and Disease in the Early History of Alaska* (Anchorage: University of Alaska Press, 1989), pp. 89–122, 161–78, 199–264, 301–14.

117. Ann F. Ramenofsky, *Vectors of Death: The Archaeology of European Contact* (Albuquerque: University of New Mexico Press, 1987), pp. 42–136.

118. Jean Louis Berlandier, *The Indians of Texas in 1830,* ed., John C. Ewers (Washington: Smithsonian Institution Press, 1969); Wood, "Changing Population of the Colonial South," p. 74.

119. David Svaldi, *Sand Creek and the Rhetoric of Extermination: A Case Study in Indian-White Relations* (New York: University Press of America, 1989), pp. 149–50.

120. Ibid., pp. 155–58.

121. Ibid., p. 172.

122. Ibid., pp. 171, 237.

123. Ibid., p. 291; Himmler is quoted in Robert Jay Lifton, *The Nazi Doctors: Medical Killing and the Psychology of Genocide* (New York: Basic Books, 1986), p. 477. Although Chivington made the phrase famous, it must be said that it did not originate with him. At least a few years earlier one H.L. Hall in California, who made a living killing Indians, refused to take other whites with him to massacres he had arranged unless they were willing to kill every Indian woman and child encountered, because, he liked to say, "a nit would make a louse." On one occasion, Hall led a group of whites in the mass murder of 240 Indian men, women, and children because he believed one of them had killed a horse. See, Lynwood Carranco and Estle Beard, *Genocide and Vendetta: The Round Valley Wars of Northern California* (Norman: University of Oklahoma Press, 1981), chapter four.

124. Quoted in Stan Hoig, *The Sand Creek Massacre* (Norman: University of Oklahoma Press, 1961), p. 192.

125. Svaldi, *Sand Creek and the Rhetoric of Extermination,* p. 291; Hoig, *Sand Creek Massacre,* p. 137.

126. Quoted in Hoig, *Sand Creek Massacre,* p. 150.

127. The following accounts are from subsequent testimony and affidavits provided by witnesses to and participants in the massacre. The full statements are contained in U.S. Congressional inquiry volumes, including *Report on the Conduct*

of the War (38th Congress, Second Session, 1865), but excerpts are printed as an appendix in Hoig, *Sand Creek Massacre*, pp. 177–92. The portion of George Bent's testimony that follows immediately is not included in Hoig's appendix, but is quoted in Dee Brown, *Bury My Heart at Wounded Knee* (New York: Holt, Rinehart & Winston, 1970), p. 88.

128. Svaldi, *Sand Creek and the Rhetoric of Extermination*, pp. 298–99.

129. Ibid., pp. 187–88.

130. Quoted in Thomas G. Dyer, *Theodore Roosevelt and the Idea of Race* (Baton Rouge: Louisiana State University Press, 1980), p. 79.

131. Herbert Eugene Bolton, ed., *Spanish Exploration in the Southwest, 1542– 1706* (New York: Charles Scribner's Sons, 1916), p.5.

132. Sherburne F. Cook disputed de Anza's dubious distinction nearly fifty years ago in *The Indian versus the Spanish Mission*, Ibero-Americana, Number 21 (Berkeley: University of California Press, 1943), pp. 23–24.

133. K.L. Holmes, "Francis Drake's Course in the North Pacific, 1579," *The Geographical Bulletin*, 17 (1979), 5–41; R. Lee Lyman, *Prehistory of the Oregon Coast* (New York: Academic Press, 1991), pp. 14–15.

134. "Diary of Sebastián Vizcaino, 1602–1603," in Bolton, ed., *Spanish Exploration in the Southwest*, pp. 95, 97, 102; "A Brief Report . . . by Fray Antonio de la Ascensión," ibid., p. 121.

135. Ibid., pp. 79–80, 109.

136. On the nineteenth-century diseases, see Sherburne F. Cook, *The American Invasion, 1848–1870*, Ibero-Americana, Number 23 (Berkeley: University of California Press, 1943), p. 20.

137. Albert L. Hurtado, *Indian Survival on the California Frontier* (New Haven: Yale University Press, 1988), p. 46.

138. Bradford, *Of Plymouth Plantation*, pp. 374–75.

139. Fray Francisco Palóu, O.F.M., *Historical Memoirs of New California*, translated and edited by Herbert Eugene Bolton (New York: Russell & Russell, 1966), Volume One, pp. 171–213.

140. Ibid., p. 211.

141. Sherburne F. Cook, *Population Trends Among the California Mission Indians*, Ibero-Americana, Number 17 (Berkeley: University of California Press, 1940), pp. 6–7, 23, 26.

142. John R. Johnson, "The Chumash and the Mission," in David Hurst Thomas, ed., *Columbian Consequences, Volume One: Archaeological and Historical Perspectives on the Spanish Borderlands West* (Washington, D.C.: Smithsonian Institution Press, 1989), pp. 365–75; Sherburne F. Cook and Woodrow Borah, "Mission Registers as Sources of Vital Statistics: Eight Missions of Northern California," in Sherburne F. Cook and Woodrow Borah, *Essays in Population History, Volume Three: Mexico and California* (Berkeley: University of California Press, 1979), pp. 177–311.

143. Robert Jackson, "Demographic Change in Northwestern New Spain," *The Americas*, 41 (1985), 465.

144. V.M. Golovnin, *Around the World on the Kamchatka, 1817–1818*, translated by Ella L. Wiswell (Honolulu: Hawaiian Historical Society, 1979), pp. 147–48. On the living space allotted for unmarried mission Indians, see Cook, *Indian versus the Spanish Mission*, pp. 89–90.

145. Cook, *Indian versus the Spanish Mission*, p. 27.

146. Golovnin, *Around the World on the Kamchatka*, pp. 150, 147.

147. For mission Indian caloric intake, see Cook, *Indian versus the Spanish Mission*, p. 37, Table 2. On slave diets and caloric intake, see Richard Sutch, "The Care and Feeding of Slaves," in Paul A. David, Herbert G. Gutman, Richard Sutch, Peter Temin, and Gavin Wright, *Reckoning with Slavery: A Critical Study in the Quantitative History of American Negro Slavery* (New York: Oxford University Press, 1976), pp. 265–68. It is important to note that Sutch's analysis is a detailed *critique* of the work of Robert W. Fogel and Stanley L. Engerman, who argued in their book *Time on the Cross: The Economics of American Negro Slavery* (Boston: Little, Brown and Company, 1974) that the average slave's caloric intake was even higher.

148. Cook, *Indian versus the Spanish Mission*, p. 54.

149. Ann Lucy W. Stodder, *Mechanisms and Trends in the Decline of the Costanoan Indian Population of Central California* (Salinas: Archives of California Prehistory, Number 4, Coyote Press, 1986).

150. Phillip L. Walker, Patricia Lambert, and Michael DeNiro, "The Effects of European Contact on the Health of Alta California Indians," in Thomas, ed., *Columbian Consequences, Volume One*, p. 351.

151. Adelbert von Chamisso, *A Voyage Around the World with the Romanzov Exploring Expedition in the Years 1815–1818*, translated and edited by Henry Kratz (Honolulu: University of Hawai'i Press, 1986), p. 244.

152. Omer Englebert, *The Last of the Conquistadors: Junípero Serra, 1713–1784*, translated by Katherine Woods (New York: Harcourt, Brace and Company, 1956). The parallel between the Spanish forced labor institutions in North and South America has long been recognized, even by professed admirers of the Franciscans and Junípero Serra. See for example, the comments of Herbert E. Bolton, "The Mission as a Frontier Institution in the Spanish-American Colonies," *American Historical Review*, 23 (1917), 43–45. In fact, Serra himself noted and used the parallel in justifying the beating of Indians; in a letter of January 7, 1780, to the Spanish governor of California, Filipe de Neve, he noted the fact that the physical punishment of Indians by their "spiritual fathers" was "as old as the conquest of these kingdoms," specifically observing that "Saint Francis Solano . . . in the running of his mission in the Province of Tucumán in Peru . . . when they failed to carry out his orders, he gave directions for his Indians to be whipped." Quoted in James A. Sandos, "Junípero Serra's Canonization and the Historical Record," *American Historical Review*, 93 (1988), 1254; Sandos's entire essay (pp. 1253–69) is a valuable contribution to the controversy over Serra's proposed canonization.

153. Quoted in James J. Rawls, *Indians of California: The Changing Image* (Norman: University of Oklahoma Press, 1984), p. 63.

154. Englebert, *Last of the Conquistadors*, p. 49; see also Fray Francisco Palóu, *Life and Apostolic Labors of the Venerable Father Junípero Serra* (Pasadena: G.W. James, 1913).

155. Palóu, *Historical Memoirs*, Volume One, pp. 86–87.

156. For details on these matters, see my earlier-cited "Disease and Infertility: A New Look at the Demographic Collapse of Native Populations in the Wake of Western Contact," *Journal of American Studies*, 24 (1990), 325–50.

157. Quoted in Ed. D. Castillo, "The Native Response to the Colonization of Alta California," in Thomas, ed., *Columbian Consequences,* Volume One, p. 380.

158. Quoted in Cook, *Indian versus the Spanish Mission,* p. 82.

159. Rawls, *Indians of California,* p. 38; the previously cited observation on severity of punishment is from J.M. Amador, "Memoria," manuscript in Bancroft Library, University of California at Berkeley, quoted in Cook, *Indian versus the Spanish Mission,* p. 127.

160. Quoted in Hurtado, *Indian Survival on the California Frontier,* pp. 74–75.

161. Rawls, *Indians of California,* pp. 96–97; Robert F. Heizer, ed., *They Were Only Diggers: A Collection of Articles from California Newspapers, 1851–1866, on Indian and White Relations* (Ramona, Calif.: Ballena Press, 1974), p. 1.

162. Heizer, *They Were Only Diggers,* p. 1.

163. Hurtado, *Indian Survival on the California Frontier,* p. 145.

164. Robert F. Heizer, ed., *The Destruction of California Indians: A Collection of Documents from the Period 1847 to 1865 in Which Are Described Some of the Things that Happened to Some of the Indians of California* (Santa Barbara: Peregrine Smith, 1974), p. 279.

165. Theodora Kroeber, *Ishi in Two Worlds: A Biography of the Last Wild Indian in North America* (Berkeley: University of California Press, 1961), pp. 84–85.

166. The estimate of the number of Indians indentured under the laws of 1850 and 1860 comes from Heizer, ed., *Destruction of California Indians,* p. 219.

167. Quoted in Rawls, *Indians of California,* p. 93.

168. Quoted in Hurtado, *Indian Survival on the California Frontier,* pp. 134–36.

169. Rawls, *Indians of California,* pp. 190–201.

170. Quoted in Rawls, *Indians of California,* pp. 132–33.

171. Quoted in John Hemming, *The Conquest of the Incas* (New York: Harcourt Brace Jovanovich, 1970), p. 348.

Chapter Five

1. Toni Morrison, *Beloved* (New York: Alfred A. Knopf, 1987), p. 180.

2. Terrence Des Pres, "Introduction" to Jean-Francois Steiner, *Treblinka* (New York: New American Library, 1979), p. xi.

3. Ibid.

4. See Richard L. Rubenstein, *The Cunning of History: The Holocaust and the American Future* (New York: Harper & Row, 1975), passim.

5. See Richard G. Hovannisian, ed., *The Armenian Genocide in Perspective* (New Brunswick, N.J.: Transaction Publishers, 1986).

6. Robert Conquest, *The Harvest of Sorrow: Soviet Collectivization and the Terror Famine* (New York: Oxford University Press, 1986), esp. chapter 16.

7. For summaries of these and other genocides, along with recent bibliographical references, see Frank Chalk and Kurt Jonassohn, *The History and Sociology of Genocide: Analyses and Case Studies* (New Haven: Yale University Press, 1990).

8. For estimates of the numbers of Romani, commonly referred to as Gypsy,

people killed in the Holocaust, see the discussion in Ian Hancock, "'Uniqueness' of the Victims: Gypsies, Jews and the Holocaust," *Without Prejudice,* 1 (1988), 55–56. There were, of course, many other victims of Nazi mass murder—homosexuals, Jehovah's Witnesses, the congenitally malformed, pacifists, communists, and others—who are not mentioned here. For an examination of the fate of these other groups, see Michael Berenbaum, *A Mosaic of Victims: Non-Jews Persecuted and Murdered by the Nazis* (New York: New York University Press, 1990).

9. The number of people forcibly exported from Africa remains a subject of intense historical controversy, but recent estimates suggest that up to 12,000,000 or even 15,000,000 captured Africans survived the ordeal of forced migration to become plantation laborers in North or South America or the Caribbean. About 50 percent of the original captives appear to have died during the forced march to the West African coast and in the holding pens there known as barracoons, while approximately 10 percent of the survivors died on board the trans-Atlantic slave ships, leaving about 45 percent of the original total to be "seasoned," sold, and set to work. However, the "seasoning" process itself appears to have killed half of those who survived the ocean journey, leaving between 20 and 25 percent of the originally captured total to actually labor as chattel; thus, for every African who survived to become a working slave, between three and four conventionally died during the enslavement process. With a total of 12,000,000 to 15,000,000 Africans surviving to become slaves, this makes for an overall death rate directly attributable to enslavement—and prior to the Africans' beginning to labor as New World bondsmen and bondswomen—of anywhere from 36,000,000 to 60,000,000. As with most estimates of genocidal mortality, these are very general estimates arrived at by extrapolation from situations where reasonably good historical data are available to situations where they are not. Thus, for example, some estimates calculate a lower death toll than the above during the within-Africa forced march and coastal imprisonment, while others suggest that death rates aboard ship conventionally were 15 to 20 and even more than 30 percent—that is, up to three times as high as is assumed above. On this, see, for example, Philip D. Curtin, *The Atlantic Slave Trade: A Census* (Madison: University of Wisconsin Press, 1969), pp. 275–82; Robert Stein, "Mortality in the Eighteenth Century French Slave Trade," *Journal of African History,* 21 (1980), 35–41; Raymond L. Cohn, "Discussion: Mortality in the French Slave Trade," *Journal of African History,* 23 (1982), 225–26; and David Northrup, "African Mortality in the Suppression of the Slave Trade: The Case of the Bight of Biafra," *Journal of Interdisciplinary History,* 9 (1978), 47–64. For discussion of the overall volume of the slave trade, compare Curtin, *Atlantic Slave Trade,* p. 268, Table 77; J.E. Inikori, "Measuring the Atlantic Slave Trade: An Assessment of Curtin and Anstey," *Journal of African History,* 17 (1976), 197–223; J.E. Inikori, "The Origin of the Diaspora: The Slave Trade from Africa," *Tarikh,* 5 (1978), 1–19; the same author's comments in J.E. Inikori, ed., *Forced Migration: The Impact of the Export Trade on African Societies* (New York: Africana Publishing Company, 1982), pp. 19–21; and Paul E. Lovejoy, "The Volume of the Atlantic Slave Trade: A Synthesis," *Journal of African History,* 23 (1982), 473–501. Conventional thought regarding the number of deaths caused by the African slave trade posits a number lower than that suggested here because it is based solely upon deaths occurring at sea between the points of embarkation from West Africa and docking in the Americas—thus ignoring the enormous num-

ber of deaths that occurred prior to the slave ships' departures and during the "seasoning" periods. If these on-land deaths are included in the overall mortality figure—as they must be to arrive at a true measure of the horrific impact of the slave trade on African peoples—even the lowest estimates of slave imports, Philip D. Curtin's and Paul E. Lovejoy's 10,000,000 or so, produce an overall mortality figure of between 30,000,000 and 40,000,000. On mortality rates during all phases of the enslavement process, drawing largely on Brazilian slave import data, see Joseph C. Miller, "Mortality in the Atlantic Slave Trade: Statistical Evidence on Causality," *Journal of Interdisciplinary History,* 11 (1981), 385–423, esp. 413–14.

10. Irving Louis Horowitz, "Genocide and the Reconstruction of Social Theory: Observations on the Exclusivity of Collective Death," in Isidor Wallimann and Michael N. Dobkowski, eds., *Genocide and the Modern Age: Etiology and Case Studies of Mass Death* (Westport, Conn.: Greenwood Press, 1987), p. 62. Wiesenthal's letter is quoted in part in Hancock, "'Uniqueness' of the Victims," 55.

11. A recent example of pertinence to the present discussion is an article on the Pequot War by Steven T. Katz, Professor of Near Eastern Studies (Judaica) at Cornell University and author of several studies on the history of the Holocaust. Professor Katz apparently became annoyed when he discovered that some historians had described the almost total extermination of the Pequot people as "genocide" and so he took time out from work in his own field to set them straight. Beginning with a rejection of conventional definitions of genocide—including that of the United Nations—and offering a substitute of his own, Professor Katz concludes his essay by observing that *some* Pequots survived the English colonists' efforts to annihilate them as a people, adding: "As recently as the 1960s, Pequots were still listed as a separate group residing in Connecticut. . . . [W]hile the British could certainly have been less thorough, less severe, less deadly in prosecuting their campaign against the Pequots, the campaign they actually did carry out, for all its vehemence, was not, either in intent or execution, genocidal." In other words, because the British did not kill *all* the Pequots they did not commit a genocide. This is not the place for a detailed critique of Professor Katz's flimsy thesis, but one can only wonder (actually, one need *not* wonder) at what his response might be to a Professor of Native American Studies taking the trouble to write an essay claiming that the Holocaust was not an act of genocide ("although the [Nazis] could certainly have been less thorough, less severe, less deadly in prosecuting their campaign against the [Jews]") because, after all, some Jews survived—a number of whom even live in Connecticut today. See Steven T. Katz, "The Pequot War Reconsidered," *New England Quarterly,* 64 (1991), 206–24, quoted words on p. 223.

12. Michael Berenbaum, "The Uniqueness and Universality of the Holocaust," in Berenbaum, ed., *A Mosaic of Victims,* p. 34. Increasingly, scholarship on genocide has recognized the necessity for comparative analysis, while acknowledging the unique particulars of individual cases. For some recent examples, in addition to *A Mosaic of Victims,* see the following: Israel Charny, ed., *Toward the Understanding and Prevention of Genocide* (Boulder: Westview Press, 1984); Leo Kuper, *The Prevention of Genocide* (New Haven: Yale University Press, 1985); Ervin Staub, *The Roots of Evil: The Origins of Genocide and Other Group Violence* (Cam-

bridge: Cambridge University Press, 1989); Wallimann and Dobkowski, eds., *Genocide and the Modern Age;* and Chalk and Jonassohn, *The History and Sociology of Genocide.*

13. Noam Chomsky, "Intervention in Vietnam and Central America: Parallels and Differences," in James Peck, ed., *The Chomsky Reader* (New York: Pantheon Books, 1987), p. 315.

14. Irving Abrahamson, ed., *Against Silence: The Voice and Vision of Elie Wiesel* (New York: Holocaust Library, 1985), Volume One, p. 33; for Wiesel on the uniqueness of the Jewish Holocaust, see Volume Three, p. 314.

15. Arno J. Mayer, *Why Did the Heavens Not Darken? The "Final Solution" in History,* Expanded Edition (New York: Pantheon Books, 1990), p. 98.

16. John Toland, *Adolf Hitler* (New York: Doubleday and Company, 1976), p. 702. See also, Richard Rubenstein, "Afterword: Genocide and Civilization," in Wallimann and Dobkowski, eds., *Genocide and the Modern Age,* p. 288.

17. Giulia Sissa, "Maidenhood Without Maidenhead: The Female Body in Ancient Greece," in David M. Halperin, John J. Winkler, and Froma I. Zeitlin, eds., *Before Sexuality: The Construction of Erotic Experience in the Ancient Greek World* (Princeton: Princeton University Press, 1990), p. 346.

18. William Guthrie, ed. and trans., *Cicero de Officiis; or, His Treatise Concerning the Moral Duties of Mankind* (London: Lackington, Hughes, 1820), pp. 70–71.

19. Elaine Pagels, *Adam, Eve, and the Serpent* (New York: Random House, 1988), pp. 99, 145. Jacques le Goff is quoted in Peter Brown, *The Body and Society: Men, Women and Sexual Renunciation in Early Christianity* (New York: Columbia University Press, 1988), p. 441.

20. Jo Ann McNamara, "Chaste Marriage and Clerical Celibacy," in Vern L. Bullough and James Brundage, eds., *Sexual Practices and the Medieval Church* (Buffalo, N.Y.: Prometheus Books, 1982), pp. 22–33. See also, P.J. Payer, "Early Medieval Regulations Concerning Marital Sexual Relations," *Journal of Medieval History,* 7 (1980), 370–71; and Jean-Louis Flandrin, "La vie sexuelle des gens mariés dans l'ancienne société," *Communications: Sexualités Occidentales,* 35 (1982), pp. 102–105. I am grateful to the late Philippe Ariès for sending me a copy of this last reference.

21. See Peter Brown, "Person and Group in Judaism and Early Christianity," in Paul Veyne, ed., *A History of Private Life: From Pagan Rome to Byzantium* (Cambridge: Harvard University Press, 1987), pp. 266–67.

22. Quoted in Aline Rousselle, *Porneia: On Desire and the Body in Antiquity,* translated by Felicia Pheasant (Oxford: Basil Blackwell, 1988), p. 170.

23. Ibid., p. 150.

24. Ibid., pp. 151–52.

25. Quoted in Frederick Turner, *Beyond Geography: The Western Spirit Against the Wilderness* (New York: Viking Press, 1980), p. 75.

26. Rousselle, *Porneia,* p. 154–56.

27. Excerpted in Roland Bainton, *Early Christianity* (Princeton: D. Van Nostrand Company, 1960), p. 153.

28. Henry Chadwick, *The Early Church* (London: Penguin Books, 1967), p. 180.

29. See Cyril C. Richardson, ed., *Early Christian Fathers* (Philadelphia: West-

minster Press, 1953), pp. 74–120; and Saint Augustine, *The City of God*, translated by Marcus Dods (New York: Modern Library, 1950), pp. 22–32.

30. Quoted in Jean Delumeau, *Sin and Fear: The Emergence of a Western Guilt Culture, 13th-18th Centuries*, translated by Eric Nicholson (New York: St. Martin's Press, 1990), p. 14. In a different context I have treated the *contemptus mundi* tradition and its theological precursors in an earlier work: *The Puritan Way of Death: A Study in Religion, Culture, and Social Change* (New York: Oxford University Press, 1977), pp. 19–27.

31. Quoted in Delumeau, *Sin and Fear*, p. 15.

32. Ibid, p. 17.

33. Norman Cohn, *The Pursuit of the Millennium: Revolutionary Millenarians and Mystical Anarchists of the Middle Ages*, Revised and Expanded Edition (New York: Oxford University Press, 1970), p. 127.

34. Caroline Walker Bynum, *Holy Feast and Holy Fast: The Religious Significance of Food to Medieval Women* (Berkeley: University of California Press, 1987), pp. 209–10.

35. Ibid, pp. 214–15, 221.

36. Ioan P. Couliano, *Eros and Magic in the Renaissance*, translated by Margaret Cook (Chicago: University of Chicago Press, 1987), pp. 209–11; Hans Peter Duerr, *Dreamtime: Concerning the Boundary between Wilderness and Civilization*, translated by Felicitas Goodman (Oxford: Basil Blackwell, 1985), pp. 52–55.

37. John Bromyard, *Summa Predecantium*, quoted in T.S.R. Boase, *Death in the Middle Ages: Mortality, Judgment and Remembrance* (London: Thames and Hudson, 1972), pp. 44–45.

38. Quoted in Philippe Braunstein, "Toward Intimacy: The Fourteenth and Fifteenth Centuries," in Georges Duby, ed., *A History of Private Life: Revelations of the Medieval World* (Cambridge: Harvard University Press, 1988), pp. 603–606.

39. The best study of this subject focuses on France: Georges Vigarello, *Concepts of Cleanliness: Changing Attitudes in France Since the Middle Ages*, translated by Jean Birrell (New York: Cambridge: Cambridge University Press, 1988).

40. J.H. Elliott, *Imperial Spain, 1469–1716* (New York: St. Martin's Press, 1964), p. 229.

41. See Leah Lydia Otis, *Prostitution in Medieval Society: The History of an Urban Institution in Languedoc* (Chicago: University of Chicago Press, 1985), pp. 25–45.

42. Duerr, *Dreamtime*, p. 55.

43. Couliano, *Eros and Magic in the Renaissance*, pp. 212–14. See also Couliano's recent literature review, "A Corpus for the Body," *Journal of Modern History*, 63 (1991), 61–80.

44. Couliano, *Eros and Magic in the Renaissance*, p. 214; Jeffrey Burton Russell, *Witchcraft in the Middle Ages* (Ithaca: Cornell University Press, 1972), pp. 94–95. On the relationship between sexuality and witchcraft in the *Malleus* and the *Tratado*, see Carol F. Karlsen, *The Devil in the Shape of a Woman: Witchcraft in Colonial New England* (New York: W.W. Norton & Company, 1987), pp. 155–59.

45. Norman Cohn, *Europe's Inner Demons: An Inquiry Inspired by the Great Witch-Hunt* (New York: Basic Books, 1975), pp. 101–102.

46. Quoted in Couliano, *Eros and Magic in the Renaissance*, p. 151.

47. Agostino Carracci did, it must be noted, also produce much more graphically sexual work that some might think borders on the pornographic. It was, however, suppressed—although even in this work he made an effort to connect with the mythical past: almost all Carracci's happily coupling couples in these latter works are named Jupiter, Juno, Hercules, Deianira, and the like. For a discussion, see David O. Frantz, *Festum Voluptatis: A Study of Renaissance Erotica* (Columbus: Ohio State University Press, 1989), pp. 118–39.

48. Thomas F. Gossett, *Race: The History of an Idea in America* (New York: Schocken Books, 1965), pp. 3–16.

49. Kurt von Fritz, "The Influence of Ideas on Ancient Greek Historiography," in Philip P. Wiener, ed., *Dictionary of the History of Ideas* (New York: Charles Scribner's Sons, 1973), Volume II, pp. 499–511.

50. Orlando Patterson, *Slavery and Social Death: A Comparative Study* (Cambridge: Harvard University Press, 1982), p. 178.

51. A. Bartlett Giamatti, *The Earthly Paradise and the Renaissance Epic* (Princeton: Princeton University Press, 1966), p. 3.

52. Homer, *The Odyssey*, translated by Walter Shewring (Oxford: Oxford University Press, 1980), p. 48.

53. Hesiod, *Theogony and Works and Days*, translated with an introduction by M.L. West (Oxford: Oxford University Press, 1988), pp. 41–42.

54. Ibid., pp. 40–41.

55. Giamatti, *Earthly Paradise and the Renaissance Epic*, p. 20.

56. Hesiod, *Theogony and Works and Days*, pp. 43–44.

57. Ibid., p. 44.

58. Giamatti, *Earthly Paradise and the Renaissance Epic*, pp. 30, 32.

59. The best study of this subject, on which much of the present discussion draws, is John Block Friedman, *The Monstrous Races in Medieval Art and Thought* (Cambridge: Harvard University Press, 1981).

60. Ibid., pp. 34–36.

61. Quoted in ibid., pp. 91–92.

62. Quoted in ibid., p. 73.

63. Richard Bernheimer, *Wild Men in the Middle Ages: A Study in Art, Sentiment, and Demonology* (Cambridge: Harvard University Press, 1952), p. 1.

64. Hayden White, "The Forms of Wildness: Archaeology of an Idea," in Edward Dudley and Maximillian E. Novak, ed., *The Wild Man Within: An Image of Western Thought from the Renaissance to Romanticism* (Pittsburgh: University of Pittsburgh Press, 1972), p. 24; Russell, *Witchcraft in the Middle Ages*, p. 50. For more on this theme, see Bernheimer, *Wild Men in the Middle Ages*, pp. 121–75.

65. Alexander Heidel, *The Gilgamesh Epic and Old Testament Parallels* (Chicago: University of Chicago Press, 1949), p. 6.

66. Paul Zweig, *The Adventurer* (New York: Basic Books, 1974), pp. 64–65.

67. Ibid., p. 75; emphasis added.

68. Bernheimer, *Wild Men in the Middle Ages*, p. 19.

69. Turner, *Beyond Geography*, p. 205.

70. Quoted in E.M.Y. Tillyard, *The Elizabethan World Picture* (New York: Vintage Books, n.d.), pp. 26–27.

71. Anthony Pagden, *The Fall of Natural Man: The American Indian and the*

Origins of Comparative Ethnology, Revised Edition (Cambridge: Cambridge University Press, 1986), p. 22.

72. Quoted in Arthur O. Lovejoy, *The Great Chain of Being: A Study in the History of an Idea* (Cambridge: Harvard University Press, 1936), p. 80.

73. White, "The Forms of Wildness," p. 14.

74. The classic brief statement on Christianity's negative view of nature is Lynn White, "The Historical Roots of Our Ecologic Crisis," *Science,* 155 (March, 1967), 1203–1207.

75. Ulrich Mauser, *Christ in the Wilderness* (London: SCM Press, 1963), p. 97.

76. David R. Williams, *Wilderness Lost: The Religious Origins of the American Mind* (London: Associated Universities Presses, 1987), pp. 26–27.

77. Ibid., p. 29.

78. For some provocative thoughts on this, though painted with an overly broad and orthodox Freudian brush, see Brigid Brophy, *Black Ship to Hell* (New York: Harcourt, Brace & World, 1962), esp. pp. 193–95.

79. See Cohn, *Europe's Inner Demons,* pp. 1–15.

80. R. Po-Chia Hsia, *The Myth of Ritual Murder: Jews and Magic in Reformation Germany* (New Haven: Yale University Press, 1988), pp. 2–5.

81. Hugh J. Schonfield, *According to the Hebrews: A New Translation of the Jewish Life of Jesus (the Toldoth Jeshu) with an Inquiry into the Nature of its Sources and Special Relationship to the Lost Gospel According to the Hebrews* (London: Duckworth, 1937).

82. Anna Sapir Abulafia, "Invectives Against Christianity in the Hebrew Chronicles of the First Crusade," in Peter W. Edbury, ed., *Crusade and Settlement: Papers Read at the First Conference of the Society of the Crusades and the Latin East* (Cardiff: University College Cardiff Press, 1985), pp. 66–67.

83. See Jacob Katz, *Exclusiveness and Tolerance: Jewish-Gentile Relations in Medieval and Modern Times* (Oxford: Oxford University Press, 1961), p. 89.

84. Abulafia, "Invectives Against Christianity," p. 70.

85. Raul Hilberg, *The Destruction of the European Jews* (Chicago: Quadrangle Books, 1961), pp. 3–4.

86. Cohn, *Pursuit of the Millennium,* p. 69. On the crusaders' ignorance of canon law and related matters, see Jonathan Riley-Smith, *The First Crusade and the Idea of Crusading* (London: The Athlone Press, 1986), pp. 50–57.

87. "The Chronicle of Solomon bar Simson," in Shlomo Eidelberg, ed. and trans., *The Jews and the Crusaders: The Hebrew Chronicles of the First and Second Crusades* (Madison: University of Wisconsin Press, 1977), pp. 28, 33, 35, 43.

88. Cohn, *Pursuit of the Millennium,* p. 69.

89. Bainton, *Early Christianity,* pp. 52–55; cf., David Little, " 'Holy War' Appeals and Western Christianity: A Reconsideration of Bainton's Approach," in John Kelsay and James Turner Johnson, eds., *Just War and Jihad: Historical and Theoretical Perspectives on War and Peace in Western and Islamic Traditions* (Westport, Conn.: Greenwood Press, 1991), pp. 124–25.

90. James Turner Johnson, "Historical Roots and Sources of the Just War Tradition in Western Culture," in Kelsay and Johnson, eds., *Just War and Jihad,* p. 7.

91. Frederick H. Russell, *The Just War in the Middle Ages* (Cambridge: Cam-

bridge University Press, 1975), pp. 19–20; see Little, " 'Holy War' Appeals and Western Christianity," p. 126.

92. The classic study on this subject is Carl Erdmann's 1935 *Die Entstehung des Kreuzzugsgedankens,* translated as *The Origin of the Idea of Crusade* by Marshall W. Baldwin and Walter Goffart (Princeton: Princeton University Press, 1977). See especially, pp. 4–32, 105–108.

93. See Riley-Smith, *The First Crusade and the Idea of Crusading* for discussion, pp. 84–85.

94. Amin Maalouf, *The Crusades Through Arab Eyes,* translated by Jon Rothschild (London: Al Saqi Books, 1984), pp. 48–49.

95. Quoted in Turner, *Beyond Geography,* p. 79.

96. Mayer, *Why Did the Heavens Not Darken?,* pp. 24–25; Roland Bainton, *Christian Attitudes Toward War and Peace: A Historical Survey and Critical Reevaluation* (Nashville: Abingdon Press, 1960), p. 112.

97. James A. Brundage, "Prostitution, Miscegenation, and Sexual Purity in the First Crusade," in Edbury, ed., *Crusade and Settlement,* p. 58. On pride as another sin responsible for defeat, see Elizabeth Siberry, *Criticism of Crusading, 1095–1274* (Oxford: Clarendon Press, 1985), pp. 99–101; Siberry also discusses the perceived relationship between sexual behavior and defeat, pp. 45–46, 102–103.

98. Brundage, "Prostitution, Miscegenation, and Sexual Purity," pp. 60–61.

99. Cohn, *Pursuit of the Millennium,* p. 87.

100. Moses I. Finley, "Was Greek Civilization Based on Slave Labor?" in Moses I. Finley, ed., *Slavery in Classical Antiquity: Views and Controversies* (Cambridge: W. Heffer & Sons, 1968), pp. 58–59.

101. Keith R. Bradley, "On the Roman Slave Supply and Slavebreeding," in Moses I. Finley, ed., *Classical Slavery* (London: Frank Cass & Co., 1987), p. 42.

102. John Boswell, *The Kindness of Strangers: The Abandonment of Children in Western Europe from Late Antiquity to the Renaissance* (New York: Pantheon Books, 1988), pp. 71, 75.

103. David Brion Davis, *The Problem of Slavery in Western Culture* (Ithaca, N.Y.: Cornell University Press, 1966), p. 38.

104. David Brion Davis, *Slavery and Human Progress* (New York: Oxford University Press, 1984), p. 55.

105. Charles Verlinden, *The Beginnings of Modern Colonization: Eleven Essays with an Introduction,* translated by Yvonne Freccero (Ithaca, N.Y.: Cornell University Press, 1970), p. 39.

106. Boswell, *Kindness of Strangers,* pp. 405–406.

107. Patterson, *Slavery and Social Death,* p. 171; Verlinden, *Beginnings of Modern Colonization,* p. 94; Charles Verlinden, "Medieval 'Slavers,' " in David Herlihy, Robert Lopez, and Vsevolod Slessarev, eds., *Economy, Society, and Government in Medieval Italy: Essays in Memory of Robert L. Reynolds* (Kent, Ohio: Kent State University Press, 1969), p. 7; Davis, *Problem of Slavery in Western Culture,* p. 61.

108. Elliott, *Imperial Spain,* p. 95. On the special dress requirements for Muslims and Jews, and the penalties for sexual liaisons with Christians, see Elena Lourie, "Anatomy of Ambivalence: Muslims Under the Crown of Aragon in the Late Thir-

teenth Century," in Lourie, *Crusade and Colonisation: Muslims, Christians, and Jews in Medieval Aragon* (Hampshire: Variorum, 1990), pp. 54–56.

109. Cecil Roth, "Marranos and Racial Anti-Semitism—A Study in Parallels," *Jewish Social Studies,* 2 (1940), 239–48.

110. See Stephen Haliczer, "The Jew as Witch: Displaced Aggression and the Myth of the Santo Niño de La Guardia," in Mary Elizabeth Perry and Anne J. Cruz, eds., *Cultural Encounters: The Impact of the Inquisition in Spain and the New World* (Berkeley: University of California Press, 1991), pp. 150–53. The story of Christobalico is only one example among many of the common Christian "blood libel" at that time of charging that Jews had crucified children to mock the crucifixion of Christ. For discussion, see L. Sinanoglou, "The Christ Child as Sacrifice," *Speculum,* 43 (1973), 491–509; and, for an early variation on the theme, see Elena Lourie, "A Plot Which Failed? The Case of the Corpse Found in the Jewish *Call* of Barcelona (1301)," *Mediterranean Historical Review,* 1 (1986), 187–220.

111. Mayer, *Why Did the Heavens Not Darken?,* pp. 459, 461.

112. Stephan L. Chorover, *From Genesis to Genocide: The Meaning of Human Nature and the Power of Behavior Control* (Cambridge: The MIT Press, 1979), pp. 80–81, 100–101.

113. Richard L. Rubenstein, *The Cunning of History: The Holocaust and the American Future* (New York: Harper & Row, 1978), *passim.*

114. Lucien Febvre and Henri-Jean Martin, *The Coming of the Book: The Impact of Printing, 1450–1800,* translated by David Gerard and edited by Geoffrey Nowell-Smith and David Wootton (London: N.L.B., 1984), p. 186.

115. Marjorie Reeves, *The Influence of Prophecy in the Later Middle Ages: A Study in Joachimism* (Oxford: Oxford University Press, 1969), pp. 259, 430–31.

116. Ibid., p. 305.

117. Leonard I. Sweet, "Christopher Columbus and the Millennial Vision of the New World," *The Catholic Historical Review,* 72 (1986), 373. The source of Columbus's claim that Joachim of Fiore had said that "he who will restore the ark of Zion will come from Spain," has long puzzled students of the subject. For discussion, and the identification of Arnold of Villanova, see John Leddy Phelan, *The Millennial Kingdom of the Franciscans in the New World,* Revised Edition (Berkeley: University of California Press, 1970), pp. 22, 134–35; and Pauline Moffitt Watts, "Prophecy and Discovery: On the Spiritual Origins of Christopher Columbus's 'Enterprise of the Indies,' " *American Historical Review,* 90 (1985), 94–95.

118. Kenneth Scott Latourette, *A History of the Expansion of Christianity* (New York: Harper & Row, 1940), Volume Three, p. 2; quoted in Phelan, *Millennial Kingdom of the Franciscans,* p. 27.

119. Probably the best account of the trial and execution of John Huss remains that of Henry Charles Lea in *The Inquisition of the Middle Ages,* available in a single volume edition abridged by Margaret Nicholson (New York: Macmillan, 1961), pp. 475–522.

120. Ibid., p. 568.

121. Quoted in Philip Ziegler, *The Black Death* (New York: Harper & Row, 1971), pp. 270–71.

122. Immanuel Wallerstein, *The Modern World System, I: Capitalist Agriculture and the Origins of the European World-Economy in the Sixteenth Century* (London: Academic Press, 1974), p. 80. On inflation, see Fernand Braudel, *The*

Mediterranean and the Mediterranean World in the Age of Philip II (New York: Harper & Row, 1972), Volume One, pp. 516–21; and J.H. Elliott, *The Old World and the New, 1492–1650* (Cambridge: Cambridge University Press, 1972), p. 62.

123. Wallerstein, *Modern World System,I*, pp. 21–22.

124. L. S. Stavrianos, *Global Rift: The Third World Comes of Age* (New York: William Morrow and Company, 1981), pp. 86–87.

125. Amidst a vast and growing literature on this topic, two older overviews remain especially helpful: Kenelm Burridge, *New Heaven, New Earth: A Study of Millenarian Activities* (New York: Schocken Books, 1969), and Michael Barkun, *Disaster and the Millennium* (New Haven: Yale University Press, 1974).

126. Quoted in Cohn, *Pursuit of the Millennium*, p. 239.

127. Barbara B. Diefendorf, *Beneath the Cross: Catholics and Huguenots in Sixteenth-Century Paris* (New York: Oxford University Press, 1991), pp. 102–103.

128. Quoted in Mayer, *Why Did the Heavens Not Darken?*, p. 22.

129. Elliott, *Imperial Spain*, p. 49.

130. "Royal Decree Ordering the Suspension of Judicial Proceedings Against Criminals, Provided they Ship with Columbus, 30 April 1492," in Samuel Eliot Morison, ed., *Journals and Other Documents on the Life and Voyages of Christopher Columbus* (New York: The Heritage Press, 1963), pp. 33–34.

131. The most detailed study of Columbus's crews on the first voyage—literally the scholarly labor of a lifetime—is Alice Bache Gould, *Nueva lista documentada de los tripulantes de Colón en 1492*, edited by José de la Peña y Camara (Madrid, 1984), and discussed in John Noble Wilford, *The Mysterious History of Columbus: An Exploration of the Man, the Myth, the Legacy* (New York: Alfred A. Knopf, 1991), pp. 115–26.

132. "The Journal of the First Voyage," in Morison, ed., *Journals and Other Documents*, pp. 48–49.

Chapter Six

1. *The Libro de las Profecías of Christopher Columbus*, translation and commentary by Delno C. West and August King (Gainesville: University of Florida Press, 1991), pp. 24, 109.

2. Pauline Moffitt Watts, "Prophecy and Discovery: On the Spiritual Origins of Christopher Columbus's 'Enterprise to the Indies,' " *American Historical Review*, 90 (1985), 82–83.

3. Ibid., p. 87.

4. *Libro de las Profecías*, p. 24; Watts, "Prophecy and Discovery," 88; Samuel Eliot Morison, ed., *Journals and Other Documents on the Life and Voyages of Christopher Columbus* (New York: The Heritage Press, 1963), pp. 22–23.

5. *Libro de las Profecías*, p. 109.

6. John Leddy Phelan, *The Millennial Kingdom of the Franciscans in the New World*, Revised Edition (Berkeley: University of California Press, 1970), p. 22.

7. For a list of Columbus's known readings, see *Libro de las Profecías*, pp. 24–25. On Mandeville's *Travels*, see the discussion in Mary B. Campbell, *The Witness and the Other World: Exotic European Travel Writing, 400–1600* (Ithaca: Cornell University Press, 1988), esp. pp. 122–61.

8. "Columbus's Letter to the Sovereigns on His First Voyage, 15 February—4 March 1493," and "Journal of the First Voyage," in Morison, ed., *Journals and Other Documents,* pp. 88, 185. In considering the veracity of Columbus's claim that the natives had told him this, it is important to note not only that the Spaniards and the Indians spoke mutually unintelligible languages but that the Indians could not have described creatures as having heads like dogs, because they had never seen any dogs and would not see any until Columbus's second voyage.

9. See Lewis Hanke, *Aristotle and the American Indians: A Study in Race Prejudice in the Modern World* (Bloomington: Indiana University Press, 1959), pp. 130–31, note 14; W. Arens, *The Man-Eating Myth: Anthropology and Anthropophagy* (New York: Oxford University Press, 1979), pp. 44–54; and R.A. Myers, "Island Carib Cannibalism," *Nieuwe West-Indische Gids,* 58 (1984), 147–84. The easy assumption (with no good evidence) of widespread cannibalism among native peoples serves the same political function among accusers as does the charge of wholesale infanticide and other allegedly savage traits. I have discussed this phenomenon in "Recounting the Fables of Savagery: Native Infanticide and the Functions of Political Myth," *Journal of American Studies,* 25 (1991), 381–418.

10. "Columbus's Letter to the Sovereigns on the Third Voyage," in Morison, ed., *Journals and Other Documents,* pp. 286–87.

11. Ibid., p. 286.

12. Germán Arciniegas, *America in Europe: A History of the New World in Reverse,* translated by Gabriela Arciniegas and R. Victoria Arana (New York: Harcourt Brace Jovanovich, 1986), pp. 44–45.

13. Leonard I. Sweet, "Christopher Columbus and the Millennial Vision of the New World," *The Catholic Historical Review,* 72 (1986), 375–76, 378.

14. "Journal of the First Voyage," in Morison, ed., *Journals and Other Documents,* p. 93.

15. Ibid., p. 48.

16. France V. Scholes, "The Spanish Conqueror as a Business Man: A Chapter in the History of Fernando Cortés," *New Mexico Quarterly,* 28 (1958), 26. For a convenient and insightful treatment of the rise of individualism in the fifteenth century, see Philippe Braunstein, "Toward Intimacy: The Fourteenth and Fifteenth Centuries," in Georges Duby, ed., *A History of Private Life, II: Revelations of the Medieval World,* translated by Arthur Goldhammer (Cambridge: Harvard University Press, 1988), esp. pp. 554–83.

17. "Journal of the First Voyage," in Morison, ed., *Journals and Other Documents,* pp. 65–67.

18. Ibid., pp. 69, 86; Leonardo Olschki, "What Columbus Saw on Landing in the West Indies," *Proceedings of the American Philosophical Society,* 84 (1941), 656.

19. Ibid., 655.

20. "Columbus's Memorial to the Sovereigns on Colonial Policy, April 1493," in Morison, ed., *Journals and Other Documents,* pp. 199–200.

21. Ibid., pp. 200–201.

22. "Michele de Cuneo's Letter on the Second Voyage, 28 October 1495," in ibid., pp. 214–15.

23. Ibid., p. 215.

24. Ibid.

25. Robert L. O'Connell, *Of Arms and Men: A History of War, Weapons, and Aggression* (New York: Oxford University Press, 1989), pp. 95–96.

26. "Michele de Cuneo's Letter," in Morison, ed., *Journals and Other Documents*, p. 220.

27. "Letter of Dr. Chanca, written to the City of Seville," in Cecil Jane, ed., *Select Documents Illustrating the Four Voyages of Columbus* (London: Hakluyt Society, 1930), Volume One, pp. 52, 70.

28. Andrés Bernáldez, "History of the Catholic Sovereigns, Don Ferdinand and Dona Isabella," ibid., pp. cxlvii, 118, 124.

29. "Columbus's Letter to the Sovereigns," in Morison, ed., *Journals and Other Documents*, p. 186.

30. "Syllacio's Letter to the Duke of Milan, 13 December 1494," ibid., pp. 236, 244.

31. Ibid., p. 245.

32. Quoted in Benjamin Keen, ed., *Readings in Latin-American Civilization, 1492 to the Present* (Boston: Houghton Mifflin, 1955), p. 78; and Tzvetan Todorov, *The Conquest of America: The Question of the Other,* translated by Richard Howard (New York: Harper & Row, 1984), p. 151.

33. Hanke, *Aristotle and the American Indians,* p. 4; Stanley L. Robe, "Wild Men and Spain's Brave New World," in Edward Dudley and Maximillian E. Novak, eds., *The Wild Man Within: An Image in Western Thought from the Renaissance to Romanticism* (Pittsburgh: University of Pittsburgh Press, 1972), p. 44.

34. J.H. Elliott, *The Old World and the New, 1492–1650* (Cambridge: Cambridge University Press, 1972), pp. 43–44.

35. David Brion Davis, *Slavery and Human Progress* (New York: Oxford University Press, 1984), p. 55; Elena Lourie, "Anatomy of Ambivalence: Muslims under the Crown of Aragon in the Late Thirteenth Century," in Lourie, *Crusade and Colonisation: Muslims, Christians, and Jews in Medieval Aragon* (Hampshire: Variorum, 1990), p. 53.

36. David Brion Davis, *The Problem of Slavery in Western Culture* (Ithaca: Cornell University Press, 1966), p. 101. Although this decision by the Priors of Florence was particularly telling, it is worth noting that in Spain a century earlier Islamic converts to Christianity continued to suffer unique indignities—such as being referred to disdainfully as *baptisats*—and they remained vulnerable to enslavement. See Lourie, "Anatomy of Ambivalence," p. 71.

37. Quoted in Elena Lourie, "A Society Organised for War: Medieval Spain," *Past and Present*, 35 (1966), 73; emphasis added.

38. C.R. Boxer, *Two Pioneers of Tropical Medicine: Garcia d'Orta and Nicolas Monardes. Diamante,* Volume 14 (London: The Hispanic and Luso-Brazilian Councils, 1963), p. 11; quoted in Joseph H. Silverman, "On Knowing Other Peoples' Lives, Inquisitorially and Artistically," in Mary Elizabeth Perry and Anne J. Cruz, *Cultural Encounters: The Impact of the Inquisition in Spain and the New World* (Berkeley: University of California Press, 1991), p. 161. The fifteenth- and sixteenth-century history of the doctrine of *limpieza de sangre* is discussed briefly but insightfully in J.H. Elliott, *Imperial Spain, 1469–1716* (New York: St. Martin's Press, 1964), pp. 95, 212–17 and Ronald Sanders, *Lost Tribes and Promised Lands: The Origins of Racism* (Boston: Little, Brown, 1978), pp. 70–73.

39. Thomas F. Gossett, *Race: The History of an Idea in America* (New York: Schocken Books, 1965), p. 15.

40. See Anthony Pagden, *The Fall of Natural Man: The American Indian and the Origins of Comparative Ethnology*, Revised Edition (Cambridge: Cambridge University Press, 1986), pp. 38–39, 47–50.

41. Lewis Hanke, *Aristotle and the Americans: A Study in Race Prejudice in the Modern World* (Bloomington: Indiana University Press, 1959), p. 47; Don Fray Bartolomé de Las Casas, *In Defense of the Indians*, translated and edited by Stafford Poole (DeKalb: Northern Illinois University Press, 1974), pp. 37–42.

42. Hanke, *Aristotle and the American Indians*, p. 65.

43. Ibid., p. 74.

44. Quoted in Pagden, *The Fall of Natural Man*, p. 104.

45. Quoted in Lewis Hanke, *The Spanish Struggle for Justice in the Conquest of America* (Boston: Little, Brown and Company, 1965), p. 11.

46. John H. Elliott, "Renaissance Europe and America: A Blunted Impact?" in Fredi Chiappelli, Michael J.B. Allen, and Robert L. Benson, eds., *First Images of America: The Impact of the New World on the Old* (Berkeley: University of California Press, 1976), Volume One, p. 15.

47. Hugh Honour, *The New Golden Land: European Images of America from the Discoveries to the Present Time* (New York: Pantheon Books, 1975), pp. 53–55.

48. Elliott, *Imperial Spain*, p. 215.

49. Stanley G. Payne, *A History of Spain and Portugal* (Madison: University of Wisconsin Press, 1973), Volume One, p. 281.

50. Kirkpatrick Sale, *The Conquest of Paradise: Christopher Columbus and the Columbian Legacy* (New York: Alfred A. Knopf, 1990), pp. 180–81.

51. Ralph Davis, *The Rise of the Atlantic Economies* (London: Weidenfeld and Nicoloson, 1973), pp. 40–41.

52. Ibid., pp. 41–42.

53. Earl J. Hamilton, *American Treasure and the Price Revolution in Spain, 1501–1650* (Cambridge: Harvard University Press, 1934), p. 34. Hamilton's figures are presented in *pesos* of 450 *maravedis;* they are converted to ducats (375 *maravedis*) by Elliott, *Imperial Spain*, p. 175.

54. Payne, *History of Spain and Portugal*, p. 283; Davis, *Rise of the Atlantic Economies*, p. 68; William McNeill, *The Pursuit of Power: Technology, Armed Force, and Society Since A.D. 1000* (Chicago: University of Chicago Press, 1982), p. 109; Charles Wilson, *The Transformation of Europe, 1558–1648* (Berkeley: University of California Press, 1976), p. 136.

55. Immanuel Wallerstein, *The Modern World-System, I: Capitalist Agriculture and the Origins of the European World-Economy in the Sixteenth Century* (New York: Academic Press, 1974), p. 179.

56. Gaspar de Espinosa's fortune is mentioned in Elliott, *The Old World and the New*, p. 67; "Harvest of Blood" is the title O'Connell gives to his chapter on the sixteenth century in *Of Arms and Men*, pp. 124–47.

57. O'Connell, *Of Arms and Men*, p. 132.

58. Ibid., p. 133.

59. Henri de la Popelinière, *Les Trois Mondes* (Paris, 1582), quoted in Elliott, *The Old World and the New*, p. 83.

60. Quoted in Todorov, *Conquest of America*, pp. 150–51.

61. There is a substantial literature on the New World Inquisition. The best and most recent review of it is by a pioneer in the subject area, Richard E. Greenleaf, "Historiography of the Mexican Inquisition: Evolution of Interpretations and Methodologies," in Perry and Cruz, eds., *Cultural Encounters*, pp. 248–76. Two other essays in this same volume, which come to conflicting opinions on certain points, deserve attention as well: J. Jorge Klor de Alva, "Colonizing Souls: The Failure of the Indian Inquisition and the Rise of Penitential Discipline," pp. 3–22; and Roberto Moreno de los Arcos, "New Spain's Inquisition for Indians from the Sixteenth to the Nineteenth Century," pp. 23–36.

62. Charles L.G. Anderson, *Life and Letters of Vasco Nuñez de Balboa, Including the Conquest and Settlement of Darien and Panama* (New York: Fleming H. Revell, 1941), pp. 163–65. On the matter of alleged Indian traits and brutishness generally, see Anthony Pagden, "The Forbidden Food: Francisco de Vitoria and José de Acosta on Cannibalism," *Terrae Incognitae*, 13 (1981), 17–29.

63. Hanke, *The Spanish Struggle for Justice in the Conquest of America*, pp. 12, 122; Phelan, *Millennial Kingdom of the Franciscans*, pp. 94–95.

64. Toribio Motolinía, quoted in Alfred W. Crosby, Jr., *The Columbian Exchange: Biological and Cultural Consequences of 1492* (Westport, Conn.: Greenwood Press, 1972), p. 52.

65. See Chapter Five, p. 166.

66. Quoted in Phelan, *Millennial Kingdom of the Franciscans*, p. 93.

67. Juan de Matienzo, *Gobierno del Perú*, edited by Guillermo Lohmann Villena (Paris-Lima, 1967), p. 1618; quoted in J.H. Elliott, "The Discovery of America and the Discovery of Man," *Proceedings of the British Academy*, 58 (1972), 108–109. It is worth noting that Elliott also points out in this essay (p. 108, note 3) that dark skin as both a negative and an immutable condition was an idea hardly original with Matienzo; among others, Francisco López de Gómara had put forward similar arguments at a much earlier date.

68. Noble David Cook, *Demographic Collapse: Indian Peru, 1520–1620* (Cambridge: Cambridge University Press, 1981), p. 114.

69. For more detailed discussion of this matter, see Appendix Two, pp. 269–78.

70. Winthrop D. Jordan, *White Over Black: American Attitudes Toward the Negro, 1550–1812* (Chapel Hill: University of North Carolina Press, 1968), p. 98.

71. Wallerstein, *Modern World System, I*, p. 271.

72. L.S. Stavrianos, *Global Rift: The Third World Comes of Age* (New York: William Morrow and Company, 1981), pp. 95–98.

73. See Harold A. Innis, *The Cod Fisheries: The History of an International Economy* (New Haven: Yale University Press, 1940).

74. Wallerstein, *Modern World System I*, pp. 225, 230–31.

75. Davis, *Rise of the Atlantic Economies*, p. 211.

76. Edmund S. Morgan, *American Slavery—American Freedom: The Ordeal of Colonial Virginia* (New York: W.W. Norton & Company, 1975), p. 17.

77. Eileen McCracken, "The Woodlands of Ireland circa 1600," *Irish Historical Studies*, 11 (1959), 271–96.

78. See the essays "Ireland as *Terra Florida*" and "The Theory and Practice of Acculturation: Ireland in a Colonial Context," by Nicholas Canny in his *Kingdom*

and Colony: Ireland in the Atlantic World, 1560–1800 (Baltimore: The Johns Hopkins University Press, 1988), esp. pp. 19, 36–37. Emphasis added.

79. Ibid., p. 53.

80. Ibid., p. 66. See also, Nicholas Canny, "Identity Formation in Ireland: The Emergence of the Anglo-Irish," in Nicholas Canny and Anthony Pagden, eds., *Colonial Identity in the Atlantic World, 1500–1800* (Princeton: Princeton University Press, 1987), pp. 159–212.

81. Frantz Fanon, *Black Skin, White Masks,* translated by Charles Lam Markmann (New York: Grove Press, 1967), p. 115.

82. Loren E. Pennington, "The Amerindian in English Promotional Literature, 1575–1625," in K.R. Andrews, N.P. Canny, and P.E.H. Hair, eds., *The Westward Enterprise: English Activities in Ireland, the Atlantic, and America, 1480–1650* (Detroit: Wayne State University Press, 1979), p. 180.

83. See Margaret T. Hodgen, *Early Anthropology in the Sixteenth and Seventeenth Centuries* (Philadelphia: University of Pennsylvania Press, 1964), p. 409.

84. Pennington, "The Amerindian in English Promotional Literature," p. 183.

85. Quoted in Arthur O. Lovejoy, *The Great Chain of Being: A Study in the History of an Idea* (Cambridge: Harvard University Press, 1936), p. 145.

86. Ibid., p. 184.

87. Keith Thomas, *Man and the Natural World: A History of the Modern Sensibility* (New York: Pantheon Books, 1983), p. 134.

88. Joseph François Lafitau, *Customs of the American Indians Compared with the Customs of Primitive Times,* edited and translated by William N. Fenton and Elizabeth L. Moore (Toronto: The Champlain Society, 1974). The illustration is on plate 3, between pages 72 and 73 in Volume One; for discussion, see Volume Two, pp. 278–79.

89. In David B. Quinn, ed., *The Roanoke Voyages, 1584–1590* (London: Hakluyt Society, 1955), Volume One, pp. 108, 110.

90. Ibid., p. 191.

91. Robert Gray, *A Good Speed to Virginia* (London, 1609), n.p.

92. Edward Waterhouse, *A Declaration of the State of the Colony and Affaires in Virginia* (London, 1622), pp. 30–31. For other examples of Spanish influence on British thinking regarding the nature and colonization of indigenous peoples, see Nicholas P. Canny, "The Ideology of English Colonization from Ireland to America," *William and Mary Quarterly,* 3rd Series, 30 (1973), 593–95.

93. Bernadette Bucher, *Icon and Conquest: A Structural Analysis of the Illustrations of de Bry's Great Voyages,* translated by Basia Miller Gulati (Chicago: University of Chicago Press, 1981), pp. 142–44.

94. Michel de Montaigne, "Of Cannibals," in *The Complete Essays of Montaigne,* translated by Donald M. Frame (Stanford: Stanford University Press, 1958), p. 220.

95. John Higham, "Indian Princess and Roman Goddess: The First Female Symbols of America," *Proceedings of the American Antiquarian Society,* 100 (1990), 48.

96. See, for example, Karen Ordahl Kupperman, *Settling with the Indians: The Meeting of English and Indian Cultures in America, 1580–1640* (Totowa, N.J.: Rowman and Littlefield, 1980), esp. pp. 169–88; and Alden T. Vaughan, "From

White Man to Redskin: Changing Anglo-American Perceptions of the American Indian," *American Historical Review*, 87 (1982), 917–53.

97. One writer (Karen Ordahl Kupperman, in *Settling With the Indians*, op. cit.) makes much of the point that those Englishmen who were most likely to have favorable things to say about the Indians were those who actually spent time with them. While the observation is correct, the conclusion that she draws from it—that among those Englishmen who settled in America racism was a later seventeenth-century development—is completely unfounded. For while it may well be that a higher *proportion* of those who visited America became friendlier to the notion of Indians as potential equals than were those who stayed in England (a common and predictable phenomenon) in *both* cases the proportion holding positive views of the natives was infinitesimal. Through the early years of the seventeenth century the number of Englishmen who lived in North America never numbered more than several hundred (as late as 1625 it still was less than 1500), while the population of Britain, where the dominant ideology was being molded, was about 5,000,000. Thus, even accepting Kupperman's premise without question—that in the early years of exploration and settlement, within the very small group of Englishmen who actually lived in North America, there was a minority (that did *not* include those who held important leadership positions) who had favorable impressions of the Indians—the observation best serves to provide a relative few exceptions who prove the rule. And that in part explains, for example, the confused statement of one of the first Jamestown settlers that the Indians "are naturally given to trechery, howbeit we could not finde it in our travell up the river, but rather a most kind and loving people." [Anonymous (Gabriel Archer?), "A Brief discription of the People," in Philip L. Barbour, ed., *The Jamestown Voyages Under the First Charter, 1606–1609* (Cambridge: Hakluyt Society, 1969), Volume One, pp. 103–104.] The realities of Indian society were forcing on this writer a befuddled reconsideration of what he—and millions of other Englishmen—had been taught for nearly a century. But he was only one among multitudes, and the others were not having similar second thoughts. On another small point, Kupperman claims (p. 40) that the British did not associate the Indians with the wild men of European cultural tradition (despite her own quoting of such comments as Robert Johnson's assertion in 1609 that the Indians were "wild and savage people, they live and lie up and down in troupes like heards of Deare in a Forrest: they have no law but nature, their apparell skinnes of beasts, but most goe naked") because, says Kupperman, "the Indian was depicted as being less hairy than Europeans," whereas the traditional image of the wild man was that "he was covered with a coat of hair." Again, the simple observation is correct, but not the conclusion drawn from it—for what Kupperman is doing here is insisting that informal sixteenth- and seventeenth-century folk knowledge meet the strict consistency criteria of the modern academic. Popular racist thought, however, invariably confounds such finicky maxims, as with the extreme and inconsistent anti-Semitic charge that Jews are *both* inferior sub-human beings (even "vermin" in certain versions) *and* enormously intelligent, powerful, and wily leaders of world-wide conspiracies. Clearly, the Indians' comparative lack of body hair was no impediment to British and other European commentators four and five hundred years ago who regarded the New World's indigenous people as brutes in the *manner* of—but not necessarily *identical* with—the creatures described in their own classic literature. Nor should it be an impedi-

ment to *our* understanding—evident in an immense body of data—of the brutal and racist ways in which the Europeans, including the British, viewed and treated the Indians.

98. Robert K. Merton, *Social Theory and Social Structure*, Enlarged Edition (New York: Free Press, 1968), pp. 474, 477.

99. Cotton Mather, quoted in John Canup, *Out of the Wilderness: The Emergence of an American Identity in New England* (Middletown, Conn.: Wesleyan University Press, 1990), p. 79.

100. Richard Slotkin, *Regeneration Through Violence: The Mythology of the American Frontier* (Middletown, Conn.: Wesleyan University Press, 1973), p. 132.

101. Quoted in Philip Greven, *The Protestant Temperament: Patterns of Child-Rearing, Religious Experience, and the Self in Early America* (New York: Alfred A. Knopf, 1977), p. 68.

102. Frederick Crews, *The Sins of the Fathers: Hawthorne's Psychological Themes* (Berkeley: University of California Press, 1989), p. 19. This insightful work, originally published in 1966, must be read in this most recent edition as it contains an important Afterword by the author addressing the excesses of its psychoanalytic approach. Greven, *Protestant Temperament*, pp. 110, 121. Emphasis added. Greven subsequently has pursued these themes across the Protestant American historical experience, up to and including the present. See Philip Greven, *Spare the Child: The Religious Roots of Punishment and the Psychological Impact of Physical Abuse* (New York: Alfred A. Knopf, 1991), esp. pp. 60–72.

103. Davis, *Problem of Slavery in Western Culture*, p. 337.

104. Benjamin Wadsworth, "The Nature of Early Piety as it Respects God," in *A Course of Sermons on Early Piety* (Boston, 1721), p. 10.

105. On the fear of contamination, see Canup, *Out of the Wilderness*, pp. 155–56, 169–72. See also, Slotkin, *Regeneration Through Violence*, pp. 116–45. On aversive attitudes of the British colonists toward Indian-European sexual encounters, including the examples cited, see Michael Zuckerman, "Identity in British America: Unease in Eden," in Canny and Pagden, eds., *Colonial Identity in the Atlantic World*, esp. pp. 145–47.

106. R.H. Tawney, *Religion and the Rise of Capitalism* (New York: New American Library, 1954), pp. 35, 125–26.

107. Hanke, *Aristotle and the American Indians*, p. 47; Thomas, *Man and the Natural World*, p. 31.

108. The quotation from More's *Utopia* is also cited in Wilcomb E. Washburn, "The Moral and Legal Justifications for Dispossessing the Indians," in James Morton Smith, ed., *Seventeenth-Century America: Essays in Colonial History* (New York: W.W. Norton & Company, 1972), p. 24; Luther is quoted in Richard Schlatter, *Private Property: The History of an Idea* (New York: Russell & Russell, 1973), p. 88.

109. Schlatter, *Private Property*, p. 89.

110. John Locke, *Two Treatises of Government*, ed. Peter Laslett (Cambridge: Cambridge University Press, 1960), section 32.

111. C.B. Macpherson, *The Political Theory of Possessive Individualism: Hobbes to Locke* (Oxford: Oxford University Press, 1962), pp. 261–62.

112. Edmund S. Morgan, *American Slavery—American Freedom: The Ordeal of Colonial Virginia* (New York: W.W. Norton & Company, 1975), p. 381.

113. See Schlatter, *Private Property,* pp. 77–123.

114. Thomas More, *Utopia,* edited by Edward Surtz (New Haven: Yale University Press, 1964), p. 76.

115. See Francis Jennings, *The Invasion of America: Indians, Colonialism, and the Cant of Conquest* (Chapel Hill: University of North Carolina Press, 1975), pp. 82, 135–38.

116. R.C. [Robert Cushman?], "Reasons and Considerations Touching Upon the Lawfulness of Removing Out of England into the Parts of America," *Collections of the Massachusetts Historical Society,* Second Series, 9 (1832), 69–70.

117. John Winthrop, "Reasons to be Considered, and Objections with Answers," reprinted in Edmund S. Morgan, ed., *The Founding of Massachusetts: Historians and the Sources* (Indianapolis: Bobbs-Merrill, 1964), p. 175. Regarding the apocalyptic beliefs of these early settlers, the leading minister and religious thinker among the first Massachusetts colonists was John Cotton, who delivered a series of highly influential sermons during the 1630s and 1640s that not only announced the imminent coming of the end of the world but even pinpointed the date—1655. See John Cotton, *An Exposition Upon the Thirteenth Chapter of the Revelation* (London, 1655), first distributed in 1639 or 1640. For discussion, see Everett H. Emerson, *John Cotton* (New York: Twayne, 1965), pp. 95–101; Larzer Ziff, *The Career of John Cotton* (Princeton: Princeton University Press, 1962), pp. 170–202; and, more generally, J.F. Maclear, "New England and the Fifth Monarchy: The Quest for the Millennium in Early American Puritanism," *William and Mary Quarterly,* 3rd Series, 32 (1975), 223–60.

118. Winthrop, "Reasons to be Considered," pp. 177–78.

119. Roger Williams, *A Key into the Language of America* (1643), quoted in William Cronon, *Changes in the Land: Indians, Colonists, and the Ecology of New England* (New York: Hill and Wang, 1983), p. 60.

120. Bartolomé de Las Casas, *The Devastation of the Indies: A Brief Account,* translated by Herma Briffault (New York: Seabury Press, 1974), p. 41. By 1720 the combined white populations of the various British colonies was approximately 400,000, according to U.S. Census Bureau figures reprinted in *The Statistical History of the United States from Colonial Times to the Present* (Stamford, Conn.: Fairfield Publishers, 1965), p. 756, Series Z 1–19. As noted earlier (Chapter Three, note 127), the comparable figure after more than a century of Spanish settlement in the New World was probably about 200,000, although it may have been less than that in view of the heavy return traffic; one study, for example, contends that an average of about 6000 Spaniards per decade left the New World and returned to Spain between 1550 and 1650. [Theopolis Fair, "The *Indiano* During the Spanish Golden Age from 1550 to 1650" (Doctoral dissertation, Temple University, 1972), p. 75.] Moreover, unlike the British colonists, most of the Spanish migration to the Americas for more than a century was overwhelmingly young, single, male, and impoverished. Magnus Mörner has demonstrated that the Spanish migrants were 95 percent male through 1540, while Peter Boyd-Bowman has shown that even after a century of migration, two of three Spanish settlers were male. Indeed, here is Boyd-Bowman's "composite picture" of the "typical . . . Spanish emigrant" near the start of the seventeenth century: "a poverty-stricken Andalusian male aged $27\frac{1}{2}$, unmarried, unskilled, and probably only semi-literate, driven by hunger to make his way to Peru in the employ of any man who would pay his

passage and had secured the necessary permit." [See Magnus Mörner, "Spanish Migration to the New World Prior to 1810: A Report on the State of Research," in Chiappelli, Allen, and Benson, eds., *First Images of America,* Volume Two, p. 744; and Peter Boyd-Bowman, "Spanish Emigrants to the Indies, 1595–98: A Profile," in ibid., pp. 729, 732.] Letters home from these men—both conquistadors and ostensible settlers—show that they shared a common goal: as James Lockhart puts it, "practically all [Spanish] settlers originally intended to return [home], and . . . the maximum ambition for all, regardless of how often it could be realized, was a seigneurial existence in Spain." [James Lockhart, "Letters and People to Spain," in ibid., pp. 795–96, note 28.] One example of the success rate for those desiring to return, which may or may not have been typical, shows that of the men who followed Pizarro to Peru—approximately 80 percent of whom have been accounted for—fully half are known to have returned to Spain to live out their lives. [James Lockhart, *The Men of Cajamarca: A Social and Biographical Study of the First Conquerors of Peru* (Austin: University of Texas Press for the Institute of Latin American Studies, 1972), p. 47, Table 12.] In contrast, not only were a much greater proportion of the seventeenth-century English colonists females and married males, but servants tended to remain in the colonies following the completion of their indentures, and even English servants in Barbados, when they achieved their freedom, tended to head for Virginia or other North American colonies rather than return to England. [See Morgan, *American Slavery—American Freedom,* pp. 298–99.] It is true that some of the earliest Massachusetts Bay colonists planned at some time to return to England, but that hope ended for most within a decade or two with the outbreak in England of civil war. [For discussion, see William L. Sachse, *The Colonial American in Britain* (Madison: University of Wisconsin Press, 1956).]

121. See Anthony Pagden, *Spanish Imperialism and the Political Imagination: Studies in European and Spanish-American Social and Political Theory, 1513–1830* (New Haven: Yale University Press, 1990), esp. pp. 16–33; another version of this analysis is the same author's essay, "Dispossessing the Barbarian: The Language of Spanish Thomism and the Debate over the Property Rights of the American Indians," in Anthony Pagden, ed., *The Languages of Political Theory in Early-Modern Europe* (Cambridge: Cambridge University Press, 1987), pp. 79–98.

122. Quoted in David Beers Quinn, *Set Fair for Roanoke: Voyages and Colonies, 1584–1606* (Chapel Hill: University of North Carolina Press, 1985), pp. 228–30; see also, Karen Ordahl Kupperman, *Roanoke: The Abandoned Colony* (Totowa, N.J.: Rowman & Allanheld, 1984), pp. 62–63.

123. William Bradford, *Of Plymouth Plantation,* ed. Samuel Eliot Morison (New York: Modern Library, 1967), pp. 270–71; Canup, *Out of the Wilderness,* pp. 21, 30.

124. Cotton Mather, *Magnalia Christi Americana,* ed. Kenneth B. Murdock (Cambridge: Harvard University Press, 1977), p. 129; second passage quoted in Forrest G. Wood, *The Arrogance of Faith: Christianity and Race in America from the Colonial Era to the Twentieth Century* (New York: Alfred A. Knopf, 1990), p. 262.

125. Canup, *Out of the Wilderness,* p. 77.

126. Mather, *Magnalia Christi Americana,* p. 89.

127. There is a good deal of literature on this, but see especially the following:

Neal E. Salisbury, "Red Puritans: The 'Praying Indians' of Massachusetts Bay and John Eliot," *William and Mary Quarterly,* 3rd Series, 31 (1974), 27–54; James P. Ronda, " 'We Are Well As We Are': An Indian Critique of Seventeenth-Century Christian Missions," *William and Mary Quarterly,* 3rd Series, 34 (1977), 65–82; Gary B. Nash, "Perspectives on the History of Seventeenth-Century Missionary Activity in Colonial America," *Terrae Incognitae,* 11 (1979), 19–27; and Zuckerman, "Identity in British America," esp. pp. 147–48.

128. Sacvan Bercovitch, *The Puritan Origins of the American Self* (New Haven: Yale University Press, 1975), p. 141.

129. Ibid., pp. 141–43.

130. From *Inaugural Addresses of the Presidents of the United States* (Washington, D.C.: Government Printing Office, 1965), p. 13.

131. Quoted in Ronald T. Takaki, *Iron Cages: Race and Culture in 19th-Century America* (New York: Alfred A. Knopf, 1979), p. 103. It is not incidental to Jefferson's willingness to exterminate Indians that at about this same time he was devising a plan to ship the nation's African Americans back to Africa. When this turned out to be excessively expensive, he proposed taking black infants away from their parents (each black baby he calculated to be worth $22.50) and shipping *them* back, leaving the adult African American population to die out "naturally." On the matter of the morality of forcibly removing an entire race of children from their parents (itself an act of genocide, so the United Nations later would decide), Jefferson acknowledged that it "would produce some scruples of humanity. But this would be straining at a gnat, and swallowing a camel." See, ibid., pp. 44–45.

132. See Chapter Four, notes 89 and 90.

133. Barry Holstun Lopez, *Of Wolves and Men* (New York: Charles Scribner's Sons, 1978), pp. 170–71. While the use of smallpox-infected blankets as a method for exterminating Indians was not as widespread (or as effective) as is popularly believed, it was an occasional practice, and as such it marked "a milestone of sorts" in military history, writes Robert O'Connell: "While infected carcasses had long been catapulted into besieged cities, this seems to be the first time a known weakness in the immunity structure of an adversary population was deliberately exploited with a weapons response." O'Connell, *Of Arms and Men,* p. 171. For an eighteenth-century example of the deliberate use of smallpox as a weapon "to extirpate [the] exorable race" of Indians—an example that killed large numbers of Delaware, Mingo, and Shawnee people—see E. Wagner Stearn and Allen E. Stearn, *The Effect of Smallpox on the Destiny of the Amerindian* (Boston: Humphries, 1945), pp. 44–45.

134. Cotton Mather, *Souldiers Counselled and Comforted* (Boston, 1689), p. 28; Rev. Solomon Stoddard to Gov. George Dudley (22 October 1703) in *New England Historical and Genealogical Register,* 24 (1870), 269–70.

135. Some of the cultural byways of these conflicting impulses are discussed in Lawrence J. Friedman, *Inventors of the Promised Land* (New York: Alfred A. Knopf, 1975).

136. Quoted in Christopher Lasch, "The Anti-Imperialists, the Philippines, and the Inequality of Man," in Lasch's *The World of Nations: Reflections on American History, Politics, and Culture* (New York: Alfred A. Knopf, 1973), p. 78. See also Drinnon, *Facing West,* pp. 307–32.

137. J.D.F. Smith, *A Tour of the United States of America* (London, 1784), Volume One, pp. 345–46.

138. Samuel G. Morton, *Crania Americana, or a Comparative View of the Skulls of Various Aboriginal Nations of North and South America* (Philadelphia: John Pennington, 1839), pp. 81–82.

139. Francis Parkman, *The Conspiracy of Pontiac and the Indian War After the Conquest of Canada* (New York: Charles Scribner's Sons, 1915), Volume One, pp. ix, 48.

140. Frederick Farrar and H.K. Rusden, quoted in Raymond Evans, Kay Saunders, and Kathryn Cronin, *Exclusion, Exploitation, and Extermination: Race Relations in Colonial Queensland* (Sydney: Australia and New Zealand Book Company, 1975), pp.14, 81–82.

141. Rev. Rufus Anderson, D.D., *The Hawaiian Islands: Their Progress and Condition Under Missionary Labors* (Boston: Gould & Lincoln, 1864), p. 276.

142. Quoted in James Belich, *The New Zealand Wars and the Victorian Interpretation of Racial Conflict* (Auckland: Auckland University Press, 1986), p. 299.

143. Quoted in Gossett, *Race*, p. 243.

144. William Dean Howells, "A Sennight of the Centennial," *Atlantic Monthly,* 38 (July, 1876), p. 103.

145. G. Stanley Hall, *Adolescence: Its Psychology and Its Relations to Physiology, Anthropology, Sociology, Sex, Crime, Religion, and Education,* Volume Two (New York: D. Appleton and Company, 1904), p. 651.

146. Quoted in Thomas G. Dyer, *Theodore Roosevelt and the Idea of Race* (Baton Rouge: Louisiana State University Press, 1980), pp. 78, 86, 159–64.

147. Ibid., p. xiii.

148. Daniel Gasman, *The Scientific Origins of National Socialism: Social Darwinism in Ernst Haeckel and the German Monist League* (New York: Elsevier, 1971), pp. 150, 39–40.

149. Robert Jay Lifton, *The Nazi Doctors: Medical Killing and the Psychology of Genocide* (New York: Basic Books, 1986), pp. 431, 441–42.

Epilogue

1. Martin Luther, "On the Jews and Their Lies," in Franklin Sherman, ed., *Luther's Works* (Philadelphia: Fortress Press, 1971), Volume 47, pp. 265–92.

2. Ibid., p. 306. Emphasis added.

3. On Marr, see Moshe Zimmermann, *Wilhelm Marr: The Patriarch of Anti-Semitism* (New York: Oxford University Press, 1986).

4. Norman Cohn, *Warrant for Genocide: The Myth of the Jewish World-Conspiracy and the Protocols of the Elders of Zion* (New York: Harper & Row, 1967), p. 171.

5. Cohn, *Warrant for Genocide*, p. 172.

6. George L. Mosse, *Toward the Final Solution: A History of European Racism* (New York: Howard Fertig, 1978), p. 108.

7. For discussion of this in Hitler's thinking and in Nazism in general, see Robert Jay Lifton, *The Nazi Doctors: Medical Killing and the Psychology of Genocide* (New York: Basic Books, 1986), pp. 481–85.

8. Joseph Conrad, *Last Essays* (London: J.M. Dent & Sons, 1926), p. 25.

The toll in Soviet military casualties from Operation Barbarossa is reported in Peter Calvocoressi, Guy Wint, and John Pritchard, *Total War: Causes and Courses of the Second World War*, Revised Second Edition (New York: Pantheon Books, 1989), p. 204.

9. Frederick R. Karl and Laurence Davies, eds., *The Collected Letters of Joseph Conrad* (Cambridge: Cambridge University Press, 1986), Volume Two, p. 16. Hitler's contempt for humanity is well known and widely discussed, but see, for example, Alan Bullock, *Hitler: A Study in Tyranny*, Revised Edition (New York: Harper & Row, 1962), pp. 398–99.

10. Albert J. Guerard, "Introduction" to Joseph Conrad, *Heart of Darkness and the Secret Sharer* (New York: New American Library, 1950), pp. 7–8.

11. The quoted words are from Chinua Achebe's brilliant essay, "An Image of Africa: Racism in Conrad's *Heart of Darkness*," in Chinua Achebe, *Hopes and Impediments: Selected Essays* (New York: Doubleday, 1989), pp. 14–15; and Marianna Torgovnick, *Gone Primitive: Savage Intellects, Modern Lives* (Chicago: University of Chicago Press, 1990), p. 141.

12. Achebe, "An Image of Africa," pp. 11, 19. In *Gone Primitive*, pp. 270–71, Torgovnick discusses the outrage that erupted in some literary circles following the original 1977 publication of Achebe's essay; Torgovnick herself (pp. 141–58) focuses on the female element in Conrad's racist vision of African primitivism.

13. Conrad, *Heart of Darkness*, pp. 105–106.

14. Chinua Achebe, "Impediments to Dialogue Between North and South," in *Hopes and Impediments*, p. 23.

15. Quoted in John W. Dower, *War Without Mercy: Race and Power in the Pacific War* (New York: Pantheon Books, 1986), p. 64. The quotations in the preceding paragraph are from ibid., pp. 108, 335.

16. Ibid., pp. 64–65.

17. Ronald T. Takaki, *Iron Cages: Race and Culture in 19th-Century America* (New York: Alfred A. Knopf, 1979), p. 96.

18. Quoted in Richard Drinnon, *Facing West: The Metaphysics of Indian-Hating and Empire-Building* (Minneapolis: University of Minnesota Press, 1980), pp. 448–49.

19. Ibid., pp. 369, 449; Frances FitzGerald, *Fire in the Lake: The Vietnamese and the Americans in Vietnam* (Boston: Little, Brown and Company, 1972), pp. 367–68.

20. Further excerpts—much more violent and obscene than this—were published in Christopher Hitchens, "Minority Report," *The Nation* (13 February 1989), p. 187, but even Hitchens could not reprint certain verses.

21. *New York Times* (28 March 1991), p. A18, columns 3 and 4.

22. The estimates of the number of children killed as a direct result of the war, and the prediction of numbers slated to die in the months ahead, come from a ten-member Harvard University medical team that visited Iraq in the immediate aftermath of the war. See *New York Times* (22 May 1991), p. A16, columns 1 and 2. See also the report of a United Nations Secretary-General investigation in London's *Guardian Weekly* (4 August 1991), p. 9, columns 1 through 5. Reflections on the U.S. war against Iraq are just beginning to appear at this writing, but one of the first books to be published that is deserving of attention is Thomas C. Fox, *Iraq: Military Victory, Moral Defeat* (New York: Sheed & Ward, 1991).

23. Arno J. Mayer, *Why Did the Heavens Not Darken? The "Final Solution" in History,* Expanded Edition (New York: Pantheon Books, 1990), pp. 365, 462.

24. Michael R. Marrus, *The Holocaust in History* (Hanover, N.H.: Brandeis University Press and University Press of New England, 1987), p. 20.

25. There is an overview of these and other practices in Rex Weyler, *Blood of the Land: The Government and Corporate War Against the American Indian Movement* (New York: Random House, 1982), esp. pp. 218–26. The best sources for up to date reports on such matters are the South and Meso American Indian Information Center in Oakland, California, which publishes a newsletter and other documents, and the International Work Group for Indigenous Affairs, home-based in Copenhagen, which publishes a newsletter and a Document Series on violence and genocide against native peoples. To date, there are several score book-length reports in the IWGIA Document Series.

26. Until the recent passage of the Indian Child Welfare Act, year in and year out between a quarter and a third of all American Indian children were removed by government authorites from their families and placed in foster homes, adoptive homes, or institutions—80 to 90 percent of which were headed and run by non-Indian persons. Article II, Section (e) of the Genocide convention defines as genocide "forcibly transferring children of the group to another group." On the problem of the forced break-up of Indian families (published prior to the implementation of the Indian Child Welfare Act), see Steven Unger, ed., *The Destruction of American Indian Families* (New York: Association on American Indian Affairs, 1979).

27. Leo Kuper, "The United States Ratifies the Genocide Convention," *Internet on the Holocaust and Genocide,* 19 (February, 1989), reprinted in Frank Chalk and Kurt Jonassohn, *The History and Sociology of Genocide: Analyses and Case Studies* (New Haven: Yale University Press, 1990) pp. 422–25.

28. For detailed discussion and analysis of the American government's ongoing refusal to join the rest of the world's nations in their unconditional condemnation of genocide, see Lawrence J. LeBlanc, *The United States and the Genocide Convention* (Durham: Duke University Press, 1991).

29. *New York Times International* (21 May 1991), p. A5, columns 1–6.

30. Edward S. Herman and Noam Chomsky, *Manufacturing Consent: The Political Economy of the Mass Media* (New York: Pantheon Books, 1988), pp. 37–86.

31. U.S. Department of Commerce-Bureau of the Census, *We, the First Americans* (Washington, D.C.: U.S. Government Printing Office, 1989), pp. 12–13; U.S. Department of Health and Human Services, *Indian Health Service Chart Series Book* (Washington, D.C.: U.S. Government Printing Office, 1988), pp. 43 (Table 4.20), 47 (Table 4.24). It must be noted that even these shocking suicide and health statistics greatly understate the desperate reality of life on many Indian reservations, for there are direct correlations between such so-called quality of life indices and the degree of cultural integrity individual Indian peoples have been able to maintain. Thus, for example, among the different Pueblo peoples of New Mexico, those who have suffered the most erosion of traditional values through forced acculturation into American life have two to three (and in one case almost forty) times the overall suicide rate of those who have been able to hold on to more of their customary lifeways. See N. Van Winkle and P. May, "Native American Sui-

cide in New Mexico, 1957–1979: A Comparative Study," *Human Organization,* 45 (1986), 296–309; and Group for the Advancement of Psychiatry, *Suicide and Ethnicity in the United States* (New York: Brunner/Mazel, 1989), p. 6.

32. Paul Stuart, *Nations Within a Nation: Historical Statistics of American Indians* (Westport, Conn.: Greenwood Press, 1987), pp. 15 (Table 2.1), 29 (Table 2.15).

33. See Susanne Jonas, *The Battle for Guatemala: Rebels, Death Squads, and U.S. Power* (Boulder: Westview Press, 1991), esp. pp. 103–13, and 145–59.

34. For overviews and analyses of some of these matters, see Peter Matthiessen, *Indian Country* (New York: Viking Press, 1984) and M. Annette Jaimes, ed., *The State of Native America: Genocide, Colonization, and Resistance* (Boston: South End Press, 1992).

35. "Columbus's Letter to the Sovereigns on His First Voyage, 15 February— 4 March, 1493," in Samuel Eliot Morison, ed., *Journals and Other Documents on the Life and Voyages of Christopher Columbus* (New York: The Heritage Press, 1963), p. 182.

Appendix I

1. For an early summary discussion, see S.K. Lothrop, "Early Migrations to Central and South America: An Anthropological Problem in the Light of Other Sciences," *Journal of the Royal Anthropological Institute,* 91 (1961), 97–123.

2. J.L. Bada, R.A. Schroeder, and G.F. Carter, "New Evidence for the Antiquity of Man in North America Deduced from Aspartic-Acid Racemization," *Science,* 184 (1974), 791–93; J.L. Bada and P.M. Masters, "Evidence for a 50,000– Year Antiquity of Man in the Americas Derived from Amino-Acid Racemization in Human Skeletons," in Jonathan E. Ericson, R.E. Taylor, and Rainier Berger, eds., *Peopling of the New World* (Los Altos, Calif.: Ballena Press, 1982), pp. 171– 79.

3. Richard S. MacNeish, "Early Man in the New World," *American Scientist,* 63 (1976), 316–27; for convenient summaries of much of the data on this matter as of the early 1980s, see the essays on specific locales in Jesse D. Jennings, ed., *Ancient South Americans* (New York: W.H. Freeman and Company, 1983).

4. See the overview discussion in Tom D. Dillehay, "A Late Ice-Age Settlement in Southern Chile," *Scientific American,* 251 (1984), 106–19.

5. See William N. Irving and C.R. Harrington, "Upper Pleistocene Radiocarbon-Dated Artifacts from the Northern Yukon," *Science,* 179 (1973), 335–40; and two reports by James M. Adovasio: "Excavations at Meadowcroft Rock Shelter, 1973– 75: A Progress Report," *Pennsylvania Archaeologist,* 45 (1975), 1–30; and "Meadowcroft Rock Shelter, 1977: An Overview," *American Antiquity,* 43 (1978), 632– 51. For the Missouri site, see M.J. Regan, R.M. Rowlett, E.G. Garrison, W. Dort, Jr., V.M. Bryant, Jr., and C.J. Johannsen, "Flake Tools Stratified Below Paleo-Indian Artifacts," *Science,* 200 (1978), 1272–75. The Warm Mineral Springs site is discussed briefly in State of Florida, Division of Archives, History, and Records Management, *Archives and History News,* 5 (July-August 1974), p. 1.

6. N. Guidon and G. Delibrias, "Carbon-14 Dates Point to Man in the Americas 32,000 Years Ago," *Nature,* 321 (1986), 769–71.

7. The most detailed discussion of these earliest sites focuses on Monte Verde.

See Tom D. Dillehay, *Monte Verde: A Late Pleistocene Settlement in Chile* (Washington, D.C.: Smithsonian Institution Press, 1989). For a non-technical review of the ferment in archaeological circles surrounding the discoveries at Monte Verde, Pedra Furada, and other early human settlements in the Americas, see Richard Wolkomir, "New Finds Could Rewrite the Start of American History," *Smithsonian*, 21 (March 1991), pp. 130–44.

8. Morris Swadesh, "Linguistic Relations Across Bering Strait," *American Anthropologist*, 64 (1962), 1262–91; Harold E. Driver, *Indians of North America*, Second Edition (Chicago: University of Chicago Press, 1975), p. 25; L. Campbell and M. Mithun, eds., *The Languages of Native America: Historical and Comparative Assessment* (Austin: University of Texas Press, 1979).

9. Joseph H. Greenberg's *Language in the Americas* (Stanford: Stanford University Press, 1988) is the most prominent and controversial of these new studies. For an important recent discussion and critique, see James Matisoff, "On Megalocomparison," *Language*, 66 (1990), 106–20. On the evolution of indigenous language change in South America, see Mary Ritchie Key, ed., *Language Change in South American Indian Languages* (Philadelphia: University of Pennsylvania Press, 1991).

10. Richard A. Rogers, Larry D. Martin, and T. Dale Nicklas, "Ice-Age Geography and the Distribution of Native North American Languages," *Journal of Biogeography*, 17 (1990), 131–143.

11. Fumiko Ikawa-Smith, "The Early Prehistory of the Americas as Seen from Northeast Asia," in Ericson, Taylor, and Berger, eds., *Peopling of the New World*, p. 23. On sea level changes and their impact on—and obliteration of—archaeological sites in the Pacific, see John R.H. Gibbons and Fergus G.A.U. Clunie, "Sea Level Changes and Pacific Prehistory: New Insight into Early Human Settlement of Oceania," *Journal of Pacific History*, 21 (1986), 58–82.

12. Jesse D. Jennings, "Origins," in Jennings, ed., *Ancient North Americans*, p. 27.

13. For a recent review of the evidence, see Sally McBrearty, "The Origin of Modern Humans," *Man*, 25 (1990), 129–43. Cf., Rebecca L. Cann, "DNA and Human Origins," *Annual Review of Anthropology*, 17 (1988), 127–43. As of this writing the most recently published research puts the date at somewhere between 164,000 B.C. and 247,000 B.C. See Linda Vigilant, Mark Stoneking, Henry Harpending, Kristen Hawkes, and Allan C. Wilson, "African Populations and the Evolution of Human Mitochondrial DNA," *Science*, 253 (1991), 1503–1507.

14. Knut R. Fladmark has long been a proponent of this idea. See, for example, his "Routes: Alternate Migration Corridors for Early Man in North America," *American Antiquity*, 44 (1979), 55–69.

15. See J. Peter White and J.F. O'Connell, *A Prehistory of Australia, New Guinea and Sahul* (Sydney: Academic Press, 1982); and J.P. White, "Melanesia," in Jesse D. Jennings, ed., *The Prehistory of Polynesia* (Cambridge: Harvard University Press, 1979), pp. 352–77.

16. There also is the possibility that very early sites do exist and are accessible along the present northwest coast, but that archaeologists—presupposing that they could not exist—have simply not been digging deeply enough. That, at least, is the conclusion drawn by one archaeologist following recent work in the area. See R. Lee Lyman, *Prehistory of the Oregon Coast: The Effects of Excavation Strategies*

and Assemblage Size on Archaeological Inquiry (New York: Academic Press, 1991), pp. 313–14.

17. These and other early estimates are reviewed briefly in Woodrow Borah, "The Historical Demography of Aboriginal and Colonial America: An Attempt at Perspective," in William M. Denevan, ed., *The Native Population of the Americas in 1492* (Madison: University of Wisconsin Press, 1976), pp. 14–15.

18. Paul Rivet, G. Stresser-Pean, and C. Loukotka, "Langues américaines," in *Les Langues du Monde,* Volume 16, ed. Antoine Meillet and Marcel Cohen (Paris: Société de Linguistique de Paris, 1924), pp. 597–712; Karl Sapper, "Die Zahl und die Volksdichte der indianischen Bevölkerung in Amerika vor der Conquista und in der Gegenwart," *Proceedings of the Twenty-first International Congress of Americanists,* Part One (Leiden: E.J. Brill, 1924), pp. 95–104; and Herbert J. Spinden, "The Population of Ancient America," *Geographical Review,* 28 (1928), 641–60.

19. Angel Rosenblat, "El desarrollo de la población indigena de América," *Tierra Firme,* 1 (1935), 1:115–33; 2:117–48; 3:109–41; Alfred L. Kroeber, *Cultural and Natural Areas of Native North America,* University of California Publications in American Archaeology and Ethnology, Volume 38 (Berkeley: University of California Press, 1939), Section 11. Although Kroeber could not have known it at the time that he was writing, his estimate was substantially lower than the likely population of North and South America even if the entire hemisphere had been inhabited only by small tribes of hunting and gathering peoples—which, as we have seen, it decidedly was not. On population densities for hunter-gatherer societies, see Richard B. Lee and Irven DeVore, eds., *Man the Hunter* (Chicago: Aldine, 1968); for discussion on this point regarding the Americas during early millennia of human settlement, see Stuart J. Fiedel, *Prehistory of the Americas* (Cambridge: Cambridge University Press, 1987), p. 49.

20. For a brief and instructive review of some of the data and technical approaches used by these investigators in one of the settings studied, see Woodrow Borah and Sherburne F. Cook, "Conquest and Population: A Demographic Approach to Mexican History," *Proceedings of the American Philosophical Society,* 113 (1969), 177–83.

21. Woodrow Borah, "America as Model: The Demographic Impact of European Expansion Upon the Non-Western World," *Actas y Memorial del XXXV Congreso Internacional de Americanistas,* Volume III (Mexico City, 1962), 381; Henry F. Dobyns, "Estimating Aboriginal American Population: An Appraisal of Techniques with a New Hemispheric Estimate," *Current Anthropology,* 7 (1966), 395–416.

22. John D. Durand, "Historical Estimates of World Population: An Evaluation," *Population and Development Review,* 3 (1977), 253–96.

23. For helpful general discussion and an estimate in the 75,000,000 range (including between 7,000,000 and 8,000,000 for the modern-day areas of the United States and Canada), see Russell Thornton, *American Indian Holocaust and Survival: A Population History Since 1492* (Norman: University of Oklahoma Press, 1987), pp. 22–25. Dobyns's conclusion that his earlier calculation for the population of the region north of Mexico was too low almost by half, and that 18,000,000 is a more probable figure, is reported in Henry F. Dobyns, *Their Number Become Thinned: Native American Population Dynamics in Eastern North America*

(Knoxville:University of Tennessee Press, 1983), pp. 42, 342–43. Dobyns's hemispheric estimate of approximately 145,000,000 was advanced in his "Reassessing New World Populations at the Time of Contact," paper delivered at Institute for Early Contact Studies, University of Florida at Gainesville (April 1988).

24. Terry L. Hunt and Melissa A. Kirkendall, "Social Complexity and Population Collapse in Polynesia" and "The Archaeology of Population Collapse in the Yasawa Islands, Fiji," papers read at Seventeenth Pacific Science Congress, Honolulu, June 1991. On the potential for explosively rapid disease dispersal among isolated indigenous peoples, see also David E. Stannard, *Before the Horror: The Population of Hawai'i on the Eve of Western Contact* (Honolulu: Social Science Research Institute and University of Hawai'i Press, 1989), esp. pp. 69–75.

25. The best and most thorough examinations of the hypothesis that massive disease pandemics that were brought by Europeans preceded their physical entry (at least in large numbers) into indigenous environments—in addition to Dobyns, *Their Number Become Thinned*—are Ann F. Ramenofsky, *Vectors of Death: The Archaeology of European Contact* (Albuquerque: University of New Mexico Press, 1987); Marvin T. Smith, *Archaeology of Aboriginal Culture Change in the Interior Southeast: Depopulation During the Early Historic Period* (Gainesville: University Presses of Florida, 1987); and Daniel T. Reff, *Disease, Depopulation, and Culture Change in Northwestern New Spain, 1518–1764* (Salt Lake City: University of Utah Press, 1991).

26. Critics of Dobyns, who nevertheless agree that "American Indian populations typically declined by 95 percent overall"—thus supporting very large pre-1492 native population estimates—include Dean R. Snow and Kim M. Lanphear, "European Contact and Indian Depopulation in the Northeast: The Timing of the First Epidemics," *Ethnohistory*, 35 (1988), 15–33; cf., Henry F. Dobyns, "More Methodological Perspectives on Historical Demography," *Ethnohistory*, 36 (1989), 285–99.

27. One of the earliest investigators to point out the demographic importance of psychological disorientation and despair among indigenous peoples, following on the devastation of epidemic disease, was J.V. Neel. See, for example, the report by Neel, W.R. Centerwall, N.A. Chagnon, and H.L. Casey, "Notes on the Effect of Measles and Measles Vaccine in a Virgin Soil Population of South American Indians," *American Journal of Epidemiology*, 91 (1970), 418–29; and J.V. Neel, "Health and Disease in Unacculturated Amerindian Populations," in Ciba Foundation Symposium Number 49, *Health and Disease in Tribal Societies* (Amsterdam: Elsevier/Excerpta Medica, 1977), pp. 155–68. On the enormous demographic importance of induced infertility as a consequence of imported disease and cultural dislocation among native peoples, see David E. Stannard, "Disease and Infertility: A New Look at the Demographic Collapse of Native Populations in the Wake of Western Contact," *Journal of American Studies*, 24 (1990), 325–50. A recent overview, linking an array of demographic factors other than genocide in the phenomenon of indigenous population decline following Western contact, is David E. Stannard, "The Consequences of Contact: Toward an Interdisciplinary Theory of Native Responses to Biological and Cultural Invasion," in David Hurst Thomas, ed. *Columbian Consequences, Volume Three: The Spanish Borderlands in Pan-American Perspective* (Washington, D.C.: Smithsonian Institution Press, 1991), pp. 519–39.

Appendix II

1. The quotation is from John Mason's account of his and his followers' crushing and burning of the Pequots in his *Brief History of the Pequot War . . . in 1637* (Boston: S. Kneeland & T. Green, 1736), p. 22.

2. For examples of exceptions to this generalization, in one way or another, see James C. Ballagh, *A History of Slavery in Virginia* (Baltimore: Johns Hopkins University Press, 1902), pp. 28–35; and Ulrich B. Phillips, *American Negro Slavery* (New York: Appleton and Company, 1918), p. viii.

3. For the most prominent such analyses, see Oscar and Mary F. Handlin, "Origins of the Southern Labor System," *William and Mary Quarterly,* Third Series, 7 (1950), 199–222; Oscar Handlin, *Race and Nationality in American Life* (Boston: Little, Brown & Company, 1957), esp. chapters 1, 2, and 4; and Kenneth M. Stampp, *The Peculiar Institution: Slavery in the Ante-Bellum South* (New York: Alfred A. Knopf, 1956), pp. 21–23.

4. Stampp, *Peculiar Institution,* p. vii.

5. Winthrop D. Jordan, "Modern Tensions and the Origins of American Slavery," *Journal of Southern History,* 28 (1962), 18–30.

6. Carl N. Degler, "Slavery and the Genesis of American Race Prejudice," *Comparative Studies in Society and History,* 2 (1959), 49–66; see also Degler's *Out of Our Past: The Forces that Shaped Modern America* (New York: Harper & Row, 1959), pp. 26–39.

7. Jordan, "Modern Tensions and the Origins of American Slavery"; and Jordan, *White Over Black: American Attitudes Toward the Negro, 1550–1812* (Chapel Hill: University of North Carolina Press, 1968). This necessarily hasty overview precludes discussion of several other historians who made significant contributions to the debate, generally supportive of Degler. One of them actually preceded Degler, though her work was focused on other matters: Katharine George, "The Civilized West Looks at Primitive Africa, 1400–1800: A Study in Ethnocentrism," *Isis,* 49 (1958), 62–72. See also, for examples of a variety of approaches, Dante Puzzo, "Racism and the Western Tradition," *Journal of the History of Ideas,* 25 (1964), 579–86; Milton Cantor, "The Image of the Negro in Colonial Literature," *New England Quarterly,* 36 (1963), 452–77; and Alden T. Vaughan, "Blacks in Virginia: A Note on the First Decade," *William and Mary Quarterly,* 3rd Series, 29 (1972), 469–78.

8. Jordan, *White Over Black,* p. 43.

9. Jordan, "Modern Tensions and the Origins of American Slavery," 30; Jordan, *White Over Black,* p. 98.

10. Alexis de Tocqueville, *Democracy in America,* translated by George Lawrence (New York: Anchor Books, 1969), pp. 341–42.

11. George M. Fredrickson, "Toward a Social Interpretation of the Development of American Racism," in Nathan I. Huggins, Martin Kilson, and Daniel M. Fox, eds., *Key Issues in the Afro-American Experience* (New York: Harcourt Brace Jovanovich, 1971), Volume One, pp. 240–41. Reprinted in slightly revised form in George M. Fredrickson, *The Arrogance of Race: Historical Perspectives on Slavery, Racism, and Social Inequality* (Middletown, Conn.: Wesleyan University Press, 1988), pp. 189–205. Emphasis added.

12. Ibid, p. 254.

13. See, for example, George M. Frederickson, *The Black Image in the White Mind: The Debate on Afro-American Character and Destiny, 1817–1914* (New York: Harper & Row, 1971); George M. Frederickson, *White Supremacy: A Comparative Study in American and South African History* (New York: Oxford University Press, 1981), esp. pp. 70–81; T.H. Breen and Stephen Innes, *"Myne Owne Ground": Race and Freedom on Virginia's Eastern Shore, 1640–1676* (New York: Oxford University Press, 1980); and Michael Adas, *Machines as the Measure of Men: Science, Technology, and Ideologies of Western Dominance* (Ithaca, N.Y.: Cornell University Press, 1989), esp. pp. 64–68.

14. One of the best studies of the emergence of racial pseudoscience in America remains William Stanton's *The Leopard's Spots: Scientific Attitudes Toward Race in America, 1815–59* (Chicago: University of Chicago Press, 1960); bringing the story from the later nineteenth century up to the present is Stephen Jay Gould, *The Mismeasure of Man* (New York: W.W. Norton & Company, 1981).

15. Richard Drinnon, *Facing West: The Metaphysics of Indian Hating and Empire Building* (Minneapolis: University of Minnesota Press, 1980), p. xxvii.

16. On the scientific illegitimacy of the idea of race, see Ashley Montague, ed., *The Concept of Race* (Westport, Conn.: Greenwood Press, 1980); see also, Stephen Jay Gould, "Why We Should Not Name Human Races—A Biological View," in Stephen Jay Gould, *Ever Since Darwin: Reflections in Natural History* (New York: W.W. Norton, 1977), pp. 231–36.

17. On Anthony Johnson, among numerous other treatments designed to make the same point, see especially Breen and Innes, *"Myne Owne Ground"*, pp. 7–18.

18. On Ellison and other nineteenth-century southern black gentry and slave owners, see Michael P. Johnson and James L. Roark, *Black Masters: A Free Family of Color in the Old South* (New York: W.W. Norton & Company, 1984), esp. pp. 124–29. For the total number of African American slaveholders and their slaves, see the classic work compiled and edited by Carter G. Woodson, *Free Negro Owners of Slaves in the United States in 1830* (New York: Negro Universities Press 1968) and Michael P. Johnson and James L. Roark, "Strategies of Survival: Free Negro Families and the Problem of Slavery," in Carol Bleser, ed., *In Joy and in Sorrow: Women, Family, and Marriage in the Victorian South, 1830–1900* (New York: Oxford University Press, 1991), pp. 88–102.

19. See Peter H. Merkl, *Political Violence Under the Swastika: 581 Early Nazis* (Princeton: Princeton University Press, 1975), p. 499; for a complementary analysis regarding the German population at large, see Sarah Gordon, *Hitler, Germans, and the "Jewish Question"* (Princeton: Princeton University Press, 1984), esp. pp. 53–67.

20. Although it is now a staple of works on racism, the term "institutional racism" appears first to have been used and analyzed by Stokely Carmichael and Charles V. Hamilton in their book *Black Power: The Politics of Liberation in America* (New York: Vintage Books, 1967), pp. 4–6, 22–23, 156–62; on "meta-racism," see Joel Kovel, *White Racism: A Psychohistory*, Second Edition (New York: Columbia University Press, 1984), pp. 211–30.

21. Jane Tompkins, " 'Indians': Textualism, Morality, and the Problem of History," *Critical Inquiry*, 13 (1986), 115.

22. Alden T. Vaughan, *New England Frontier: Puritans and Indians, 1620–1675* (Boston: Little, Brown, 1965), pp. 62, viii.

23. See, for example, Bernard W. Sheehan, *Seeds of Extinction: Jeffersonian Philanthropy and the American Indian* (Chapel Hill: University of North Carolina Press, 1973), esp. p. 43, note 48. Sheehan, it must be said, takes this notion to a truly amazing extreme, claiming that the murderous destruction of American Indian peoples in the late eighteenth and early nineteenth century was caused simply by "naivete, perhaps even an excess of good will, but not the intentional inflicting of pain on a less powerful people" (p. 12). On the otherwise insightful Jordan's "clouding of vision" when it came to Indians, see Drinnon, *Facing West*, pp. 80–81.

24. Vaughan, *New England Frontier*, p. viii.

25. Wilbur R. Jacobs, *Dispossessing the American Indian: Indians and Whites on the Colonial Frontier* (New York: Charles Scribner's Sons, 1972); Francis Jennings, *The Invasion of America: Indians, Colonialism, and the Cant of Conquest* (Chapel Hill: University of North Carolina Press, 1975); Richard Drinnon, *Facing West*; and Neal Salisbury, *Manitou and Providence: Indians, Europeans, and the Making of New England, 1500–1643* (New York: Oxford University Press, 1982).

26. Alden T. Vaughan, "From White Man to Redskin: Changing Anglo-American Perceptions of the American Indian," *American Historical Review*, 87 (1982), 917–53. Vaughan himself notes (p. 941) that British colonists in the early 1620s—when there were not many more than a thousand white settlers in Virginia and barely a hundred in New England—were referring to the Indians as creatures "having little of Humanitie but shape," as "more brutish than the beasts they hunt," and as "naturally born slaves." These, however, are not racist opinions, Vaughan thinks, because they do not mention skin color.

27. Hugh A. MacDougall, *Racial Myth in English History: Trojans, Teutons, and Anglo-Saxons* (Hanover, N.H.: University Press of New England, 1982).

28. W.E.B. DuBois, *Dusk of Dawn* (New York: Harcourt, Brace, 1940), p. 139.

29. Frank Chalk and Kurt Jonassohn, *The History and Sociology of Genocide: Analyses and Case Studies* (New Haven: Yale University Press, 1990), pp. 8–9.

30. The Convention contains 15 additional Articles that are not reproduced here because they are procedural, and procedural action has never been taken against any member state.

INDEX